THE BEDFORI
HISTORICAL R
SOCIETY
1995

Frontispiece: Wrest Park: The Staircase
(*Drawing: J.C. Buckler, 1831*)

THE PUBLICATIONS OF THE BEDFORDSHIRE
HISTORICAL RECORD SOCIETY
VOLUME 74

Inventories of
Bedfordshire Country Houses
1714–1830

Edited by
James Collett-White

PUBLISHED BY THE SOCIETY   1995

First published 1995 by the Bedfordshire Historical Record Society, Bedford.

This volume has been published with the help of grants from the Friends of Chicksands Priory, the Scouloudi Foundation in association with the Institute of Historical Research, the Marc Fitch Fund and South Beds. District Council.

Cover design by Justin March, Park Farm Studios Ltd., Riseley Road, Bletsoe, Bedford MK44 1QU

Printed and bound by
Stephen Austin and Sons Ltd, Hertford

In Loving Memory of my Parents

Harold Edwin Collett-White (1902–1989)
and
Patience Winifred Collett-White (1910–1991)
with whom I first enjoyed visiting
country houses.

CONTENTS

	Page
List of illustrations	viii
Preface and acknowledgements	ix
Abbreviations and symbols used in transcription	xi
Bibliography	xii
GENERAL INTRODUCTION	1
THE HOUSES	
Ampthill Park House	12
Chicksands Priory	23
Colworth House	32
Hasells Hall	73
Hinwick House	89
Houghton House	103
Houghton Manor House	123
Ickwell Bury	132
Leighton Buzzard Prebendal House	146
Melchbourne House	165
Northill Manor	184
Oakley House	193
Sharnbrook House	205
Southill Park House	212
Toddington Manor	234
Wrest Park	243
Glossary	274
Names Index	284
Subject Index	286

LIST OF ILLUSTRATIONS

Plate		Page
	Ampthill Park House, NW view 1827	Cover
	Staircase of Wrest Park 1831	Frontispiece
1	Chicksands, SE view 1730	23
2	Chicksands Library c.1820s	25
3	Chicksands, view 1829	26
4	Colworth House, E Elevation c.1770s	39
5	Colworth House, Octagonal Table 1938	43
6	Colworth House, E view 1820	44
7	Colworth House, W view 1890s	45
8	Hasells Hall, Ground plan 1814	74
9	Hasells Hall, S & E view c.1920s	79
10	Hinwick House, S view 1820	90
11	Hinwick House, Cabinet 1928	92
12	Hinwick House, Portrait of John Orlebar c.1740	94
13	Houghton House, view c.1750s	105
14	Houghton House, W view 1843	111
15	Houghton Manor, S view c.1775	123
16	Ickwell Bury, Library c.1910	132
17	Ickwell Bury, E view 1736	134
18	Ickwell Bury, c.1820	134
19	Ickwell Bury, E & S view c.1910	136
20	Leighton Buzzard Prebendal House, S view c.1800	146
21	Melchbourne, NW view 1820s	166
22	Melchbourne, The Old Schoolroom 1861	171
23	Oakley House, S view c.1820s	195
24	Sharnbrook House, W view c.1820s	206
25	Southill, S view c.1740	213
26	Southill, Ground Plan before alterations 1795	215
27	Southill, Hall 1930	217
28	Toddington Manor, Old kitchen 1843	236
29	Toddington Manor, Copy of view of 1806	238
30	Wrest Park, N view 1735	245
31	Wrest Park, Library 1831	247
32	Wrest Park, SE view 1831	250

Sources of Illustrations

All the pictures are reproduced from originals or copies held in the County Record Office apart from the copy of A. Devis's portrait of John Orlebar, supplied by the National Portrait Gallery (12), and the elevation of Colworth in the 1770s kindly provided by Dr. H.M. Colvin (4).

Owners who have kindly allowed reproduction of their material include N. Bagshawe (Fisher Collection) (2), H.M. Colvin (4), S.R. Houfe (5, 20 and 27), the owner of A. Devis's portrait of John Orlebar (12), Lord Pym (28 and 29), Sotheby Parke Bernet & Co. (15), the Vicar of Toddington (28 and 29) and S.C. Whitbread (26).

Preface and Acknowledgements

It is always a great pleasure to acknowledge with gratitude the help given in various ways to an editor of a volume of this kind. Her Majesty's Stationery Office has allowed the publication of documents held at the Public Record Office that are crown copyright. These are the inventories of Colworth (C114/176), Houghton Regis (PROB3/42/35) and Northill (C107/145). The 1749 inventory of the Prebendal House, Leighton Buzzard is held at the Shakespeare Birthplace Trust and is published by kind permision of the Stoneleigh Abbey Preservation Trust. The inventories of Houghton House, Ampthill Park House and Oakley are included by the kind permission of the Marquess of Tavistock and the Trustees of the Bedford Settled Estate. Similar authority to publish is gratefully acknowledged to Lord Pym and Unilever PLC for the inventories of the Hasells and Colworth 1723 and 1774. The remaining inventories are either directly owned by the Bedfordshire Record Office or have been deposited there for so long that the present owner is unknown. Special mention should be made of the inventories of Southill and Wrest, formerly part of the manuscript archive of the late Lady Lucas and now in public ownership but still deposited at the Bedfordshire Record Office. I would like to pay tribute to her generosity in letting scholars study the archive for many years and her unfailing interest in what use they made of it. I would like to thank her and her family for all the help they gave me as the archivist administering their papers for over fifteen years.

In writing this book I have had a great deal of help from a number of people. I should particularly like to mention the following who have helped with information on individual houses or on architectural matters generally: Nicholas Bennett, Anne Buck, Howard Colvin, Anthony Crossley, Alan Hunter, Michael Jones, June Masters, Ann Mitchell (Archivist at Woburn Abbey), Marita Prendy, Lord Pym, Stephen Sartin and Andrew Underwood. Simon Houfe has let me use material from the Richardson Collection, which is of great value to Bedfordshire. His own great knowledge of Bedfordshire country houses has been of great assistance to me. Ian Davies's help in liaising with Justin March over the design of the cover has been much appreciated.

The staff of institutions have eased my research considerably. These include the Public Record Office (Chancery Lane Branch), Royal Institute of British Architects, Sir John Soane Museum and Stoke City Museum, Ceramics Department.

The support of the editorial team has been tremendous throughout. Gordon Vowles in addition to his duties as General Editor has proof read the introductions and made many helpful suggestions for their improvement. Patricia Bell has been equally painstaking in her proof reading the texts themselves and in transcribing the Houghton House inventory. Don Cox very kindly undertook the arduous task of compiling the index. Christopher Pickford has always been at hand with friendly advice and help on technical matters. As ever, the biggest burden has fallen on Pauline Newbery, who has typed the whole text on to the word processor. Her endless patience with an often difficult manuscript and the endless minor corrections needed has been remarkable in this, the fourth B.H.R.S. volume with which which she has been involved.

I am also grateful to my colleagues in the Record Office for the support and help they have given me, either directly or in easing my work load, so that I could complete the volume. Nigel Lutt, as usual, has been of great assistance in getting the illustrations sorted out.

The Warden and Staff of Ecton House, Retreat House for the Diocese of Peterborough, provided a comfortable and peaceful setting for the writing of the first drafts of this book.

Above all I must pay tribute to my long-suffering wife Ann and our three children. My absences either in the study or elsewhere have been accepted without complaint. Ann's help with identifying objects mentioned in the inventories, either from her knowledge or from her excellent collection of reference books on decorative arts, has been invaluable. My family's interest, love and support have made this volume possible.

ABBREVIATIONS

BCRO	Bedfordshire County Record Office
BHRS	Bedfordshire Historical Record Society
BNQ	*Bedfordshire Notes and Queries* (3 Vols. 1886–1893)
B.Mag	*Bedfordshire Magazine* (1947-date)
c.	circa (e.g. c.1700)
CL	*Country Life*
Colvin	H.M. Colvin's *Dictionary of British Architects*
EF	*Encyclopedia of Furniture* by Joseph Aronson
HFB	*Home Fires Burning*
Millard	A.M. Millard's *Glossary of some unusual words in the London Port Books for certain years between 1588 and 1640* (available at PRO)
N. Evans	Nesta Evans
OED	Oxford English Dictionary
Pevsner	Pevsner's *Building of England Series* volume for Bedfordshire and Huntingdonshire
PCC	Prerogative Court of Canterbury
PDDA	Penguin Dictionary of Decorative Arts
PRO	Public Record Office
M. Reed	M. Reed's *Ipswich Probate Inventories* (Glossary)
SBT	Shakespeare Birthplace Trust
VCH	*Victoria County History* for Bedfordshire

All references are to documents in the Bedfordshire County Record Office (BCRO) unless otherwise stated.

NOTES ON TRANSCRIPTION

Where possible the transcription reproduces the punctuation, spelling and use of capitals found in the original documents. Where there was difficulty in determining whether a capital was intended in an original, all available instances were compared, and a decision made to use lower or upper case as appropriate, in the transcription.

SYMBOLS USED IN TRANSCRIPTION

Cancellation or deletion	(^{c})
Insertion	(^{i})
Marginal note	(^{m})
Addition by the transcriber	[ ]
Omission by the transcriber	. . .
Illegible or torn parts of the manuscript	– – –
Line breaks (in line-by-line transcripts)	/

BIBLIOGRAPHY

a) Bedfordshire

Note: Works on individual houses are not included in this bibliography, but will be cited in the footnotes relating to each house.

For Bedfordshire Inventories see section **b)ii** of the Bibliography

ANDREWS, C. BRUYN (editor) *The Torrington Diaries* containing the Tours through England and Wales of the Hon. John Byng, later the 5th Viscount Torrington, between the years 1781 and 1794 (reprint 1970) Vols.2 pp271–298 and 4 p.1–86 relate to Bedfordshire

CHAMBERS, B. *Printed Maps & Town Plans of Bedfordshire 1576–1900* (BHRS Vol.62, 1983)

CONISBEE, L.R. and THREADGILL, A.R. *A Bedfordshire Bibliography* (Bedford 1962) and three supplements (1967, 1971 and 1978)

GODBER, J. *The Marchioness Grey of Wrest Park* (BHRS Vol.47, 1968)

GODBER, J. *History of Bedfordshire* (1969, reprinted 1984)

HARVEY, WILLIAM MARSH *The History and Antiquities of the Hundred of Willey* (1872–1878)

HOUFE, SIMON R. *Through Visitors' Eyes: A Bedfordshire Anthology* (Book Castle, Dunstable 1990)

MARSHALL, LYDIA M. *The Bedfordshire Hearth Tax Return for 1671* (BHRS Vol.16, 1934 republished 1990)

PARRY, J.D. *Select Illustrations, Historical and Topographical of Bedfordshire* (1827)

PEVSNER, NIKOLAUS *"Bedfordshire, Huntingdon and Peterborough"* in *The Buildings of England* series (Penguin Books, Harmondsworth 1968)

Victoria County History of the County of Bedford (VCH) 3 vols (1904, 1908 and 1912) and Index (1914)

b) Books on Inventories

i General

MULLINS, E.L.C. *Texts and Calendars: An Analytical Guide to Serial Publications* Vol.I (1958) and Vol.II (1983) provides a useful indication as to what inventories have been published by national and local societies.

ii Bedfordshire Historical Record Society

Vol.11 BLUNDELL, JOSEPH H. editor *Toddington Manor House 1644* (1927)

Vol.20 EMMISON, F.G. editor *Jacobean Household Inventories* (1938)

Vol.32 FREEMAN, C.E. *Elizabethan Inventories* pp 92–107 of *Harrold Priory: A Twelfth Century Dispute and other articles* (1952)

Vol.38 CURTIS, EVELYN editor *Inventory of Furniture at Houghton House c.1726–1728* (1958)

Vol.65 LEE, ROSS editor *Text of Inventories and Rentals from Add. Ms. 5494* in his Law and Local Society in the time of Charles I: Bedfordshire and the Civil War (1986)

iii Buckinghamshire Record Society

Vol.24 REED, MICHAEL editor *Buckinghamshire Probate Inventories 1661–1714*

iv Furniture History Society

THORNTON, PETER AND TOMLIN, MAURICE editors Ham House (1980)

v Suffolk Record Society

Vol. XXII REED, M. editor *The Ipswich Probate Inventories 1583–1631* (1981)

Vol.XXXV EVANS, NESTA editor *Wills of the Archdeaconry of Sudbury 1636–1638* (1993) (This has a useful glossary)

c) General Books relating to Houses

BINNEY, MARCUS AND MARTIN, KIT *The Country House: To be or not to be* (Save Britain's Heritage 1982)

CARTER, GEORGE, GOODE, PATRICK and LAUNE, KEDRUN *Humphrey Repton, Landscape Gardener 1752–1818*

COLVIN, HOWARD *A Biographical Dictionary of British Architects 1600–1840* (1978 edition)

DOWNES, KERRY *English Baroque Architecture* (1966)

DUTTON, RALPH *The English Country House* (2nd Edition, 1943–44)

ELTON, ARTHUR, HARRISON, BRETT and WARK, KEITH *Researching the Country House: A Guide for Local Historians* (1992)

GIROUARD, MARK *Life in the English Country House* (1979)

HARRIS, JOHN *The Design of the English Country House 1620–1920* (1985)

KINGSLEY, NICHOLAS *The Country Houses of Gloucestershire Volume Two 1660–1830* (Phillimore 1992)

LLOYD, NATHANIEL *A History of the English House* (Omega Books, Ware, Herts., reprint of 1985)

STROUD, DOROTHY *Henry Holland 1745–1806* (1950)
STROUD, DOROTHY *Henry Holland, His Life and Architecture* (1966)

d) Ceramics

CHARLESTON, ROBERT J. *World Ceramics, An Illustrated History* (2nd impression 1975)
CHARLESTON, ROBERT *English Ceramics 1580–1830* (1977)
DUCRET, SIEGFRIED *The Colour Treasury of Eighteenth Century Porcelain* (1976)
GARNER, SIR HARRY *Oriental Blue and White* (3rd Edition 1970)
JENKYNS, SOAME *Later Chinese Porcelain* (4th Edition 1971)
WATNEY, BERNARD *English Blue and White Porcelain of the 18th Century* (reprint 1979)

e) Decoration

BEARD, GEOFFREY *Decorative Plasterwork in Great Britain* (1975)
FLEMING, JOHN AND HONOUR, HUGH *The Penguin Dictionary of Decorative Arts* (1977)
GUNNIS, RUPERT *Dictionary of British Sculptors 1660–1851* (revised edition, n.d.)
HONOUR, HUGH *Chinoiserie, the Vision of Cathay* (1961; reprint 1973)
SNODIN, MICHAEL (ed.) *Rococo: Art and Design in Hogarth's England* 1984

f) Dress

BUCK, ANNE *Dress in Eighteenth Century England* (1979)

g) Furniture

ARONSON, JOSEPH *The Encyclopedia of Furniture* (1970 reprint)
MUSGRAVE, CLIFFORD *Regency Furniture* (2nd Revised Edition 1970)

h) Equipment

HARTLEY, DOROTHY *Food in England* (1985 edition)
SAMBROOK, PAMELA *Laundry Byegones* (Shire Publications 1983)
WRIGHT, LAWRENCE *Clean and Decent: The History of the Bathroom and the WC* (1966 edition)
WRIGHT, LAWRENCE *Home Fires Burning: The History of Domestic Heating and Cooking* (1964)

GENERAL INTRODUCTION

Bedfordshire Inventories

This volume contains eighteen inventories relating to sixteen Bedfordshire country houses, made between 1714 and 1830. The value to social and architectural historians of inventories has been known for many years and a number of historical societies have published selections of them.[1] The Bedfordshire Historical Record Society has published some too, dating from the sixteenth and seventeenth centuries.[2]

Although most of the surviving inventory series from the Archdeaconry of Bedford have been published, unpublished inventories in the Bedfordshire County Record Office include inventories attached to wills and inventories held in individual archives. At the Public Record Office is a considerable group, part of the Prerogative Court of Canterbury archive, dating from 1650. Any of these could have been used to make a substantial volume.[3]

Why were inventories relating only to country houses chosen for the volume? One of the weaknesses of editions of inventories already published is the failure to identify an inventory with a specific building. Country houses are readily identifiable and often have a considerable data of other information so that the inventory can be used to its full advantage.

Selection of inventories that list most rooms in detail has meant that many of the PCC inventories have had to be left out. Fairly short inventories of Bilberry, the Old House Aspley Guise and Cockayne Hatley Hall have been omitted. Regrettably, the very long Southill inventory of 1816 could not be included on grounds of space.

It is hoped that architectural historians will be able to look in a new light at the country houses discussed and that the social historian will have sufficient data to analyse the contents of a country landowner's house. Design historians will be interested in the changing fashions in fittings, furniture and decoration. These changes have to be seen in their Bedfordshire context – of a county under a hundred miles away from London, greatly influenced by her but still able to lead a provincial life of its own. Change is more obvious in the principal rooms but considerable detail is given to the service areas of kitchen, pantry and brewhouse as well as to the bedrooms of the servants who worked there.

The General Introduction is designed to bring these themes together while the specific history of each house is discussed before its relevant inventory. The Glossary attempts to explain some of the more obscure words.

Inventories and their Function

Before looking at the historical and social background of Bedfordshire country house inventories it is important that they are evaluated as a class of records and their strengths and weaknesses ascertained.

Inventories have been kept since the thirteenth century. From 1529 they had to be produced to accompany wills being presented for probate.[4] They were also kept for other purposes as a checklist on the transfer of property from one member of a family to another or perhaps from a landlord to a tenant. More rarely the contents of a house were included in a sale or mortgage and an inventory was drawn up. Inventories contain detailed lists of the goods of a person in their house (often listed room by room), in their service buildings and in their barns. Such records give valuable information on the layout of houses and their contents, as well as much useful information on prices and social conditions.

The most comprehensive type of inventory is normally that prepared for probate. Heirlooms and specific bequests in the will can be omitted from the inventory. Some of the best furniture and pictures were often kept in the testator's London house and so are omitted from the Bedfordshire inventory. Inventories prepared for leases may not cover all the house, such as the one for Ickwell Bury in 1823. Nearly always china and plate were omitted from this type of inventory, as well as the most valuable pictures.

Inventories should be used with all other relevant records. They should be seen in the context of the estate that produced the money to maintain the house. The whims and tastes of the country house owner should not be underestimated. At their best inventories shed a powerful light on the evolution of the country house and the way of life carried on there.

Building campaigns on Bedfordshire Country Houses 1660–1830

The period from 1714 to 1830 saw the building and remodelling of a number of country houses in Bedfordshire including most of the houses described in this volume. The building activity did not start in 1714 but was part of a process going back to the restoration of 1660. Nicholas Kingsley in his book on Gloucestershire country houses[5] has estimated there were 440 of what he calls building campaigns in Gloucestershire between 1660 and 1830. Over a similar period there were under 60 in Bedfordshire. A county two and a half times the size of Bedfordshire produced seven times the number of building campaigns. Bedfordshire's comparatively small total is perhaps explained by the concentration of land into the hands of a relatively few owners, and Gloucestershire gentry were more wealthy by virtue of their links with Bristol.

The pattern of building of Bedfordshire country houses was affected by two important factors, one local and one more general. Sir Robert Chernocks of Hulcote in 1668 wrote a list of a staggering 114 names of "Gentlemen of Quality that have sold their Estates and are Quite Gone out of Bedfordshire within lesse than the space of 50 years."[6] Not all the families listed had sold up: a number such as William Paine of Podington had died without male issue and were represented in 1668 by another gentry family such as the Orlebars. The Tyringhams of Hinwick Hall were ultimately replaced by another gentry family the Livesays, so Hinwick Hall remained a gentry estate.[7] Other estates such as that of Beverley at Cainho and Boteler at Higham Gobion were bought up by larger landowners, such as the Dowager Countess of Kent at Wrest Park. A further eight estates were sold between 1668 and c.1725.[8]

By 1668 Chernocke reckoned there were only 55 gentry families remaining in Bedfordshire, probably an underestimate but indicating some measure of the major shake-up in the seventeenth century of Bedfordshire estates. Among the 55 were newcomers from London with substantial City wealth behind them such as Humphrey Brandreth and Humphrey Monoux. Interestingly, the first three building campaigns were undertaken by them at Houghton Manor and Wootton House respectively. The Dowager Countess of Kent's purchases around Wrest Park in the 1650s and the building of the new north front at Wrest in the 1670s were financed by the fortune she inherited from her father Sir Anthony Benn, Recorder of London.

The newcomers were not satisfied with the Renaissance or vernacular houses of the sixteenth and early seventeenth centuries. They wanted the new classical ideas of Palladio and French or Italian Baroque incorporated into their new houses. These ideas which before 1640 were only supported by a tiny coterie around Inigo Jones had now become part of the universal culture of the educated and the rich as a by-product of the return from exile on the Continent of Charles II's supporters. Some of them, like John Evelyn, kinsman of the Earls of Kent, had taken the opportunity to go on a leisurely Grand Tour. After 1660 this became the norm for the well to do young man. John Harvey and successive members of the Grey family of Wrest Park went from Bedfordshire on Grand Tours in the 1690s[9] and thereafter.

Surprisingly it was only in the 1690s, in the more stable conditions that followed the Revolution of 1688, that country house building took place on a large scale in Bedfordshire. Ampthill Park, Ickwell Bury and Hasells Hall date from this period, as well as Houghton Hall, another Brandreth house. A further period of inactivity was followed by the building of three houses close to one another: Colworth, Hinwick House and Hall in the years around 1714. The period from then to 1830 showed a similar pattern of long periods of inactivity succeeded by a sudden burst of building on a number of properties, reverting to inactivity thereafter. This irregular pattern underlines the fact that building was very expensive and a whole host of conditions were required to enable a landowner to contemplate it. A marriage to a rich heiress, a lucrative government post, a rise in rents either rural or urban could act as a spur.

The 1730s saw major building work on only two country houses in the County but they were important ones – the Leighton Buzzard Prebendal House, transformed by James Gibbs, and Southill Park.

The 1740s to early 1750s provided one of the peaks in country house building activity in Bedfordshire. Both Woburn Abbey and Melchbourne were remodelled, Oakley House built and Chicksands transformed by Isaac Ware.

The 1760s provided another time of activity,[9] Robert Adam's Luton Hoo being the major house built in the period. Although admired it was not imitated. The busiest architect locally was Sir William Chambers, who did work on the Duke of Bedford's properties including Houghton House and on a garden building for the Marchioness Grey at Wrest Park. The 1760s were succeeded by the relative inactivity of the 1770s when the extension to Colworth, probably contemplated in the 1760s, was the only item of note.

The late 1780s and 1790s saw the most building at any time between 1714 and 1830. This activity was led by the Duke of Bedford and Samuel Whitbread II and centred on the architect Henry Holland, who did work at Woburn Abbey, Oakley and Southill. Sir John Soane's Mogerhanger Park, and the remodellings of Hasells Hall and Wrest Park complete the decade. The Napoleonic Wars saw the continuation of Southill and a further remodelling of Colworth House on Holland-like lines. To sum up, between 1714 and 1830 twelve country houses were built in Bedfordshire and a further nine remodelled, often more than once.

Against this pattern of rebuilding and improving of country houses in this period should be set the fact that three out of the sixteen houses studied were pulled down or left as a ruin. A fourth, Toddington Manor, was severely reduced in size and a fifth, Wrest Park, was demolished soon after the period ended. Ironically, three of these houses were among the five largest houses in 1671.[10] By the 1800s they were unsuitable for the way of life gentry families led then.

Changing tastes in furniture – the contents of the principal rooms

Parallel with changes to the structures of the houses, changes in the decoration and furnishing of the rooms took place. Rejigging an existing room to comply with the latest fashion was a cheaper alternative to rebuilding. Obviously most houses were newly fitted out when they were built, such as Colworth House in the years 1715 to 1720. Often the principal rooms were refitted subsequently and the inventories can give a clue as to when this might have been. The introductions to the individual houses and the inventories themselves give sufficient detail for analysis of the contents of the houses. This section is intended merely to indicate the approximate date for any major refitting and to relate this to a broad pattern of cultural change.

The inventories of Chicksands and Houghton Manor suggest that they were furnished before 1700. There is no mention of walnut furniture, and at Houghton Manor there are cane chairs, old fashioned by 1743. At Chicksands there were a number of tapestries on the walls, popular wall coverings in the late seventeenth century. Colworth House was initially fitted out from 1715 to 1720. Being recently furnished Colworth had more modern equipment. Antonie had a Norway oak table, Holland linen and Delft dishes from Europe and china plates from China, as well as a tea set. His marble table is of interest as white marble was only beginning to be popular for table tops in 1720. Antonie had a number of pictures and prints, but the main decorations of the walls were still tapestry.

Hasells Hall was probably furnished by Heylock Kingsley in the 1720s with both oak and walnut intermingled. Much of the furniture at Northill Manor in 1731 was walnut but Bromsall did have gilt sconces, which indicate a possible Rococo influence. Ampthill Park House, whose furniture was probably purchased soon after Lord Fitzwilliam bought the house in 1727, stands in marked contrast to these smaller houses. There was plenty of mahogany furniture at Ampthill in 1737, as well as the first painted furniture mentioned in these inventories. New curtain materials were being used, such as calico, camblet and caffoy. Striped furniture and room decorations make a first appearance.

Wrest, being an older house which had evolved over the centuries, shows a greater age span of fittings. Some of the rooms had "old" furniture, but a significant number of fashionable pieces appear in the more important rooms. Some mahogany furniture, a rose wood table, an escritoire – probably walnut – and an ebony cabinet with tortoiseshell inlay being the most stylish pieces. These possibly date from after the Duke of Kent's second marriage in 1729. Although the fittings were being modernised, when the family was painted as a group in c.1735 it was in a magnificent Baroque room, possibly "My Lady Duchess Room".

Charles Leigh of the Prebendal House, Leighton Buzzard had a reputation as a convivial host. Although there were pieces of furniture made of a variety of woods at Prebendal House, they were put together as little as possible. The saloon, Leigh's principal room for entertaining, was fitted exclusively with mahogany. The side tables had marble tops. These pieces were probably purchased just after James Gibbs's remodelling of the house in the 1730s.

There are no relevant inventories between 1749 and that of 1761 for Hasells Hall. To the fittings of the 1720s had been added a few mahogany pieces. Hinwick in 1766 by contrast was a house in transition with walnut, oak and mahogany furniture. The Mortlake tapestries probably date back to the initial furnishings of 1710. Sharnbrook House shows a similar contrast of woods used for making the furniture.

The same types of differences, that we had seen earlier between Ampthill and smaller houses in the 1730s, existed between the Duke of Bedford's houses and the rest. As a result of the Duke and his son's sojourn in Paris during his embassy there in 1763, French rococo pieces were introduced into all the family's Bedfordshire houses[11] – Woburn, Oakley and Houghton House. Inventories to the two latter houses are published here and detail the furniture the Duke and the Marquis of Tavistock bought in the 1760s. The French rococo did not have a complete carte blanche in Bedfordshire country houses in the 1760s. Colworth was remodelled and extended by the Palladian, John Woolf, who no doubt produced more restrained interiors than in the Russell houses. Leighton Buzzard Prebendal House shows little change between 1749 and the inventory in 1774.[12] Some classical bustos and some candlebranches (possibly girandoles and therefore French influenced) seem to be the only additions of note. Southill in 1779 was furnished virtually entirely with mahogany furniture. This represents a refitting, probably done in the 1760s, since the house was built between 1724 and 1732.

Changes between 1780 and 1816 unfortunately cannot be gauged accurately, as there are no suitable inventories for Bedfordshire country houses in the period. The great rebuilding for the Whig landowners of the 1790s of their house exteriors was accompanied by equally radical transformations within. Their common political faith, their social links through hunting and through their London clubs and a common admiration for the taste of the Prince Regent led them to adopt a common style of interior design. Features at Southill are repeated at Oakley; furniture at Colworth echoes furniture at Southill, made by the same group of craftsmen. Although the initial inspiration for this common style was Henry Holland, after his death the style modified and developed in the hands of the cabinet makers, interior decorators and sculptors he had gathered together. French influence was again apparent but in the more restrained style of Louis XVI rather than in the exuberant rococo of the 1760s.

Melchbourne was owned by the St.Johns, who had intermarried with the Whitbreads and do not seem to have been as strongly influenced as other Whig patrons by the prevailing Holland taste. In c.1810 the house was refitted. Mahogany reigned supreme in all the principal rooms, with walnut and oak banished into the others, according to the 1817 inventory. Ickwell Bury, too, in 1823 had a predominance of mahogany on the principal floors, as well as some fashionable painted furniture. In the attics, walnut and oak were to be found, as at Melchbourne.

To sum up, Bedfordshire country houses started the eighteenth century with oak furniture, added to in the early decades by walnut in the solid Augustan style of Anne and George I. As early as 1737 mahogany became the principal wood for the furniture of the grander houses, an ascendancy which only increased as the century progressed. Painted wood, first appearing in 1737, became increasingly important. The style of furniture evolved from early Georgian, via a brief flirtation with rococo in the grander houses in the 1760s, to the more restrained Regency, again influenced by French design. Bedfordshire played its part in these national trends in an uneven way and with a considerable time lag between changes in the greater houses and those in the smaller.

Changing tastes in furniture: bedrooms.[13]

Changes to the furniture of the bedrooms paralleled those in the reception rooms. At Northill in 1731 in the hall chamber Bromsall had a bedstead, presumably a four-post, "with Crimson Mohair Furniture fring'd with silk", a case compass rod with curtain and counterpane, both stuff, a feather bed, bolster and pillow; four blankets, one quilt. The curtains were good for keeping out draughts and a warming pan made the bed less icy. There were no carpets or rugs to step out on to. By 1779 at Southill there were different designs of beds. In addition to the four-post, there was a small tent bed and a turnup bed. In 1816 Lee Antonie seems to have preferred the traditional four-post bed in mahogany. Even the bedrooms had carpets, and the yellow room had a fitted carpet.

Paintings

Although tapestry still provided an important wall covering in early eighteenth century country houses in Bedfordshire, by c.1723 Marc Antonie had a good collection of paintings including a painting by Pieter Wouverman. Northill Manor in 1731 had a dozen paintings. The 1740 inventory of Wrest shows that the basis of its important collection of portraits had already been made, some of which remain in the staircase hall of the present house. The Duke of Kent had some landscapes and at least one "History piece". Charles Leigh at Leighton had an impressive collection in 1749.

By the 1760s large collections of paintings were much more common. John Bullock in 1768 had a total of sixty-six at Sharnbrook House including religious pictures from Italy and Dutch land and seascapes. Hinwick at the same date lists few pictures but at least two portraits of John Orlebar by the well-known Arthur Devis have survived. Southill in 1779 was full of pictures including fifty-three in Lady Torrington's dressing room. To the small collection of Marc Antonie's in c.1723 were added further pictures by the time of the 1771 inventory. This was extended in its turn by 1816. Unfortunately William Brown, the valuer of Colworth, at that date was more interested in the picture frames than their contents! Owning pictures and collecting them became an important way of emphasising the cultural interests and tastes of the country house owner.

Ceramics

By the beginning of the eighteenth century the European craze for porcelain had begun. Initially this was linked to the parallel craze for tea, so that every polite household had to have a tea set made of Chinese export porcelain. At the centre of *The Conversation Piece of Wrest*, 1735, is a tea table. By c.1723 Marc Antonie had several china basins and dishes. Owen Bromsall by contrast in 1731 had a considerable collection of blue china with plates, dishes and basins as well as coffee and tea cups. The Duke of Kent had plenty of cups in Chinese blue and white but no dinner service in 1740. His widow five years later left "Dresden" china.

The effect of the 1740s and 1750s was to produce porcelain in England and the rest of Europe in such quantities as to make it much more readily available. Parallel to this was the development of stoneware and earthenware, especially in Staffordshire. By 1771 Richard Antonie had made a large collection of ornamental figures. Unfortunately, the description is insufficiently detailed to indicate where the pieces came from, but it no doubt included Chelsea and Bow as well as Meissen and some Chinese export "Nanking ware". The Marquis of Tavistock, in addition to his purchases of French furniture in the 1760s, was a patron of "Staffordshire Creamware". By 1817 Melchbourne had an "Indian breakfast set with arms" and Nankeen soup bowls and breakfast cups with saucers. The main dinner service was blue and white with some dishes in white and gold, both Worcester porcelain. From being a minor plaything to the coffee and tea drinking classes, china either porcelain or pottery became all-pervasive by the end of the eighteenth century. A similar pattern could be detected in the increased use of glass. Unfortunately, the inventories give even less detail about glass than they do on china.

Silver

Inside a house possibly nothing said so much about the wealth and importance of its owner as a large and impressive display of silver. In c.1723 no silver is specifically mentioned at Colworth. Wrest, by contrast, in 1740 has a long and impressive list of silver with its weight. Little detail as to the design of the silver can be gleaned, but the Duke's "eight silver salvers scollop'd" could be in the rococo style, possibly by one of the French Hugenot craftsmen such as David Willaumes, settled in London. Hasells Hall has a comprehensive list with the value added for each piece as well as the weight. By 1817 at Melchbourne silver had been put to every kind of use: tureens, candlesticks, a muffinere, asparagus tongs, a salad fork, a cream basket, as well as countless spoons and forks.

Kitchen and Service Rooms and Buildings

So far this introduction has concentrated on the principal rooms and their contents. What happened behind the green baize door? Was the pace of change and concern for comfort as great there as in the family's apartments? Any large house had, as well as the kitchen, a number of auxilliary rooms within the house and one or two independent buildings outside to serve the household. A fairly modest house, Houghton Manor had in 1743 a kitchen, pastry, pantry, bacon room, "Lobb Hall", warehouse, laundry and brewhouse. Underneath the house there were cellars. In addition, most larger country houses had a steward's room, a servants' hall and a housekeeper's room where the linen was kept.

The eighteenth-century cook was primarily concerned with cooking meat. As a result, the spit was the important cooking agent.[14] This was incorporated into a range by the eighteenth century. The spit was turned by a smoke jack with a multiplying wheel added later in the century. The range was used for baking and for the cooking of puddings. The stewing and sauce pans were heated on the hobs. Houghton Manor, home of Rebecca Price the author of *The Compleat Cook*, had a wind-up jack, three complete spits, two bird spits and a frame.

Needing a well-equipped kitchen for his entertaining, Charles Leigh had a large range, a crane and three hooks, eleven large spits and four lark spits, two beef forms and a large beam and wooden scales, in 1749. Although the cooking equipment had not substantially changed by the time of the Southill inventory thirty years later, numerous moulds and cake pans, for more exotic puddings, appear. Preserving pans for fruit are also in evidence. At Melchbourne in 1817 the smoke jack had a multiplying wheel. To supplement it was a wrought iron oven, set in brick, a range of charcoal stoves and a copper boiler. Fish kettles and turbot kettles were now popular, showing a slight trend away from an almost wholly meat based diet.

It is impossible in this space to describe all the additional rooms and buildings. Most houses had a brewhouse and washhouse. Some had a bakehouse. The country house was supported by an estate, an extensive vegetable garden and an orchard. It was self-sufficient in a way that is foreign to our experience.

Sanitation[15]

At the beginning of the eighteenth century sanitation was crude to non-existent. Washing was in a basin supplied by a hand jug and a close stool or chamber pot served the function of a modern lavatory. As early as 1737 there was a bathing room at Ampthill Park House. This was unusual for its date. The Byngs at Southill were clearly concerned about sanitation, as they had both a bathing room and a gentleman's water closet. At Colworth in 1816 there were a number of bidets, no doubt bought at the instigation of Madame du The, Lee Antonie's mistress. Such improvements were not standard and it was not until well into the nineteenth century that most country houses had proper plumbing.

Heating

Technological change helped make the country house more comfortable in winter. In the early eighteenth century each room had an open fire, mainly using large logs supported by dog irons. These needed large chimneys. As a result the chimney tended to get warmed rather than the room. This did not matter so much as long as the family of the house stayed in London for the winter season. Once the owners had decided to hunt in winter and stay down in the country, the situation changed. The Marquis of Tavistock hunted regularly in Bedfordshire and soon payment was made for a Bath stove at Houghton House. Various types of stove appeared in country houses during the next sixty years. The idea of the stove was to restrict the amount of heat going up the chimney. Although a marginal improvement, they were still very inefficient and smoky. Melchbourne in 1817 was completely kitted out with them.

Other Contents

Although costume is left out of most inventories, useful lists of men's clothing occur in those of Hinwick House, Houghton House, Houghton Manor and Northill. Every inventory gives detail on materials used for curtains, bed hangings etc. A little can be gleaned on the equipment of nurseries, but as many of the owners of the houses were elderly when they died, these are comparatively few.

Clocks are mentioned occasionally including one by Tompion. Those interested should look in the index under clockmakers. If they wish to find out more about an individual clockmaker they should study Christopher Pickford's *Bedfordshire Clockmakers* (BHRS Vol.70). At Southill there was even an alarm clock. There was a good set of astronomical instruments at Wrest in 1740.

Conclusion

Both the interiors and exteriors of country houses underwent dramatic change between 1714 and 1830. The pace of change varied from house to house but all country houses were profoundly different in 1830 to what they had been in 1714. One house, Colworth, epitomises these changes. Newly-built in 1715 as a modest double pile country house, fitted with early Georgian furniture, it was extended and refitted in the 1760s and 1770s to make a grander gentleman's seat. By 1816 it had been transformed into one of the larger country houses of Bedfordshire, refitted in the most up-to-date Regency style. The pace of change can be gauged from inventories. It is hoped that, by publishing these local examples, researchers will obtain a clearer picture of the house they are studying and its place within general cultural developments in a specifically Bedfordshire context.

While this in no way claims to be a definitive study, the editor's labours will be more than rewarded, if this volume prompts further research into, and better understanding of, Bedfordshire country houses.

NOTES

References to inventories appearing elsewhere in this book are not given in these footnotes.

1. See Bibliography b)i.
2. see Bibliography b)ii.
3. PRO Classes PROB 3–5.
4. Michael Reed editor: *Buckinghamshire Probate Inventories 1661–1714* (Buckinghamshire Record Society Vol.74)
5. Nicholas Kingsley: *The Country Houses of Gloucestershire* Volume Two 1660–1830 (Phillimores 1992) pp.7–8.
6. BNQ Vol.I pp.213–220.
7. VCH III p.83.
8. Purchases L 4/16–17, L 9/14–15, Rebuilding of Wrest L 31/228–243.
9. References to Greys: L 30/2/1–16; L 30/8/28/1–55; John Harvey's diary 1688–1689, BHRS Vol.40 pp.1–35.
10. BHRS 16 (reprinted 1990)
11. *Apollo* June 1988.
12. Shakespeare Birthplace Trust Record Office (DR 18/4/42) (photocopy also available at BCRO ref. FAC 77/3)
13. For the various types of beds see *Glossary.*
14. Lawrence Wright *Home Fires Burning: The History of Domestic Heating and Cooking* (1964); David J. Eveleigh *Firegrates and Kitchen Ranges* (Shire Albums 99) (1983).
15. Lawrence Wright: *Clean and Decent: The History of the Bathroom and the W.C.* (1966 edition).

AMPTHILL PARK HOUSE

Park House to 1737

The present Park House was built in the late 1680s to replace the Great Lodge, built c.1525–1550 as a residence for Sir Francis Bryan. It is not clear if Park House is on exactly the same site but the earlier house, too, could have used the escarpment with its dramatic view to the North. Park House was intended as a dower house for the Dowager Lady Ailesbury (d.1689) and the future seat for her younger son, Robert Bruce. Her eldest son Thomas, 2nd Earl of Ailesbury (1656–1741), lived at Houghton House.[1]

Preparations for building the house were made in 1685 soon after the death of the 1st Earl. Board for wainscot – 2248 feet – was sawn (paid for in May 1686). The building seems to have been designed by Robert Grumbold (1639–1720), mason of Cambridge. Robert Bruce was at Queens' College in 1683–1684 and would have known of Grumbold from the number of collegiate buildings he was involved in at the time, including the Wren Library at Trinity College, where he was master mason to Sir Christopher.[2]

Grumbold's design was for a double pile house (a rectangular building two rooms thick) with basement, two principal floors and an attic. The house was to have a pediment and a central cupola (similar no doubt to the earlier one on the north front at Wrest Park). The base of the cupola survives in the roof and the cupola itself was probably transposed to the Moot Hall in Ampthill in the late 1760s.

Simon Houfe in his important series of articles on Park House comments on the "conventional even conservative" ground plan. The entrance hall led into the great parlour with rooms connected by corridors around this central area. The first floor had a central corridor connecting two staircases at either end. The main construction of the house seems to have been completed by October 1687 when a bill was submitted for "270 foot of cornish and 421 foot of guttering under the lead", which indicates that the cornicing must have gone round at least three sides of the house, if not the fourth. Grumbold built a typical late seventeenth century house influenced by Sir Robert Pratt and Wren but by the late 1680s already a little old-fashioned.

On the death of the Dowager Lady Ailesbury on 8 April 1689 all work on the interior was suspended. Her death and the political eclipse of the 2nd Earl meant that Robert no longer needed Park House, having to concentrate on running Houghton House. In February 1690 he sold the lease of the estate, originally taken out in 1661 for forty years, to John, 1st Lord Ashburnham, for £6,500.[3]

Lord Ashburnham was deeply interested in architecture and ultimately intended to change or replace Park House. In the 1690s he concentrated on creating extensive gardens and the building of a new court on the Bedford side of the house. All the time he was considering the more radical transformation of the house, consulting many architects including Hawksmoor. Having reluctantly rejected Hawksmoor's suggestion for a total replacement in the Baroque style, in 1704 he finally chose John Lumley of Northampton, who had been working on Burley-at-the-Hill for Ashburnham's friend, the 2nd Earl of Nottingham. Lumley was no doubt cheaper and could, as Simon Houfe suggests, be more easily controlled by Ashburnham, who was an exacting patron.[4]

Lumley seems to have been in sole command till April 1706 when William Winde, architect of Buckingham House, was given an advisory role. By the time Winde became involved, the east front had been completed but Winde's influence with the craftsmen he brought from Buckingham House is most noticeable in the key north front. Like Buckingham House, Park House was given two supporting pavilions attached to the central block by arcading. A crude representation of this is shown on Gordon's map of Bedfordshire of 1736.[5] Lord Ashburnham discussed with Winde putting classical statues on the parapet, similar to Buckingham House, sculpted by John Van Nost, who did work at Wrest Park. In the end he made do with urns, designed by Lumley himself. Thomas Archer, Baroque designer of the Pavilion at Wrest, was also consulted before the work started in earnest. In May 1707 Lumley's great door and steps were completed, giving a French Baroque centrepiece to the house.

Despite the house being completed in 1708, the Ashburnhams hardly ever lived there as the 1st Earl died in 1710 and his son and daughter-in-law died soon after from smallpox. The family sold Ampthill Park to Earl Fitzwilliam in 1727.

The 1737 Inventory

The 1737 inventory was prepared as part of the sale of Park House to Lady Gowran by Earl Fitzwilliam.

Although a number of garrets are not fully furnished, being used as lumber rooms, the contents of the principal rooms seem to have been reasonably intact with the house being sold with a full complement of furniture.

The first rooms fully described seem to be in the highest of the principal floors of the house. The colour (and fabric) of the bedhangings give the name to the room: "White Bedchamber", "Strip'd Holland" and "Strip'd Sattin". They show that striped as opposed to monochrome coloured fabrics were coming into vogue at this time. In the area of the "Red Bedchamber" was an early example of a bathing room. Unfortunately, its furniture is not listed.

Further rooms on this floor include "My Lord's Bedchamber", the "Yellow Mohair Room", as well as dressing rooms. The arcade contained a walnut-cased month clock by Thomas Tompion, the famous clockmaker from nearby Ickwell.

At this point the inventory probably moved to the piano nobile or lower of the two principal floors. The stone parlour and "My Lord's Dressing Room" were probably near the great hall, which led into the great parlour. Beyond that was a withdrawing room. Nearby was the "Atlas Bedchamber" and its dressing room. The rooms on this floor were completed with a vestibule, stone room, gallery and library.

On the ground floor were the kitchen, bakehouse, housekeeper's room, powdering room (for wigs), servants' hall, steward's room, distilling room, dairy and brewhouse, slaughter house and laundry. Below this floor were cellars.

The furniture of the house shows that it was in an interim phase with plenty of wainscot (oak), walnut and mahogany, as well as a significant number of japanned pieces. Marble was also used extensively for table tops. The stone parlour, for instance, had a mahogany table and dumb waiter, a marble table with an oak frame, a japanned copper fountain and cistern and a pair of walnut armchairs.

For 1737 the house had quite a collection of china, almost certainly Chinese export. Apart from the usual blue and white service set, Fitzwilliam had a red china coffee pot and a number of jars and bottles including a large one decorated in blue and gold. In "my Lord's Dressing Room" were six china figures, showing his personal taste. The next item, a Hercules on a pedestal, could have been porcelain but unfortunately the material of which it was made is not mentioned. The two Chinese images in wood on the "Atlas Dressing Room" are intriguing. They could be majolica work from Italy.

In a number of rooms there were plaster busts, the subjects mainly not listed apart from Palladio and Inigo Jones[6] – conscious echoes of classical architecture – in the gallery. A number of rooms had pictures but none of them described. Although the kitchen was fully equipped, Lady Gowran was expected to bring her own silver.

Ampthill Park after 1737

Lady Gowran was a sister-in-law of the Duke of Bedford. On her death in 1744 the estate passed to her son John, 1st Earl of Upper Ossory. On his death in 1758, his son aged only thirteen inherited the estate. Till he came of age he lived with his guardian, the Duke of Bedford. After a lengthy Grand Tour in 1764, he decided to remodel Ampthill Park on neo-classical lines. Naturally, he turned to Sir William Chambers, the architect of alterations at Woburn, employed by his ex-guardian. In 1769, the year that Ossory married the divorced wife of the Duke of Grafton, the improvements began.[7]

It would appear that Chambers remodelled the already existing arcades and pavilions (shown on Gordon's map of Bedfordshire of 1736). His intention was to create a self-contained suite of rooms in the east pavilion and a service/kitchen wing in the west. In doing so he harmonised the central block with the two pavilions. Redecoration of the old parlour to convert it into the drawing room was the major feature of Chambers' work. The plasterwork of the ceiling was done by Joseph Rose. Chambers introduced a number of fine chimney pieces including a Doric one in the dining room, probably by Joseph Wilson R.A., who did a similar one at Peper Harrow, another Chambers house. The work was almost complete by 1771. The 2nd Earl of Upper Ossory lived at Park House till his death in 1818.[8]

The estate passed to his nephew Henry Richard Fox, Lord Holland. In 1820 he purchased from the Crown the estate that had formerly been let. Although liking Ampthill, his wife, the celebrated hostess, preferred London. The house fell into neglect.[9] In 1837 it was leased to Sir James Parke, later Lord Wensleydale, and on Holland's death was sold by his widow and his son to the Duke of Bedford for £145,000.[10] Thomas Butcher, the steward of the Russell estate, at first considered pulling the house down for building materials and commented that the more he looked at the house the worse it seemed.[11]

Despite this, Lord Wensleydale and his family remained as tenants at Ampthill Park till his widow's death in 1879. It was then leased to the 1st Lord Ampthill, brother to the 9th Duke of Bedford. He died in 1884 but his widow lived there till her death in 1927.[12] Their two daughters the Hon. Constance and the Hon. Romola Russell lived in the house till 1941 when it was occupied by the Army. After the second World War the Duke of Bedford sold Ampthill Park to Bovril Limited, as a headquarters for their extensive operations in Ampthill. In 1967, on the firm leaving the town, Lord Luke presented Ampthill Park to the Cheshire Homes for disabled servicemen who had been there since 1955. Subsequently, it has been divided into multi-occupation housing units.

AMPTHILL PARK HOUSE 1737

Sale of the goods in Ampthill Park House and Garden 28 May 1737 by Richard Viscount Fitzwilliam to the Rt. Hon. Ann Baroness Dowager of Gowran

In the Garrets:

No.1: A Corded Bedstead with Stuff Furniture, a Feather Bed and Bolster, three Blankets and a Rug, three Old Chairs and a Table, a Lock and Key.

No.2: A Bedstead and Sacken and Striped Linnen furniture, a feather Bed, Bolster and small pillow, three Blankets, a Quilt, a Table and Lumber in the Closet.

No.3: A Cane Couch and Old Curtain, two Mattrasses and pillow, two Blankets and an Old Counterpan, a Table, One Chair and Cushion and an Old Six leaved Screen.

No.4: A Dressing Glass with Drawers and a tin basket, two pair of Stuff Curtains and Vallens, a Japanned Board and Seven Saucers, two flox Mattrasses, a flox Bed and bolster, a Feather Bed and Bolster, two Old Quilts and a Rug, two Velvet Cushions and a Cloath and three kneeling Cushions, two Bibles, three Common Prayer Books, a Cushion, two Stools, two Elbow Chairs and a Table, a long Deal box, Old hangings and Grate, a Broom, an old Map, a Lock and Key.

No.5: A Bedstead and Sacken and Drugget furniture, a feather Bed, bolster and pillow, three Blankets and a Quilt, One Chair and Stool and Cushion, a table, a Grate and fender, some Guilt Leather and paper hangings and a brass Lock and Key.

No.6: A Corded Bedstead and ticken furniture, a Feather Bed, a Quilt and Mattrass, a Chair, a Stool and a Table.

No.7: A Corded Bedstead and Curtains, a Feather Bed, Bolster and pillow, two Window Seats, three Blankets and a Linnen Counterpan, two Chairs and a Table.

No.8: A Bedstead and Linnen Damask furniture, a Feathered Bed and two Bolsters, a Rug and two Blankets, a Table and three Chairs.

No.9: Two Iron bound Chests and a Lock and Key to the Door.

No.10: A parcel of Lumber.

No.11: A Bedstead and Sacken and plad furniture lin'd with Stuff, a feather Bed and Bolster, a Mattrass, three Blankets and a Quilt, three Chairs, a Stool and Cushion, a long Stool, a Table and a Lock and Key.

No.12: A Bedstead and Sacken and Old Satten furniture, a Feather Bed and Bolster and Rug and table, Iron work and Rolers for six Umbrelloes.

In the Gallery: Four large pictures in frames and four without frames.

In the Attick Rooms: A Bedstead and Sacken and green Camblet furniture, a feather Bed and Bolster, a Mattrass, a White Quilt and three Blankets, an Easy Chair and dressing chair, five Matted Chairs, a Glass in a Tabernacle frame and Table, three pair of Camblet Window Curtains, Vallens, and Rodds, a Stove, Grate, Shovel, tongs, poker and fender, a Table and two Cane Elbow Chairs and two Stools and Cushions, two brass Locks, Keys and bolt.

In the Passage Room to the White Apartment: Two Cane Elbow Chairs, two Stands and a table and a brass Lock and Key.

In the Dressing Room to Ditto: A steel hearth Doggs and Iron back, a cane Elbow Chair and six Matted Chairs, a table and two Stands, a Chimney Glass and Walnut tree Arms, a looking Glass, the frames Ornamented with Brass, a Wainscott Close Stool and pan, a brass lock and Key and brass Bolt.

In the White Bed Chamber: A Wainscot Bedstead and Sacken and

White Marseilles Quilted furniture Lin'd with Sprigg'd Calicoe, a feather Bolster and two Small pillows, a Check mattrass, a White Quilt and three Blankets, two pair of Sprigg'd Calicoe Window Curtains, Vallens, Cornishes, and Rods and Six Cases for Cushions, a Crimson Damask Easy Chair, a Cane Elbow Chair and Six Matted Chairs and Cushions, two Walnuttree Stools with Needle Work Seats, a Table and two Stands, a Glass in a Tabernacle frame, a Chimney Glass and two Walnut tree Arms, a Steel hearth compleat, a Brass Lock.

In the Strip'd Holland Room: A four post Bedstead with Strip'd Holland furniture, a feather Bed and Bolster, four Blankets, a Mattrass and White Quilt, two pair of Strip'd Holland draw up Window Curtains, a Table and Glass in an inlaid frame, a Walnut tree Desk, a Cane Elbow Chair and two Matted Chairs, an Iron hearth compleat, a brass lock Key and bolt to the Door.

The Strip'd Satten Bedchamber: A Wainscot Bedstead and Sacken and Strip'd Satten furniture, the Curtains lin'd with Persian, a Feather Bed, Bolster and pillow, a Check Mattrass, a White Quilt and three Blankets, two pair of Yellow Silk Window Curtains lin'd with Stuff, Vallens, Cornishes and Rods, an Easy Chair cover'd with thread Satten, a Cane dressing Chair and Satten Cushion, four Matted Chairs and Six Satten Cushions, a Glass in a Tabernacle frame, a table and dressing Glass with Drawers, a Chimney Glass and Iron hearth compleat, a Wainscot Close Stool and Pan, a brass lock and Key and brass bolt.

The room Adjoining: A large Wainscot Nest of Drawers, three Cane Elbow Chairs, a Glass in a Guilt frame and two Tables, a Case Rod for a Bed, an Iron back, Shovel, tongs and fender and brass bolt.

The Red Bedchamber: A Wainscot Bedstead and Sacken and Crimson Harrateen furniture, a feather Bed and Bolster and three pillows, a Mattrass, three Blankets, a Quilt and a Counterpan, two pair of Crimson Harrateen Window Curtains, Vallens, and Rods, a Table Bedstead, a Feather Bed and Bolster, three Blankets and an old counterpan, a Cane Elbow Chair and three Matted Chairs, a Small Wainscot Chest of Drawers, a dressing Glass with Drawers, a Close Stool and pan, an Iron hearth compleat, a brass Lock and Barr to the Door.

In the Room Opposite the Red Room: A four post Wainscot Bedstead and Sacken and Strip'd Holland furniture, a feather Bed, Bolster and Small pillow, a Strip'd Holland Quilt and Blanket, two pair of Crimson Window Curtains, Vallens and Rods, a dressing table, a Glass broke, a Cane Elbow Chair, Six Matted Chairs an Iron hearth, Doggs and back, brass Shovel and tongs and a brass Lock and Key to the Door.

In the Room next to the Bathing Room: Twelve Wooden Chairs, a Dove Cage, a brass Latch and Bolt.

In the Arcade: A Month Clock in a Walnuttree Case made by Tompion, a Glass Side light in a Walnuttree frame, and a Glass Bell to Ditto and a brass Latch and Bolt.

My Lords Bedchamber: A Wainscot Bedstead and Sacken, four Mahogany posts, blew Camblet furniture lin'd with Linnen, a feather Bed, Bolster and two pillows, a thick Mattrass and a Check Mattrass, four Blankets and a White Quilt, two pair of Camblet Window Curtains lin'd with linnen, Vallens and Rods, a Mahogany dressing table and a Glass in a tabernacle frame, painted and Guilt, an Easy Chair, four Matted Chairs and an Old Writing Desk, two heads, two plaister figures and six pictures, a brass Lock and Key and Iron bar to the Door.

The Dressing Room: Two pair of Camblet Window Curtains lin'd with White Dimity, Vallens and Rods, a Cane Dressing Chair and Needle Work Cushion, four Square Stools and two round Ditto with Needle Work Seats, a large Wainscot Nest of Drawers, a Wind stove, a brass Latch and Bolt and two pictures.

The Passage Room: A fourpost Bedstead and Sacken and blew Camblet furniture, a feather Bed and Bolster, a Close Stool and pan, a brass Lock and Key and Iron barr and two black Japann'd tables.

The Servants Room: A Crimson China field Bed, a feather Bed, Bolster and pillow, a White Mattrass, Three Blankets and a White Quilt, One pair of Crimson China Window Curtains and a Rod, a Wainscot Close Stool and pan, Six Cane Chairs and a Table, a Chimney Glass and Iron Doggs, a brass lock and Key to the door.

The Yellow Mohair Bedchamber: A Wainscot Bedstead and Sacken and Yellow Mohair furniture, Shalloon Case, Curtain Rod and Counterpan, a feather Bed, Bolster and One pillow, a White Mattrass, four Blankets and a White Quilt, two pair of Yellow persian draw up Window Curtains, lin'd with Stuf, Vallens and Cornishes, a Yellow Mohair Easy Chair and Seven Chairs, backs and seats cover'd with Mohair and Cases to Ditto, a dressing table and Japann'd dressing Glass and Boxes to the same, a Glass in a tabernacle frame painted, a Chimney Glass and two Glass Sconces, three pieces of forrest tapistry, three Old pictures, a Steel Hearth compleat, two brass Locks and Key.

The Dressing Room: Two pair of Crimson persian Window Curtains lin'd with Stuf, Vallens and Rods, a Crimson Damask Easy Chair, Eight Matted Chairs and Cushions, a Jappan'd tea table and Stands, a Chimney Glass and four Glass Sconces, a brass Hearth and Doggs compleat, a brass lock and ten pictures.

The Stone Parlour: Two pair of Crimson Harrateen Window Curtains, Vallens and Rods and a Glass in a tabernacle frame painted, a Mahogany table and Dumb Waiter, a Marble table and Wainscot frame, a Japann'd Copper Fountain and Cistern, two Elbow Chairs Cover'd with blew Cloath and Eight matted chairs, a pair of Walnuttree Arms and One Double One, an Iron Stove compleat, two Old floor Cloaths and two Japann'd bottle Stands, two brass Locks and one Key and ten pictures.

My Lords Dressing Room: Six Russia leather Chairs, a Mahogany table and a Deal table a Wind Stove a Chimney Glass and a Weather Glass, a plaister Bust and six China figures, a Hercules on a pedestal and three brass Locks.

The Great Hall: Twenty four Cane Chairs with Carv'd frames, two portland Stone tables on Deal painted frames, ten Plaister heads and two Vazes, two plaister figures, an Indian Umbrello, an Iron back and Doggs, fireshovel and tongs, three floor Matts, two brass Locks, two handles and a brass Latch.

The Great Parlour: Three pair of Dutch Caffoy Window Curtains lin'd with Stuff, Vallens, Cornishes and Rods, twelve Walnuttree Chairs with Laid Seats, four pieces of painting in the pannels Over the Doors, two Marble Sideboard tables on Iron Bracketts and Shelves Over them, two large Marble Cisterns with handles, a Marble fountain and Cistern, two Marble tables on Single Iron Brackets, two Glasses in tabernacle frames painted and Guilt, a Chimney Glass in a Guilt frame, a Brass hearth and Iron back compleat, four brass Locks and Keys.

The Closet: A Deal Table, a Backgammon table and Draft board.

The Withdrawing Room: Two blew Taffety draw up Window Curtains lin'd with Silk, an Easy Chair covered with blew Damask and Lacquer'd frame, Six Chairs Cover'd with Ditto, a Walnuttree Settee with a false Seat cover'd with blew Damask, a Marble table on a Gilt frame, a large Glass in a tabernacle frame Carv'd and Guilt, a Chimney Glass in a glass frame and two Gilt arms to Ditto, a Small fire Screen and a Six leav'd India Screen, a Brass hearth and Iron back compleat, two pieces of Iamage Tapistry, three plaister Vazes and a brass Lock and Key.

The Atlas Bed Chamber: A Wainscot Bedstead and Sacken and Gold Atlass furniture, the Curtains lin'd with flower'd taffety, an Atlas Counterpan, a Shalloon Case Curtain and Rod, a Feather Bed, Bolster and One pillow, a Mattrass, a White Quilt and three Blankets, two Taffety draw Up Window Curtains lin'd with Stuff and a pair of Silk door Curtains, a Settee and Eight Chairs with Laqueur'd frames cover'd with Gold Atlass and two Walnuttree Stools Ditto, a Commode table with a Marble top broke, a Pier Glass in a Glass frame and a Chimney Glass Ditto and a pair of brass Arms wrought, two Indian figures and four plaister Sphynxes and two pieces of painting in the Pannels over the Doors, a brass hearth and Iron back compleat, three pieces of Tapistry and two Bedside Carpetts, a brass Lock and Key, a brass Latch and three bolts.

The Dressing Room: A Yellow silk Draw up Window Curtain, a Walnuttree Dressing Chair and four Stools cover'd with Needle Work, a Dressing table and a Set of Dressing boxes Japann'd, an Oval Chimney Glass, three China Jarrs, two Beakers, one Bottle, two China Images in Wood, a large China Bowl and Cover, the Bowl broke, a Close Stool and pan, a brass Lock and Key and brass Bolt.

The Vestibule: An Indian Tea Table, a China tea pot and Stand, a

Slop Bason and Milk pot, four China Cups and Saucers Colour'd and four Ditto, two of them broke, two Colour'd Sugar dishes and Covers, one broke, four Colour'd Chocolate Cups, Six Coloured Caudle Cups and Saucers and four Covers to Ditto, four small blew and White Cups and Saucers and One Single Saucer and a Red China Coffee pot, two brass Locks and Keys, two Japann'd Card tables and four stone Pedestals.

In the Stone Room: Seven Walnuttree Chairs with Laid Seats and two Japann'd tables, a Steel hearth and Iron Back, Doggs, Shovel, two plaister figures of Palladio and Inigo Jones and a brass Lock.

The Gallery: Fourteen Walnut tree Chairs and two Settees Cover'd with Dutch Caffoy, three pieces of Brussels Tapistry, two Slabbs on Carved and Gilt frames, a Table with Drawers Inlaid, a large Glass in a Tabernacle frame Carv'd and Gilt, a large China Jarr, blew and Gold, and two Beakers Ditto, two Colour'd China Jarrs and One Beaker and two Square China bottles, a brass hearth and Iron back compleat, two brass Locks and Keys.

The Library: Two Walnuttree Elbow Chairs on Castors Cover'd with Scarlet Cloath, a Walnuttree Writing table on Castors with drawers and a Standish, four Walnuttree Chairs with Laid Seats, a stove Compleat and an Iron back to the Chimney and a brass lock.

The Kitchen: A Range with Seven Barrs and an Iron Back, Cheeks, Crane and five hanging Irons, Shovel, tongs, poker, fender, and Ash Grate and Spit Wracks, four Spits, an Iron Dripping pan and Stand, twelve Trevits, a Grid Iron, four flat Irons, a Box Iron and two Heaters, a pair of Steel Yards, two Cleavers and a Chopping knife, three Iron Scewers, a Jack with a Multiplying Wheel, Lead weight lines and pullies, two Iron Candlesticks, three pair of Snuffers and two Salamanders, a Copper and Iron Work fixt and leaded at top, a brass Cock and lead in the Sink, two Copper Tea Kettles, two Frying pans, Seven Stew pans, four Saucepans and two Covers, two pottage pots and Covers, a Cullinder and pudding pan and Drinking pot, a Coffee and Chocolate pot, two Copper patty pans, ten Ditto small, a Chaffing Dish, twenty four tin patty pans, two brass Skymmers and Ladle, a Skillet, two preserving pans, four brass Candlesticks, one broke, Eight flat Candlesticks and Snuff Dish, a Dish kettle, two beef forks and basting Ladle, a Marble Mortar, pestle and Block, a Bathing tub and lead pipe, a Dinner bell, a plate Warmer, a Copper Lamp and plate Rack, eight pewter Dishes and Two Dozen and Eleven plates of the best sort, ten Dishes, twenty three Old plates, a Copper Warming pan and a Kitchin table.

The Bakehouse and Larders: Two Iron Oven Stoppers and Raker, a kneeding Trough and Spice box and Drawers, a flower Tub, a powdering trough lin'd with lead, two Tables, two Sieves, four flesh hooks and a Chopping block, a Table and two forms.

The Butlers Pantry: A Writing Table, four blew and White Cups and saucers, two large blew and White China Dishes, One Ditto less, Seven Small ditto, Seventeen Soop plates and twelve Odd Plates, Eight Plates, a sugar Dish, broken China, a China Mug, a China Chamberpot and five Cups and saucers, a Cistern lin'd with Lead and brass Cock, a Table, a Waiter and Napkin press, One Chair and a Tub for Glasses, fourteen tin fenders, four Water Candlesticks and two Safe Ditto.

The Housekeepers Room: Two pair of brass Scales and Nine brass Weights, a hand Bell, two Sieves, two Tables, a Cistern lin'd with Lead and brass Cock, a Coffee Mill, a Grate, Shovel, tongs, poker and fender and a Drying stove for Sweetmeats.

The Powdering Room: Two Wig Blocks, a Table, a Deal leaf, a Cistern lin'd with Lead and a brass Cock and Some Old Lead.

The Servants Hall: A long Table and two forms and four old Settle Beds, a Beam Scales and Weights, a Grate fixt and two Cupboards and some Lumber.

The Stewards Room: An Iron Grate Doggs and a shovel, twenty four Leather Stools and forty eight Leather Buckets.

The Distilling Room: A Copper Alembick fixt, a Cold Still of pewter, three Chaffing Dishes and an Iron Grate, a Jelly frame, three Chairs, a brass Cock, a Table Dresser, a Shelves.

The Cellars: Seventeen Iron bound pipes, Six Stillings, a Form, a Tunnell, four Tubs, a Cistern lin'd with Lead and Brass Cock.

The Dairy: A Copper and Iron Work fixt and a Slice, a Cheese press, two Churns and frames, two Stands, two Yokes, two handbowls, three Tubs and two Covers, a Small Churn, two large Wooden Bowls, and four Butter Tubs, five Cheese fatts and two Cheese plates, a pair of Butter Scales and Weight and five pair of Cheese tongs, a safe and Lock and Key, twelve Milk Leads and frames, a Cistern lined with Lead and Brass Cock, six Milk pails and a Piggon, two Water pailes and Eight Earthen pans, a Hog trough lin'd with Lead and two pails.

The Brew House: A large Copper and Iron Work, a less Ditto and Iron Work, a large Mashing fatt and Spout, a pewter tap and brass Cock to Ditto, an Under back, lined with Lead, two large Working fatts, three Coolers and frames and a large Tub, six Turning Churns with Iron handles, a Tunnell, two Jetts and three Covers, an Iron fork and Rake and two Iron Crows, two Deal Troughs and two Mashing Rakes, a Leaden Pump and Iron handle and Sucker, a large brass Cock and One Smaller, a Timberchain and an Iron Candlestick and Brass forcer and three New Iron bound pipes painted.

The Slaughter House: A cistern lined with Lead, a Chopping Block and Hooks, a Cyder press lined with Lead and a Mill to Ditto. and a Bushel Measure.

The Laundry: A Range and Cheeks fixt and hanging Iron, Shovel, tongs, Fender and Ash Grate and a Stove for the Heaters, a Press Bed and Sacken, a Drying frame, Pulleys and Lines, a Horse for Cloaths, a

Copper and Iron Work fixt and Leaded at top and two Brass Cocks, Seven Tubs, two forms and a horse, a Cistern at the Stable door lined with Lead, Four Bells fixt to Call the servants.

The Garden: A sun dial fixt and all the Utensils belonging to the Garden.

BCRO: R.O. 1/118

NOTES

1. Undoubtedly the fullest account of the history of Ampthill Park House is found in Simon Houfe's articles entitled: *The Building of Ampthill Park* Part I *Robert Gumbold* (B. Mag XIII pp.72–80), Part II *John Lumley* (pp.113–120), Part III *Sir William Chambers*(pp.202–207), Part IV *Capability Brown* (pp.241–246). A plan of the previous house is found in the Fisher Collection, Cecil Higgins Art Gallery FB 677, p.38 (Micf 66).
2. Simon Houfe, B. Mag XIII pp.72–80; Colvin pp.367–8; The Ailesbury archives held at Wiltshire Record Office are partly microfilmed (Mic 120, 121, 123); Mic 32.
3. RO 1/3.
4. Simon Houfe, B. Mag XIII pp113–120. He relies heavily on Ashburnham papers, held at East Susses Record Office. The letters 1696–1707 have been microfilmed (Mic 180). BRO have an earlier account book for 1683–9 (S/AM 153).
5. MC 2/8. Enlarged photograph of sketch of Park House (Z 50/143/180).
6. Colvin pp.467–474.
7. Simon Houfe B.Mag XIII pp.202–207.
8. Accounts of Lords Upper Ossory 1737–1804, RO 32/13–25; Accounts of work done for Earl of Upper Ossory 1761–1766.
9. R.H. Catalogue introduction: *The Holland Estate 1818–1842*; R 4/608/18 letter about proposed alterations 1819.
10. Sale Catalogue RH 9/1–9; Conveyance and Papers RH 9/59–66.
11. R 5/4402, 4418–4420, 4435; Some of James Parke's daughter Cecilia's letters and journals have been transcribed (*Cecilia Parke* 130 Ampthill). The originals are at Northumberland Record Office.
12. A. Underwood's *Home Rule for Ampthill* (1974) pp.116, 135, 138.

CHICKSANDS PRIORY

Chicksands Priory up to 1721

Chicksands Priory[1] was founded in the 1150s by Rohisa, widow of Geoffrey de Mandeville, Earl of Essex, and wife of Payn Beauchamp. Chicksands was a Gilbertine house with male canons serving a community of nuns. The present house represents the canons' cloister. To the north of it lay the church and to the north of that lay the nuns' cloister, conforming to the layout prescribed by Gilbert of Sempringham in his "Order". The nuns and canons were kept totally apart with a stone partition between them dividing the church in two.[2]

The arrangement of the rooms in the surviving cloister in the Middle Ages is not completely clear. A drain leading from the south-west corner of the house to the nearby stream[3] indicates that the rere-dorter and by implication the dorter were in the west side of the cloister rather than the more usual east. On the south side of the cloister was the frater with kitchens, no doubt attached. The use of the east side is more problematical but could have included the Prior's rooms in the centre with accommodation for the lay brothers. It is suggested that the chapter house lay to the east of the present house.

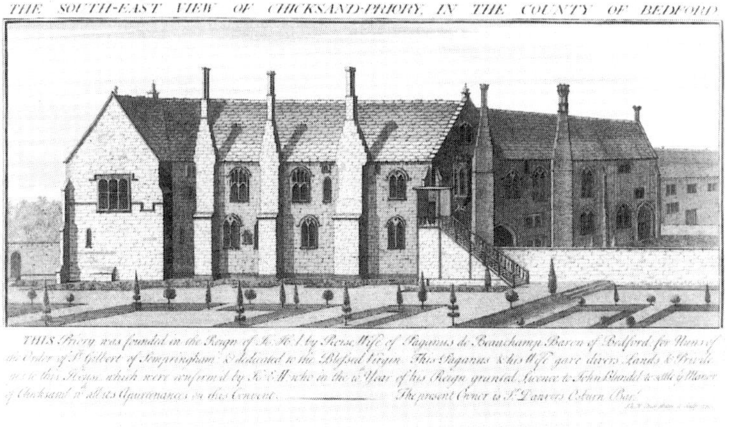

Plate 1: Chicksands Priory: This view shows that a substantial portion of the mediaeval house survived virtually unaltered into the early eighteenth century.
(*Engraving: S. & N. Buck, c.1730*)

On the Dissolution in 1538, Chicksands passed to the Snow family who demised it to Peter Osborn and his son John in 1576.[4] The freehold was conveyed in 1587.[5] From a seventeenth century plan[6] it would seem the Osborns used existing rooms rather than undertaking wholesale alteration. The entrance hall was on the east, the new chapel at the south-east corner and the dining room, possibly the old frater, above a number of small "chambers". A store house was part of the west range. S. and N. Buck's engraving of 1730[7] shows that externally Chicksands remained unchanged from mediaeval times.

Inventory of Chicksands 1721
The death in 1720 within a few months of each other of Sir John Osborn and his heir, also called John, meant control of the estate passed to Sarah Osborn,[8] a Byng of Southill, during the long minority of her son, Sir Danvers, 3rd Baronet. In 1721 the house was leased to Hildebrand Jacob of St. Anne's, Westminster, on a year-to-year tenancy at a rent of £50 p.a.[9] The inventory is important as it shows Chicksands prior to the major alterations of the eighteenth century. Using the earlier plan referred to above, and the c.1907 reconstruction of the ground plan in the VCH,[10] the location of some of the rooms mentioned can be attempted. The second corner room, the "Great Hall" and "the Chapel Closett" were in the east range. The "withdrawing room" was probably in the south range and the "Matted Chamber" in the south-west part of the house. The parlour was in the north-west corner with the store room in the undercroft. The passage with the two dining room tables probably connected up to a series of service buildings on the site of the former church. The exact location of the chambers can not be determined but it is significant that there was still a long gallery. The "Long Bed Chamber" may well refer to the former canons' dorter. The inventory reveals a house on which there appears to have been little recent internal alteration. Room uses have changed to synchronise with the new service wing.

Chicksands seems to have been furnished in the late seventeenth century, consistent with evidence of the Osborns being stretched financially in the years prior to 1720.[11] Despite the popularity of walnut furniture, there was none at Chicksands in 1721. Cane chairs were popular in the late seventeenth century but by 1721 looked old fashioned. The black and japanned furniture mentioned also could date from the 1690s.

The large number of tapestries again have a 1680s to 1690s feel rather than 1720. The fine embroidery work in both "Turkey work" and "Irish stitch" is a feature of the inventory.[12]

Unusually, the quantity of tapestries was accompanied by an impressive collection of paintings, totalling 41 in number. Unfortunately, no artists are given and only a few references to the subjects. There were at least two "landskips" and eight "family pictures".

As the inventory accompanies a lease, no mention is made either of plate or china, so no clue as to the Osborn tastes can be gained from those useful indicators. The only slight bowing to modern taste that can be detected are the "Red China Curtains", hinting at the current craze for chinoiserie.

Chicksands after 1750

Although Sir Danvers reached his majority in 1736 and there is a stray reference to Mr. Ware advising him in 1739,[13] it is probable that Isaac Ware's alterations to the house took place in the 1740s. After Sir Danvers had commanded the Bedfordshire Regiment in the suppression of the 1745 rebellion, he decided to stand as MP for Bedfordshire, being elected in 1747. Consistent with his new importance, he wanted to have Chicksands modernised and turned to Isaac Ware, whom he already knew, to do the work.

Exactly what Ware did and what James Wyatt did in 1813 is difficult to unravel. Fortunately, there are three drawings of the exterior looking towards the south and east facade dated 1730 (i.e. pre-Ware), 1781 (post-Ware and pre-Wyatt) and 1827[14] (post-Wyatt). Both Pevsner and Gomme thought that Wyatt was responsible for removing a number of

Plate 2: Chicksands Priory: The Library.
(*Pencil sketch: Thomas Fisher, c.1820*)

the mediaeval features and regularising the facades,[15] yet most of the work had already been done by 1781. It was Ware who removed the prominent Tudor chimneys, a projecting wing on the south-west corner and the external staircase at the south-east corner of the house. It was he who regularised the south and east front into seven bay symmetry. It was he who also introduced the pinnacles at the corners. The only piece of unregularised Gothic that was allowed to remain undisturbed was the fifteenth century oriel window near the south-east corner.

What internal rearrangements were made by Ware are not clear but it may be that the creation of the library in the south-west corner might be his work. In the 1730s mention is made of fitting a chapel at Chicksands[16] and this may be the date when the chapel moved to the position it was in c.1907.

The death of Sir Danvers Osborn in 1753 meant another long minority for Sarah Osborn to cope with. Sir George, when he finally came of age in 1763, seems to have done little to the house initially, contenting himself with Gothic garden buildings.[17] In 1813, somewhat unexpectedly, he decided on further improvements to Chicksands.

Why a seventy year old man decided to do this is unclear. It could well be that the marriage of his son and heir John in 1809, with possibly a large dowry from the well to do Davers family of Rushbrooke Hall in Suffolk, spurred him on. More particularly the birth of a son, his

Plate 3: Chicksands Priory: Note the large service block to the north of the main building. (*Engraving: J.P. Neale, 1829*)

namesake George, in 1813 meant that the male line was assured.

What did Wyatt do? To the exterior of the east wing he added a fine Gothic porch while apparently doing little else to the south and east sides. The large service block to the north of the older part of the building, shown on Neale's engraving of 1829 may well be his work, although it is still just possible Ware was involved. On the north side is a brick octagon, not illustrated in any contemporary engraving. The window and vault in it are thought to be by Wyatt.

The Osborns continued to own Chicksands till 1935 when it was sold to the Government. From 1939 onwards the estate has been an R.A.F., later U.S.A.F., base. Since 1962 this has included the early warning system, which dominates the local landscape.[18]

CHICKSANDS PRIORY 1721

The Schedule or Inventory whereof Mencion is made in the Indenture to which the same is annexed.

In the Great Hall: Eighteen Turkey work't Chairs, two Tables, five lacquard Sconces, One leather six leave Skreen, One Pair of Bellows, One Hearth Brush, Two iron Breast Plates, two back Plates, two Caps and one Halberd, three Pictures, three Mapps, One Scutcheon, One long Matt, One little Matt.

In the Chappell Closett: One Table, One Stool and a Cushion upon itt, One long Cushion upon the Seat below Two Hassocks, One fire Pan to Air the Roomes.

In the withdrawing Roome: six Elbow Cain Chairs, Eight other Cane Chairs, Fourteen Green and irish stitched Cushions, two Pillion Stools, Two large looking Glasses with Japan Frames, Two japan Tables and two pair of Stands, leather Covers to the Tables and Stands, One Tea Table, One Card Table. Three Callicoe window Curtains with Cornishes, One Pair of Bellows and a Hearth Brush, Two Coarse Cloaths to lay in the Windows, Five Peices of Tapestry Hanging, Two Long Matts, One little Matt, Tenn Pictures, One Pair of Steel Andirons and One Pair of Doggs, One Fire Shovell, One Pair of Tongs.

In the Matted Chamber: One Damask Bedstead, Curtains Vallains, Bases and Counterpin, One Feather Bed and Boulster, Four Pillows, Three Blankets, One Callico Quilt, Two Silk easy Chairs with Cushions Ten Cain Chairs, Ten Red Damask Cushions, Two Glass Sconces, One Pair of Bellows and hearth Brush Three White Callico Window Curtains and Vallains, Four Peices of Tapestry hanging, One Pair of Steel Andirons, One Pair of Doggs, Seven Pictures, One fire Shovell and Pair of Tongs.

In the Yellow Chamber: One Yellow Stuff Bedstead, Curtains and Valains, Bases and Counterpain, One Feather Bed and Boulster, Four Pillows, Three Blankets, Two Yellow Stuff Elbow Chairs, Four Yellow

Stuff Stools, Two Yellow Stuff Window Curtains with Vallains, One Table, One Pair of Stands, One Looking Dressing Glass, One Leather Six leave Screen, One Pair of Bellows and a hearth Brush, three Peices of Tapestry Hanging, Eight Pictures, One Pair of Brass Andirons, One Pair of Doggs, One fire Shovell, One Pair of Tongs.

In the Closett: One Close Stooll and Pan.

In the Corner Room: One Elbow Chair and Cushion, Four Green Stuff Chairs, Three Red Velvet Stools, One Tea Table, One Pair of White Callico Window Curtains, Two Peices of Tapestry Hangings, One Pair of Steell Andirons, One Pair of Doggs, One fire Shovell, One Pair of Tongs, Eight Familly Pictures, One Pair of Bellows and Hearth Brush.

In the Lobby: One Close Stooll and Pan and a Stand.

In the Green Bed Chamber: One Green and White Stuff Bedstead Lin'd with White Diaper Curtains, Vallains, Bases and Counterpain, One Feather Bed and Boulster, Two Small Pillows, Three Blankets, One Elbow Irish Stich Chair, Five other Irish Stich Chairs, One Pair of Green and White Stuff Window Curtains, One Pair of Bellows and a Hearth Brush, One Brass Hearth and Fender, One Pair of Brass Andirons, One Pair of Doggs, One fire Shovell, One Pair of Tongs, One Pair of Small Black Stands, One Table, Tapestry Hangings round the Room, Two Pictures.

In the Dressing Room: Six Green Stuff Chairs, One Chest of Draws upon a Frame, One Wanscote [– – –], One Dressing Table, One Corner Cubord, One Glass Sconce, One Pair of Bellows and Hearth Brush, One Pair of White Callico Window Curtains, One Pair of Brass Doggs, One Fire Shovel, One Pair of Tongs, Three Pictures, Tapestry Hangings round the Room.

In the Long Bed Chamber: One Green Cloath Bedstead Curtains, Vallains, One Yellow Stuff Counterpain, One Feather Bed and Boulster, Three Blankets, Two presses, Three stools, one Chair, One Pair of Callico Window Curtains.

In the Room within: One Cubord, One Dressing Table, Five Black Chairs, One Chest of Draws.

In the Canopee Room: One Small Table, Seven Wooden Stools, One Stand.

In the Pasage: One Press Cubord.

In the Long Gallery: One Large Linnen Press, One large Leather Trunk with Two Keys, One Square Deall Chest for Foull Linnen, One Large Table, Twelve Cain Chairs, One Pair of Iron Doggs, One Long Handle Brush, One large Painted Saill Cloath.

In the Room over the Pantry: One Bedstead, curtains and Vallains, One Feather Bed, Two Boulsters, Three Blankets, One Quilt, Two Chairs, One Table, Two Stools, One Sadle which belongs to my Sister.

In the Pantry: One Table, One Napking Press, Three Forms, One

Picture, Two Whetting Bords, One Glass Basket, One Stool, One Dust Pan.

In the Pasage: Two Dineing Tables, One Lanthorn, Two Pieces of Tapestry.

In the Parlour: One Ten Inch Eight Day Clock and Case, One Weather Glass, Two little Tables, Eight Cain Chairs, Three Velvet and Four other Cushions, One Cain Couch with Irish Stich Squab and Pillow, One Painted Fountain and Pedestal, Two Pair of Red China Window Curtains, One Landskip over the Chimney, One Pair of Bellows and Hearth Brush, One Pair of Tongs, One fire Shovell and Fender, One Pair of large Strong Doggs, One Pair of Black Stands for the Chimney, Five Peices of Old painted Hangings.

In the Closett: One Table, Two Stools.

In the Parlour Chamber: One Workt Dimothy Bedstead, Curtains, Vallains and Bases and a Camblet Case to Draw round, One Feather Bed and Boulster, Two Pillows. One Mattrass, Quilt, Three Blankets, One White Quilt, One Cotten Counterpain.

In the Parlour Chamber: Four Workt Dimothy Chairs with Covers, Two Workt Dimothy Stools with Covers, One Strong Box on a Frame, One Walnut Tree Chest of Draws, One Japan Table, One Japan Framed Looking Glass, One Pair of Bellows And Hearth Brush, One Pair of Black Stands, One Landskip over the Chimny, One Iron Fire Hearth, Two Matted Chairs, One Pair of Andirons, One Fender, Two Pair of White Callico Window Curtains.

In the Closett: One Table, One Close Stool.

In the Stoor Room: Seven Pair of Brass Andirons and Doggs, Six Pair of Iron Andirons and Doggs, Seven Pair of Tongs and fire Shovels, Three Fenders, One Trevit One Roleing Pin, Nine Tins to bake Cakes, One Marble Pestle and Morter, Four large Cordial Glasses, One Pair of Brass Scails and Five Brass Waits, One Dinner Bell, One Coffee Mill, One Quilting Frame, Three Suger Barells, Two Trays for Cloaths, One Cake Hoop, One baking Board, One Iron Peell, Two Pewter Still Bottoms and Tops, One Alimbeck Pot and Trevet, One large Skillet, One Pewter Bed Pan, One Iron Dust Skuttle and Three Leather Sives, Four Flower Potts, Three Old Potts and a Pitcher, One Nest of Draws for Druggs, One Large Chest of Draws.

In the Maids Room: One Bedstead, Two Feather Beds, One Boulster, Three Blankets, One Rug, Two Chairs, One Stool.

In the Corner Room: Four Leather Chairs, One Hearth Brush, One Pair of Iron Doggs.

In the Inward Room: One Bedstead of Blue Stuff and Counterpain, Three Feather Beds, Three Boulsters, Eight Blankets, One Rug.

In the Dairy: Three large Forms, One Table, One Dresser, Three Chairs, One Pair of Bellows, One Pair of Potthooks, One Pair of Andirons.

In the Landry: Two Tables, Two Chairs, Two Stools, One Rack for

Napkins, One Four Leafe Drying Horse, Two Fire Shovels, Two Pair of Tongs, One Poker and One Horse for Irons, One Pair of Bellows.

In the Wash House: Two Copers, Three Washing Stands, One large Tub, One paill, One Rack, One large Leaden Cestern.

In the Larder: One Hair Cubord, One Boyler and Cover, One Iron Driping Pan, One Chafing Dish, Two Cullinders, One large Pottage Pott and Cover, One Table, Two Earthen Milk Pans, One Pott, One Kimnell to Salt hams, Two Wooden Trays, One Cleavour, One Block, One Pewter Salt, One Stool, One frying Pan, One Sauce Pan, One Beef Fork, One Powdering Tub and Cover, One Choping Knife, One Bowll, One Leaden Cesturn.

In the Pastry: Two Bings, One Dough Scraper, One Stone Morter, One Table, One old Tubb.

In the Bake House: Two Iron and One Wooden Peall, One Pair of Wooden Scaills One Iron Beam, Three half Hundred Waits, One Quarter Hundred Wait, Five Smaller Waits, Four other Waits, One Table, One Form.

In the Kitching: One iron fire Grate, One Rack, One pair of Andirons, One Crane, One Pair of Tongs, One fire Shovell, One Poker and Two Cheeks, One Iron Morter and Pestle, Two Spitts, One Lark Spit, Two Tables, One Coper Pot for Bear, Two Forms, One Iron Horse for Dishes, Three Stools, One Choping Block, One Gridiron, One Cubord, One Pair of Bellows, One Bacon Rack, One fire Screen.

In the Hall: One Table, One Form.

In the Yard: One Bottle Rack, One Chicken Pen.

In the Celler: Ten Hogsheads, Two half Hodgsheads, Nine Barell Stalls.

In the Brewhouse: Two large Mashing Fats, Two Coulers, Four Brewing Tubs, Six large Kimnels, Two less Kimnels, Two Sives, One jette, Two Pails, One Shovell, One Cole Rack, One Pudler, Two Copers, One Leaden under Back, Two Wooden Spouts, Two Tunnels.

In the Stoor Room in the Yard: One large Candle Chest, One large Candle Box, One Scruing Press, Three Stools, One Flower Chest or Bing.

In the Stewards Room: Three Red Chairs, One Table, One Grate, One fire Shovell, One Pair of Tongs and Poker, One Pair of Bellows, One Hearth Brush.

In the Men's Chamber: Three Bedsteads, One old Table, Two Chairs, One Great Clock over the Stable.

In the Room over the Sink House: One Bedstead with Green Curtains, One Feather Bed and Boulster, One Quilt and one Blanket.

BCRO: O 44.

NOTES

1. The main archive relating to Chicksands is the Osborn (O) Archive held at BCRO.
    There are a number of printed works relating to Chicksands. These include Dr. A.
    Gomme's Notes on Chicksands, May 1982 (CRT 130 Chicksands 6); R. Humphrey,
    P. Lajoie and August Trottman *Chicksands Priory 1150–1958*; Pevsner pp.67–69;
    R.W. Ward's *A Brief History of Chicksands*, 1977; VCH Vol.I pp.390–393; VCH
    Vol.II pp.271–276; For the early mediaeval period G. Herbert Fowler's *Early
    Charters of the Priory of Chicksand* BHRS Vol.1 pp.101–128 (1913) is useful.
2. Gomme p.1.
3. mentioned in VCH Vol.II p.274.
4. O 4/8.
5. O 4/10.
6. reproduced in VCH Vol.II p.274.
7. S. and N. Buck's engraving *Chicksands from the South East* reproduced in VCH
    opposite p.272.
8. E.F.D. Osborn editor: *Political and Social Letters of a Lady of the Eighteenth
    Century 1721–1771* (c.1949).
9. O 44.
10. see note 6 and 1907 Reconstruction VCH Vol.II p.272.
11. Sir John Osborn (1659–1720) in the decade before his death had to provide for his
    wife and himself and their eight children who had survived to adulthood. In 1719
    the yield of the rents was £1852 8s 4d, leaving £269 9s 8d for household expenses
    (O 185/12). In 1718 he had assigned his mortgage of £1200 to Mrs. Leigh of
    Leighton Buzzard. This caused a court case after his death (O 155–159).
12. Margaret Swain *Covered with Care* CL 14 March 1991.
13. E. Osborn page 49 but see note by H.R. Colvin that this letter should be dated 1739
    (CRT 130 Chicksands 8).
14. 1730 S. and N. Buck (see note 7); 1781 W. Watts *Chicksands Priory in Bedfordshire,
    the Seat of Sir George Osborn Bart* (Z 49/148); R.C. Stratfold's view of the east
    front in Parry's *Selected Illustrations* 1827; 1829 J.P. Neale: *Chicksands Priory,
    Bedfordshire* (Z 49/19).
15. Pevsner pp.67–68; Gomme p.2.
16. E. Osborn pp.69 and 72.
17. Torrington Vol II p.312, IV p.26.
18. William C. Grayson, *Chicksands: A Millenium of History* (1992) esp. p.228.

COLWORTH HOUSE

Colworth up to 1720

The chantry of Lowick and the lands, including the manor of Colworth, was granted to Sir Edward Montagu of Boughton, Chief Justice of Common Pleas, in 1546.[1] It passed to a junior branch of the Montagu family who held it till 1691.

The Montagus' house at Colworth was probably built by the family. W.O. Corbett found Elizabethan red brick walling about eight feet down near the centre of the present house[2] during the restoration work done on the house by Unilever in 1949. The map of the estate of 1715 shows a classic E-shaped house on the site of the present house.

In 1691 the Montagus decided to concentrate their resources on the other estate at Lackham in Wiltshire. They sold the Colworth estate to John Wagstaff, citizen and mercer of the City of London. In 1715 he sold it on to Marc Antonie, steward to the Duke of Montagu.[3] Antonie was born at Stamford, Lincolnshire, married Anne Beke from a well-to-do Buckinghamshire family and had worked for the Montagus of Boughton since the 1680s. This had included long journeys with various members of the family to the Holy Land, France, Spain, Italy and Germany. He went on Winwood Montagu's fatal trip to Hanover in 1702, where drinking to the Hanoverian succession proved a little too much for him. This seems to have been Antonie's last trip abroad and for the rest of his life he was based in England either at Boughton House or at Montagu House (on the site of the present British Museum). His London house seems to have been near there with no country house of his own. In addition to supervising the running of the Montagu estates in Northamptonshire, Beaulieu and London, Antonie paid the various artists and craftsmen employed at the Duke's residences[4] including all the finest French Huguenot artists.

In 1714, Antonie decided to rebuild Colworth. With all his knowledge of continental styles and particularly his connections with Huguenots, one would have expected him to build in the French style, a mini-Boughton perhaps. In fact he had built a simple square house of three storeys with eight rooms on each floor (represented by the centre block of the present house). Even the entrance front lacked a pediment, if Gordon's tiny sketch on his map of 1736 is to be believed.[5] The west front survived virtually unchanged till the 1890s. A photograph of that date underlines the plainness and simplicity of the original exterior design. Not a sign of anything French anywhere.

Antonie used local workmen exclusively. His son Richard wrote: "In 1714 and 1715 Mark Antonie Esquire Began to Build his House at

Colworth & Mr. John Sumpter of Higham ferrys in the County of
Northamptonshire, plaistere, [was] the Hed foreman, Stone Cutter &
Builder about this House for my Father".[6] It was probably late in 1715
that Marc Antonie started the rebuilding of Colworth, as he did not
own the property till mid-June 1715.

In a note of 1762 Richard Antonie records that "Old Hayes was the
Carpenter at the Building of Colworth House and the present Mr. John
Scrivener of Sharnbrook his Father was the Bricklayer at the Building
of the said Colworth House."[7] Thomas Hayes was a Sharnbrook man,
too. He was buried there on 24 April 1770.

There is no mention of a London architect, although it is just possible
payment could have been made through Antonie's London banker. It is
more likely, however, that Sumpter as Head Foreman designed the
house with help possibly from Richard Knight. Whoever the architect
was, he was clearly influenced in his design by the newly built Hinwick
House in the nearby parish of Podington. A comparison with the early
picture of Hinwick (made c.1715) reproduced in *Country Life*,[8] and the
front of the central part of Colworth reveals a number of striking similarities. Both are three storey houses arranged with a central section of
three windows, flanked by two windows either side. Both use the device
of a low-pitched roof running the whole length of the entrance front. At
Hinwick this is skilfully screened by balustrading. Colworth, although
clearly influenced by Hinwick, is no mere replica. So far as can be ascertained today Colworth was intended to have only one "grand" front.
Hinwick had three. The central section of Colworth is much smaller and
simpler in ornamentation than Hinwick and lacks Hinwick's fine front
doorway, pilasters and balustrading. The connecting link between the
two houses occurs in the person of Richard Knight of Weldon,
Northants, who was the principal stonemason at Hinwick and supplied
stone from his pits, probably for the front of the central part of
Colworth. In a document copied by John Lee in 1817,[9] it is recorded
"1718 Mr. Richard Knight delivered from Wilden [Weldon] pits a quantity of stone for the use of Mr. Antonie at Collworth." Edward Sumpter
was employed at Hinwick in a minor capacity and it could be that John
Sumpter was a former apprentice of Knight who had branched out on
his own. The stone for the back part of the new house at Colworth "was
dug out of Mark Antonie's Stone quarries in his Manor or Lordship of
Colworth". Nos. 134 and 135 on the map with the 1861 sale catalogue
of Colworth are named as "Stone Pit Spinney". They lie almost due
north of the house.[10]

Marc Antonie died in 1720 after a long illness and was buried on 20
October at Sharnbrook. The house was still unfinished as a letter written to him by his wife Ann in September 1720 shows: "the tylers have
don(e) one side of Roof and part of another; the man att Olney had not
got all the Chimney stone ready . . . so the masons have gon on with

the Hall that is over the Cornish and finished at the Southend."[11] Bayes
had been digging stone from the stonepits and Johnson was going to lay
the foundation for an unnamed building, possibly a stable.

After Marc's death, so far as we can see, everything was done that
absolutely had to be done but no more. In 1723 an inventory (published
below) was made and much of the contents, presumably newly bought,
were sold by Marc's widow. The family had a considerable amount of
money in South Sea stock which had sunk dramatically as a result of
the Bubble bursting in the month before Marc's death.[12]

The 1723 Inventory

The inventory of 1723 lists the contents of Antonie's square and simple house. As it gives the amounts items fetched it provides a useful
guide to the value of household goods in the early eighteenth century.
The inventory totals £305 3s, of which £198 9s 9d were for items in the
house and over a third (£103) for items in the yard; with subsequent
sales bringing the total to £365. The comparatively low figure is
explained by the fact that there were a number of pictures that remained
unsold. By contrast, the contents of Antonie's house in Great Russell
Street, London, was valued at £723 6s, including two South Sea Bonds
valued at £100 each and his wife's jewels.[13]

The ground floor of the house seems to have included on the entrance
or east front the north parlour, hall and south parlour (on the 1874 plan
of the house included in the hall). Behind these three rooms was the
main staircase. The very large kitchen area occupied much of the west
side of the house. The servants' hall and passage was probably on the
north side of the house, lying west of the north parlour. In 1723 the
house was compact and small. Its transformation into one of the larger
Bedfordshire houses lay in the future and clearly was not part of the
original owner's plan.

The furnishings of the house are fairly typical of the period. The furniture includes a number of cane chairs that were then fashionable but
there is no specific mention of walnut, the wood most likely to be used
for the better pieces. Antonie certainly had a number of walnut pieces
in London. In the parlour was a Norway oak table, product perhaps of
the increased trade between Britain and the Baltic and beyond, resulting
from the Treaty of Utrecht in 1713. There were a considerable number
of pictures in the house, including 27 black and white prints. The pieces
of tapestry in the first floor room over the servants' hall also did not
sell initially as tapestries were beginning to lose popularity. However, an
offer came in subsequently.

Antonie had a number of china dishes and basins, no doubt exported
from China in this early stage of the craze for porcelain. The Delft ware
came from Holland. The parallel craze for tea and coffee drinking is
also reflected in the inventory with a "Cheany (teapot?) and Teatable"

in the hall and two coffee pots in the kitchen. The prices given indicate that much the most valuable items in houses were not, as one might have expected, tables and sideboards but the beds with their furnishings and hangings. The "Bedstead with Yellow Callimanco Bed" fetched sixteen guineas, while the marble top table in the hall, clearly a valuable piece, fetched four guineas. The Norway oak table only raised nine shillings. The principal cooking equipment of jack, spits and waits was worth just £1 10s. The contents of the house echoed its unpretentious exterior, modest but modern.

Colworth House 1720–1771

Following the sale the new owner John Antonie, Marc's eldest son, and his mother, Ann, seem to have lived exclusively in London and taken little interest in Colworth. John lived in Southampton Row and became Councillor and Chief Clerk to the Court of King's Bench, Westminster. He died at Bath where he had gone to take the waters for his health on 17 May 1760 aged 48.[14]

The estate was inherited by his younger brother Richard, who had an altogether more colourful career. After an apprenticeship cut short by the death of both his masters, Richard set up on his own as a linen draper in 1738, in which trade he continued till 1745. In 1748 he went to Jamaica where he was probably involved in a sugar plantation. Richard was living at Mount Cheerful when he heard of his brother's death.[15]

Richard set off for England with his favourite slave, whom he subsequently freed and sent back home.[16] Unlike his brother, Richard settled happily into life at Colworth. His notebooks,[17] either originals or copies made by John Lee in 1817, are full of information relating to Colworth and the surrounding area. As might be expected, the house needed considerable repair after so long a neglect. In 1761 John Scrivener, son of the bricklayer at Colworth in 1715, "Began to Repair the said House at Colworth for Mr. Richard Antonie (when he) came to live at it".[18]

John Sumpter, of Higham Ferrers, Northants, stone cutter, almost certainly the son of John Sumpter who built the main part of Colworth in 1715, was paid £21 for providing "5 Stannick chimneys" [coming from Stanwick, Northants.] in February 1762.[19] These were for the hall, parlour, dining room and two bedchambers. Sumpter was also paid for making one with stone for the study: "£2 2s & one for the stable". He was also paid for laying 19 feet 10 inches of stone steps for the servants' hall at 1s 6d per foot: £1 9s 9d. The labour costs for putting up the chimneys, which took 15 days, were – for John Sumpter himself £1 10s for 15 days work, for his brother for 11 days, £1 2s and for his son for 7 days, 4s.

The next account of John Sumpter's is dated 19 September 1764[20] when he was paid £1 1s for 14 feet of "Harthstone" for the chimney in the hall and a grindstone. Further labour accounts follow: £1 4s for himself for 12 days' work, and 12s for his son for 12 days' work.

The notebook records under June 1762[21] two walls split by the "China" work in the middle, forming a continuous length of fencing of 202 feet, the exact length of the two wings, colonnades, and centre of the house. The latter he describes as the "grass wall". The two walls are described as "the stone wall the front of House Next hill Ground side is 72 foot long" and the other "the Stone Wall the front of my House Next the Dove house & the Pond side is 70 foot long." Unfortunately, we do not know how high the fencing and walls were but they were probably fairly low forming part of a scheme of promenades around the house. Mention is made of "the said Walk" and one on the garden side is described as being "14 foot in breadth" so it is probable the walk in the front was the same size. Mention of the "front of the house" in relation to the two walls might perhaps be thought to imply that the two wings were actually in existence in 1762. However, in Antonie's notebook there is no mention of the large expenditure it would have involved. It is clear, however, that Richard Antonie intended to do some major work on precisely the same scale as was eventually achieved.

The "China" work is of importance in itself. It appears to have been a low fence of oak railings made in the Chinese style. Richard Antonie elsewhere in his notebook wrote, "Richard Antonie Made a New China Work the front of his house here & all new Rails this side of this said house & Old Hayes of Sharnbrook made all the above of oak".[22] Chinese style or chinoiserie was becoming fashionable and examples of this style occur on many estates during the period. At Wrest Park, for instance, the original Chinese pavilion was built in c.1761.[23]

From maps of 1715 and 1762,[24] it appears as if Colworth never had large formal gardens to set off the house. The various ancient enclosed fields surrounded the house throughout the early part of the eighteenth century. This is in marked contrast to Wrest Park, whose surviving Great Garden mainly dates from this period. Antonie planted a number of fruit trees to enhance the orchard but there is no mention of other planting.

The 1771 Inventory

The addition of two wings to the main part of the house was probably started in Richard Antonie's lifetime but the inventory made after his death on 26 November 1771 shows few changes from the 1723 inventory.

On the top floor in 1723 and 1771[25] were four garrets. In 1723 they are described as south, middle and north garrets and the garret over the servants' hall. In 1771 they are described as best garret, men's room, maid's room and garret passage. On the first floor in 1723 the rooms were: a room over servants' hall, a south chamber, a middle room and a north chamber. In 1771 on the same floor were a bedchamber, green bedchamber, a green bedroom and a yellow bedroom.

On the ground floor in 1723 were the north parlour, hall, south parlour, kitchen, servants' hall and passage and linen room. In 1771 these rooms were called the best parlour, hall, dining parlour, kitchen, servants' hall, pantry and passage and linen room. A cellar is mentioned in both inventories. In 1771 a study is mentioned which does not appear in 1723.

The furnishings of the house listed in the 1771 inventory would mainly have been installed in 1761 or after. While many of the pieces would have been purchased at that date, some no doubt came from John Antonie's London house in Southampton Row. As a whole they provide, however, useful insight into what a country gentleman with London connections might have purchased and collected in the 1760s.

Colworth in 1771 was in the transitional phase in the long replacement of the principal pieces of walnut furniture by mahogany. At Colworth the two stood side by side in complete contrast to, say, Melchbourne in 1817 where mahogany predominates and walnut, old fashioned and out of favour, languished in the garrets.

In the best parlour where mahogany was most in evidence Antonie had a square mahogany dining table, a mahogany card table, a marble slab and mahogany frame and eight walnut chairs with one elbowed arm chair. In the dining room, an oval mahogany dining table, a walnut card table and six walnut tree chairs are all listed together. The dining parlour was not used wholly for dining. Guests could play cards there or listen to music from the chamber organ. Mr. Antonie could sit down and write up his numerous note books here rather than in the study, which had no escritoire. Equally, the best parlour was not used entirely as a drawing room as it had the dining table and chairs, mentioned above.

Both rooms displayed Antonie's considerable collection of pictures and ornamental china. Antonie had a few classical pictures of such subjects as Hercules, "Two Views of a Temple" and "Eight Prospects of Rome". A larger part of the collection appears to be Dutch. "Five Dutch Pieces in black frames" were hung in the dining parlour. "Nine Sea Pieces and Flowers" could well have been painted by Dutch artists, who favoured both subjects. His fine historical prints show an interest in the past, which comes across in his notebooks. He seems to have had but two small landscapes and one named portrait of Sir William Lee, Chief Justice of the King's Bench. Sir William was grandfather to Antonie's ultimate heir, William Lee Antonie (1764–1816). Antonie had a remarkable and unusually large collection of china. In the two parlours and three of the four principal bedrooms were 125 pieces of ornamental china. Although there is no indication as to which factories the pieces came from, it is likely that they came from a variety of sources: China itself, continental centres (such as Delft, Meissen, and, possibly,

France) and also from English manufacturers (such as Derby and Bow). To complement the ornamental china, Antonie had a considerable number of domestic china plates and dishes in the china closet. Some of this was probably Chinese export as two dragon China dishes and Nankeen basins are mentioned in the inventory.

Colworth 1771–1778

In 1771, on the death of Richard Antonie, Colworth passed to a cousin, William Lee of Totteridge, Herts. In the short occupancy of William Lee (he died in 1778) the second major phase of the building of Colworth was completed. A picture was painted of hounds running in front of Colworth. A copy appears as a plate in Miss J. Godber's *History of Bedfordshire.*[26] It has been attributed to John Hunt and dated c.1780. However, the notebook in which John Lee copied snippets from earlier account books records "Memorandum of Mr. W. Lee 29 Sept 1772: Paid Read for a hunting picture £7 7s 0d – Gave Read extra 16s." Against this entry John Lee comments: "This is probably the painting of Mr. Lee and his friends hunting in front of Colworth".[27]

This may help resolve a number of difficulties about the picture being dated c.1780. Mr.William Lee of Totteridge died in 1778 and his son was thereafter always called William Lee Antonie, as he had been forced to take the name as a condition of inheriting the estate. In any case, in 1780 he would have been only 16 years old.

The picture shows the central part of the house with the classical pediment. On to the central block are added the two colonnades and two wings, as they are today. These extensions had not been completed by the 19th and 21st December 1771 when the inventory was made of the goods of Richard Antonie, as they are not mentioned. In September 1775 a large bill was sent to William Lee by the architect John Woolfe, newly appointed Clerk of Works at Whitehall, Westminster and St. James.[28] He was no doubt responsible for the undated elevation of the house showing the centre of the house with the two pavilions, as in Read's drawing but lacking the central pediment.[29]

Woolfe's billed items only start in 1772.[30] The entries from then till the end of 1773 all relate to bills for plastering and "wainscoting" (probably for windows). They do **not** include any bills for moving stone or paying stone masons. The assumption must be that the shell of the two new pavilions and connecting wings to the central part of the house must have been built by May 1772. It is just possible that they were built from the beginning, immediately after Richard Antonie's death, but it is more likely that the project was at least agreed on well before his death and represents a joint initiative between Richard Antonie and William Lee, father of Richard's eventual heir, William Lee Antonie.

A number of new chimney pieces were installed between 1772 and 1775, probably for the main house as well as the pavilions. Some of

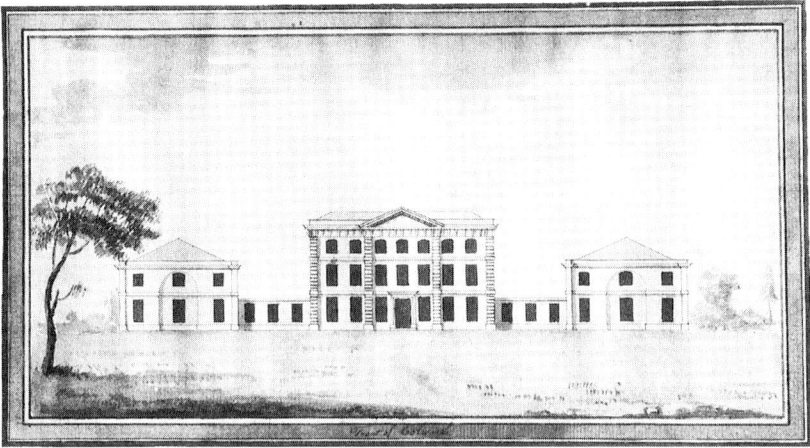

Plate 4: Colworth House: The east elevation showing the central portion dating from c.1715 and the wings added by John Woolfe in the 1770s.
(*Watercolour: Anon, c.1770s*)

these were carved by Richard Lawrence, who had made carvings for Greenwich Palace in 1770 and thus was known to Woolfe who was a clerk for the palaces. Others were sent ready-made by Nathaniel Goldsmith from London.[31]

Lawrence sent in a detailed bill to John Woolfe for his work at Colworth on 31 October 1772. He charged for "8 ft 2 inches of hollow carv'd with Straps work't in an Ogee, a stone lip ditto and bands to upper moulding of cornice, 8 ft 2 inches of Ovals to ditto, clove, egg & tongue, 4 ft 10 of Antique water leaf in a very quick Ogee to bedmould of ditto, 16 feet of clove fluting to hollow round marble, 15 ft 6 of plain leafe and stork to a quick Ogee, 15 ft 3 ilix beeds to it".[32] The tablet to the above was also described in detail: "Tablet to Ditto, a very rich vase, with foliage, three Lyons heads, festoons of husks etc., pattarn to ditto with festoons of Laurels etc. finished very neat, two end freezes very rich foliage etc." There is also a good description of the dining room chimney piece installed in 1764. Although rich and ornate, they did incorporate a vase, probably inspired by Wedgwood's designs, heralding the new simplicity in ornamentation of the neo-classical.

The building of the extensions to Colworth seem to have taken from c.1771 to 1775. The very leisurely speed with which it all progressed can be explained by the fact that the eventual heir, William Lee Antonie, was only a child and unlikely to need the house for some time to come. William Lee's picture of himself riding past Colworth with his hare hounds disguises the fact that the house portrayed was just a shell and could not have been inhabitable for another three years.

Colworth 1778–1814

On William Lee's death in 1778 control of Colworth passed to the guardians of his son, William Lee Antonie. By c.1790 Lee Antonie was established at Colworth in the winter with an establishment of up to eighty horses to enjoy the hunting. Between then and 1792 he spent over £5,000 improving and restoring the house, his extravagance causing much head-shaking by his trustees.[33] In 1802 he became M.P. for the Borough of Bedford in the Whig interest, having previously been M.P. for Maidenhead from 1790. As a Whig he was a close political ally of Samuel Whitbread II, (1764–1815) the owner of Southill. As a Whig and a devotee of hunting, he was closely concerned with Lord Tavistock of Oakley House in the affairs of the Oakley Hunt.

At first, Lee Antonie was content with Colworth as it was but in c.1808 he decided to improve the back of the house. It was with the intention of altering only a few rooms and making the ground behind neat and pleasant "that he consulted his fellow M.P. Samuel Whitbread",[34] whose Southill House had been dramatically altered by Henry Holland between 1796 and 1802. Instead of advising him to employ Robert Smirke, the up-and-coming architect at the time, he suggested Samuel Reynolds, an out-of-work artist and engraver, whom Whitbread generously supported. Inevitably, Reynolds did not like Lee Antonie's plan, writing: "I think it much too formal & not at all suitable to the Place and were it executed I am sure you would not approve it . . . I think more might be done with it, and at less expence than the plan gives me an idea of."[35] Reynolds won the day.

As Lee Antonie wrote in a letter of 1810 to Reynolds: "It is from having Your assistance in the plans & Moreover the inspection of the work that has tempted me to undertake as much as I have done."[36] Reynolds' plan for the entrance front was to add colonnades with a large central porch with balustrades, exactly on the model of Holland's Southill.[37] To this he wished to add two arches, one on each end with "service" buildings to connect them to the main house. Reynolds' most radical plans, however, concerned the rear or west part of the house. The back of the house Whitbread described as "worse than nothing" as it was entirely composed of kitchens and other service rooms. Reynolds determined to move the kitchens behind Woolfe's south wing, build a new reception room behind the main hall and change the main staircase, so that it came down into the inner hall rather than the outer. Externally, he planned to build a glass conservatory the whole length of the reception part of the house, ending in a large, probably mainly glass, orangery. Through Reynolds' letters to Antonie the progress of the "improvements" can be traced.[38] On 11 January 1810 Reynolds reported that "the two new rooms are finished".[39] Exactly which these are is unclear, but changes were made to the drawing room, library and billiard room. By March the walls of the orangery were up and earth put ready for planting.

August 1810 saw a serious crisis that could have produced a rift between Lee Antonie and Reynolds. Lee Antonie complained bitterly: "I have been witness to the . . . prevailing and shameful idleness of the Workmen with so much pay, and without there is some confidential person to superintend their proceedings during your absence. It would be better to throw the money into the River Ouse than be the means of encouraging such imposition and idleness".[40] Reynolds smoothed things over by suggesting, on Whitbread's recommendation, the appointment of George Cloak as Surveyor. Cloak had been involved in a number of commissions both on the Woburn estate and in Bedford with John Wing, the chief mason at Colworth.[41] By August Lee Antonie was writing warmly praising Reynolds again, and the crisis was over.[42]

The veranda was completed on 13 August. On 10 October Reynolds was "chimney piece hunting" in London, presumably successfully, as all the Lawrence ones were ripped out and replaced by less florid and simpler designs, echoing the plainness of the Holland chimney pieces at Southill.[43]

By June 1811, the north arch appears to have been built and the project of the south one abandoned.[44] The partition between the billiard room and the breakfast room had been broken down and the new oven installed in the kitchen. Reynolds was still having labour problems, "half crazy with the Workman's neglect". The men spend more than "half their time at the Village Feasts . . . even Bribery has lost its effect".

While the improvements were going on to the house, Reynolds was hard at work landscaping the park. A new canal was built and planting took place on a large scale.[45] The approach road to the new lodges was diverted as a result of the Sharnbrook Enclosure Act of 1809 so as to give a straight vista up to the lodges to show them off to their maximum advantage.[46] Behind the arches was a large extension to the park awarded as a result of enclosure from what had been old strips of common field land. The ancient Yelnoe Lane was diverted round the outside.

All this work was incredibly expensive and on 4 March 1812 Lee Antonie had had enough and wrote to Reynolds: "My expenses at Colworth are going on much too great for my means – I must therefore decline for the present any new project of Alteration."[47] The total cost of the improvements had come to a staggering £46,357 of which no less than £12,000 remained to be paid. This included £3,500 owed to Tatham, Bailey and Company who supplied the wall paper and no doubt much of the furniture.[48] This was still owing on 2 January 1813 despite a curt note from Thomas Tatham, a member of the well known cabinet making family,[49] who had been employed at Southill during Holland's alterations from 1795 to 1802.

The 1816 Inventory

The inventory of Colworth taken in 1816 in the year after the death of William Lee Antonie reveals the house as extended by Samuel Reynolds less than four years after completion. The old dining room and old study although downgraded were still important rooms and in 1816 were still filled with substantial and important furniture. The drawing room and private sitting room were clearly now the most important rooms in the house because they were both sumptuously furnished. On the first floor, Mr. Lee's bedroom seems the most luxuriously fitted and could even be over the drawing room. Even the attics were furnished to a comfort well above the principal bedrooms in many country houses. The north attic had a very handsome chest of drawers and a very handsome chimney glass as well as a number of items merely "Handsome". The occupant of the room slept on an "exceedingly good goose feather" bed. Even allowing for the over enthusiasm of William Brown, the Bedford valuer,[50] it is clear that the furnishings of Colworth House in 1816 were of superb quality, in excellent repair and almost certainly much of them very new. It seems likely that the house was refitted after the extensions of 1811–1812 had been completed. Support for the idea came from the extensive bills to Tatham & Bailey in 1813.[51] Unfortunately, the bills are not itemised but certainly a number of pieces in the inventory were made by Tatham during this period. Some pieces have survived and their quality gives some idea of how dazzling the effect of these rooms must have been in 1816. The inventory's importance is that it shows how a man of fashion, prepared to spend almost without limit, furnished a house in the early Regency period.

As one might expect there are a large number of mahogany pieces in most of the rooms. The housekeeper slept in a "Handsome Mahogany four post Bedstead with Handsome Chintz furniture." In the breakfast room was a "Handsome Mahogany Elbow Chair with Cushion and Cover on Casters". The "Valuable and Costly Library Table, Octagon shape with Four Draws cover'd with best Spanish Leather Carved and Gilt in Spanish Wood with Large Pillow and four Claws Richly gilt" turned up in the salerooms in 1994.[52] The mahogany dining room chairs could well be those that are now at Brighton Pavilion, collected because of their being high quality Regency work.[53] There was a "Very Handsome set of Dining Tables" to match them.

Increasingly, however, the principal pieces were being made in other woods. Lee Antonie had a "Rich and Costly Drawing Room Table Richly inlaid Verigated Yew Tree Wood on four Pillows most Magnificently Gilt in the highest Taste and fashion". Satin wood was growing in importance either on its own or used with rose wood inlay. In the library were six satin wood glazed cupboards. In the boudoir were another two as well as "Two Beautiful Stands (with handsome China Dishes) carv'd brass mounted in sattin wood Very elegant."

Plate 5: Colworth House: Octagonal table from the Library.
(*Photograph: 1938*)

In the private sitting room was a "Beautiful Ladies Work table in Sattin and Rose Wood made in the Highest Taste and Fashion Comprised of the Best Materials on Castors". This is no doubt where Madame du Thè, Lee Antonie's mistress, did her sewing. In Mr. Lee's bedroom were two "Complete and Handsome" gentlemen's dressing tables "with Large Rising Glass in sattin wood Handsomely Inlaid with Rose Wood". In the dressing room were "six very Handsome Sattin Wood Chairs Neatly Inlaid Cane Seats".

Colworth 1816-date.
Colworth in 1816 clearly had a good collection of paintings and prints. The best, however, were unidentified either by painter or subject. William Brown listed: "Six Valuable and Elegant Paintings In Valuable and Costly Gilt Frames By the most esteemed Artists." A number of the identified pictures are in the "Bath Room", in itself an innovation. The bath room was clearly used by Lee Antonie, as he could enjoy pictures of horses and dogs as he reclined in his bathing tub. The "Old Dining Room" had "A handsome Painting of Hunting", possibly Read's of Lee Antonie's father. Elsewhere were two religious prints and the inevitable one of Charles James Fox – this time with the Duke of Bedford.

The fittings of the house were up to date as well with sofa beds in both the pink and yellow rooms and tent beds for servants such as the valet. Fine Brussels and Turkey carpets were found in the principal rooms with the one in the yellow room "Form'd to the Room", i.e. fit-

Plate 6: Colworth House: This shows the house with the additions made for
W.L. Antonie. (*Watercolour: Thomas Fisher, c.1820*)

ted. In the list of fixtures are a number of Bath and register stoves.

Lee Antonie had fine china, glass and plate. How much of the china originated with Richard Antonie and how much he added himself is not known. The numerous china vases on stands were new as was the blue and purple gilt edged china dish. The ornamental china that was such a feature of the 1771 inventory is not mentioned unless it is hidden by the "29 pieces of old china" in the housekeeper's room. Lee Antonie's collections of cut glass and plate were both extensive.

Brown valued the contents at the impressive figure of £6,162 19s, including a library valued at £327 17s 6d and fixtures such as bells (£371 4s), representing 8% of the total known expenditure on the improvement of Colworth by Lee Antonie.[54]

On his death, the estate passed to his nephew John Fiott, who assumed the name Lee to inherit the Hartwell estate, Bucks. He was an astronomer, antiquary, ecclesiastical lawyer and philosopher, who held a festival in promotion of peace, brotherhood and temperance in his park.[55] He lived at Colworth till 1826 after which he concentrated on his Buckinghamshire estates.

Underlinings in red made in 1826 in the 1816 inventory indicate that most of the contents stayed there till then. On his leasing Colworth to Hollingworth Magniac in 1826, some of them, such as the octagon library table and the chairs now at Brighton Pavilion, went to Hartwell House. Much of it must have stayed behind.[56] When Hollingworth Magniac, a partner of Jardine, Matthesson of Macao, bought out the lease in 1861, it may be he purchased some of the items.[57] They could then be found in the sale of the Magniac Collection in 1893 on the death of Hollingworth's son Charles,[58] (M.P. for Bedford 1880–1885), in financially embarrassed circumstances. The bulk of the contents of the sale was the magnificent collection of art collected by Hollingworth Magniac.

Colworth was sold at the same time to William Clarence Watson, who had the back of the house remodelled to, it is said, the designs of Harold A. Peto and Sir Ernest George.[59] Subsequent owners included Sir Albert Bowen, a race horse owner, who sold Colworth in c.1930. Edgar

Plate 7: Colworth House: The rear of the centre of the house survived unaltered until the alterations by Peto & George for W.C. Watson after 1893. (*Photograph: c.1890*)

Clayson followed the Bowens and exploited the value of the estate by cutting down large numbers of trees. Lord Melchett, businessman and friend of Winston Churchill bought the estate in 1935. His widow sold it in 1948 to Unilever Limited, who transformed the house into offices and used the grounds for further offices and agricultural experimental work.[60]

COLWORTH HOUSE, SHARNBROOK c.1723

Inventory of Colworth House, c.1723

South Garett Sold: 1 pair of dogs, tongs & shovell 6s 6d; a harth Broom 10d; a pair of Bellows 1s 9d; 2 Setts of Window Curtains 15s; 6 Chairss 13s; a Looking Glass 5s; picktures [nothing^c] 3s; 1 Quiltt £1 5s; A Screwtore £3 3s; the hangings of the Room £1; a Carpett 2s; Table not sold 3s; 2 Blanketts 17s; 1 Blankett 4s 6d; Bed weightt 48 pound £4; A Table 4s; a Bedstead, Curtains & Counterpin £5 10s. (£18 12s 10d)

Midle Garett Sold: Bedstead & Curtaines & Matriss £1 2s 6d; Red Curtaines & Blue Curtains 16s; Drogett hangings 15s; A Bed 75 pound at 7[1/2] per pound £2 6s 10d; a Looking Glass 6s; 6 Chearss 6s; 16 peices of paper £3 7s; Window Curtains 10s; [Bedstead, head & Teaster £2^c]; one pair of Bed Curtains 10s; A Blue Callimancos Bed which was all salved on maide the wood work Callimanco & Lace att £8 17s 10d, £9 4s; 3 Blankets & 1 Rug £1; A Draw Nett Nott Sold. (£20 3s 4d)

North Garrett: Bedstead & Curtaines £1 2s 6d; Bed & Bolster 57 at 8 per pound £1 18s; a Bedstead 3s;[61] A Looking Glass 3s; 2 Chairss 9d; Bed & Bolster 82 pound at 8 per pound £2 14s 6d; 3 Blanketts 1 Coverlid 12s; 3 Blanketts 1 Coverlid 12s; 1 Chair 6d. (£7 6s 3d)

Garrett over the Servantts Hall: [a feather Bed 73 pound at 10 per pound £3 0s 10d^c] 2 Little Rugs 8s; A Bedsted & Curtaines £1 4s; 3 Blanketts & a Rugg £1 2s; 3 Blanketts 17s; 1 feather Bed & Bolster Weight 75, £2 10s; 1 feather bed & Bolster Weight 72 pound £3. (£9 1s)

First Floor room over the Sarvants Hall: [Blew Bed^c]; Green Bed Curtains & bedstead 18s; 1 Coverlid & 3 Blanketts 13s; 5 peices of Tapestry not sold; the Feather Bed & Bolster Weight 88 pound £3 0s 10d. (£4 11s 10d)

South Chamber Sold: [a pair of Dogs Shovell and tongs^c] 6 Chairss at 3s 6d per Chair £1 1s; the Yellow Callimanco 56 yards £5 16s; Bedstead Yalow Callimanco bed £16 16s; with 1 pair of pillows 10s; 3 Blanketts £1 5s; 3 Looking Glasses £1; 14 picktures not sold;[62] a Closstoole & pan 10s; a Cane Couch £1; 2 peicees of Tapstery Not Sold; 1 Matriss 10s; 1 feather Bed & Bolster Weight 54 £4 10s (£32 18s) 1 pickture sold forgott 7s 6d (£33 5s 4d)

Midle Room Sold: A Bed 73 pound at 10 per pound £3 0s 10d; A Bedstead with Curtains Imbossary £3 10s 0d; one feather bed & Bolster £3 10s; 3 Blanketts 15s; 6 Chearss £1 1s; 6 Curtaines not sold; 12

picktures not sold att 0; 1 pair of Dogs, tongs, belows 7s; 2 tables 11s (£12 14s 10d)

North Chamber Sold: A Worst quilt Callico bed Curtains & Head £13; Window Curtains & hangings £4 14s; A Mattriss 12s; 3 Blanketts 18s; a Cotton Counterpin £2; fier Shovell, tongs & Brush 7s; one Looking Glass 14s; 2 Cheany jarss not sold; A Bell 3s; a Matt gave to the Blue bed 0; 5 picktures not sold; 1 feather Bed & Bolster Weight 73 £4 (£26 8s) 1 table forgott 4s [6 overwritten] (£26 14s)

North Parlor: The Chimney Glass £2 10s; picktures not sold; 8 Cane Chairess £3;[63] 1 table 6s; fier Shovell tongs & Dogs Belows 10s; one Grate & fender 8s; Cheany & Teatable not sold (£6 14s)

Hall: 4 picktures not sold; 8 Cane Chaires £2 8s; a Marble Table £4 4s; one Glass stand & 40 glasses 12s; 10 litle Cheany plates £1 5s; 6 larg Cheany Dishes £1 15s; 4 Cheany Basons 2s; 15 Costard Cups 7s 6d; 6 pickell Saucers 3s; 2 Cheany mugs 8s; Delf Dishes 4s; 2 plate Basketts 3s; 1 Dozen of Soop plates £1 2s; 3 Cheany Cassters 3s; Cheany £4 10s not sold. (£12 17s 6d)

South Parler Sold: a Table of Norway Oake 9s; 1 pair of Dogs, tongs & Bellows 10s; 8 Cane Chaires £2 6s; one Table for a Sydeboard 5s; 27 Black & White prints not sold; 6 Cushins & one Elbow chair 15s; 2 Decanterss & one Larg Glass 6s 6d; Beer Glasses & Watter Glass 11s; 3 Setts of Green Harateen Curtains £1 16s (£6 18s 6d)

Kitching: 1 Larg Kettle att 12 per pound £1 4s; 1 Little Brass Kettle att 12 per pound 8s; Coper Chafindish 2s; 1 Iorn Chafindish 2s 6d; tin Collender pott & drodger 11d; 3 candle Sticks 11d; Chopping Kniff & Cleaffer 1s 6d; 8 Kniveffs and forks 4s; frying pan, Tongs 3s & jack, spitts and waites £1 10s; 1 Coper Sestorn 16s; 6 Chaires 3s; 1 Coper stew pan 4s 6d; 2 Coffee Potts & a Tea Kettle 12s; 1 Brass pattipan & 30 little tin 4s 6d; 6 Brass Candlesticks 4s 6d; a Brass pestle & Mortar 2s 6d; one Marble Mortar & pestle 10s; Sauce pans 11s; 1 Little porig pott 6s; 1 Larg porig pott 16s; a frying pan & Grid Iorn 2s; Pewter sold £5 7s 6d; a pair of Scaills & Waits 4s; 8 Black handle knives & a Cullinder 8s 6d. (£14 8s 10d)

Sarvant Hall & Passage: Sold a Table 3s; a Larg Table 7s; Candle Box & 3 Leather Chairss 2s; a Bell 1s, Scaills & Waitts 4s 6d, 5s 6d; 1 table, 1 Clock not sold; 1 picture [nott[c]] sold 3s; a Warming pan 8s. (£1 8s 6d)

The Sellar: 2 hogsheads £1 16s; 3 hogsheads £1 16s; half hogshead 5s 6d; 1 half hogshead & 2 hogsheads £1 2s; 1 Botles 12 Quartts 2s; 3 Little Barrell 11s; 1 half hogshead 5s; Bottles £1 (£6 17s 6d)

Lyning: 3 pair of Sheetts 17s 6d; 3 pair of fine flaxen sheetts £3; 2 pair of fine holland sheetts £3 5s;[64] 2 pair of flaxen sheetts £1 14s; 5 pair of Sarvantts sheetts £3; 1 Dosen of holland Diaper £1 2s; 18 Damask Napkins 15s; 2 table Cloths & 1 Syde Board 13s; 6 Diaper Napkins & a table Cl[oth] 6s 6d; 1 Dosen of Sarvantts Napkins 3s; 1 table cloth 3s;

8 towells 3s; 1 fine Damask table cloth & syde Board 9s; 1 Dosen holland Diaper Napkins & table cloth £1 2s; 18 Damask Napkins 15s; 2 Damask table cloths 13s; 6 Napkins & one table cloth 6s 6d; 1 fine Damask table cloth 9s; 17 Kitching Napkins 3 table cloths 15s; 2 pair of fine holland Sheetts £3 5s; Callimanco & Lace sett down in the Midle Garrett 0. (£22)

[Detailed list of things in the yard totalling £103 14s 3d.]
BCRO: UN 91

COLWORTH HOUSE, SHARNBROOK 1771

A Catalogue of the Effects of Richard Anthonie Esq; of Colworth 1771

An Inventory of all the Household Furniture Chena Plate Books Fixtures & Other Effects belonging to Rich[d]Anthonie Esqr as taken at his House at Colworth the 19th and 20th & 21st Days of December 1771.

Lot No.1 Best Parlour: Stove Grate fender Shovel Tongs & poker; A Chimney Glass 4 foot 4 inches by 19[1/4] Inches; A Pier Glass in a Gilt frame 26 by 18; Ditto; A Square Mahogany Dining Table; A Mahogany Card Table; A Marble Slab, and Mohogany frame; Eight Walnuttree Chairs Leather Seats and one Elbow Ditto; A Pillor & Claw Mohogony Tea table; Three Bells 1 Brush 2 Hand Screens; a Teakettle and Lamp & Mohogoney Stand; Three Crimson Damask Window Curtains Lines and Tossels Compleat; Twenty one Pieces of Ornamental China and two Jars; four Window Blinds; Hirculous &c. in a neat Covrd and Gilt frame; Two Views of a Temple; Two flower Pieces; Two small Landscapes; Two small Paintings in Gilt Frames; Sir William Lee and a Curious Piece of Needle Work.

Lot No.2 The Hall: Pare of Iron Dogs fender Shovel Tongs & poker; Oval Mohogony Dining Table & Cloath; Six Walnuttree Chairs Rush bottoms; A Walnuttree Smoaking Chair leather seat; A Mohogoney Dumb Waiter brass Casters; A Japan Table and Ambirella, two Painted Table Carpets; A Cat and Candle Shade; Two Long Glass Lanthorns; A Wether Glass and 2 Sconces; Three Baskets and 2 Jars; Six fine Historical Prints; Eight Prospects of Roome; Eleven fine Engravings; Two Bells; Floor Matts.

Lot No.3 Dining Parlour: A large Bath Stove fender Shovel tongs & poker; A Larg Chimney Glass in a frame and Gilt and 2 Glass Sconces and Arms; A Pier Glass 29 Inches by 19; A Mohogoney Ovel Dining Table; A Walnuttree Card Table and Carpet; Six Walnuttree Chairs Leather seat & one Arm Ditto; A Pembrook Table Drawers &c.; A Ceder Table and Mahogany Wrighting Desk Two Candle Stands & Ebeny Ink Stand; Three window Carpets; A Fire Screen; A Chamber

Organ; Three Window Curtains Green Damask; Two Bird Cages Lines & Pulleys; An Old Turkey Carpet; A Corner Cubbard Three Bells & a Hand Bell; A Tea Chest; A Pillor and Claw Table; Thirty two pieces of Ornamental China; A Bellows and Brush; A flower & fruit Piece over the Chimney and four other flower Pieces all in black frames; Nine Sea Pieces and flowers; five Dutch Pieces in Black Frames; Erasmus and its Companion; Two Scripture Pieces; Maps of Bedfordshire by Gorden; Six blue & White Cups and Saucers; Anteen Chocolate Cups; four Coffee Cups 6 Coulourd Ditto 5 Saucers; four basons 2 Tea pots 6 Ornamentle Cups; A Box of Chania handles knives & forks; A Ditto of Agget handles, one Carving knife.

Lot No.4 In Studdy: A Bath Stove; Chimney Glass; Pier Glass; a Dining Table Mohogoney; Three Heads; Couch & Squab; Six Cherry Tree Chairs Horsehare seats one Elbow Ditto; A Corner Cubbard; A Pair of Window Curtains; a Book Case, Walnuttree Plate glass Doors, Diamond Cut; 2 Bells &c; Two Tea Boards; A Floor Cloath.

Lot No.5 Stair Case: Ten Pieces of Paintings; A Lanthorn and Pulley; a Clock.

Lot No.6 Bed Chamber: Bath Stove Shovel Tongus and Fender; Bedstead and Chints Curtains Lin'd; Feather Bed Bolster two Pillows; Mattress; 4 Blankets, Counterpan, and Quilt; Six Walnuttree Chairs Rush Botams & Cushins; An Easy Chair; Dressing Table Walnuttree, with Drawers; Chest of Drawers and Cabinet; White Sattin Quilt; Three pair of Muslin Window Curtains; A Pier Glass 17 by 30; a Dressing Glass; Twenty one pieces of Ornamental Chaney; Fire Screen; a Pair of Brackets and Bellows; An Agget Head pocket Glass &c; A painting Over the Chimney; Two Ditto over the Door; five Heads; Two paintings; Ink Cabinet; Carpet & Bells; China & Drawers.

No.7 Green Bedchamber: Stove, Fender, Tongs, and Poker; Green Harrateen Bedstead; Feather Bed, Bolster, 2 pillows; 3 Blankets a Needlework Quilt & Coverlid; Two pair of Needle Work Window Curtains; Six Chairs and an Ebbard &c; a Close Stool; a Pair of Pier Glasses; a Mohogoney Cloaths Press; Two Ebeny Dressing Boxes; Inlaid Cabinet; Card Table; 21 pieces of Ornamental China; Paintings over the fire; Twelve Picktures; Seven Glaz'd Ditto; A Cut pickture; Two Pictures and a Loadstone set in silver; Hanger and Bell; Stool and G Flute.

No.8 Kitchen: Range Iron Back & Trevets; Crain and pothooks; Jack and Weight; Fender Shovel Tongs and poker; Two Clevers 1 Choping knife Beef fork Iron Skewers 2 Iron Candle Stick 3 foot Men pair Stylards; Six Brass Candlesticks; five flatt Candlesticks; Brass Pestel & Morter 2 Druge Boxes 1 peper Box 2 Quart 1 pinte Coper Mugs; Slice, Toaster, Stand, Basting Ladle; three Spits; 6 flat Irons 2 Lock Irons & Rest; Two Screens; Six Kitchin Chairs & a Arm^d Ditto; Four Tables; Ladle Slice Tin Saice Pan &c; Three Bells and a Spit; Nine Water plates;

four Water Dishes; 24 Dishes 2 fish Dishes 1 Cheese plate; Six Dozen of Hard Metle Plates; Pewter Cullinder 2 Dutch Ovens, Tin Cullender 2 Puding panns 2 Tin Coffee pots Pewter funnel fish Dish; five Tin Covers 2 Cake Hoops 4 Tin Sauce panns 2 graters & a Candle Box; Japan Plate Wormer 5 Old Tea Boards; a Looking Glass and Corner Cubbard; Clock in Black frame; Warming pan and Coal Skuttle; Two Fish Kettles; Four Stewpans 1 Cover; Two Confec'n panns Slice and Sauce pan; one 2 Gallon Sauce pan & 4 Other Sauce Ditto; one Tea Kettle 1 Ditto & Lamp 1 Chocolate pot; two Brass Boilers; one Coper Ditto; two Ditto; Two Sauce Pans and Iron Frying Pan; Brass Pail 1 Skilet 2 Sauce pans and one Belmetle pot; fire Screen Blowers Driping pan and Stand; A Press; Nine Oval Dishes 3 Dozen Plates; Two Teakettles

No.9 Servants Hall: A Corner Cubbard; Two Oak Tables; Two Guns; one Chair, Pair of Steps; Bellows Tongs shovel Dogs and Bell; Boiler 2 Pothooks.

No.10 Pantry & Passage: A Pair of Iron Racks; Three Diner Trays 2 Knife Boxes; Pickle Pans and Other Earthenware; Eight Baskets; Marble Morter 2 Choping Blocks; Steps Safe flower Tubb Common Knives; Bell Cubbard &c; a Large Six Leave Screen; Cubbard 2 Lanthorns.

No.11 Dairy: Two Pails 5 Milk Pans; Seven Milk Leads; Two Milk Covers Cheese Vats and Bowls; Milk Pails; Milk Pans & Cream pots; Barrel Churm.

No.12 Green Bed Room: Mohogony Bedstead Green Damask furniture; Feather Bed Bolsters 2 Pillows; 2 Mattroses; 3 Blankets one Quilt one Counter; Stove fender Shovel Tongs & Poker; Six Walnuttree Chairs Crimson Damask; Two Pier Glasses; Larg Dressing Glass; Three Pair of Green Damask window Curtains Lines & Pulleys Compleat; Curious Tortershell Cabinet; Dressing Table and Toslet; Wash Bason Stand Bason and Bolle; Wallnuttree Bureau; Thirty Pieces of Ornamentle China; China Candle Cup & Jarr; Painting over the fire; Eleven Historical Prints in Red; a Counter Pan Silk Workd; Three Pictures in Black frame and a Small Sword Silver Hilt & Belt; a Carpet & 2 Side Ditto; Five Baskets 3 Bells.

No.13 Yelow Room: Stove Shovel Fender Tongs and Poker; Bedstead and Furniture; Feather Bed Bolster and 2 Pillows; four Blankets and Curtains; Six Chairs and a Easy Ditto; Wollnuttree Bureau; Small Cabenet; Chest upon Chest; Japan Corner Cubbard and Pillar & Claw Table; Case Horse Pistols 2 Small Scabards; Turkish Scabor set in Silver; Chinay Glass; Pier Glass; Carpets; China Over the Drawers.

No.14 Best Garret: Two Stoves fender tongs fireshovel & poker; Yelow Bedstead and furniture; Feather Bed Bolster and one Pillow & Mattress; Blue; Feather Bed Bolster and Pillow; four Blankets 2 Quilts 2 Counterpans; Old Drawers Oak; Walnuttree Draws; Six Chairs 1 Elbo

Ditto; Picktures; Chimney Glass; Glasses; Trunks; Beautiful Counterpan; Crimson Furniture for a Tent Bed; Three Pair of Window Curtains.

No.15 Maids Roome:
Bedstead & Curtains; feather bed Bolster & Pillows; Three Blankets a Quilt Coverlid & Tick; Stump Bedstead pair of Steps, Wheel; Pictures.

No.16 Garret Passage: five India Pictures; Corn Binns, a press, a Bushel, & Half Bushel; a larg Turkey Carpet; Ditto & two Matts.

No.17 Mens Room: A Bureau Bedstead feather & Bolsters; Bolsters & Cover lid; 4 post Bedsteads Serge Curtains; Feather Bed Bolster and Pillows; Two Blankets & Coverled; Bath Stove &c; Four Seives; Lumber in the Store Roome.

No.18 Linnen: Twelve new Damsk Napkins; one new Damask Table Cloth; Three Pair of Hollond Sheets; Two Pair of Old Ditto; Three Pair of fine Old Sheets; Two Pair of fine Ditto; Eight Pair of Irish Servants; Seven Pair of Coarse Sheets; Damask Table Cloaths; Eleven Damask and Diaper Table Cloaths; Ten Huckaback Table Cloaths; Twelve Ditto Towels; Eighteen Diaper Napkins; Ditto; Five Dozen Ditto; one Dozen Damask Napkins 6 Diaper; Twenty Eight Damask and Diaper Towels & Napkins; Thirty three Damask and Diaper Towels & Napkins; 1 Dozen 6 Old Napkins; Russia Towels; Eleven Irish Pillow Drawers; Six Ditto; Six Old Ditto 12 Old Holland; Nine Huckaback Table Cloaths.

No.19 Books in Studdy: See Catalouge

No.20 Cellar: Ten Bell Hogsheads Iron Bound; Two Pickling Jarrs; Half a Hogshead 3 Cask; five Bell Hogsheads 1 Pipe 2 Hogsheads; Two Tap Tubs 2 Little Tunnels Six Brass Coks; Iron Rake 2 Wooden Ditto; Cross Cut Saw; Iron Crow Pick ax 3 forks; Two Corn Bings.

No.21 Plate: To 590 ounces at 5/6 £162 5s.

No.22 Plate: Case of China Knives and Case; To Pare Plated Candle Sticks; Case for Salver; Gilt Cup Silver; Set of Casters.

No.23 China &c in Best Parlour: Twelve Small Dishes; Six Couloard Plates; Twenty Eight blue and white plates; Eleven Soup plates; Small Tureen 2 Basons 4 Chocolate Cups 1 Jarr & Sundry other Articles; Twelve fruit plates 28 Saucers; Two Plates 1 Bason 2 Salad Dishes 4 pickling pots; Stone Dishes 12 Plates; Three Dozen & 6 Wine Glasses 2 Rumm Ditto 3 Gill Ditto a pair Candle Sticks a Glass Can 8 Watter Glasses 2 Cut Tumblers; Dutch Kettle and Lamp Tea board 2 Juggs.

No.24 Corn: Three Quarter of Oats; one Quarter of Barley.

No.25 China in the Hall: Sixteen fruit Dishes; Twelve Custard Cups 4 Chocolate Cups 6 Coffee Cups 10 Small Cups; Ten Od Saucers, 8 half pinte Basons; Six Cylabub Glasses 6 Stands 4 plates 2 Cups; Brown China Tea pot Silver Spout; two fish plats; four large Enamel Dishes; Three Large Do; Large Soup Dish 1 Smal blue and Gold; Large Blue Soup Dishes 2; Twelve Different China Dishes; Three Soup Dishes Coloured China; Two Dragon China Dishes; A Set of China Cups &

Saucers &c; Six Cups & Saucers Coffee Cups Slop Bason Sugar Dish Tea pot and Stand, Cream Ewer; Two Nankeen Basons, 1 Jarr; Three Botles & Stone Pots; Three Bowls 2 Basons 2 Plates &c.

No.26 Brewhouse: Large Coper 108 Gallons; Small Coper – 13 Gallons; Long Cooler & Stand; Larg Mash fat and Stand; Ditto; Two Working Fats; Under Back; Hogshead; Slips Hop Sive, Jet Mash Rool; Cheese Press, Portland Stone; four Washing Tubs, 4 Cloath horses; Irning-Broad, Trusels &c; Three Cheekin Pens 1 Rabit Hatch; Leigh Rack, Cloaths Stand, pothook, & Bellows; Napkin Press.

No.27 Yard, Coach house &c: [*detailed list of 21 lots*]

The Above Household Furniture, Plate &c. belonging to the late Richd. Anthonie Esqr; of Colworth in the County of Bedford, were the 19th, 20th and 21st of December 1771. Appraised by Us whose Hands are hereunto Subscribed, between Buyer and Seller, for the Sum of Six Hundred and fifty-four Pounds, 13s.

[signed] Batholomew Hyatt, Negus Eston

Summary of Valuation

No. 1	28	0	0	Brought Forward	£277	0	0
No. 2	7	0	0	No.15	5	5	0
No. 3	34	10	0	No.16	3	10	0
No. 4	16	10	0	No.17	8	10	0
No. 5	8	0	0	No.18	32	10	0
No. 6	31	10	0	No.19	15	10	0
No. 7	26	10	0	No.20	14	0	0
No. 8	32	10	0	No.21	162	5	0
No. 9	2	5	0	No.22	4	5	0
No.10	4	10	0	No.23	8	10	0
No.11	3	10	0	No.24	3	18	0
No.12	44	10	0	No.25	13	10	0
No.13	20	10	0	No.26	17	0	0
No.14	17	5	0	No.27	89	0	0
Carried Forward					£654	13	0
	£277	0	0				

BCRO: UN 184

COLWORTH HOUSE, SHARNBROOK, 1816

An Inventory and Appraisement of all the Neat and Valuable Household Furniture China glass Linen Plate Library of Books Fixtures And other Valuable Effects The Property of the late Wm. Lee Antonie Esq. Colworth House near Sharnbrook in the County of Bedford Febry 9th, 1816, And Following Days by William Brown, Bedford.

Old Dineing Room: Handsome fender and fire irons Brass ornaments handsome Mahogany side board with Drawer Brass ornaments silk blinds etc. complete One handsome Do. to Corrispond Three pair of Elegant Morine Window curtains with velvet border handsome fringe, Brass french Rods. Completely fitted up with Handsome Cornice's, very handsome Turkey Carpet 5 Yards and half by 4 yards and ¾, Full size Pembrook table Handsomely inlaid (fine wood), Pair of Elegant and ornamental Side tables in Mahogany brass Mounted, and in best Preservation Large mahogany Plate warmer Lined with tin, Handsome Celleret Cupboard in Mahogany Very Handsome and Elegant Side board table in Mahogany and inlaid seven foot and half, Brass mounted etc. complete, one fine Pole & Claw fire screen Harth rug and small Marble cistern Large and handsome wine Cooler Lined with Lead,[65] mahogany fire Screen with slide two stools And hearth brush Seven very handsome mahogany Chairs with two Elbows to match with morrocco seats and Double Brass nailed, Handsome Painting A Hunting piece in A neat Gilt Frame very Handsome Painting (Four Dogs) in an Elegant Gilt Frame, Two Elegant Paintings in Recesses (Flowers, Fruits etc.) in Very Handsome frames Three Large Paintings and two smaller in handsome frames Two Bell pulls and two fox Dusters Very Elegant and Valuable sett of Mahogany Dineing tables on Pillows and Claws (fine Wood).

Breakfast Room: Handsom steel fender, sett of Fire Irons, Harth brush and Gard, two handsome Pole Fire screens and Harth Rug, Two Leav'd fire screen Very Handsome convex Mirror in neat black frame, two Beautifull Lustres and Chimney Ornaments, Gentleman's Weighing Machine, Two Handsome Japand Ornamental tables with Draws, Mahogany stand and two stools, Handsome Mahogany writeing table with Draws etc. Complete, A very Handsome Brusels Carpet twenty one foot by Sixteen foot and half, Two Prints in gilt frames, Fox and the Duke of Bedford, Six Handsome Japand Chairs and four Elbows to Corrispond – With Cane seats and backs to Ditto, One Handsome mahogany Elbow Chair with Cushon And Cover on Castors Complete Painted sofa with Large hair Mattress Squabs and Pillows on Casters and Handsome neat Cover (On Casters) with neat fringe to Ditto, Handsome Couch (Japand) with Cane bottom and back with hair Mattress, Elegant and Handsome Chimney Glass in A neat gilt Frame seven foot by four foot, Beautiful brilliant Plate to Ditto, Three Pair Handsome window Curtains and Rods – Venitian Window blinds in both Rooms.

The Old Study: Piear Glass in A Gilt frame Small mahogany table writeing Table with Draws etc. Complete, Handsome Mahogany Wardrobe And Bookcase with glazed Doors Painted [mahogany^c] Sofa on castors With cushions swabs etc. Two Handsome Pole fire screens *And one Elbow chair*, Fender And fire irons, Four Mahogany Chairs with cane seats, two Pair window curtains and stool, Brussels Carpet twelve foot square.

New Dineing Room: Two pair of Very Elegant China Vases on Handsome gilt stands Very Handsome Brussels Carpet Twenty four feet and Half by sixteen feet and Half Very Handsome set of Mahogany Dineing tables, Eight handsome Mahogany Chairs with best Morocco seats and Double brass Nailed Eight very Handsome Japand Chairs Cane seats handsome Polished steel fender and set of Best fire Irons With ornaments, Three Handsome Chemny Ornaments Very fine toned Hand Organ two Chairs Cane seats Handsome Painting (Ruins of Athens), One Dutch Painting eight leav'd Screen Three flower stands Marble tops twenty five yards Of Oil Cloth in two Pieces Pair Elegant Chandiliers.

In the Pink Study: Very Handsome and Valuable French time Piece, very Costly Made up Carved figures glass Cover and stand Richly gilt.

New Dineing Room: Beautiful and Costly Festoond Window Curtains Richly made Up Fitted up with French Rods to Ditto Lines and tassels all to Corrispond being aboute one Hundred and twenty five yards Of the very best and Rich Buff Morine with Rich silk Border And fringe to Ditto, the Whole Comprised Of the very best Materials.

Library: A Valuable and Costly Library Table Octagan shape with Four Draws cover'd with best Spanish Leather Carved and Gilt in Spanish Wood with Large Pillow and four Claws Richly gilt, Ten very handsome Library Chairs blue and gilt with two Elbows Ditto to match and two Cushons Handsome Brussels Carpet Twenty foot square, Six sattin Wood Glazed China Cupboards Handsome wallnuttre Pillow and Claw Table Library Step Elbow Chair in Mahogany With Cushon and Cane Seat, Pair of very Elegant And superbly Rich Gilt Fire Screens very Handsome and Elegant time Piece In A Gilt and Marble stand And Glass Cover to Ditto Very handsome Library Chair Elegantly gilt,[66] On brass Castors, Port Folio, Very Handsome and Elegant Book Case Brass mounted in Sattin wood Brass wire Pannels Silk blinds With ornaments Atop. In the Recess Left hand side Going into the New Dineing Room, Ditto Adjoining the Chemny Piece Much Larger And on the same Principle And elegance and made with the very best and valuable Materials one other Ditto on the Other side Of the Chemny Piece One othe Ditto the Right hand Going into the Drawing Room And two Ditto the Left hand side All to Corrispond with the best Materials and Workmanship Harth Rug etc.

In the Boudoir: Very handsome and Elegant Back gammon and Draft board Table on pillow and Claw fine Wood In the Very best Preservation Two Elegant and Handsome China Cupboards Glazed in sattin Wood Very Handsome and valuable Couch and Mattress with Pillow's Squabs etc. Complete, Two Beautifull stands (with handsome china Dishes) Richly carv'd brass mounted in sattin Wood[67] Very elea-gant Brilliant Mirror in Handsome gilt frame Thirty three Inches Diameter, Dutch Painting in an Elegant frame Handsome Picture frame

Valuable and gilt ornamental Ink stand With three Sconces And Pedestal Elegant Mounted with best cut glass stands and Beautifull shade to Ditto Sett of Best fire irons and fender Very Elegant Chimny glass Beautifull Brilliant Plate six feet by four feet In very handsome satin wood frame Brass mounted in A superb taste.

Drawing Room: Two Large and Beautifull China Vases on very Elegant gilt fluted And brass mounted Pillows being Of the first Description and Elegance Two Ladies work-tables Rare and Beautifull Wood inlaid on sattin Wood Handsome stands And Richly gilt ten Handsome Chairs blue and Gilt with cane Seats very Handsome sett Of fire Irons and fender with brass Rim Large and handsome harth rug Pair of Elegant fire Shades superbly Gilt with Bracketts Coverd with Velvet Costly made and Of the best Materials Pair of Very Elegant Carved and Gilt stands of superior Workmanship, Large and Handsome China Dishes to Ditto, Costly made And in the most fashionable Taste And Elegance One most elegant And Superb Grecian chair Cover'd with Rich silk, Cane seat And and [sic] Cushion, gilt in the most Elegant and Costly fashon four very Elegant elbow chairs all to corrispond very Handsomely gilt And in the best Preservation[68] Pair of very Handsome fire shades with Brass Pole and Superior gilt Pillow and Claw in the most Elegant taste, Pair of very Rich and Costly Stands Or Burners for Lamps Got up In the most elegant taste and fashon Richly Gilt and Carved in the most superb taste and Beauty, Rich and Costly Drawing Room Table Richly inlaid Verigated Yew Tree Wood on four Pillows most Magnificently Gilt in the highest Taste and fashion, A very Costly And elegant Chandiliar, A very Handsome and Rich Brussels Carpet Twenty eight feet by eighteen feet, Rich Pattern and in the best Preservation *Twelve yards of Carpeting*, Two very Elegant sofas Seven feet Long by two feet and Half wide being very Costly and Magnificent Richly carv'd And Gilt Cover'd with costly blue silk Richly Ornamented Rare and Costly Mattress cover'd with Rich silk and Costly ornamented Pair Valuable Rich blue sattin window Curtains Lined with silk Troughout, yellow Silk Border and trimings and Handsome brass French Rods to Ditto, Containing 48 Yards, One Other Pair Ditto to Corrispond Containing All the best Materials and got Up in the most workmanship like manner, Containing 48 yards Very Elegant Chimny Glass Brilliant Plate six feet by four feet three inches In a very Rich and Costly Gilt and Carved frame with Handsome Circular top to Ditto Very Elegant Piear glass In one most Beautifull brilliant Plate Seven foot and Half by four foot In A very Elegant carved And gilt frame With Circular top eighteen Inches Deep with Transparent Glass to the Floor, three foot six by two Feet Ornamental tablet on Rich and Costly gilt Bracketts, Very Beautifull and Valuable time Piece upon A very Superior French plan Rich and costly Gilt and Enamell'd Handsome Glass cover to Ditto Richly sett in Diamonds with every Ornament to

Corrispond Elegant Piear Glass six Foot six inches by four foot Nine Inches in A Handsome Gilt Frame And circular top to Ditto Very Handsome China Jarr blue And White and gilt stand, Very elegant and Valuable time Piece Richly sett and carved in Marble, Beautiful ornamented In Highest taste and Elegance With Handsome glass cover to Ditto.

In the Library: Twenty four yards of Shambray Muslin Lined with blue Gooloon made up to the windows for curtains Twenty four Yards to corrispond Lined and made for Curtains in the best manner Very Handsome Festoon Window, Curtain thirty two Yards Handsomely Fringed And Lined throughout with Gooloon, The Curtains to the Pink Study Thirty six yards of Ell wide Chintz Lined with Pink Callico, And Festooned Done up in A very Complete manner.

Private sitting Room: Fender and fire irons and harth Rug Twelve Neat Chairs Cane Seats, Very Handsome Elbow Chair With cushon and Cover Complete With stool and hair Mattress, Very Elegant Knee hole writeing Desk or table with Draws etc. complete Coverd with best green spanish Leather with handsome gilt Ornaments in sittin Wood, five Foot and Half Long by three foot And Half made in the best Workmanship Like manner and the Whole comprised of the best materials[69] Very Handsome and Elegant Cabinet in sattin Wood Very Handsome Gilt ornaments With mouldings and two Cupboards Escrutoir front with Private Draws Complete made of the best materials And in the highest taste of Fashon[70] With a very Handsome And Ornamental Alabaster Urn two Foot high by fifteen inches Diameter Pair of very handsome brass Pole Fire screens elegant gilt stands With handsome silk blinds in Gilt frames Beautifull Ladies Work table in Sattin and Rose Wood Made in the Highest taste and Fashon Comprised of the best Materials on Castors elegantly gilt And green cover, Mahogany Pillow and Claw stand, And best Harth rug And Brush A very Handsome and elegant Sofa on Castors seven foot long by three foot wide, Capital hair Mattress stuffed with the best Curled hair covered with canvas With squabs Pillows and Cushons, Fine Holland cover to Ditto and Very Handsome Chints cover to Ditto, Very Handsome Brusels carpet, eighteen feet by fifteen feet. A very elegant Patterns Beautifull Coulers Very Handsome Chemney Glass four foot four Inches by two foor six inches in A very Elegant Carved and Gilt frame Very elegant Piear Glass six foot by four foot four Inches Brilliant and fine Plate in A superb Carved and gilt Frame.

Articles in Different Places: Seven Homespun Sheets two Pair Window Curtains to the Library Jaconet Muslin one yard three Quarters Wide with broad and Handsome Needle work border (twenty Yards) Four Pair beutifull Curtains Handsome Pattern to Ditto Forty yards, 4 very Handsome sprig muslin Curtains forty eight Yards three muslin Covers to Chandeliers eighteen yards of New Muslin and eighteen yards of Bedfurniture, forty yards Of fine Chintz Different Patterns, Fourteen Yards of Pink Cotton Lineing, Fifty four yards of Blue Sarcenet Cotton, three yards and half Of broad Yellow cloth, one hundred and fifty Yards of fine brown Holland, Two Whole Pieces of fine brown Holland, Two Large Window Curtains, Curtains for a Tent Bedstead Complete and two window curtains to Match (Chintz), Four muslin Curtains in Dressing Room Clost, Worsted and bell Rope Curtain Fringe.

In the China Closet: Sixty six Blue and White Plates, Nine Blue and White Plates and Three basons, five yellow plates And two covers, ten small blue And White Plates, five black tea Pots and eight Coulerd Plates, Mahogany Wine Cooler brass mounted, Large ovil tea tray And three Clay's Round tea boards, Pair very Handsome Dishes, Covers and Stands, ten large Breakfast and six Cups, ten very Handsome gilt edged Chocolate Cups, Two handsome coulerd bowles and ten sausers and eight Breakfast Cups and sausers very elegant, Blue and Purple gilt edged China Dish With two Handles, two couler'd Pitchers, two pair bottle stands, Bread basket snuffer and Japand tray, One Clays bread basket, one gold Borderd Octagon waiter and one Ovil Ditto with two Handles Ovil Basket and Large pickling Jarr Mahogany Dinner tray small One Ditto, Knife box and tray stand, Two Large Dinner trays and Leather Plate baskett, two Leavd mahogany table, two Chairs With Rush seats twelve very Handsome and best cut glass Wine coolers, eleven very best cut Glass water bottles and ten Ditto Tumblers, twenty Handsome and best cut wine Glasses, One Pair of best cut glass cruets, six small Cruets, pair of best cut glass salts, six small Cruits, pair of best cut Glass salts, soy bottle, butter Dish and Cover, six finger glasses with Handles, four best Rummers, four Cut Glasses, one Large beer Glass And five Cyder glasses, Eleven best Cut finger glasses, six best cut glass Wine coolers, two very handsome best cut glass Dishes and two Ditto Cream Jugs, twenty seven Wine and Punch Glasses, four Champaign Ditto, Two best glass cruits three very Handsome Brown pitchers and one pair of best mustard pots and Covers All with silver Rims, Dozen of Blue and White China Plates, Large Yellow Jarr and stand wood Bowle and Wood ware, pair of best cut glass De Canters, one other Pair Ditto, Two pair of Handsome best Cut glass De Canters, Pair glass Pitchers, One Large water bottle and two pair smaller Ditto best Cut glass sugar Bason and Cover to Ditto and sundrys Two pair of Clarit wine De Canters.

In the Kitchen and Pantrys Adjoining: Table china etc. Consisting of Nineteen Dishes Various sizes two Tureens and covers three Vegetable Dishes and covers and five soop Ditto And Stands Fish Plate and Two round Dishes and sundry pieces to corrispond several sandish Dishes and covers Large tureen and cover, Several ovil Dishes various sizes, Twenty four plates and sundry Pieces of Odd Earthenware salt tub And

Cover, Flower Tub, three basketts And two pieces of Marble, Pair steps, excellent Marble slab Four feet by two feet on A Handsome Mahogany stand, two salting tubs and Covers to Ditto, Handsome blue Marble slab, one Inch and half thick, Six foot long by three foot Wide on A Handsome Mahogany stand, Milk Lead And Stand Pitchers Jarrs etc., Exceeding good Eight Day Clock In a neat Mahogany Case, seven Roasting Spitts, Pair stilliard and tin salt box, three Copper Calldrons, And Covers to Ditto and one Large Round one and Cover, three small Round ones and Covers, seven very Best French copper stew pans And Covers, A very good six Quart copper, three stew pans with handles, One Copper fish Kettle and Cover, Seven French copper Stew pans And Covers and one large Ovil Copper Stew pan and Cover Two ovil Copper Stew Kettles with two strainers, Three stew Kettles and Covers, six small french stew pans and Covers, Three smaller Ditto Pudding mould etc., Three Copper Pans, five meat Choppers And one Rasp, one Large Copper stew pan and Cover, Large Lot of tin Ware Sheet of Copper, And three pudding pans and Driping Pans, small brass Mortar and Pestall, Eleven best Meat Covers Sorted, Tin Cullinder and tin Coffee Pott And sundry tin ware, eight Pewter Dishes and seven small Ditto, Two Large Vension Dishes pewter, One Large ovil Dish, two large Round Dishes, seven Common Plates, Two water Plates, twelve best Pewter Plates two salt stands, spurgers, And tin ware Ink stand and Cheese Toaster, Large fire screen Lined With tin, Stout Kitchen table And Chopping block, tea Boiler, Tea Kettle and sausepan, Large Fender and sett Of fire irons, one Elbow Chair, three Rush bottom Chairs And one Wood bottom Ditto, Marble Mortar, Wood Pestal and stand, Large meat cover, fork, Beef tongs, hook and sallamander And Japand Coal Scope, two small forms and table [*Two small forms and table*[c]] Coffee and Pepper Mills, five large Copper sausepans and two Quart Copper, A four Quart Copper and One Quart Copper, A Copper tea Kettle, Copper boiler and Cover, Frying pan, Gridiron, Meat Chopper, Ladles And sundry Old tin ware Driping pan And stand and ovil Tub, iron bound tub and Hog tub, Iron bound tub, pail and Jett, Choping block, coal shovil and Old Brass Kettle, iron bound tub And Pail and Step Ladder And Sundrys over the oven.

Linen: Six pair of Large and Handsome Sheets, Two pair sheets, six Pair various marks (fine), Thirty five pair of stout usefull sheets, twelve Large and best Pillow cases, six small Ditto, Twelve second best seventeen Common Ditto and twenty two Various.

Table Linen: Fifteen New Damask table Cloths, Nine very good table Cloths, four Old table Cloths, Twenty one Side table Cloths, Sixteen Hall table Cloths, four Huckaback table Cloths, thirty six Napkins, thirty six best Ditto, twenty four fine Napkins, Thirty six not marked, twelve Best Ditto, thirty six small ones, Twelve old, twenty five much used, Six Toilett Cloths marked as New, Eleven Ditto being in Use,

twenty four towels, Forty eight much in Use, Thirty six smaller, twenty
five marked, thirty six Course, twenty five much used, twenty Round
towels, 30 Glass towels & 40 Knife Cloths. Twenty four New Light
Doilets, twenty four new Dark Ditto, twelve Light Doilets much Used
And twelve Dark doilets much Used, eighteen various sizes, A Cover To
Bathing tub, seven Powdering Sheets, Eleven China Cloths, twelve
Dusters, twelve Dairy Ditto, four House cloths, six Dresser Ditto, thirty
Kitchin Cloths etc. etc..

House Keeper's Room – China etc.: Twenty best Desert Plates,
Beautifull Paintings and burnt in Gold, fourteen Best burnt in Inamelld
Plates All Various, six best Old China Plates, Eighteen Beautifull
Dishes, one Handsome China Baskett, four valuable & best Cut Glass
Dishes, Six common Ditto, eighteen Best China Cups and sausers Burnt
Inn and Gold Eged, six Ditto all Burnt in and Gold Eged, one
Handsome Pickle Dish Gilt in an Elegant Manner one slop bason and
five Broth Ditto, twelve White Custard Cups, twenty six Red and White
Soop Plates, twenty Nine red and White Plates and nine smaller Ditto,
Four small tureens and Covers, Four China butter boats, twenty two
(Foreign China) Dishes various sizes, Two Large tureens and covers,
Ten very Handsome blue and White Dishes, Eleven Blue white and Red
Ditto, Fifteen best blue and White Plates, Fourteen fruit Dishes, one
Vetegable Dish, Twenty China Jarrs, Two Large china Jarrs, one China
stand, one milk pot, one Cream pot, One China mug, two White sugar
Basons and two China basons, Three China Ornaments, two Pickles,
Twenty Nine pieces of Old China, One slop bason, one tea Pot and
Eleven Handled Cups and Sausers, Nine tea Pots, seven Jelly Cups, And
five blue and White mugs, Six blue and White Jelley cups, Three
Strainers, six White cups And sausers, one bason & Coffee Pot, Three
Ale Glasses and thirty one Ditto, Twenty two Jelley glasses, one Trifle
and two Coffee cups, six Breakfast cups And Sausers, eleven smaller
Ditto, one bason, one Cream Boat and two tea Pots, sugar boat, Three
Large Tea Canisters, three Sugar canisters, four small tea Ditto, twelve
preserving glasses, Three China Bowles, one Handsome China Bowle
and cover, one bason And Jug, Twenty one preserving Jarrs Two Ice
Pails and two Ice Paddles.

Furniture In the same Room: Two Handsome mahogany Dineing
Tables, Mahogany Bureau, Six Mahogany Chairs, hair seats, One
Elbow Ditto to Match, Polish'd Fender and sett of Fire Irons, Carpet
and Harth Rug, two Pieces Of Oil Cloth, two pair window Curtains,
Handsome Piear glass in A neat Gilt frame, Ebony writeing stand, Four
Japan'd candlesticks and three Ditto (tin).

Servants Hall: Full size Oak Wardrobe Bedstead, The Hall Bell,
Feather bed Bolster and Mattress, Minner Nett and small Cast Nett and
sundry Spittoons, Long Deal table And form, small table and Cloaths
Horse, Poker And fender, Nine Valuable Patent Lamps and glasses And

one bed Chamber Ditto and sundry's.

Butler's Pantry: Mahogany Writeing Desk and stand, Port Folio and Ink stand wallnuttree Settee or sofa Mahogany Cellerett, mahogany table, Mahogany Elbow Chair, Clay's waiter and snuffer trays, Three bird Cages, mahogany front Wardrobe etc. complete, Double Door Cupboard With Draws and shelves, Complete Corking machine, steps and sundrys, small stand, Large and Handsome Ovil Clays tea tray, China Punch Bowle, Pair of Clarit De Canters, Pair of the best Rummers, Six best Cut glass water bottles, six Common Water bottles and five tumblers, Two best cut glass sugar basons and Covers, Pitcher, Cream Jug and mug, four best Rummers, twenty four Beautifull Cordial glasses, thirty four Large Ditto, six beer glasses and one Rummer, Five Handled Beer glasses, twenty three Wine glasses, one De Canter And two pints Sundry Glass.

Maids Room: Sett of fire irons and fender, Pillow and Claw table, tea board & five Chairs, Sugar canister and Candle box, Carpet, Rumford Stove and Coal scope.

Footman's Room: Sacking bottom turn up Bedstead Half Tester Plaid furniture turnup Bedstead With neat Plaid furniture, Mahogany Wardrobe with shelves, Quilt and three blanketts, one Other Quilt and three blanketts, Dressing And Swing Glass and Window Curtain Tent Bedstead And Plaid furniture Feather bed, Bolster and one Pillow Quilt And three Blanketts, small Chest of Draws, Dressing glass and One Chair and Window Curtain, etc.

The Valet's Room:

Tent Bedstead with Plaid furniture, Good feather bed bolster and one Pillow, three blankets and White counterpan, one coulerd Ditto, Four post bedstead with Stripe Furniture, Good feather bed bolster and one pillow, three blanketts and Counterpane and Coulerd Quilt, two Basons, and two Jugs, two Leaved Mahogany table, swing glass, two Chairs and bed side Carpetts, Four Dimity Elbow Chair Covers sett Of Bed furniture Complete and sundrys One Other sett of Bed furniture, New and Complete Very Handsome and Elegant Piear glass, A very fine and Brilliant Plate Six foot by four foot in a Handsome frame With Circular top.

Middle Room in the Gallery: Handsome four post Bedstead in Mahogany with Stripe furniture Handsomely fringed Pair window curtains to corrispond exceeding good Feather bed Bolster and two Pillows, A Very Good mattress Handsome Counterpan and Large and fine blanketts, Night Chest of Draws in Mahogany, Elegant Piear glass in Handsome gilt Frame, Mahogany Biddett, very Handsome Chimney glass in Neat White frame, four Chairs, Rush Seats, Handsome Elbow chair, One fire shade, Fender and A Complete Sett of fire irons Very Handsome Mahogany Chest of Draws in the Best Preservation, Painted Dressing table, one other handsome painted Dressing table, Pitchers basons etc. etc., Large and Handsome ovil swing Glass, Pair Window Curtains, Carpetting Round the Room and Piece of Carpett.

Chintz Room: Fender and sett of fire irons Chimny Ornaments very Handsome Sofa, Four post bedstead with Chintz Furniture, Neat Mahogany Table and Ink stand, Mahogany Biddett, Gentlemen's Dressing table wash bason Handsome mahogany Chest of Draws, Dressing Table with Cupboard and Folding Doors etc. Complete Mahogany Pott Cupboard, Cloaths horse & harth Rug, Very Handsome Brussells Carpet, six Handsome Japands Chairs A Very Handsome four Post Mahogany Bedstead, Double screws with very Elegant and Beautifull Chintz Furniture lined with blue Very Handsome and Large Goose Feather Bed bolsters and one Large Down Pillow, Large Wool Mattress, Exceeding good Mattress in Excellent Stripe Case, Large Counterpane, three Large And Good Blanketts, Pair of Handsome Festoon Window Curtains To Match the Bed furniture, Very Elegant Piear glass Handsome Brilliant Plate, three foot by two foot, In a Handsome Gilt Frame.

In the Pink Room: Very Elegant Sofa, Bedstead with Very Handsome Chintz Furniture Lined with Pink Coach top Head all Lined throughout, Exceeding Good goose feather bed Bolster and One Down Pillow, Large and Handsome Counterpane, three Blanketts, Wool Mattress, one other Exceeding Good Mattress in A Neat Stripe Case, three Pair Window Curtains To Corrispond with the bed, Handsome Glass in three Pieces in A neat gilt Frame, A very Handsome Grecian Couch Mattress Beautifull Cover with Pillow etc. very Complete, Dressing Table Handsome and Large swing Glass in a Neat Mahogany frame, A very Handsome Mahogany table with Draw, Inkstand etc., Complete, A very Handsome Gentleman's Dressing chest in Mahogany, Riseing Glass in Mahogany complete, A Very Handsome Brussells Carpet Fashionable Pattern and in the very Best Preservation, six Chairs & one Stool, Fender and fire Irons and Harth Rug.

Closits and Dressing Room: Neat Dressing table and Dressing Glass, Mahogany Biddett, mahogany Three Leav'd Horse, Large Bason & Jug, Piece of oil Cloth, Mahogany Chest of Draws, Painted [Mahogany^c] Pott Cupboard, Neat Mahogany Horse and boot stand.

Passages and Stair Case: Seven Yards of Oil Cloth, Rich Pattern And Coulers, Five foot wide Oil Cloth to the Broad space to Passages, six Yards And Half by five Yards; Piece of Oil Cloth Along the Passage to the Portico six Yards Long by two Yards wide; Large Piece of Matting under the Carpetting; Thurmometer in handsome Case in the Passage, three Door carpetts And five Door Rugs, Two very Handsome Dumb Waiters in Mahogany fine wood in best Preservation, A Very Handsome Dutch Painting in Handsome gilt frame, A Large Baskett to the Passage, Elegant Passage Lamp, Oil Cloth in the Passage to the Conservatory Handsome Pattern twelve yards long by one Yard And

Half Wide; twenty eight Yards best stair Case Carpeting Yard and Half Wide and twenty four Stout brass Rods, very Handsome and Elegant, Month Clock Clock [*sic*] in the best stair Case in a Beautifull Inlaid Case, Handsomely gilt and on Costly ornamental Stands, Painted seat.

Dressing Room: Fender and Harth Rug sett of fire Irons And fire shade, Mahogany Night stool, gentleman's Painted Wash Hand stand, Painted Dressing table, Very handsome swing glass, six very Handsome sattin wood Chairs Neatly Inlaid Cane seats, hair Cushons and Covers, Small Turkey Carpet, A small Mahogany [Dineing^c] table, Very Handsome gentleman's Dressing Glass [Chest^c] in Handsome sattin wood Frame thirty seven inches by Twenty Inches fine Brilliant Plate Pair of Green Venetian Blinds Very Handsome Mahogany Bureau And Book Case complete with Handsome Dental cornice, Mahogany Bureau, small Book case in Wallnuttree With Glazed Doors, Mahogany Wardrobe with Draws Complete, Handsome Chimney Glass Plate in Three Pieces in a Handsome gilt Frame and sundrys etc. etc..

Mr. Lee's Bed Room: A very Handsome full Sized Four post Mahogany Bedstead With very neat and Handsome Dimity furniture A very excellent Goose feather Bed, Handsome borderd tick Bolster and four Large Down pillow, Large and handsome Counterpane One very Large and Handsome Mattress In A fine Case to Ditto, one other Mattress In A fine Raised Case, three Large and fine Blanketts, A Handsome Brussells Carpett Beautifull Pattern And Fashon Seventeen foot Square, Six very Handsome staind Chairs Cane seats with Cushons etc., Complete Very Handsome Commode Chest Of Draws in Sattin Wood inlaid Night Table in Sattin Wood and Pott Cupboard In Sattin Wood, A very Complete and Handsome Gentleman's Dressing Table With A very Handsome rising Glass In Sattin Wood handsomely inlaid With Rose Wood, one other Gentleman's Dressing table with Large Rising glass, Handsomely inlaid with sattin & Rose Wood, Three [Two pair of^c] Venetians green blinds, Three (Two^c) pair Dimity Window Curtains, Elegant Chimny glass in three Handsome and Brilliant Plates, sixty-three inches by twenty inches in very neat and Handsome Gilt-Ornamental frame, A very Elegant Piear glass in a Handsome Gilt Frame, thirty six inches by twenty four Inches, one Other Ditto A most Brilliant Plate in A very Handsome Gilt ornamental frame thirty Six inches By twenty four Inches Large harth Rug and Fender, Easy Chair and Cushon and Cover, Complete Pott Cupboard.

In the Dressing Room: Fender and fire irons, Large Harth rug And Carpet, Oak Dressing Table, Handsome Painted Dressing table and Draw to Ditto, Very Handsome swing glass in Mahogany, Pair Venetian green Window Blinds, two pair Window Curtains, A Very Elegant Piear glass Beautifull Brilliant Plate thirty six inches by Twenty four Inches in A very Handsome Gilt frame, Very Handsome Dressing Glass fine Brilliant Plate Beautifull Inlaid With A Handsome Sattin Wood frame

Very Handsome Mahogany Commode Chest of Draws, A very Elegant
And Handsome sofa Japand in Sattin Wood with Large hair Cushon or
Mattress, Squabs and Cushons Complete, A Very Handsome Chimney
Glass three Brilliant Plates in a Very Elegant and Ornamental Gilt
frame fifty inches by eighteen Inches, Mahogany two Leaved table (fine
wood), Mahogany horse, coal Scope and Mahogany Biddett, four
Flower Gasses [sic], Harth Rug and Venetian Blind, Mahogany Wash
hand Stand, Wash Basons and Pitchers.

In the Green Room: A very elegant and Handsome Lofty Four post
Mahogany Bedstead, Very Handsome stripe Cotton, Furniture Lined
through out with Green Callico, Circular Head full Vallens Handsome
fringe, Head And tester Lined Very full with green Callico and full
Bastings Complete Most Excellent And Large Goose Feather Bed fine
Raised borded Tick Large Goose Feather pillow and Bolster, A very
fine large Counterpane, Three Large and fine Blanketts, Large and
Handsome fine Wool Mattress in a Neat White Case, Large and good
Hair Mattress In A neat stripe Borded tick, Mahogany night table,
Wallnuttree Elbow Chair Silk Cover and brass naild, One Other Elbow
Chair Handsome Cover And brass naild Mahogany Cloaths Horse, very
Handsome mahogany Chest of Draws in best Preservation, Sett of fire
Irons and Harth Brush, Six Handsome painted Chairs, Rush Seats,
Large harth Rug, one [two°] Pair Venetian window blinds, two pair
Handsome window blinds Lined With green Callico Through out with
Full Vallens and Cornice as fixt, Handsome Brussells Carpet, eighteen
feet by fifteen feet, green Pattern and Excellent Coulers, very Neat
Painted Dressing table with Draw, Very Handsome Swing Glass in
Mahogany With three Draws, Very Handsome Piear glass thirty Six
Inch by twenty Inch in a Very Handsome gilt frame, Mahogany table,
A Very Elegant Chimny Glass In three Beautifull Plates in A Very
Handsome Gilt Frame, Handsome painted washhand Stand, Pitchers
and Basons, Mahogany Biddett.

In the White Room: Very Handsome mahogany four post Mahogany
Bedstead, Neat White Furniture, full Vallens Handsome Fringe and
bastings Complete with Handsome Cornice, Excellent feather Bed,
Bolster and two Down Pillows, Large and handsome Counterpan And
three Large blanketts handsome Mahogany Night table, two Mahogany
Elbow Chairs with neat White Dimity covers, two Pair of Venetian
Window blinds, two Pair Dimity Window Curtains, full Vallens fringed
And Cornice Complete, Neat Mahogany table, Six Handsome painted
Chairs With Cane Seats.

In the Dressing Room: Handsome fender & sett of Fire Irons and
Harth Rug Wash Hand corner bason stand Painted, Pitchers, Basons
and Glasses etc. etc., Handsome Mahogany writing table, Answers to a
Dineing table etc., Mahogany Chest of Draws (fine Wood), Handsome
Mahogany sofa on brass Casters and Socketts, six foot long by three

foot wide, large hair Mattress, cushons, Swabbs etc. and Covered with Canvas With Handsome Dimity Cover, Four very handsome Elbow chairs In Mahogany, Hair seats, and backs Covered with best Canvas and Handsome Dimity Covers to Ditto, Painted Dressing Table with A Draw, Handsome swing Glass in Mahogany, Elegant Piear Glass, thirty six inch by twenty four Inch in A Very Handsome gilt frame, Mahogany Biddett, Cloaths Horse and 50 yards of Carpetting in both rooms, Ink Stand.

Bedroom South Attick: A Very Handsome four Post Mahogany Bedstead with Handsome Stripe Furniture lined through out with Blue Callico Circular Head & Bastings, Very Excellent Goose feather bed, Bolster and one Pillow, Large and Handsome Counterpane And three Blanketts, Large Mattress, A Plain Case one Other Ditto in A Handsome Stripe Border'd Case, Handsome Mahogany Bureau, four Wallnuttree Chairs Fender, fire irons & harth Rug, Wallnuttree Elbow Chair green silk Cover [Blind'], Painted Dressing Table and Pott Cupboard, Swing glass in Mahogany with Draws, two Pair Venetian Window blinds, two pair Window Curtains to Corrispond With the Bed, One Other Elbow Chair in Wallnuttree, Handome [*sic*] Chimney Glass in three Pieces in A very Neat Gilt frame, Very Good Brussells Carpett, Six Yards by five Yards, Very Handsome Chimney Glass, In three Brilliant Plates and In A Very Handsome gilt frame, Elegant Piear Glass thirty six Inch By twenty four Inch in A very Neat guilt frame.

North Attick: Lofty four post Mahogany bedstead With Handsome flowerd furniture, Lined throughout with white Callico Furniture Circular Head fringed, Full Vallens and bastings Complete, Two Pair Handsome Window Curtains to Corrispond one [two'] Pair Venetian Window Blinds, Two Elbow Chairs In Wallnuttree green silk Covers,Painted pot Cupboard, Mahogany Biddett, one Elbow Chair & two Others, Mahogany bason stand and basons, Mahogany Pembrook table with A Draw ovill swing Glass, two Leav'd ovill Table in Mahogany, Very Handsome Mahogany Chest of Draws, Fender and Neat Sett of Fire Irons, Ink Stand etc., An Exceeding good Goose feather Bed, Bolster and two Down Pillows, Large and Handsome Counterpane And three Very Large and fine Blanketts, Large Mattress in A fine White Case, Large Hair and Wool Mattress in Handsome Borderd Case, Kidderminster Carpett, five Yards Square, Handsome Pattern and in the best State of Preservation, A Very Handsome Chimney Glass Fine Plate in three pieces forty four Inches by seventeen Inches In a very Handsome Gilt frame.

Room Adjoining the Attick: Neat Fender and Sett Of fire irons Wallnuttree Elbow Chair in A Silk Cover, two Elbow Chairs with Hair Seats, two Rush bottom chairs, Neat mahogany bason stand, Pitcher and bason and sundry's, Very Neat Mahogany Pillow and Claw table and swing Glass in Mahogany wallnuttree Beaureau, Ovill Glass in A neat Gilt frame, Handsome Mahogany four Post Bedstead Handsome Cotton furniture Lined With White Callico Circular Head And fringed and bastings, Complete Large and Handsome Quilt And three Large And fine Blanketts, Exceeding Good Goose feather bed, large Goose feather bolsters and one Pillow, Whole with Handsome borderd Bed round Carpett, Two Pair Window Curtains and Sundrys.

Bath Room: Bathing tub, Wallnuttree Settee And Elbow Chair, Mahogany Pott Cupboard, sett of fire Irons and fender, Very Handsome Eight Leavd screen, Piece of carpet, Painting of a Dog, Ditto A Castle & Fort Ditto Of a Horse, Handsome Painting of A Cottadge Appearance in A Handsome Gilt frame, One other Ditto, fine painting of a Grey Horse, one Other Ditto of a Black Horse, one Other Ditto of A Bay Horse, Air Baskett for the Bathing Tub.

Valetts Room in the Atticks: Handsome four post Stain'd Bedstead Coulerd furniture, Exceeding good Feather bed, bolster And one Pillow, Counterpan and three Blanketts and Coulerd Quilt, Large Wool Mattress in A neat Brown Case, Two Wallnuttree Chairs, One Brown seat and one Green Seat, Mahogany bason stand, Pitcher and bason, Dressing table And Glass, Handsome Wallnuttree Double chest of Draws, four Post Beech Bedstead, Coulerd furniture, Exceeding good feather bed, bolster and one pillow, Large Mattress in A neat Stripe tick, White Counterpan, Neat Coulerd Ditto And three Blanketts, two setts Bed Room carpetts, six neat Black Chairs, fender And Chimny Board and two pair Window Curtains.

The Maids Room: Neat four Post Bedstead with check Furniture, Exceeding good feather Bed, Bolster and one Pillow, Good Mattress in A Stripe Tick, Large White Cotton Counterpan, Large Coulerd Quilt and three blanketts, Two Setts of Bed Room Carpetts, Six black Chairs, Fender and Chimney Board and two pair Window Curtains.

The Other Maid's Room: Four Post Bedstead Neat Check Furniture, exceeding good feather bed Bolster and two Pillows, Handsome Coulerd Quilt and three Blanketts Large and good Mattress, Four Post Bedstead with Handsome Chintz Furniture, good feather bolster and Two pillows, Large Coulerd Quilt And three Blanketts, Good Mattress, Piece of Carpett and three Chairs, Wallnuttree Chest of Draws, and Two window Curtains Wallnuttree Chest of Draws and Stove Grate, Dressing Glass.

In the Room Adjoining: Neat four Post bedstead, Stripe Furniture, Exceeding good feather Bed, bolster and two Pillows, Large Quilt, and three Blanketts, Mattress Neat turnover Leaf table in Mahogany, Very Handsome Chimney Glass in A Neat Gilt frame Wainscott Chest of Draws, Two Elbow Chairs And two Others, window Curtain, Handsome Print of Samuel & Eli, Ditto Of Our Saviour from the Cross.

House Keepers Room: Handsome Mahogany four Post Bedstead with Handsome Chintz Furniture Lined with White Calico And Bastings etc.

Complete Exceeding Good Feather bed, bolster and two Pillows in A Handsome Raised Border'd tick Large Counterpan, And three Blanketts, Two Very Good Mattress, Bason, stand, Pitchers, Basons etc., Double Chest of Draws In Wallnuttree, Neat Wallnuttree Bureau, Neat mahogany Dressing table and Swing Glass, two pair Window curtains to Corrispond with the bed, Very Handsome Piear glass In A neat Gilt frame, An Aarm Neat Stove grate and sett Of fire Irons, Elbow chair and two Others Bed Round Carpett and sundry Prints.

Yellow Room: Elegant full sized sofa Bedstead With very Handsome blue furniture Lined with Yellow Callico with Coach top Head Lined, Head and Tester Complete, Large and Handsome Goose Feather bed and one Large Down Pillow in A very fine Raised Borderd tick, large and Handsome Counterpan and three Large and fine Blanketts, Two Large Mattresses In two fine Cases, Handsome Mahogany table with A Draw, Handsome Fender And Sett Of the Best Polished Fire Irons, Gard and Harth Rug, A Very Handsome Grecian Couch on Casters Complete, Elegant Chimney Glass in A very Handsome Gilt Frame, six Handsome Chairs Cane seats And One stool Very Handsome, Gentleman's Dressing Chest Painted, Basons, Pitchers etc., Neat Painted Dressing Table, Large and Handsome Dressing glass, two pair Window Curtains Very Handsome Brussels Carpet, Rich Coulers and Border, Form'd to the Room, Very Handsome Mahogany Chest of Draws (fine Wood), Mahogany Horse, Mahogany booth Horse and Painted Pott Cupboard, Piece of Oil Cloth, Painted Table and Glass, Mahogany Biddett, Pitcher and bason, Ink Stand and Piece of Oil Cloth and Sundrys.

In the Front Hall: Sixteen Yards of Buff Cloth, Curtains with Lines and tassells, Bell Ropes etc. being the best Broad Cloth.

In the Passages from the First Floor to the Atticks: Twenty eight yards Handsome Brussels Carpeting One Yard and Half Wide, two Slips Oil Cloth twenty Eight Yards Long Each, Handsome full size Pembrook table and four Neat Chairs, Large Passage Baskett, Dinner Tray and Large Passage Rug, Forty eight yards Handsome Stair Case Carpetting three Quarters Of A Yard Wide to Stair Case, And Sundry Wires, Piece Of Carpet Eleven foot by six foot and Half, One Other Piece the same Pattern very Handsome and excellent eight Day Clock in a Handsome Case, Two Elegant Paintings on the stair Case In Valuable gilt Frames and the Map of Bedfordshire.

In the Drawing Room: Six Valuable and Elegant Paintings In Valuable and Costly Gilt Frames By the Most esteemed Artists, Four Very Handsome (Ditto Smaller) Two Others very Handsome Ditto, Two Very Handsome Paintings in the Library much Larger.

In the House Maid's Closit: Sundry Pieces of Carpets, Door and Harth Rugs, Boxes, Cloaths horse, Foot Baths, tea kettles and sundry Odd things, Large Quantity Of Stair Case Carpeting in the Closit etc.

etc. Several thousand Yards of fine Brown Holland to cover the furniture in all the Different Rooms and Some Pieces not made up and Pieces of Carpetts and Other Odd things In Different Closits and Places.

Plate: Pair of High and Elegant Candlestics With a Pair Of Handsome branches to Ditto, Two Pair smaller Candlestics, One cheese toaster, Egg Boiler and Cover complete Egg Cups and stand And spoons gilt insides, Large and Handsome waiter and small Ones Ditto, Three Very Handsome and Imboss'd Ditto, Coffee Pott and Lamp, Very Elegant and Beautifull Cruit stand with eight best Cruits and Ladles, A Very Handsome and large Cruit Stand with four very Elegant Cruits and Ladles, four Handsome sause boats with Covers, Very Large sause boat or tureen With Lamp Complete, Ink stand In Glasses silver seal and Ivory Handle, Pair flatt Candlestics and Extinguisher, one Other Ditto much Larger, four Very Handsome salts Gilt inside with Particians, Fourteen salt Spoons, two Soop Ladles, four large Gravy spoons, Forty two Large and Handsome Table spoons Forty two Large and Handsome forks, thirty Desert Ditto, Twenty four Handsome Desert spoons, Three Handsome Marrow spoons, And four Skewers, four wine Labels Sixteen tea Spoons, two pair sugar tongs and one butter Knife, one Pair Candlestics, Pair flatt Ditto, two Oyster forks, Case Knives etc. two sugar Spoons, Six silver Desert knives, twelve Table Knives silver Handles two Carvers And two forks Very Handsome Bread basket Pair Very Handsome Ovil Dishes and Covers to Ditto With Plated Stands to Ditto, two Very Handsome soop Dishes And Covers, Capital Toast Rack tea Pot And stand Very Handsome Imbossed tea Kettle and Lamp and tea Kettle stand in Mahogany, Plated Inside, One Other Handsome tea Kettle Imboss'd and Lamp, Stand etc..

Plated Articles: Six Dish Covers, two stands and Lamps, tea Kettle, four flatt Candlesticks, six Ditto for Dressing Rooms, Six Other Ditto for Dressing Rooms, one handsome Liquor stand best Cut Glass and Silver Labels.

In the Attick: Mahogany plate warmer, Old painting and prints, Painted table, three Venetian blinds etc., ten Good and Usefull Blanketts and five Old Ones, Twelve Very Good Feather beds , ten Bolsters and four Pillows, two Mattress, Four Chairs, one easy Chair and one Elbow Chair, Piece of green Baise to Cover Carpett Box and Bed Furniture to the Stable beds and Piece of Green Baise two Down Pillows, Four pair best and Large Blanketts, two Quilts and coverlets some Valuable and Costly China both for use and Ornament to the several Rooms etc. Comprising three Chimney ornaments, two China stands, Two Vases and two smaller Ditto and Handsome glass Covers to ornaments, Two Very Handsome and Elegant brass gates.

Next Room to Housekeepers Room: Sundry Pieces of New Carpetting, Four Rolls of new Carpetting (Bordering), two pieces of new Brussels

Carpetting bed round Carpetting and Sundry Pieces of Carpetting, Door mat, Two Large carpetts out of Use, ten Chair Cushon, Elbow Chair and one Other, sundry ornaments, Boxes etc., three Biddetts, one Night stool, one Other Ditto Servants bedstead, two Small mahogany stands and Dumb Waiter Basons and Pitchers, bason Stand in Mahogany, Wallnuttree Chest of Draws (Chest upon Chest), Two brass lamps with Lustre's and Burners, Handsome Passage Lamp, swing glass two Gilt Stands, glass cover and Lustres And sundry Boxes, four Door Rugs, Scrapers, Brushes and sundry's.

Articles at Mr. Baxter's House: Mahogany Bureau, Mahogany Dineing table, Neat four post Bedstead with Plaid furniture, two Good feather Beds, two Bolsters and Two Pillows, four Blanketts, Half Tester Bedstead with Plaid furniture, Eight Leather bottom Chairs etc.

At Mr. Phillips House: Three Common Bedsteads and One Feather Bed, Large table With three Draws and Sofa Bedstead.

Blacksmith's Shop: Large Anvil and Block Pair bellows And Cold trough, Blacksmith's Vice Cupboard as fixt, Quantity of Old And New iron, Hammer, Pintchers And All the sundry tools in the shop.

In the Lumber Room over Stables: Nine Common bedsteads, Large Pictures and three Lamps, Elbow chair Hair from Sofa and four Old Chairs, Large beam and Scales, Quantity of Old Lead, Two boxes of Papers, six Draws, two tea Chests and one box Ditto, Fire Screen Lined with tin, Oak Chest of Draws, Large Churn and Frame (6 dozen), A Cover to A Marque, Lines etc., Two Large Oil Carbines, sundry Hampers and Packing boxes, Two Marble tops for tables, three foot by two foot each, three black marble Plints, Mahogany Dineing table, Bed and Window Cornices and sundry Usefull Wood, Carpenters Benches Usefull Wood etc., Large Buffet Cupboard, Large Vice, Nail box and Sundrys, Piece of Oil Cloth and Matting, A large Quantity of Sashes, Fameings amd Moddells A Large Quantity Of very Usefull Stuff Cut out for Different Uses, etc. etc..

All the Valuable Fixtures

Bells etc. on the Premises, A Valuable and Large Brewing Copper with Large tapp to Ditto with Excellent Grate as fitted Up, Complete Iron bound Masshing Vatt And Stand as fitted up, Four Iron bound Working tubs, Long And Short Spouts, Jett Mash, Rules and sive and Leather Pipes, A Large And Good Cooler on Stand, A Shorter Ditto, ten Iron bound Casks, Underback steps, truck And two Stands etc. etc..

In the Dairy etc.: All the Valuable fittings up in the Dairy, Dish Stands and Table, Good Copper, with Lead Curb And Grate to Ditto Lead Sink fixt.

In the Larder: Two Well fitted up Dressers etc..

In the Saddle Room: Small Grate as fixt, thirty gallon Copper as fixt, Grate as fixt in the Coachman's Room.

In the Kennells: Two Iron Furnaces and Grates As fixt, Cooler Stand and frames And an Exceeding good Lead Pump.

Washouse: Good Copper with Lead Curb as fixt, Most excellent Copper as fixt with Capital Cistern Above, very Complete, A very Capital forseing Pump to the Cistern made up in the Best Stile Complete, All the Lead pipes from the Cistern all Round the Washhouse With all the Brass taps Complete, A Complete sett Of Wash trays, A Long Spout to Ditto, Large Ironing Stove and Pipes Complete, Frames and Pulleys and Ironing Boards as fixt, A Very Complete Patent Mangle etc. etc..

In the Kitchin: A Very Handsome Polished Kitchin Range, Fall Down barr and iron back, Spitt Racks etc. Altogether Complete, Very Capital Patent Smoak Jack, Multiplying Wheel as fixt Complete Peacheys Patent Oven with the Whole of the Apparatus Complete, Five stewing stoves as fitted up, all the Range of Dressers, draws and Shelve Completely fitted up Round the Kitchin etc. etc. (A Bacon Rack)

Pantrys: Flour binn as fixt, Oven Door & frame, Very good Copper and Grate with Large Lead Curb to Ditto, Plate Rack and Stone Sink, A Dresser and shelves as Fixt, Dressers, Draws and shelves, Large Binn, Large cupboard with folding Doors, Draws and shelves Altogether Completely fitted up etc.

Servants Hall etc., etc.: Stove, grate, shelves and pegs.

Housemaids Room and Closit: Grate and Dresser as fixt, dresser as Fixt.

In the Butlers Room: Lead sink, Deal Press cupboard With Folding Doors etc.

Dineing Room's and Study: Very Handsome Polished Regester Stove Completely fitted Up, One other Ditto, a very Elegant and Costly Regester Stove, Ditto, Neat Regester stove and book Case.

Footman's Pantry: All the Store Cupboards with folding Doors, Dresser with Draws & Shelves, Painted Buffett Cupboard.

Housekeeper's Room: Polished stove grate as fixed All the Valuable store Cupboards as Fixt Round the Room With folding Doors and shelves complete.

In the Pink Study: Very handsome Polished Regester Stove.

In the Drawing Room: A Very Handsome Regester Stove As fixt, All the Very Handsome And Elegant Book Cases Neatly Fitted up with silk blinds, brass Wires and brass Ornaments and fronted With Rose Wood.

New Dineing Room: Handsome Regester Stove.

In the Breakfast Room: Very Neat Bath Stove.

In the Dressing Room: Handsome bath stove as fixt.

Principal Bed Room: Bath Stove, one Other Ditto.

Next Room: Rumford Stove and bath Stove as fixt in the Other Room.

In the White Room: Bath Stove.

In the Room in The Atticks: Bath Stove.
South Attick: Bath Stove.
North Attick: Bath and Rumford Stove as fixt.
In the Yellow Room: Bath Stove, Middle Room.
In the Gallery: Rumford Stove.
Pink Room: Handsome Bath Stove.
In the Chintz Room etc.: Neat Bath Stove, All the Bells, Wires, Cranks etc. All over the House, All the Cupboards with folding Doors And Shelves in the Passage to the Housekeepers Room as fixt, A Very Handsome Brilliant Table. The Large Bottle Rack in the Cellar.

The End

[gap]

All the Valuable household furniture, Plate, Linen, Fixtures, Books, Hot house and green House Plants In and On the Premises Specified in the Inventory At Colworth House, near Sharnbrook in the County of Bedford have been View'd, Valued and Appraised At the Sum of £6586 9s 6d By Me W. Brown.

[gap]

Separate Valuation		
Valuable Library of Books	£324	17s 6d
All the Valuable Plants, Orange Trees etc.	£424	10s 6d
All the Valuable household Furniture,		
Linen, Plate and Other Effects	£5465	17s 6d
All the Valuable fixtures, Bells etc.	£371	4s 0d
	£6586	9s 6d

Index of Rooms

Note in different hand:
In Chancery Lee against Ryder

On the first of September of this Year, one thousand eight hundred and twenty six, the contents of this catalogue were compared with the Furniture in this house and I believe that all the Articles in this Catalogue except those marked with a red line are now in the house and for which I am willing to be accountable. John Lee Colworth House near Bedford, 1826, September 6.
Signed by Us in pursuance of the Decree Lee against Ryder F ? Ryder, Edward Arrowsmith

PRO: C 114/176

NOTES

1. The main archive relating to Colworth is Unilever (UN). The earlier deeds of Colworth are found in Montagu Archive at Northamptonshire Record Office. Later deeds are also found in the Garrard & Allen (GA) Archive. Personal papers of the Antonie family are found in AD 1734–1750, BS 448–463, 576–607, 1176–1288, 2022–2143 and X 800; James Collett-White's *Colworth House*, B.Mag Vol.17 No.130 pp.47–53; W.O. Corbett's *The History of Colworth 1278–1947*, c.1977 (UN 578); M. Jones *Yesterday's Witness*. The following CRTs amplify the published sources: CRT 130 Sharnbrook 11, *Colworth House 1546–1977*, CRT Sharnbrook 26, *Descent of Colworth in Montagu Family 1556–1691*, CRT 130 Sharnbrook 27 *Manor of Colworth up to 1604*; VCH Vol III p.92.
2. 1546 deed Cal S.P. Dom 1546 p.345; W.O. Corbett.
3. Conveyance Montagu to Wagstaff 1691 (BS 2023–4); Conveyance Wagstaff to Antonie (BS 2042).
4. UN 63, X 800; Montagu of Beaulieu Archive (held at Beaulieu Palace, Hampshire); Montagu Correspondence Volumes (Northants CRO); *Montagu Correspondence of the Duke of Buccleuch* HMC Volume 1 pp.347 and 351.
5. Gordon's Map of 1736 (MC 2/8); Enlarged photograph of thumbnail sketch of house (Z 50/143/235).
6. BS 2143/2 pp.66–68.
7. BS 2143/2 p.67.
8. A. Oswald *Hinwick House, Bedfordshire* CL Vol.128 pp.619–621, 676–679 and 730–733 (1960).
9. BS 2143/4, last page.
10. Hinwick House Building Accounts (MIC 111); Sale Catalogue of 1861 (GA 889).
11. BS 2069.
12. A number of reference to South Sea Stock in BS 2143/4. A patent had to be sold to raise the £1000 legacy due to Marc's younger son Richard.
13. UN 86.
14. BS 2143/2 p.67.
15. UN 105.
16. X 800/34.
17. BS 2143/1–4.
18. BS 2143/2 p.67.
19. BS 2143/2 p.26.
20. BS 2143/2 p.24.
21. BS 2143/2 p.13.
22. see note 18.
23. Joyce Godber *Marchioness Grey* pp.62 and 68.
24. 1715 Map (GA 2955); 1772 Map (GA 2958).
25. Compare with useful inventory of 1763 (BS 450/9) which gives some indication of where rooms were.
26. J. Godber *History of Bedfordshire* (1969) plate 66, between pp.360 and 361. The animal hunted is in fact a hare not a fox!
27. BS 2143/4.
28. For Woolfe's career see H.M. Colvin p.916. At the end of his career he did work at Wrest Park.
29. CRT 130 Sharnbrook 27. I am grateful to H.M. Colvin for this reference.
30. UN 228.
31. For the career of Richard Lawrence see R. Gunnis p.236.
32. UN 240.
33. Letter by John Fiott to Sir William Lee, 16 June 1792: Bucks. CRO D/LE/D3/71.
34. Letter of 18 August 1810.
35. Undated letter UN 364.
36. Letter of 10 August 1810 (UN 507).

37. UN 364.
38. UN 510–555 covering 1788–1815.
39. Letter of 11 January 1810 (UN 368).
40. Undated letter (UN 508).
41. Letter from Reynolds to Lee Antonie 13 August 1810 (UN 370 and 566).
42. Letter of 18 August 1810 from Lee Antonie to Reynolds (UN 507).
43. UN 373. Reynolds had information on two or three at a statuary near Kingsland (east of City of London).
44. Letter of 13 June 1811 (UN 379) and 18 June (UN 380).
45. UN 370, 373, 379.
46. MA35/3 and Award Book.
47. UN 510.
48. UN 563.
49. UN 393.
50. William Brown Auctioneer of Bedford in commercial directories 1792–1839. He was buried at St. Peter's, Bedford 18 February 1847 aged 84.
51. UN 563.
52. Illustrated in *Sale Catalogue of Hartwell House, Bucks. 26 April 1938* (Book Classification 200) plate XVII.
53. *The Royal Pavilion, Brighton.* Item 133 in Regency Exhibition 1980.
54. see note 48.
55. H. Hanley.
56. Sale Catalogue of Hartwell House, 1938. See note 52.
57. 1861 Sale Catalogue (GA 889).
58. Lease of 1839, with useful list of rooms (GA 2945).
59. See photograph UN 581.
60. Corbett, M. Jones *Yesterday's Witness* (UN 636).
61. Probably servants' bedstead purchased by Antonie from Wagstaff for 5s. (X 800/24).
62. Antonie gives details of thirteen pictures he bought 1717–1719, including a number of Dutch pictures. These include a Peter Wouverman: *A Seaport* and a Moses Wittenbrook: *Landskip with Cattle*. A number of Dutch pictures occur in the Hartwell House Sale Catalogue of 1938, some of which came from Colworth. *The Wayfarers by a Rocky Stream* by Wouverman could be that described in 1717 as *A landscape & Grotto*, bought for 20s. (X 800/24).
63. The three sets of cane chairs were purchased from Wagstaff for a total of £10 4s.
64. Antonie bought 11 ells of Holland from Wagstaff for £1 15s.
65. Wine Cooler probably one described in Hartwell Sale Catalogue 1938 No. 244. Like the one of Melchbourne it was of sarcophagus form.
66. Probably No. 265, Hartwell Sale Catalogue.
67. Probably No. 219, Hartwell Sale Catalogue.
68. Probably Nos. 254,255, Hartwell Sale Catalogue.
69. Probably No. 257, Hartwell Sale Catalogue.
70. Probably No.258, Hartwell Sale Catalogue.

HASELLS HALL

Hasells Hall up to 1761

In 1634 the former Chicksands Grange of Hasells was purchased by Robert Britten of Waresley, yeoman. His grandson, Baron Brittain began to rebuild Hasells in c.1698, according to evidence for a legal case of 1722.[1]

What Brittain pulled down is not clear. It is possible that the mediaeval core of the original house lasted till c.1698. It would have been extensively remodelled in either the Tudor or Stuart period. It seems as if the new house incorporated nothing of the older house. It is possible that the western part of Brittain's house was a remodelling of an earlier house. This would explain the odd positioning of the kitchen in relation to the block of principal rooms. This idea is strengthened by the mention of "Old Parlour" in this area in the 1761 inventory. The principal block formed the central section of the south facade of the present house. A hall was flanked by a drawing room on the east end and a parlour on the west, with the kitchen behind them somewhere on the north side of the house. The new house was probably not very large. Indeed, Brittain did not live in the house and the tenant of the previous house, John Dunn, remained in the new house till 1710. After the house was built, Brittain increased his debts substantially, owing £1465 in 1721 on mortgage.[2] The largest single increase was in 1713, so it is unlikely the building of Hasells Hall was a major factor. Three recently built cottages mentioned in 1721 no doubt contributed to this. The collapse of the South Sea Bubble in 1720 probably caused the mortgagees financial difficulties, forcing them to press for the return of their capital. Brittain offered all his family property including Hasells to William Astell of Everton for £4,200. The deal fell through and on 28 and 29 September 1721 Hasells was sold to Heylock Kingsley of Furzen Hall near Biggleswade for a mere £2,342, leaving Brittain with £876 after the debts had been paid.[3]

Heylock came from a well-to-do family of Hitchin haberdashers. His wife Elizabeth was to be the joint heiress of her father, Robert Jenkin. Heylock's grandmother was a Heylock of Abbotsley, another substantial local family.

Between 1721 and Gordon's map of Bedfordshire in 1736,[4] Kingsley added two projecting wings to the central block on the south side of the house. From a sketch on Gordon's map it would appear that the central section of the house was recessed very slightly further than the two wings. During the 1720s Heylock bought and enclosed land round the house to make formal gardens and terracing to enhance the impact of the south facade.[5] He died in 1749 and his wife Elizabeth in 1761.

73

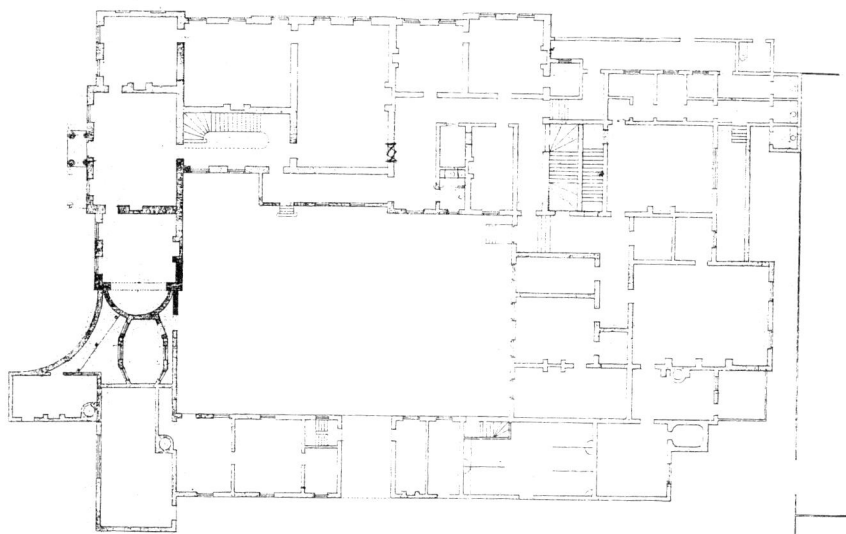

Plate 8: Hasells Hall: Ground plan, 1814. (*Plan, 1814*)

The 1761 Inventory

Using the 1736 Gordon map of Bedfordshire and plans of 1814 and 1892,[6] it is possible to work out an approximate ground plan of the house in 1761. At the western end of the main south facade was the end parlour (1892 morning room). Moving east, in the centre, was the hall (1892 dining room) and the drawing room. At the east end of this side of the house lay the great and common parlours. If the inventory had been taken in strict order, the room at the corner would have been the great parlour, but it seems too small a room. It may well be that the common parlour occupied this position and the great parlour was on the site of the future front hall.

The inventory then moves up the "Best Staircase" to the principal bedrooms. The exact position of specific bedrooms can not be determined, as there is no indication as to what rooms were underneath them. Most had dressing rooms and therefore it is likely that the blue room was in the centre of the south facade, as it did not have a dressing room. The only bedroom on the 1814 plan without a dressing room is in that position. Mrs. Kingsley's bedroom and dressing room therefore lay in the eastern part of this facade. The long room looked out north and was over the butler's pantry in the 1892 plan. Mr. Pym's room and the nursery were over the servants' hall and rooms nearby.

The inventory then moves on to the garret or attic floor. These rooms again cannot be located individually but there was a gallery running down the centre giving access to bedrooms leading off it. The inventory then returns to the ground floor to the large kitchen, which then, as in 1892, took up two floors. There were a good number of specialist rooms/buildings listed, such as the brewhouse in the north range. In the western part of the house were the study, dressing room and old parlour (possibly on the site of the later housekeeper's room). The butler's pantry lay on the north side of the house and the servants' hall near the kitchen in the south-west of the house. Both are marked on the plan of 1814.

The word "old" is repeated frequently throughout the inventory. Most of the furniture was old, worn and out of fashion. It is likely that it dates from the early 1720s when the Kingsleys first came into the house. By 1761 it was beginning to look shabby and run down. In the drawing room, for example, was a settee and six chairs with old gold-coloured seats (the similar set in the great parlour had the settee seat damaged) and an "old Japan'd Tea Table"; the steel hearth and shovel for the fire were "very old". Mrs. Kingsley's own bedroom was perhaps the worst. Everything in this room, apart from the four-post bedstead and its furnishings and the pair of window curtains, was described as "old"; even the white quilt and blankets that covered her were "old".

As one would expect much of the furniture that is specifically designated is either walnut or "wainscot" oak, being the fashionable woods of the 1720s. In Mrs. Kingsley's bedroom was an old walnut bureau and in the dressing room an "old Wainscot Nest of Drawers". There were also six "old Cane Chairs" in the end parlour, that would have been fashionable in the 1720s.

Some mahogany had been introduced, probably in the intervening period, as none of the mahogany pieces are described as "old". The most valuable was a mahogany dressing table, valued at £2 2s. in the blue room. A corresponding walnut table was valued at £1. A mahogany pillar and claw table in the common parlour was worth the same. The other mahogany was at the cheaper end of the market. A mahogany pillar and claw table in the end parlour was worth 1s 1d. A "Scallop'd Mahogany Tea Board upon a pillar and claw" was valued at 5 shillings and was one of the items sold.

There is only one picture mentioned in the house and that is not identified. To compensate for this was a large and impressive array of china. Sixty eight-inch blue and white plates start the list with a corresponding series of plates of different sizes. As well as the blue and white cups and saucers are enamelled ones. It is likely that these items were Chinese export ware. If they were bought in the 1720s, as seems most likely, they are almost certainly Chinese; if bought in the 1740s or 1750s there would be just a possibility of their being European. As the house does not seem to have had anything spent on it after Haylock's death in 1749, the earlier suggestion must be the most likely.

There was an equally impressive collection of silver containing coffee cups, candlesticks, mugs and tea spoons as well as more unusual items such as the single most valuable piece in the house – a tea table weighing just over 7 lbs. and valued at £28 18s. Two silver patch boxes were worth £25. There were perfume boxes and powder boxes and two salvers "the neatest pair of any there were".

In a letter to his co-executor William Pym, Elizabeth Kingsley's son-in-law wrote "part of the furniture is very old and therefore some of it I don't propose to keep."[7] The inventory marks which items were sold soon after Elizabeth's death. The selection of items for sale seems to have been fairly random. The eight old cane chairs in the end parlour were sold as well as the old yellow damask curtains there. From the area of the best staircase went "an old card Table" and a "Scallop'd Mahogany Tea Board". In the bedrooms there was a general clear-out of the old window curtains, as well as some of the old quilts and coverlets.

At the end of the inventory are two interesting items not often found in inventories of the period – the amount of ready money in the house and the large sums due on rent and other debts. Elizabeth had a total of £689 3s 7½d in the house, showing that even at this late date a gentry family kept so much money in the house rather than earning interest in a bank. It is well that no one raided the house as the four old guns and pistols in the dressing room were unfit for use. The sum of over £1170 was owed Elizabeth at her death. Part of it was rent due at Michaelmas 1760. The rest of the total no doubt was money lent out on mortgage (earning 5%) or on bonds. Borrowing privately rather than through a financial institution was very common in the eighteenth century.

The Hasells after 1761

On Elizabeth Kingsley's death the estate passed to her daughter Elizabeth and her husband William Pym (1788) of Norton, Herts. The 1760s saw the creation of a park to the design of Nathaniel Richmond,[8] one of the many landscape advisers that flourished during the time of Capability Brown. At the same time the third walled garden was added. The pavilions at the end of the terrace (one of which has a classical front and a rustic rear elevation) could well date from this period. Edward Stevens built the bath house at Wrest Park in 1767, and the back of the south pavilion has certain stylistic similarities to it.

On William's death in 1788, the Hasells estate passed to Francis Pym (1756–1833). Having married a rich heiress, Anne Palmer, in 1784,[9] Francis had designs on a position of greater social and political importance. The house at the Hasells was too insignificant and by 1790 the park looked old-fashioned, being in the Brown style. To keep up with his Whig friends, he had to radically alter both house and garden. To achieve this he consulted Humphrey Repton, the most fashionable garden designer of the period. The alterations were conceived of as a whole: the remodelled house was designed to complement the remodelled park. In his Red Book of 1791,[10] Repton wrote that the purpose of the park was to present the house in a "pleasing point of view". Equally, the park and surrounding countryside were to "make a delightful Landscape", when viewed from the house "where the Eye dwells upon the tame foreground with increasing pleasure, while the imagination bounds forward to a supposed romantic Country in the distance". The easiest side to achieve this effect was on the east; so the house needed to be refronted.

Instead of the hall being in the south side of the house, a new one was made on the east. To the north of it was built a new library, an important sign of the culture and wealth of the owner of a house. The old hall on the south side was converted into a dining room. It is likely that there was a certain amount of remodelling of the service area in the west part of the house and the courtyard to the north was given a formal central entrance arch and gatehouse. Upstairs modern fireplaces were put in the principal bedrooms. A number of these are still in place.

To harmonise the old and new parts of the house, the whole exterior of the house was filled with twelve paned, sashed windows. The old front door was redundant and replaced by a window. Above it was added a pediment and the Pym coat of arms. The entrance and classical porch was added at this stage. Work started in 1789, being described in the insurance policy registers of the Sun Fire Office in September as "not quite finished". Lord Torrington when he visited the house in the same month in 1790 commented: "I came to the Hasells a pleasant dry, shaded seat of Mr. Pym, which is soon to be put under taste by Mr. Repton and where Mr. Pym has employed a large sum of money in building a new house."[11] The redesign of the outside of the house could well have deceived Torrington into considering that the house was new built. The works were completed in October 1790 and Francis Pym recorded in his wine book that he put down some cases "upon my return to the Hasells after the house had been repaired and part rebuilt."[12]

The clerk of works and probably the architect was Martin Cole. He was the Pyms' London agent and later drew up plans for their Aldersgate Street properties there. In the London rent books Francis Pym recorded that "The taxes, insurances and other disbursements are by Mr. Martin Cole's desire reserved to be accounted for in the next half year's payment to Lady Day 1789 and the whole amounts of the rents (viz. £528 10s) on the opposite half year to Michaelmas 1788, I have this day deposited in his hands and for which he has given me a proper receipt, towards the expence of the buildings which he is now employed to do for me at Hasells Hall."[13] In February 1789, Bennett, the Pyms'

Bedfordshire steward, advanced Mintrin, a local Bedfordshire builder, £20 "for the new building and altering the house at the Hasells".[14] In the accounts there are references to ladders, scaffolding, fetching coals for the brick clamp and straw for the bricks. Probably the majority of the bricks were made on the estate but some were fetched by carrier from Clophill and Eaton Socon. In July 1789 a further £525 was added to Cole's £528 10s. Mintrin was paid weekly. John Edrop, carpenter, and John Waters, brickmaker, were also employed.

Repton's detailed advice on the landscaping of the Hasells was only partly acted on. The park was thoroughly Reptonised, as a series of undated watercolours (probably 1840s) show.[15] "Naturally" grouped clumps of mainly deciduous trees were planted with the occasional cedar to add variety. The old road from Everton to Sandy was stopped up in January 1792 as a direct result of Repton's advice. The lodges at the main entrance he had suggested were not built. Instead one was built at the other entrance to the Hasells, near the present Everton Park.[16]

With his house built and his park naturalised, Francis Pym turned his attention to politics. He was Member of Parliament for Bedfordshire for twenty years from 1806 with one short break. Politics were expensive – he had to pay out on election expenses over £10,000 between 1820 and 1822.[17] Improvements to Hasells Hall of necessity took second place. In 1814 however, plans were drawn of the house, showing proposed alterations to the north west of the gate house range to accommodate a new laundry and washhouse.[18] In 1817 a water closet cistern was added to improve the house's sanitation. Plans were drawn up for a Greek Revival Doric Temple.[19] Unfortunately, they are undated but probably date from this period and show Pym's willingness to contemplate adding a classical building to Repton's landscape.

Francis's son, also called Francis (1790–1860), succeeded to the Hasells in 1833 and moved from Long Stow in Cambridgeshire in 1835. He lived at the Hasells till 1858 when he moved to the family's Hertfordshire home, Radwell House in Norton parish. Francis was a hardworking Chairman of Quarter Sessions from 1832 until 1848 when he was forced to give up due to ill health. His conscientiously kept notebooks[20] have survived. He was Chairman of the Bedfordshire Agricultural Society and a keen supporter of the evangelical British and Foreign Bible Society. His improvements to the farm, later called Park Farm, and the alteration of various drives on the estate are the most noteworthy changes he made. Little alteration seems to have been made to the house, which despite the death of Francis's wife, Lady Jane, in 1848 still housed 18 people on census night in 1851.

In 1858 Hasells Hall was let to the playing card manufacturer, Thomas de la Rue. As was customary, an inventory was made to provide evidence for the endless wrangles over dilapidations that so often followed the termination of a lease.[21] While there were one or two items made of mahogany, overwhelmingly the largest number of pieces were made of rosewood, indicating that the house was refurnished in the nineteenth century. Before that rosewood was used mainly for veneers and ornamental inlays. The refurnishing of Hasells seems therefore to be dated quite a few years after Cole's remodelling.

Two of the paintings are by well known seventeenth century Italian artists: *Magdelen* by Guido Reno and *Judith and Holofernes* by il Guernico. Interestingly, there is a *Magdelen* by Guido Reni at the National Gallery.[22] Even if these two pictures are copies or misattributed they indicate an interest in seventeenth century Italian art, either of Francis Pym (1756–1833) or his son.

The death of Francis Pym (1790–1860), and his son Francis Leslie (in a railway accident in the same year), meant that the estate passed to another Francis (1850–1927) who was still only ten years old. It therefore seemed sensible to continue the letting of Hasells Hall, while the family continued to live at Radwell House and from 1861 at Brighton. On de la Rue's death in 1866, the house was leased to Colonel (later General) Thomas Hooke Pearson. "who had seen much service in India".

Plate 9: Hasells Hall: View from the south east. The original entrance was on the south (i.e. left) side. The present eastern entrance was added in 1789–90. (*Photograph: c.1920*)

On his death in 1892, the newly married Francis Pym returned to live at the Hasells. Although the family had not lived in the house since 1858, there had been a number of improvements during the time the house was let. By 1873 the lodge at the end of the main drive had been built and a third one added in 1877 to the designs of Samuel Redhouse.[23] Before 1885 a new single storey building replaced the library and breakfast room marked on the 1814 plans. By the 1880s the present game house had been erected and covered ways from the house constructed. Pym's first act as soon as he came into residence in 1892 was to install hot water central heating. After becoming High Sheriff in 1903, Francis became an invalid, latterly confined to a bath chair. On his death in 1927 the estate passed to his brother Frederick, then in his sixties. The period between 1900 and 1941 saw little change at the Hasells apart from the removal of the plaster on the exterior, thus revealing the rich colour of the brickwork. The war brought requisitioning and bad internal damage. The disastrous fire at Ginns in Bedford saw the destruction of most of the surviving furniture held in store.

The lease was continued to the Government till 1948 when the Hall became an annexe to Bromham Hospital. Drastic conversion, such as installing concrete partitions in the hall, was so badly done that fortunately the joins did not dovetail into the the panelling and when they were removed the panelling was intact.

The 1980s saw an attempt to demolish the house, empty since 1968 on the sudden termination of the lease by the hospital authorities. It was the subject of one of the principal articles in *The Country House: To be or not to be* by Marcus Binney and Kit Martin. In 1981 it was sold to Kit Martin for a nominal sum and expertly restored. It has now been divided into separate dwellings in as sensitive a way as possible to the room lay out of the original structure.

HASELLS HALL, SANDY 1761

A true and Perfect Inventory of the Goods, Chattells, Credits and Personal Estate of Elizabeth Kingsley late of Hasell Hall in the Parish of Sandy in the County of Bedford, Widow Deceased made the 23rd Day of February 1761 by the Appraisors hereunder named.

[*In the original, the values are tabulated in two columns:* (i)   "The Value of the Goods taken & sold out of the several Rooms as undermentioned" *marked in transcript with* *; (ii) "The Value of the Goods now remaining in the several Rooms". *A few items were not valued.*]

In the End Parlour: One couch with a squab and four Cushions very old 10s; A Picture in a Gilt Frame 12s 6d; A Pair of Old Bellows & a Brush 2s 6d; An Old Stove Grate fender fire Shovel Tongs & Poker 7s; A Mohogany Piller & Claw Table 1s 1d; One Small Pier Glass Broke;

2 Pair of Brass Sconces 4s; 6 Old Cane chairs & Cushions 14s*; 2 Elbow Ditto Ditto 7s*; 2 Pair of Yellow Damask Window Curtains £1 1s*.

In the Hall: Two Leather Bottom'd chairs 2s; 2 old Elbow Chairs 4s; A Pier Glass £1 1s; A Marble Slab and frame £3; 7 Brass Sconces 7s; A Pair of old Bellows & a Brush 1s 6d; A Stove Grate, fender, fireshovel, Tongs & Poker 10s; 8 old Leather Bottomed Chairs 8s*.

In the Drawing Room: One Settee with an old Gold Coloured Seat 10s 6d; 6 Chairs Ditto £2; 1 Large Pier Glass with Gilt Frame £5; 1 Small Ditto £2 10s; 1 Chimney Ditto £2 10s; 1 Card Table with a leather Cover 5s; 1 old Japand Tea Table 5s; a Steel harth with Brass facings, Brass fireshovel and Tongs very old 10s 6d; A Pair of Bellows & Brush 3s; 2 Pair of Silk Damask Window Curtains £3.

In the Great Parlour: 2 Pier Glasses & 1 Chimney Glass with Gilt Frames £8 8s; 3 Pair of Damask Window Curtains £5 5s; 2 Card Tables £1; 1 Settee Chair with a Gold Colour'd Seat Damaged 10s 6d; 9 Chairs Ditto £3 3s; A Steel Harth Brass Shovel and Tongs 10s 6d; A Pair of Bellows and Brush 3s.

In the Common Parlour: A Marble slab & Iron Bracket £2; 1 old Pier Glass £1 10s; 1 Chimney Glass £2 2s; 2 Mahogany Piller & Claw Tables £2 2s; 1 old Walnut Tree Oval Table 4s; 6 old Chairs & 2 Smoaking Chairs 15s; 2 Pair of Blew Damask Window Curtains £1 10s; 1 floor Carpet £1 15s; 1 old Stove Grate, fireshovel, Tongs, Poker, fender, Bellows & Brush 10s.

In the best Staircase: One Eight Day Clock £4 4s; 2 old Chairs 2s; One old Oval Table 4s; One two leaved Wainscoat dining Table 10s 6d; One old Brass Lanthorn; 2 Brass Arms 2s; One old Card Table 8s*; One Scallop'd Mahogany Tea Board Upon a Piller & Claw 5s*.

In the Green Room: 3 old Blankets 10s 6d; 1 Feather Bed, 2 Pillows, 1 Bolster & a Mattress £3 3s; 1 Easy Chair covered with Red Velvet & a Cushion £1 10s; 2 Small Bed Carpets 3s; 1 old Steel harth Brass faced, a Pair of Tongs, Fireshovel, Bellows & Brush 15s; 1 dressing glass 10s; 1 Bedstead with Sacking Bottom & Green Hangings £2 10s*; 1 old Quilt 2s 6d*; 8 Covered Chairs & 2 Stools £1 12s 6d*; 2 Pair of Green Window Curtains £2*; 1 old Dressing Table 4s*.

In the dressing Room: 1 Bedstead with a half Teaster & old red hangings £1 10s; One old Blanket 2s; 3 little Sconce Glasses 2s 6d*; 1 Elbow Chair 2s 6d*; 1 red Window Curtain 2s 6d*; 1 close Stool 6s*; 1 old Feather Bed, 1 Bolster & an old Quilt £2 2s 6d*.

In the White Room: 1 feather Bed 1 Bolster & 2 Pillows £3; 1 White Quilt, 3 old Blankets £1 10s; 1 old dressing Glass in a Black frame 6s; 1 old Tin fender 2s; One old White Elbow Chair 2s 6d*; 6 old Comon Ditto 6s*; 1 Bedstead with Sacking Bottom & white hangings very old £2 5s*; An old Crack'd Iron harth 4s*; 2 Pair of old red Window Curtains 14s*; 1 old Table 4s*.

In the Yellow Room: One Bedstead with Yellow Silk Damask hangings £20; 1 feather Bed, 1 Bolster, 1 Pillow, 3 Blankets & 1 Silk Bed Quilt £3; 1 Easy Chair covered with Yellow Silk Damask £1 5s; 6 Chairs Covered with Ditto £3; 2 Pair of Window Curtains £3 10s; A Walnut Tree dressing Table & Glass £2; A Chimney Glass £2 10s; An old steel harth Brass faced, brass fireshovel, Tongs, Bellows & harth Brush 15s.

In the dressing Room: One half headed Bedstead with old Blue hangings £1 10s; One old Quilt 5s; One old Elbow Chair 2s; A Grate, fireshovel, Tongs, Poker & fender 10s; One old Feather Bed, one Bolster, one Blanket £1 8s*; One old Blue Window Curtain 3s*; One Close Stool & 1 old Chair 6s*; One old Sconce Glass 10d*.

In the Blew Room: One Bedstead with Sacking Bottom & Yellow Damask Hangings £5; One Feather Bed, 2 Pillows, 1 Bolster, 3 Blankets & 1 Counterpain £4; 2 Pair of Window Curtains £1 10s; a Mahogany Dressing Table £2 2s; a Walnut Tree dressing Table £1; 6 Chairs & 1 Elbow Chair £1; a Tea Board & 2 Carpets 5s; 1 old Japan'd Tea Table 1s; 1 old Steel harth brass faced, fireshovel, Tongs, Bellows & Brush 10s.

In Mrs. Kingsley's Room: 1 four post bedstead with Sacking Bottom £2; Blew Serge Hangings £2 10s; One feather Bed, 1 Bolster, 2 Pillows, 1 Mattres & 3 old Blankets £4; one old White Quilt 3s; 2 Pair of Window Curtains £1; 8 old Chairs 16s; one old Chamber Clock £3 3s; 2 old Chests of Drawers £1; 1 old Walnut Tree Beaureau £1; 1 old Pier Glass 10s; 1 old Steel harth fire shovel, Tongs, Poker, Bellows & Brush 7s; 1 old Dressing Table 1s 6d; 1 old blanket 2s.

In the Dressing Room: 2 old Chests of Drawers upon Frames 15s; One old Wainscot Nest of Drawers, Table 10s 6d; One old Chair & One Oval Table 4s; A Fireshovel, Tongs, Poker & fender 3s; One old Close Stool 5s*.

In the Long Room: One Feather Bed £2; 3 Blankets 9s; One Quilt 9s; A Dressing Table & Glass 12s; A Bedstead with old Yellow Hangings £1 10s*; 1 Bolster & 2 Pillows 5s*; One old Iron harth, fireshovel, Tongs, a Crack Ironback & 2 dogs 10s 6d*; 2 Pair of old Yellow Window Curtains 3s 6d*; 6 old Broken Cane Chairs 2s 6d*.

In Mr. Pym's Room: One Bedstead with Sacking Bottom & old Wrought Hangings £3 3s; One feather Bed, 2 Pillows, 1 Bolster, 1 White Mattres, 1 White Quilt & 4 Blankets £3 10s; A Wainscot Nest of Drawers Table 7s 6d; A Dressing Table & Glass 9s 6d*; 2 Pair of old White Window Curtains 8s*; 1 old Stove, Grate, fireshovel, Tongs, Poker, Bellows & Brush 10s*.

In the little White Room: 1 Feather Bed, 1 Bolster, 2 Pillows & 3 Blankets £3; A Close Stool Chair 6s; A Stove Grate, fireshovel, Tongs, Poker & fender 7s 6d; A Bedstead with White Camblet Hangings £3*; 2 Pair of old Window Curtains 8s*; 1 old Quilt 3s*; One Table and dressing Glass 12s*; One Sconce 1s*; 3 White Chairs 3s*; One old Easy chair & Cushion 5s*; 1 old Eight day Clock £1 17s 6d*; 1 Dutch Teakettle & Lamp 5s*.

In the Nursery Room: One Bedstead with Sacking Bottom & old Blew hangings, 1 Feather Bed, Bolster, 3 Blankets & 1 Quilt £4; One Bedstead with old Hangings, 1 blanket, 1 Quilt & 2 Pillows £1 1s; One old Looking Glass, 4 old Cane Chairs & one old Table 3s; One other Bedstead with Sacking Bottom & very old Hangings, 1 Blanket, One Quilt, One Bolster & 2 Pillows £1 1s; One old Feather Bed, One Bolster & 2 Blankets £1 10s*; One old Feather Bed £1 2s 6d*; One old Close Stool Pan 1s*.

In the Little Garrett: One old Chest of Drawers 2s 6d; One old Settee Bedstead 6s*; One old Close Stool 3s*.

In the Maids Room. 1st Room: One Bedstead & old Yellow Hangings 18s; One old Brass bed & feather Bed £1 16s*; 2 feather Beds & 1 Bolster £2 14s*; 1 old Rug 1s*.

Second Room: One Rug 3s; One old Bedstead with old Green Hangings £1 2s*; 2 feather Beds & 1 Bolster £2 16s*; 2 old Blankets 2s*.

Third Room: One Pillow 2 shillings, One Quilt 5s: 7s; One old Bedstead with old Blew Hangings £1 2s*; 2 Feather Beds & 1 Bolster £2 15s*; 2 old Blankets 2s*.

In the Gallery: One old Chest 3s; A Globe & frame not Compleat £1 1s.

In the Gardeners Room: One old Bedstead with a Sacking Bottom & old Yellow Hangings £1; One feather Bed, 1 Pillow, 1 Bolster & 3 old Blankets £1 14s; 1 old Table & 2 old Chairs 1s 6d; Two old Window Curtains 2s*; 1 old Close Stool 5s.

In the Middle Room in the Gallery: One Feather Bed & 1 Bolster £1 10s; 1 old Coverlid 2s 6d; 1 old Table, an old Case of Drawers & a Grate 9s; 1 old Bedstead with old Brown Hangings & Quilt 10s 6d*; an old Coverlid & 2 old Blankets 3s 6d*; 2 old Window Curtains, 2 old Chairs & 4 old Cushions 6s 6d*; 1 old stove Grate 4s*.

In the End Room in the Gallery: One old Bedstead with old Yellow Hangings £1; 2 Window Curtains 2s; An old nest of Drawers & an old Close Stool 5s; One old feather Bed & 1 Bolster £1 1s 6d*; 3 old Blankets 3s 6d*.

In the Store Room: 12 Stone Dishes 6s; a Soop Poole & Cover 2s; 14 Stone & 1 Earthen Pickle Pots 10s 6d; 2 China Baking Dishes 1s 6d; An old Copper Still & Iron Work unfit for Use 14s; One Pair of Small Steps 1s.

In the Kitchen and Scullery: One old Smoak Jack £1 15s; 2 Roasting Irons 5s, A Range & fender £1 1s, £1 6s; An old Iron Crane & 3 Pothooks 10s; a Gridiron 1s, 2 Ironhorses 1s 6d, fireshovel Tongs & Poker 6s, 8s 6d; 1 Bell metal Mortar & Iron Pestal 5s; 1 Quart, 1 Pint & 1 half Pint Copper Pots 5s 6d; 1 Chaffing Dish 1s 3d, four Iron Candlesticks 9d: 2s; 2 flat Tin Candlesticks 1s; 1 Beef fork, 1 Brass Slice & 4 Iron Scures 1s; 2 Copper Pasty Pans 8s 6d; 1 Tin Pudding Pan 1s; 6 Chairs & 1 Coffee Mill fixt 6s; A Kitchen Table & 3 Forms 12s; 1 large, one lesser & 4 small Pewter Baking Dishes 15s; 1 Dozen of hard mettle Pewter Plates 11s; 1 Marble Mortar 7s 6d; 4 Copper Saucepans 12s; 1 Brass Baking Pan 7s 6d; 1 frying Pan 2s 6d, One fish Kettle 4s: 6s 6d; 1 Copper dripping Pan 8s; 1 Brass Kettle 10s 6d, 1 Pair of Brass Scales 6d: 11s; 3 Old Pewter dishes 2s 6d; 4 Spits 5s, 1 Gridiron 6d, 1 Horse & 2 Trivetts 2s: 7s 6d*; 1 Old Brass Saucepan 1s, four old Brass Candlesticks 2s, 3s*; 3 Iron Candlesticks 6d, One Dozen of Pewter Plates 10s 6d, 11s*; 1 Brass Kettle 4s, two Dozen of Patty Pans 1s: 5s*; 1 old fender 1s, one roasting Screen 4s 6d: 5s 6d*; 1 dozen of Soop Plates 13s*; 18 Pewter Plates 13s 6d, two Water Plates 3s: 16s 6d*; 1 Copper Chaffing Dish 1s, one Pair of Stake Tongs 6d: 1s 6d*; One Brass Saucepan 1s 6d, two old Coffee Pots 2s 6d, 4s*; 8 Pewter Dishes, 1 Cheese Plate, 1 Mazeren & 1 fish Plate £1 0s 6d*; One old Brass Cauldron 9s*; 2 Small Pewter dishes 3s, one pair of Brass Scales 5d: 3s 5d*; One Brass Warming Pan 2s, one Iron Horse 1s 6d: 3s 6d*; 1 Pewter fish plate 2s, one old Brass Warming Pan 1s 4d: 3s 4d*; 1 old Brass Candlestick 6d, one Stew pan & Fish Kettle £1 4s 0d: £1 4s 6d*; One Pottage Pot 9s, One Plate Warmer 2s: 11s*; 7 Pewter Plates & 1 Small Dish 5s*; 1 Brass Pottage Pot 15s*; 1 old Chaffing Dish 1s, One old Stew Pan 1s 2d: 2s 2d*; 1 Chocolate Pot 1s, Six Pewter Plates & 1 Dish 5s 6d: 6s 6d*; 2 Pewter Plates & 2 Dishes 2s 6d*; 1 old Brass Warming Pan 2s 6d, One Pottage Pot 3s 6d: 6s*; 1 Water Plate 2s, One Bell metal Pottage Pot & Mortar 16s: 18s*; 1 old Frying Pan 3s, one Trivett & a Pair of old Bellows 1s: 4s*; 2 Water Dishes 8s, One pewter dish 2s 6d: 10s 6d*; 3 Small Pewter Dishes 4s, four water Plates 7s: 11s*; 1 Tin Dripping Pan 2s*; 1 Trivet & Plate Warmer 10d*; 50 lb of old Pewter £1 5s*; 1 old Copper Cistern 10s*; 1 old Salamander 10d*; 1 large Boyler 15s*.

In the Pastry Room: One Old Square Table 2s.

In the Cheese Chamber: 1 old Tub, 1 old Churn, a Cheese press, a Cheese Frame and shelves 10s.

In the Dairey: 8 Cheesevats & 2 Cheeseboards 5s; One old Cheese tub, 2 Milk Tubs 5s; five Milk Pans, 1 Cheese rack & Tongs 3s 6d; one Cheese press, 1 Pair of Wooden Scales 11s; one Meal Tub, 1 hand churn & 2 Pails 9s.

In the Larder: A Wire Safe & a Pair of Steps 5s 6d; 2 Salting Jars 10s, one Salting Tub 7s: 17s; One Iron Meat rack & Some Earthen Ware 2s; 2 old Tea Kettles 6s; One Mincing Knife & block 1s 4d*; 1 Salting Tub 4s, a Pair of old Stilyards 3s: 7s*; A Dinner Bell 4s 6d*.

In the Studdy: An old deal writing Table 3s; an old Painted floor Cloth 2s 6d; a fireshovel, Tongs, Poker & Fender 3s; 2 old window Curtains 2s 6d*; 1 old brass reading Screen 2s 6d*

In the Dressing Room: four old Guns & Pistols not fit for use £1 1s; An old Peer Glass 10s; an old Corner Cupboard 5s; an old Cushion & Couch & Table 9s 6d*; two Pair of old window Curtains 2s*.

In the old Parlour: one old Peer Glass 10s; Seven matted bottomed

Chairs 5s*; two pair of old window Curtains 2s 6d*; two old Tables 3s*; one old Stove Grate, fire Shovel, Tongs & Poker 4s 6d*.

In the Common Entry: two old Tables 12s 6d; One old brass Sconce 6d*.

In the Butler's Pantry: two Wainscot knife boxes, 2 Cole Tubs & 1 Chair 3s; one white Stone 2 Quart Decanter & 1 Quart Ditto, 1 Delf Punch Bowl & an old brass Candlestick 5s; One old Copper Cistern 10s*; One Glass Tray 2s 6d*.

In the Butler's Lodging Room: One Bedstead, Sackin Bottom with old Yellow hangings 15s; One feather Bed, one Bolster, one Pillow £1 10s; 1 Chest of Drawers, 1 old Chair, 1 old Small writing Desk 12s; one old Quilt 6s*.

In the Brewhouse: one Liquor Pump £1 16s; 1 large Ironbound Marsh Tub & a Working Tub £10; 3 old working tubs £2; 6 old Tubs of different sizes & a bearing Tub £1 1s; 4 troughs, Spout, Strom & Jett etc. £1 6s.

In the Servants Hall: one old Table & form, 1 old Cloaths horse & an old Pillion & Pillion Cloth 9s 6d.

In the Carpenters Shop: One old Timber Jack £1; 1 old water cart & Vessell £2.

In the Ale Cellar: two Iron bound Pipes £2; 8 Ditto £2; 2 hogsheads 16s; 1 hogshead 5s; 1 half hogshead, 1 Small Cask 5s; 2 Tap Tubs 2s.

In the Small Beer Cellar: 2 old Pipes iron bound £1 1s; 4 Ditto £1 10s; 2 old Ditto 10s; 1 hogshead 10s 6d; Glass bottles 14 Dozen of good Wine Bottles £1 8s; 4 Dozen of Pint Ditto 6s; Some old Bottles 15s 6d.

In the Laundry: 1 old rough Table & frame 7s 6d; 1 Lock iron 2 Pads & some hair line, 1 Close Basket & an old fireshovel & tongs 10s 6d.

In the Wash House: 2 old Tables, 2 old Slabs & one Drink Stall 6s; 2 old Brass kettles & 1 pair of Pothooks 13s; 2 old Wash Tubs & 3 old Wash Trays 11s; 2 Cloaths horses 1 Lye rack & one old Tub 8s 6d.

In the Coachman's Room & Boys Room: One Bedstead Mat & Cord with old Green hangings, 1 Pillow & 2 Blankets £1 5s; 1 old Bedstead Mat & Cord & 1 Bolster, all very bad 3s; 2 old naked Bedsteads at the Farmhouse 5s; one old Rug 1s*; 2 old Feather Beds £1 15s 6d*; 2 old Blankets 1s 8d*; 1 old Coverlid 1s*.

Glasses: One Dozen of Wine Glasses, 10 large Glasses, 1 Decanter, 8 Tumblers, 10 Water Glasses with Dishes & 1 Pair of Cruets £1; 63 odd Glasses 11s*.

In the Garden: [*List of implements*]

China: 60 Eight inch blue & white plates, 20 Eleven Inch Ditto, 3 Twelve Inch Ditto, 13 ten Inch Ditto 9 Nine Inch Ditto £7; 2 Eleven Inch Enameld Dishes & 6 Plates Ditto £1 10s; 30 blue & white Cups & Saucers £1; 24 Enameld Ditto £1; 8 blue & white Coffee Cups 4s; 6 Enameld Ditto 4s; 2 blue & white Tea Pots 4s; 2 Enamel'd Ditto 5s; 10 blue & White Small Basons 10s; 3 Ditto Sugar Dishes 2s; 3 Enameld

Slop Basons 4s; 2 Ditto Sugar Dishes 2s; 1 twelve Inch Enameld Punch Bowl 7s 6d; 3 ten Inch blue & white Punch Bowls 12s; 2 Enameld fruit Plates 4s; 3 Ditto desert Dishes 7s 6d; 1 Enameld Spoon Pan 1s; 2 Ditto Salvers 2s

Stone: 12 Soop Plates 3s; 30 Comon Dishes 7s 6d; 2 brown jugs 1s; 1 ditto Tea Pot 9d.

Glass: One Glass Salver 2s; 50 Jelly Glasses of different Sizes & very old Fashioned 5s.

Linnen: 4 Damask Table Cloaths £2; 2 large Ditto £2; 1 small Ditto 10s; A Piece of Huckerback containing 26 yards unwhiten'd for Table Cloaths £1 6s: Napkins: 30 Damask £1 10s; 12 large Diaper 12s; Six small Ditto 3s; 12 Diaper 9s. Sheets: 2 Pair of Holland £2; 20 Pair of Flax £12; 8 Pair of Hemp £3 12s; 4 Pair of Flax Sheets not made up £3 10s; Pillowbeers 20 Holland £2.

The above mentioned Linnen pretty much worn.

The under mentioned of an Indifferent Sort & Very much worn.

Table Cloths: 6 Damask £2 5s; 20 Diaper £5; 20 Huckerback £4; 4 Ditto Servants 10s; Napkins: 12 Damask 9s; 42 Diaper £1 1s; Sheets: 8 Pair of Holland £4; 13 Pair of Flax £5 4s; 7 Pair of Hemp £2; Pillowbeers: 10 Holland 10s; 12 Flaxen 6s; Towels 13 Damask 13s; 15 Huckerback 7s 6d; 9 Servants Ditto 4s 6d.

Plate:

	Weight			Value		
	oz	P	D	£	s	d
a large Coffee Pot	23	0	0	5	15	0
A Cream Jug	7	10	0	1	17	6
2 Small Candlesticks	6	10	0	1	12	6
2 half Pint Mugs	14	12	0	3	13	0
A Punch Ladle	3	5	0		15	3
3 Plain Casters	22	16	0	5	14	0
A Tobacco Sieve	8	0	0	2	0	0
A Soop Spoon	5	0	0	1	5	0
A Strainer	5	3	0	1	5	9
2 Pair of Tea Tongs	1	6	0		6	6
A small Coffee Pot	16	10	0	4	2	6
6 Salts, 4 Spoons	15	2	0	3	15	6
2 Pint Mugs	22	15	0	5	13	9
12 Spoons	27	16	0	6	19	0
12 Ditto	19	11	0	4	17	9
12 Ditto	12	12	0	3	3	0
a Salver	24	9	0	6	2	3
4 Candlesticks	41	3	0	10	5	9
2 Salvers	18	2	0	4	10	6
14 odd Spoons	24	3	0	6	0	9
A Marrow Spoon	1	13	0		8	3

A Papspoon & boat	3	5	0		16	3	
A Saucepan	9	10	0	2	7	6	
13 Tea Spoons	4	9	0	1	2	3	
a Snuffer dish	7	10	0	1	17	6	

Plate Specifically devised							
One Gold Watch & Chain				12	12	0	*
A Tea Table	115	15	0	28	18	9	*
a Dressing Box	32	0	0	8	0	0	*
2 Powder Boxes	19	10	0	4	17	6	*
2 Salvers	28	0	0	7	0	0	*
2 Cawdle Cups	18	0	0	4	10	0	*
a Pincushion Case	7	0	0	1	15	0	*
2 Patch boxes	9	0	0	25	0	0	*
2 Perfume boxes	5	10	0	1	7	6	*
2 Candlesticks	16	4	0	4	1	0	*
Some Silver round a Small Broken							
Glass & 2 comb brushes	-	-	-	-	-	-	
4 Plain Candlesticks	55	10	0	13	17	6*	
a Pair of Snuffers & Case	11	15	0	2	18	9*	
2 Salvers the neatest pair of							
any there were	45	5	0	11	6	3*	
a Tea Kettle	55	16	0	13	19	0*	
a Lamp	38	0	0	9	10	0*	

[*Detailed list follows of animals in the stable and yard; produce in the barn and equipment in various buildings*].

Money in the house   £689 3s 7½d
Arrears of Rent & other Debts
  due to the Deceased   £1,173 10s 0½d

Examined by William Pym junior 6 February 1771

BCRO: PM 2578

NOTES

1. The main archive relating to Hasells Hall is the Pym archive (PM). Published sources include James Collett-White's *Hasells Hall, Sandy* BCRO publication 1983, Marcus Binney and Kit Martin's *The Country House to be or not to be*, SAVE 1982, and Marcus Binney and James Collett-White's *Rescue of the Hasells* CL 4 July 1985. The 1634 deed (PM 196) and the 1722 Legal Case (PM 1804).
2. PM 236–237.
3. Offer to Astell (PM 235); conveyance to Kingsley (PM 236–7).
4. Gordon Map (MC 2/8); Enlarged photograph Z 50/143/233.
5. PM 1736.
6. 1814 plans (PM 1/5–6); 1892 plans (PM 1/64).
7. PM 1957.
8. PM 2380.

9. See photograph of painting *At Mr. Palmer's House* by Mortimer Hunt c.1784, where Francis Pym is portrayed at his father-in-law's house.
10. There is a copy of the text of the Red Book held at BCRO (CRT 130 Sandy 16).
11. Torrington Diaries Volume II p.289.
12. Michaelmas 1790 (PM 2290).
13. PM 2383.
14. PM 2833.
15. Photograph of painting of South Front of Hasells c.1840 (Z 50/99/4).
16. PM 1918–1919. The lodge is illustrated in the corner of an estate map of 1855 (PM 1/40).
17. PM 2608.
18. PM 1/5–6.
19. PM 1/7–9.
20. PM 2629–2644.
21. PM 1615.
22. National Gallery Italian Schools 1937 plate 177, p.304.
23. PM 1/86.

HINWICK HOUSE

Hinwick to 1766

The Manor of Brayes in Podington, including the site of the present
Hinwick House, descended to the Orlebar family through the marriage
of George Orlebar and Margaret Childe in c.1620. The existing Turret
House and attached outbuildings are all that remain of the previous
manor house. The Orlebars continued to rent property in Harrold.
Richard Orlebar (1671–1733), however, married Diana Astry, daughter
and coheiress of Samuel Astry of Henbury, Gloucestershire, a relation
of the Astrys of Wood End, Harlington.[1] As the Clerk of the Crown to
the Court of the Exchequer, Astry accumulated a considerable fortune.
He used it to create a substantial estate based on the Great House,
Henbury, which he rebuilt. Samuel had been born in 1632, a member of
the Harlington Wood End family. On the death of Sir Samuel's widow
in 1704, Richard and Diana were entitled to a third share of Sir
Samuel's estate.[2]

By 1708, the work had started on their great joint project: to rebuild
Hinwick. Meticulous accounts were kept of payments to the individual
workmen, who were paid on a day-to-day basis.[3] The work was controlled by master mason Richard Knight of Weldon, Northamptonshire,
who performed a similar task at Colworth House, (built from 1715
onwards), and probably at Hinwick Hall. Much of the stone came from
local pits but a number of loads came from Weldon. The gates to
Hinwick House, and probably Hinwick Hall, were provided by the well
known ironsmith Thomas Warren of Cambridge.

Creating a house from scratch was a rare event in Bedfordshire. What
sort of house did Knight build?

Although totally unlike Henbury in most ways, Hinwick does include
something of the new Baroque, as well as features from earlier types of
house. The Baroque full entabulature over the pilasters on the entrance
front has been noted by Dr. Andor Gomme in his notes on the history
of the house.[4] This is in contrast to the long gallery mentioned as being
on the second floor, very much more a feature of an Elizabethan house.

The entrance or east front is based on a scaled down version of
Buckingham House, a favourite for master masons such as the Smiths
of Warwick to imitate and modify. A picture formerly in the house,
reproduced in Arthur Oswald's article in *Country Life* and William
Gordon's map of 1736, show that there was a three- walled enclosure
in front of the house. Both show all three storeys in place in the
1720s and 1730s, so that the house was clearly of this height from the
beginning.[5]

Plate 10: Hinwick House: This shows the entrance (i.e. east) front as it would have looked at the time of the 1766 inventory. (*Watercolour: Thomas Fisher, c.1820*)

A similar front was built on the south side of the house at right angles to the entrance front. In place of the front door flanked by a window on either side is a single central window flanked by two shallow niches. This is repeated at first floor level. At the attic level is a vigorous carving of Diana, the Goddess of Hunting, added after the death in 1716 of Diana Orlebar, whose money had provided for the building of the house. The carver was John Hunt of Northampton, who also executed the memorial in Podington Church.

The back of the house was not so satisfactorily completed and proves that in spite of the showy magnificence of the main facades and the U-shaped ground plan favoured by him, the house was not designed by Francis Smith or anyone of such stature. Dr. Andor Gomme comments on the lack of symmetry of the windows of the two rear wings: one wing having one wide window and the other two of conventional size. He goes on: "Worse still from a purist's viewpoint the window architraves nearest to the re-entrant angles disappear into the projecting walls . . . the back is frankly something of a cobble, possibly even reusing older features . . . just the sort of thing to happen to a house put up by an enthusiastic and only moderately wealthy owner in the absence of a supervisory architect or really competent master mason."[6]

Richard Orlebar continued to live in the house after his wife's death and the house passed on his death in 1733 to John Orlebar, M.P. for Bedford 1727–1734.

The 1766 Inventory

What does the inventory tell us about the layout of the house in the 1760s? Can any change be detected since the house was finished in 1710 and have any of the furnishings been replaced since that date? In working out the layout of the house in 1766, the plans prepared by F.C. Penrose before his major alterations and extensions of 1865–1866 are most useful.[7]

In 1766 the ground floor had an entrance hall much as today but without the main staircase leading from it. At the south-east corner of the house was the best parlour (drawing room on F.C. Penrose's plan). This led to the tapestry parlour (morning room on the plan). Although not specifically mentioned in the inventory, the library must have existed to house John Orlebar's collection of 1493 books. On Penrose's plan the library was immediately west of the hall, sharing a wall with the tapestry parlour/morning room. It is probable that this was where it was sited in 1766. At the south-west corner of the house on Penrose's plan was the main staircase, leading out of what subsequently became the library. The fine staircase, probably made by Daniel Wayman, replaced by Penrose in the hall area in the 1866 refit was clearly not intended by Richard Knight to have a dramatic impact on the main part of the house, tucked away as it was in a wing and only reached by going through at least one room to get to it from the hall. We are very far from the dramatic staircase of Holkham leading straight out of the hall into a piano nobile. Across the hall at Hinwick House lay the service area of the house in Penrose's day.

In the wing opposite the staircase, i.e. on the north-west corner of the house, lay the servants' hall both in 1766 and 1866. To the east of it lay the kitchen with a pantry (butler's pantry on Penrose's plan) between it and the library. In 1866 a back stairs led up to the north part of the first floor. Leading off the kitchen in 1866 was the housekeeper's room; in 1766 this was the dining room. At both dates there was a pantry attached to this room. In the north-east part of the house there was a tiny room, unidentified on Penrose's plan but almost certainly the writing closet mentioned in 1766. Certainly, the ground floor appears as if there has been little change between 1710 and 1766. The only partition walls that might have been added are in the area of the dining room and would have involved comparatively minor alterations. The tapestry room and the best parlour could have been one room but that is unlikely, as tapestries were much more popular in the 1710s than subsequently.

The first floor is much more problematical, as although Penrose made a plan of the first floor he did not identify any of the rooms by

Plate 11: Hinwick House: The Japan cabinet and stand. It may have come from Henbury, and it is probably included in the 1766 inventory. (*Photograph: 1928*)

name. Curiously, too, there were two unfinished rooms, whether from the initial building or as a result of later alteration it is difficult to say. Much the most valuable items on this floor were kept in the wrought bedroom which seems to have been the principal bedroom suite. It is likely that the bedroom itself was on the south-east corner of the house with windows looking out on both fronts. The ante-chamber was probably behind the left window of the central section of the eastern facade. Naturally there was an interconnecting door between it and the wrought bedroom itself. Behind the right wing of the central section lay the second of the two green bedchambers with its one pair of window curtains. The yellow bedchamber possibly lay on the north-west.

The garret/attic area of the house included a long gallery, a very old fashioned feature, normally found in Elizabethan and early Jacobean houses. They were designed to allow the residents of the house to take exercise under cover during bad weather. A number of long galleries were introduced or adapted to act as picture galleries. This does not seem to have been the case at Hinwick House although other wet weather amusements were catered for in this area with a bookcase, a writing table, a reading stand and maps, as well as a couch for the exhausted to lie on. The fittings of the tapestry room, too, probably date from the building of the house. The nursery was on this floor, much used by the Orlebars, who had large families in succeeding generations.

The inventory of 1766 shows a conservative addition of pieces to the furnishings rather than wholesale replacement under the pressure of changes in fashion. There certainly are pieces of mahogany in the chief rooms such as a marble side table with a mahogany frame in the best parlour, and in the tapestry parlour a mahogany oval dining table, a mahogany claw table and two-leaf screen. These do not, however, predominate and throughout the house there are pieces in walnut and oak (here called wainscot). Next to the marble side table was "a walnuttree settee and 8 chairs covered with flowered silk & cases". The hall contained eight walnut chairs as well as a two-flapped wainscot table. Somewhere in the inventory, though not instantly recognisable, must be the famous Hinwick counting table.[8]

John Orlebar clearly was a considerable collector of paintings, having a total of 38 (seven portraits[9]) and 53 prints. This was not so large as his near neighbour John Bullock of Sharnbrook but still represents a substantial collection. Possibly he did not buy more as he had inherited a number of tapestries, probably the Mortlake ones relating to Ulysses, mentioned in Michael Orlebar's *Hinwick House*, c.1970.[10] By the 1760s these would have looked old fashioned but at Hinwick they were retained and not cut to accommodate new doors, like those at Hardwick.

Among the pictures, which by and large are not identified, are two portraits of William III and Mary II. These are noted by Michael

Plate 12: Hinwick House: Portrait of John Orlebar of Hinwick.
(*Oil painting: Arthur Devis, c.1740*)

Orlebar.[11] This emphasises John Orlebar's role as M.P. and Government official, wedded to the Whig Party for whom William and Mary were the chief hero and heroine of the age and of the Revolution of 1688, the greatest event in recent English history. The one other identified picture, of Venus, was clearly not highly regarded as it was dumped unframed in a dressing room (No.10) with the old swords and blunderbuss.

The dressing room combined the functions of the later man's dressing room (with pewter shaving pot and plate and possible pin up) with the later gun room. The fowling pieces were used for rough shooting on the estate while the swords and pistols remind us of the connection the Orlebar family had with the regular army and local militia from at least the early eighteenth century.[12] The blunderbuss could well have been used by the family coachman to deter highwaymen.

Apart from shooting, other amusements were catered for in the house such as backgammon and draughts. The family did however have intellectual interests as well. While it is true that many of John Orlebar's books related to legal and parliamentary matters, many of them did not. Richard, John's son, became a Clerk to the Privy Council and was educated at Eton College. John believed in educating his daughters. Mary, the eldest, certainly went to school and it is likely that the others did as well. Mary's studies included French and German. She played the harpsichord and was the family bard producing poems for all family and national occasions. Her sister Constantia was an expert on weather and the third sister Elizabeth read Italian.[13] The library was therefore well used and the pewter ink pots did not remain idle.

The linen cupboard reveals some of the clothes worn by John Orlebar and his family. The blossom coloured coat, waistcoat and breeches are particularly interesting as an "Apple Blossom Suit", supposedly worn by Richard Orlebar as Clerk to the Privy Council, is mentioned by Michael Orlebar as forming part of the Hinwick clothing collection. An earlier date for this must now be suggested. Unfortunately, no mention is made of the "seven magnificent waistcoats . . . dating c.1760".[14] These were either later or came from a different ancestor of the Orlebars.

John Orlebar had a considerable number of pieces of silver, totalling £178 7s 3½d in value, but his china and earthenware was less extensive. The only china ornaments seem to have been blue and white jars, one identified as Delft.

Hinwick House 1766–1994

It is probable that even by the death of John Orlebar, the family was in financial difficulties. John's son Richard reorganised the finances of the family as soon as he came into the ownership of the estate. He became Clerk to the Privy Council and this should have re-established the family. Richard (1736–1803), however, had a large number of children by his two wives. All of these had to be found means of support such as army commissions, marriage portions or plain maintenance. He tried farming for a short time and was the first member of the family to go to France to cut his expenses. He went in 1785 and prudently returned before the French Revolution.[15]

His son Richard (1775–1833) also had financial problems, partly inherited from his father, and partly as a result of having children himself. During the 1820s he left Hinwick House to be looked after by his youngest brother William Augustus Orlebar. He and his family went to France, returning at the first sniff of the 1830 Revolution. It is probable that Richard purchased the French furniture and the Belgian fireplace in the drawing room that date from this period.

Richard Longuet Orlebar (1806–1870) succeeded to Hinwick in 1833. He married Sophia Parrott, daughter of Jasper, of Dundridge, Devon. On his death, Richard and Sophia used their share of the inheritance to add a service wing to Hinwick House, restore the dining room to its former place and bring the staircase up from the hall. These expensive schemes were put into effect by Francis Cranmer Penrose, architect in charge of St. Paul's Cathedral and a relation by marriage of the Orlebars.

Such a grand, enlarged house could be maintained so long as the rents of the Bedfordshire and Devon estates remained high. In 1874, the Great Agricultural Depression started and rents sank. For much of their ownership of the house Richard (1833–1920) and Frederica (1838–1928) could not live in it.[16] In 1880 there was a scheme to make it into a private lunatic asylum.[17] Fortunately, tenants were found, including A.S. Orlebar, a cousin, who ran a preparatory school there before World War I. Richard's son Rouse, who took over the estate in 1891, was advised in 1896 to sell Hinwick.[18] He tried but failed to find a buyer. It was not until 1994 that the house was in fact sold, after the family had surprisingly been able to live there for the last eighty years of their ownership.

HINWICK HOUSE, PODINGTON 1766

An Inventory of Sundry Household Furniture, Plate, Linen, China etc. of John Orlebar Esq. Deceased, taken at His late Dwelling-House at Hinwick in the County of Bedford these 27th, 28th and 29th days of January 1766

No.1 Small bed Chamber, 2 pair [of Stairs]: A 4 post Bedstead with Green Cheney furniture, a feather-bed, bolster, one pillow, 3 Blanketts, a quilt, 3 Matted Chairs, a stool and a Chamber-table, 28 Prints, a picture and a Map, and 7 odd China Cups £3 18s.

No.2 Long Gallery, 2 pair: A walnuttre Couch cover'd with leather, a Squabb & 3 pillows, a Walnuttre Writing table with green Cloth cover, a windsor Chair and 7 other Chairs, a Reading Stand, a pair of Steps, 3 pictures, 5 Maps, a wainscot double Chest of Draw's with folding doors and desk draw'r and book Shelf over Ditto, 1 Large Wainscot Bookcase with Glazed doors, 2 Ditto less, a wainscott Press with folding doors £10 8s.

No.3 Tapestry Room, 2 pair: A Bedstead with blue Stuff furniture, a feather bed 2 bolsters, 1 pillow, 2 Blanketts, a quilt, 2 Stuff window Curtains and rods, the Tapestry Hangings, 7 Cane Chairs and a table, an old grate and a trunk. £3 3s.

No.4 & 5 The Maids' Room and Boys' Adjoining, 2 pair: Two Bedsteads with half Canopy, Stuff furniture, 2 feather-beds, 2 bolsters, 2 pillows, 5 Blanketts, 2 quilts, 1 pair blue and 1 pair Yellow Curtains, 2 pictures, a Small Glass and a Pewter Ink Stand, a 4-post Bedstead with blue lindsey furniture, a feather-bed, bolster and 1 pillow, 3 blanketts, a quilt and one Chair. £4 9s.

No.6 Store room, 2 pair: Two Copper Kitchens, 2 Stewpans, 1 cover, an Iron plate warmer, 2 bird cages, a tea kettle stand, a box with some bees wax, a quilting frame and Tressells, a cloths horse, a looking glass, a Stand with Shelves Containing a parcel of broken China and Earthenware, 2 basketts, a side-saddle Cloth, 7 blue and white Coffee Cups, a coloured teapot and sugar dish, and a punch bowle, 84 sundry pieces of Glass ware. £2 10s.

No.7 The Nursery, 2 pair: A Bedstead with old wrought furniture, a feather bed, 3 bolsters, 2 pillows, 3 blanketts and a quilt, a Bedstead with old Stuff furniture, a feather bed, 1 bolster, 1 pillow, 3 blanketts and a quilt, 2 pair of Stuff window Curtains and rods, a Walnuttree Escrutore, a large Cyprus Chest,[19] 8 Chairs, 2 Stools and a table, 2 small Dressing-Glasses, 6 Glazd prints, a pair of Steele doggs, shovle and tongs, tin guard, fender and bellows. £10 3s.

No.8 Little blue Room, 2 pair: A 4-post Bedstead with blue lindsey furniture, a feather-bed, bolster, 3 blanketts and a quilt, 3 chairs, a small table, a round Night Stool and pewter pan, 3 prints and a small glass. £3 3s.

No.9 Linen bed chamber, 2 pair: A Bedstead with linen furniture, 2 pair of Stuff window Curtains and rods, a feather bed, bolster, 1 blankett, a white mattrass and a quilt, a walnuttre Cabinett with Glazed doors, 5 Matted Chairs and a table, a pair of doggs, shovle, tongs and brush. £7.

No.10 Dressing room, 1 pair: A Cane Couch with a Squabb and pillow, a Walnuttre Escrutore,[20] 2 Matted Chairs, a stool, a table, a dressing Glass, a stove grate, Shovle, tongs and bellows, an Iron Chest, a Picture of Venus (no frame), 2 pictures in black frames and 9 prints, a brass barrell blunderbuss, a Rifle barrell Gun and powder horn, 5

Fowling pieces, 4 pair of Pistols, 4 old Swords with Mettle hilts, 4 old whips, a french plate, Tea Kettle and lamp, and a dish stand Ditto, a pewter shaving pott and plate. £10 10s.

No.11 Green bed chamber, 1 pair: A 4 post Bedstead with Green Camblett furniture and 2 pair window Curtains, a feather bed, bolster, 1 pillow and a white Cotton Counterpain, an India- Japanned Cabinet, a walnuttre Chamber table and 5 Matted bottom Chairs, a Dressing Glass, a piece of Tapestry, a steele harth, back and doggs, shovle, tongs and bellows, 3 pictures, 2 China bowls (1 Cracked) 1 bason, a pair of Japan'd blue and Gold Cups, a Jugg and cover, 21 odd pieces, some broke, 2 Striped China bottles, 4 blue and white Jarrs and a Candlestick Ditto. £13 14s.

No.12 Dressing Room and leather Closet, 1 pair: A Glass in a black frame and 2 Slip Sconces, 1 pair of Green window Curtains and rod, a Stool, 4 pictures & 8 prints, a Fine Needlework Counterpin, a walnuttre bookcase with looking glass doors, an Easy Chair and Cushion, a stool, 2 window Curtains and rods and a window seat, the Gilt leather Hangings, 2 pictures, 1 print, 5 Needlework Cushions and the top of a table and toylett. £9 9s.

No.13 The two Unfinished rooms, 1 pair: An old Settea covered with green Mohair, 4 feather pillows and Ditto hair, 5 high back Chairs, 3 odd Chairs, 4 Bedsteads, 8 rods, a gaurd Iron and 15 window Rods, a walnuttre bed Chair, 7 Chairs, a Roling Map, part of a bedstead & rod, 2 pictures, an old table, 2 teapotts and Stands, a brass fender and a pair of doggs. £3 1s.

No.14 Yellow bed Chamber and passage, 1 pair: A Bedstead with Yellow furniture and 2 pair of Window Curtains, a feather bed, bolster, 1 pillow, 3 blanketts, a quilt and a white Mattrass, 3 Chairs, a stool, a Dressing table and Glass, a glass in a black frame and 2 prints, a pair of steele doggs and back, shovle, tongs and bellows, the Tapestry Hangings, an Eight-day Clock £12 7s.

No.15 Green bed Chamber, 1 pair: A bedstead with green Cheney furniture, a feather bed, bolster, 1 pillow, 2 blanketts, a quilt and a Mattrass, a Chamber table and dressing Glass, a Matted chair, a bed waggon, 1 picture, 14 prints, a pair Steele doggs, shovle and tongs £5 5s.

No.16 Wrought bed Chamber, Anti-Chamber and Closett, 1 pair: A 4 post Bedstead with Needlework furniture lined with Persian and 2 pair of Silk window Curtains, a feather-bed, bolster, 2 pillows, 3 blanketts, a white Quilt and a Mattrass, 4 Chairs, 2 Elbow Ditto, and 2 Stools cover'd with Needlework and Chequa Cases, a Chimney Glass in a gilt frame, a picture over Ditto and 2 others, 2 turkey bedside Carpetts, a pair of Steele doggs and back Shovle, tongs, tin gaurd fender, bellows and brush, a piece of Tapestry, a small Chest of draws and dressing Glass, a round Night Stool and pan, 2 bottle stands, a pair of Iron doggs, Shovle and tongs, a Japan'd Cabinett and Dressing Glass,[21] 6

Cane Chairs with feather Cushions, a dressing table & toylett, 7 pictures, 25 prints, a pair steele doggs and back Shovle and tongs, 1 blue and white Delph Jarr and 2 bottles, 2 China Chamber potts and a bason Ditto. £39 17s.

No.17 Large hall: A Steele Stove, 3 Iron backs, fender, shovle, tongs and poker, 8 Walnuttre Chairs, 2 Elbow Ditto, a 2 flap't wainscott table,[22] 4 Carved bracketts, a Barometer, King William, Queen Mary, and one other portrait. £7 17s.

No.18 Best Parlour: A Steele Chair stove grate, moulding, fender, poker, shovle, and tongs, a Chimney Glass with brass arms, 2 Pier Glasses, a Marble Side Table with a Mahogany frame, a walnuttre settea and 8 Chairs Cover'd with flowered Silk & cases, an old Turkey Carpett, 1 picture and 4 portraits in black & Gilt frames. £21 11s.

No.19 Tapestry Parlor: A brass hearth and doggs, shovle, tongs, bellows and Iron back, a Chimney Glass with Glass arms and a picture over Ditto, a Mahogany Ovall Dining table, 3 Cane Chairs, a tea table, 3 pieces of Tapestry, a Mahogany Claw table and a 2 leaf Screen, a wainscott Oval table, a back gammon table, boxes and men, a bell lamp shade and hook, 8 Maps, a leg stool and cushion. £11 1s.

No.20 Dining parlor and writing Closett: A Steele Stove, shovle, tongs, poker, fender, bellows and brush, a Chimney Glass, a Mahogany 1 flap dining table, a wainscott Claw table, a walnuttre Card table, 1 Elbow Chair, Cushion and case, 6 Matted bottom Chairs, a tea Chest, 1 pair red Cheque window Curtains and rod, a 2 leaf Canviss Screen, 5 pictures, a painted floor Cloth, a pewter Ink Stand, a Slip Sconce, a Slate table, a draftboard and men, 2 Cane Chairs, 1 Cushion, a wainscott cupboard. £7 17s.

No.21 Pantry: 47 sundry Glasses, 4 decanters, 12 blue and white China Saucers, a Copper bottle Cistron and Coal Scoup, a Napkin press with draw's, a Voider, 4 bottle boards, a dutch tea kettle & lamp, 3 dozen & 9 white hafted knives, 3 Dozen and 6 forks & 3 Shagreen Cases, A Shagreen case with 9 China hafted knives & 8 forks, 4 knifeboxes, a Copper tea Kitchen with an Iron & Cock. £4 11s.

No.22 Kitchen: A Rainge fix'd with hanging barr, shovle, tongs, poker and fender, an ash grate, a hanging Iron, 2 pigg irons, 4 Trivetts, 3 Gridirons, stake tongs, a House wife and 7 Iron Skewers, a Chaffing dish, 2 flatt Irons, a Crane and hooks, A Smoake Jack Compleat, 8 Spitts and a pair of Spitt racks, an Iron Stand to a Dripping-pan, a Salamander and a Rake, a pair of stilliards & weight, a bell metle Morter and Iron pestle, 2 Iron Candlesticks, a pair of bellows, a Cookhold, 2 Cleavers, a Chopping Knife, 5 pottage potts and Covers, 5 Saucepans, a fish Kettle and cover, 4 Stew pans, 2 brass Kettles, 1 frying pan, 2 brass ladles, a Scummer, a Copper Oven, 2 Coffee Potts, a Chocolate Pott, a Preserving Pan, 2 Drinking potts, 2 tea Kettles, a Skillett, 9 brass Candlesticks, a pair of snuffers & stand, a dredger, a pair brass scales and weights, a tin Drippin pan, and 20 pieces of tin-ware, 46 Sundry pewter Dishes, 130 Sundry table Plates, 2 Cullenders, 2 fish plates, 2 Cheese plates and a head to a Limbick, 9 water plates, a Meat Screen, 6 Chairs, a small table, a Marble Morter and pestle. £18 18s.

No.23 Servants' Hall, the Kitchen parlor and Pantry: A large table, a deal leaf, a form, 7 Matted Chairs, a boot Jack, 9 old Guns, an Iron harth, fender, tongs & poker, an Ovall wainscott table, 5 Cane Chairs and 1 Cushion, a deal table, 1 Small Ditto, a Nest of spice draws, a Chair, a pye peal, a large Stone Morter, an old Copper fish Kettle, and a lamp Ditto, an Iron plate warmer, a toasting-stand, 3 Coffee Mills and some odd pieces of Stone ware, 15 Stone dishes, 38 plates and 18 pieces of Earthen ware, 2 old Colour'd China Dishes, 3 blue and white Ditto, 1 Ditto Crack'd, 6 Ditto, 12 fine Coloured Japan'd plates, 12 blue and white Ditto, 4 Ditto Crack'd and 1 odd plate, 12 Enameld tea Cups, 12 Saucers, a tea pott & stand, a Milk pott, a sugar dish and cover and Slop bason, 54 Sundry Pieces of Glass Ware, 5 blue and white basons, a Ditto tea pott with Silver spout, 10 Coffee Cups, 23 Sundry tea and Coffee Cups and 33 Saucers, a round banister'd tea-board and 2 plain Ditto. £10.

No.24 & 25 Scullery and Brewhouse: A Copper fix'd, cirb'd with lead and Ironwork with brass Cock, 5 tubbs, 4 pails, a barrell Churn Compleat, a plate rack and some wood ware, a large Copper and Ironwork fix'd, a Mashing tubb, 2 working Ditto, 3 backs, 2 Shoots, a pail, 2 ladles, an Oar, a hop bask and a ladder. £24 8s.

No.26 & 27 Laundry, Wash House, and Room over Ditto: Two Oak tables, 2 Cloths horses, a fender, shovle and tongs, 2 Chairs, 2 box Irons and heaters, 3 Flat Irons, 3 Stands, 3 flasketts, a pair of Steps and a sive, a Copper fix'd and Ironwork, a Nedding Trough, a flour binn, a long board, 11 sundry tubbs, a peele, a pair steps, a Meat Screen, a Cloths horse, some hampers, tubbs and 1 Iron shovle. £3 6s.

No.28 Outhouses, stables etc.: The Terrett Clock Compleat with lead weights, bell and diall, a Ladder and Sundry old Iron. Coachman's Room: a Bedstead and Curtains, a flock bed and bolster, 3 blanketts, a rugg, a feather bed, bolster & pillow, a table, 4 chairs and a wigg block. Next Room: a Bedstead, 2 flock beds, 1 bolster, 1 old Covering, a Chair and stool. Next Room: a Bedstead and old Curtains, a feather bed and flock bolster, 2 Blanketts, a quilt, 2 Chairs, a Cushion, a stove and fender. Room Next the Park and Summer house: a Bedstead and Curtains, 3 Chairs, an old Mattrass, 2 blanketts, a rugg, a feather bed, bolster and 2 pillows, 4 Cane Chairs, a looking Glass, a Corner Cupbord, 4 Cane Chairs, a Japan'd table, 5 high back Chairs, a round table with a Stone top.

[*Park, garden & farm equipment, listed in detail*] £73 15s.

Silver plate: 3 Salvers, 2 Sauce-boats, 3 flatt Candlesticks, 1 cup and cover, 1 Ditto less, 1 Ditto less, 1 two handle cup & cover, 2 basons, a pap-boat, a box with french Counters, a Carrell, a pair candlesticks' nossells, Snuffers and Stand, 1 pair Candlesticks and Nossells, a Coffee-pot,[23] 2 pint potts, top of a tea Kettle Stand, a Soup Spoon, 13 table spoons, 12 Desert spoons, 21 tea spoons, a pair tea tongs and Strainer, a Small Saucepan, 4 Salts, 4 Shovles and a pepper Caster, a Sett of Casters, a Strainer, a Cup, a Marrow Spoon, an Extinguisher, 4 Skewers and 2 bitts of old Silver. The whole weight is 600 oz. 15 dwts. O grs.@ 5/6 per oz.

2 Shagreen Cases with 24 Knives, 24 forks with Silver handles, 1 case Ditto with 12 Knives and 12 forks with Silver handles, 12 old Knives, 12 forks with Silver handles, a Cocoa Nut Sugar dish Tip't with Silver and foot to Ditto, a pair of Silver Spurs. £178 7s 3½d.

Linen, Wearing Apparel, etc.: 8 pair and 1 Holland Sheets, 7 pair of pillow beirs, 1 pair of Irish sheets and 8 pair of pillow beirs, 3 pair Hemp Sheets, 14 Pair of Hemp and flax and some old pillow beirs, 8 Damask table Cloths, 6 fine Diaper Napkins, 42 Coarser Ditto, 9 Diaper table cloths, 30 Napkins, 6 Huccaback Napkins, 7 old Ditto, 8 Coarse round towels, 20 Dusters and towells, 4 Huccaback Kitchen table Cloths, Glass Cloths etc., 1 Green Silk & worsted Damask window curtain, 4 silk Cushions filled with feathers, 17 full trim'd Shirts, 5 plain Shirts and 18 Stocks, 2 Shaving Cloths, 2 Cambrick Handkerchiefs, 5 silk Handkerchiefs, 4 quilted Night Caps, 7 pair of thread, Cotton and worsted Stockings, 10 hand-towels, a Blossom colourd Coat, Waistcoat and breeches, a brown Surtout Coat and a pair of Flannon drawers, 1 pair of boots, 4 pair of shoes. £20.

Books: 1,493 Volumes Sundries, 2 Books of Anatomy, Ovid's Matamorphoses, General-View of the World of Trade, 1 Book of plans and Sections, 1 Book of the Installation, Antiquity Explained, Echard's History of England in one volume. £50 10s.

All the Within-mentioned Goods are Appraised and Valued at the sum £570 18 shillings and 3½d.
per Sills. Watkins; Sam. Watkins

BCRO: OR 2071/244

NOTES

1. The principal source for the history of Hinwick House is the *Orlebar Archive* (OR) held at the Bedfordshire Record Office. Important secondary sources include: F. St.J. Orlebar's *The Orlebar Chronicle in Bedfordshire and Northamptonshire 1553-1733 or the Children of the Manor House and their Posterity*, Mitchell, Hughes and Clarke 1930; R.R. Orlebar's article in *Bedfordshire Magazine* Vol.1 pp.181–184; A. Oswald's article *Hinwick House, Bedfordshire* (CL Vol.128 pp.618–621, 676–679 and 730–733), 1960; Dr. Andor Gomme's *Hinwick House* (Notes) May 1982 (CRT 130 Podington 11) and M. Orlebar's *Hinwick House (a Guide)*, n.d. c. early 1980s. Further information can be gleaned from standard works for the area such as

Pevsner, Listed Buildings, and W.M. Harvey's *Hundred of Willey* published 1872–1878 pp 394–395. The main deeds relating to the descent of the estate to the Orlebars are OR 190–210, 1331–2, 2060.

2. See Margaret McGregor's *Astry and Orlebar Correspondence from the Ashton Court Papers (1709–1721)* in BHRS Vol.72 pp.116–128.
3. Hinwick House building accounts 1708–1714; Microfilm copy held at BCRO (Mic 111).
4. Gomme p.2.
5. Oswald p.618. W. Gordon's Map of Bedfordshire 1736 fully described in BHRS Vol.62 entry 23 (BCRO MC 2/8)
6. Gomme p.2.
7. F.C. Penrose, Architect to St.Paul's Cathedral was a cousin of the Orlebars by marriage. His plans have the BCRO reference OR 2078/1–16.
8. The Hinwick counting table is illustrated in Oswald p.677.
9. The portraits probably included the two of John Orlebar himself, painted by Arthur Devis and illustrated in *Polite Society* see note 20 below.
10. M. Orlebar p.12
11. M. Orlebar p.4
12. BHRS Vol.71 (1992)
13. BHRS Vol.72 (1993), my article *My Choice: A Poem written in 1751 by Mary Orlebar*.
14. M. Orlebar p.15
15. For the Orlebars' visit to France in the 1780s see OR 2071/326A following and OR 2211/1, 2214. The 1820s visit is covered in OR 2223/18–51 letters from Richard to W.A. Orlebar.
16. See their letters and diaries OR 2236 following.
17. PLH 102, 1–3, OR 2280/1–2284/15.
18. OR 2304/6, X 662/4.
19. "Cypress chest" illustrated in F. St.J. Orlebar opposite p.16
20. "Walnut escritoire", probably the one featured in the portrait of John Orlebar by Arthur Devis illustrated on p.76 of *Polite Society by Arthur Devis 1712–1787* (exhibition catalogue 1983–4). This is more likely to be the one chosen by John Orlebar for his portrait as the other walnut escritoire was not in one of his own rooms.
21. Japanned Cabinet, F. St.J. Orlebar p.153, probably correctly identifies it as originating from Henbury. The base is Baroque and the mirror Rococo. It could well be that they were both moved to the Drawing Room from the Wrought Room where they were in 1766. They are illustrated in F. St.J. Orlebar opposite p.153.
22. The "Hinwick Counting Table" is illustrated by F. St.J. Orlebar opposite p.16. An article by Richard Turner in *Bedfordshire Times and Standard* for 2 February 1940.
23. A fluted porringer, coffee pot and pair of candlesticks, all early C18th, with Orlebar arms engraved upon them are illustrated by F. St.J. Orlebar opposite p.214. These all appear to be listed in this section of the inventory.

HOUGHTON HOUSE, AMPTHILL

Houghton House 1615–1767

Probably the history of no building in Bedfordshire has provoked so much speculation and so much disagreement as Houghton House. The Park of Dame Ellensbury, split between the parishes of Ampthill and Houghton Conquest, was granted in 1615 by James I to Mary Herbert (1561–1621), wife of Henry, Earl of Pembroke, and sister of the famous poet, Philip Sydney. Her uncle had been Robert Dudley, Earl of Leicester, and favourite of Queen Elizabeth. She was well-educated, translated French poetry and was in contact with a wide range of artistic and cultural people, including the Earl of Arundel, the foremost promoter of Italian classicism in England.[1]

Between 1615 and her death in September 1621 the present Houghton House was built in probably two distinct stages. On her death, her son sold it back to the King. By 1624 the Bruce family, close supporters of the Stuart regime, were installed there.

Tradition has it that Houghton House is the model for Bunyan's Palace Beautiful in *Pilgrim's Progress*. Whether this is correct or not, Houghton House certainly had the air of a palace, flamboyant and arrogant, lauding it over the landscape below.

Although clearly designed to emphasise the importance and social dominance of its owner and possibly upstage the rival Ampthill Great Lodge on the ridge opposite, Mary George is probably correct in seeing its origins as a hunting lodge.[2] This is indicated by the unusual feature of the principal rooms facing north, yet with a south entrance. From these principal rooms, Mary Herbert and her friends could have a superb view of the hunting in the park.

The first phase of the building of the house was the creation of the H-shaped core of the house – a conventional Jacobean plan and only incidentally a graceful gesture to the Herbert family. It included a piano nobile. This probably was started in 1615 or soon after but Dr. Andor Gomme[3] thinks that it may well predate Mary Herbert. If so that would mean that James I commissioned it and that is unlikely as no mention of such work has so far been found in Royal accounts or in State Papers Domestic. The first phase did not include the loggias and porch.

From plans made in 1793,[4] it is possible to get a good idea of structural walls and their probable relationship to an original ground plan. Although the internal design is conditioned by the need to preserve a Renaissance symmetry on the outside, the room layout appears to be quite conservative. For symmetry, the entrance porch is in the centre of

103

the south facade but traditional features, such as a large great hall (later subdivided), and a grand staircase leading to a north gallery off which led almost certainly a large great chamber (1793 library), survive. Personal accommodation was arranged on both ground and bedchamber level into groups of two or three apartments: dressing room, bedchamber and closet.

The architect, who designed the first phase in which traditional elements were only slightly modified to accommodate new Renaissance fashion, remains unknown. The main candidate is John Thorpe. Despite Sir John Summerson seeing Thorpe as mainly a land surveyor rather than architect, various houses are still attributed to him. Some of the more unusual features of Houghton House are repeated in these houses. Shaped gables appear in three of Thorpe's designs and the characteristic, but rare, concave pyramid roofs that cover the four flanking towers, appear at Aston Hall (1618–1635) and Holland House (1606–7), both attributed to Thorpe. Chastleton (c.1603) has flanking towers similar to Houghton House.[5]

Mary Herbert's interest in France may have led her to favour the pyramid roofs and spirelets (on the south facade); also the French light type windows, which first appear in England at Somerset House in c.1610. All the above evidence shows that it is perfectly possible Thorpe was the first architect at Houghton House. Orlebar Marsh, soon after 1792, mentions that Thorpe's designs for Houghton were in the Earl of Warwick's collection.[6] Thorpe is known also to have worked at two local houses, Toddington Manor (c.1615) and Ampthill Great Lodge (1606). It may be right that Thorpe was the architect but the least that can be said is that whoever he was, he knew Thorpe's work. The north wing is similar but not identical to an elevation of John Smythson, who knew Inigo Jones's work.[7]

Sometime about 1620 a radical reinterpretation of the building took place and Mary Herbert decided Houghton must have some architectural features from the new Italian style, inspired by Palladio, that was becoming so fashionable with her cultured friends. A new architect, possibly Inigo Jones, was appointed. The gaps in between the projecting wings of the north front were filled in. The north was given a classical Italian centrepiece, based it has been argued on the unexecuted design for St. Paul's Cathedral by Inigo Jones, dated c.1620 by John Harris, who states that anything in Italian style before 1621 must be by Jones.[8] Randall, however, argues that the top sections of the drawing of St. Paul's and the centrepiece of Houghton, which are the features most similar, could have been found in any Italian church of the period.

The west side had three superimposed open loggias with the colonnades being Doric, Ionian and Corinthian. The heraldic devices relate to the Herbert family and Mary's Sidney and Dudley ancestors, indi-

Plate 13: Houghton House: The north and west fronts of the house as it
appeared just before the Marquess of Tavistock lived there.
(*Engraving: M. Griffiths, c.1750*)

cating that this front was built before 1621.

The impressive porch on the south side with its large keystone above
the doorway probably dates from 1621, as this is when James I visited
the house. It is just possible that this feature relates to his visit of 1624
but it seems unlikely as the Bruces do not seem to have added to the
building elsewhere.

Do these Italian classical features add up to a likely attribution to
Inigo Jones as the architect? They fit awkwardly into the general design
and in the case of the west facade, seem to be an exercise in showing off
the architect's knowledge of the three forms of classical columns rather
than providing a unified and harmonious front.

Randall very sensibly compares Houghton with the mature works of
Inigo Jones that he had already built such as the Queen's House,
Greenwich and the Banqueting Hall, Whitehall.[9] He compares the
masculine and unaffected outlook of the Banqueting Hall with the
spindliness and angularity of Houghton House. He rightly points out
that Jones was far too busy on the King's works to even supervise the
building of Wilton House for Mary's son Philip, having to leave the
details to Isaac de Caus. Houghton House should be seen as a house
built when traditional elevations were challenged by styles of different

traditions. Like many buildings constructed during times of change, Houghton House took ideas from the traditional French and Italian but used them without producing a coherent and integrated design. Full of exuberance and innovation, Houghton House could not aim for the unified order of a Jones design. The architect, however, clearly knew Italian designs. To sum up, it was built in the style of Inigo Jones rather than by the master himself.

In 1621 Mary Herbert died and her son soon after surrendered house and park to the King who granted it to Robert, Lord Bruce, son of James's ambassador in London when King of Scotland and thus a key person in the smooth takeover following Elizabeth's death. The Bruces were rewarded by the Stuarts, to whom they were unfailingly loyal.

After the difficult years of the Civil War the Restoration saw the heyday of Houghton House. The late seventeenth-century accounts show this and have been quarried skilfully by Andrew Underwood and Evelyn Curtis.[10]

In 1671 the house was recorded as having 53 hearths, one of the largest houses in the County. The death of Robert Bruce, 1st Earl of Ailesbury, in 1685 meant that his widow and younger son Robert moved to Ampthill Great Lodge (see Park House, Ampthill), while his elder son Thomas stayed at Houghton. Thomas, 2nd Earl of Ailesbury, was a strong supporter of James II. Under William III and Mary II he spent 327 days in prison for treason, 1696–1697, and in 1698 was finally exiled to the Continent. He died at Brussels in 1741 aged 85.[11]

It appears that Thomas's son, Charles, looked after the family estates which included Warwick House, London, Tottenham Park and Savernake in Wiltshire and Tanfield in Yorkshire, as well as Houghton House. Although Thomas's unmarried brother, Robert (1669–1736), lived there, an inventory of c.1725–6 shows the house to have been sparsely furnished. Mary Curtis in her introduction to the inventory rightly comments "most of the furniture described would have been of the seventeenth century, dating from the heyday of Houghton House: it is unlikely that much refurnishing or redecorating would have been carried out after Lord Ailesbury's flight into exile."[12]

The inventory does suggest some alterations to the interior of the house since the early seventeenth century, probably during the years 1660–1698. Rooms such as the withdrawing room, alcove room, smoking room, the great dining room appear. Some of these no doubt were rooms renamed but it is likely that the old great chamber had been broken into smaller rooms. It is likely that at this date the great dining room was separated from the great hall by the thin partition wall marked on the plan of the ground floor of the house, dated 1793. This dining room would have been on the site of the old dais where the high table for family and guests would have stood. Still preserved were the ground floor bedrooms and apartments of the early seventeenth century. Similar arrangements were found on the first floor. This arrangement suited the new formal lay out of rooms described in M. Girouard's *Life in the English Country House*.[13]

In 1738 the Bruces sold the house to the Duke of Bedford, who greatly expanded his Bedfordshire estates in this period.[14] From then until c.1764 the park and the house were let to tenants, first to James Erskine and then Benjamin Line.[15] The Duke's son Francis, Marquis of Tavistock, came of age in 1760 and married Lady Elizabeth Keppel on 8 June 1764.

Supported by a generous marriage settlement, the couple decided to renovate and modernise Houghton House. P. Russell and O. Rice in their book *England Displayed* state that: "In the year 1765 Houghton House underwent another reformation under the inspection of the 'celebrated Mr. Chambers'."[16]

No documentary evidence is given and no plans survive. It is, however, highly likely that the alterations, undertaken between 1764 and 1765 for which the bills survive in the Russell Archive, were indeed to designs by Chambers. In 1766 he was doing work at nearby Wrest Park and in 1767 he was rebuilding the south wing at Woburn for Tavistock's father.

The vouchers suggest that work started in July 1764, just a month after the wedding.[17] The principal alterations seem to have been putting new chimney pieces into most of the rooms. The principal rooms were all given marble ones and the less important, Totternhoe stone. "The Dineing Room North Front" had a new marble "slab", 10 feet 4 inches at 5s 6d per foot – £2 15s 10d. The bed chamber had a new marble slab, a fire hearth and coves of Totternhoe stone and a Bath stove and polished grate with a "freet (fret) and facing 4 Barrs high, cast (iron) Cheeks and Back". The Steward, Mr. Bridgman, who passed all the accounts for the work, was given a Totternhoe stone chimney piece and a Bath stove. Clearly, the Tavistocks intended to be warmer than their predecessors, while the marble fireplaces added to the elegance of the interiors. The Marquis was keen on hunting, so this meant staying in the country during the winter, at the very least for long weekends. The house had to be better heated than when the owners of country houses spent their winters in London.

The chimney pieces were carved and installed by Nathaniel Bayliss, who worked at Woburn Abbey doing similar work from 1762 till his death in 1768. If Chambers had a hand in improving Houghton House, he must have produced the designs for the chimney pieces, as it seems unlikely that he altered the room shapes. There is no structural evidence of any partitions being built at this period.

The rest of the vouchers indicate that the house was in poor repair and major renovation was needed. Windows were reframed; part of the roof reslated and woodwork restored (using 672 feet of oak from Maulden Wood). William Marshall, a painter's apprentice, spent two days cleaning and puttying the pinnacles on the four turrets and the cornice. The brewhouse was repaired. All these were important items in the restoration of an old building but hardly needing an architect of Chambers' standing to supervise them.

On 22 March 1767, the Marquis of Tavistock was killed out hunting near Dunstable. His widow died on 2 November 1768 from what sounds to be tuberculosis. Their children, including the future 5th and 6th Dukes of Bedford, were whisked off to Woburn to be brought up by their grandmother, Gertrude. Tavistock's father died in 1771, which meant that the Woburn estate was subject to a long minority. Houghton House's role as a dower house was clearly redundant, so it was let to tenants.[18]

The 1767 Inventory

The listing of the rooms found in the inventory when used with the plans of all three floors prepared in 1793[19] can give the location of the various principal rooms. On the ground floor at the south was the great hall. By 1793 this had been subdivided to make an extra room, which would seem to be the eating room. In the centre of the house was the little marble hall and the great staircase, the latter dating from 1688 and installed in 1794 in the Swan Inn, Bedford. The west side of the ground floor still seems to have been used for suites of outer reception rooms, bedchambers and closets, retaining their original seventeenth century use. They led on to a central stone hall. At the east end and looking north to appreciate the superb views lay the drawing room. The service wing also included a basement. The kitchen probably lay in the southeast part of the house with a servants' hall, back stairs and steward's dining room in the centre of the east with the blue and white bedchamber, housekeeper's room and china cabinet in the north- east area of the house.

On the first floor in 1793 were two large rooms taking in the whole of the centre of the house. The southern one was the library, a room not mentioned in c.1728 inventory. It was probably the original great chamber and had been recently converted to become a library by the Marquis of Tavistock. The other room was the north gallery, again not mentioned in c.1728 but probably described there under another name. A house like Houghton House would have originally had a gallery and it is possible Tavistock had some smaller rooms using the area cleared to restore the north gallery to its original proportions. In the north-west area of this floor seems to have been the blue drawing room, with the rest of the west front filled with the cotton bedchamber, my lord and lady's dressing rooms and closet.

As Tavistock's family was growing, the old nursery, probably on the south-east of the house, proved inadequate, and a new nursery with adjoining child's bedroom was prepared. The Marchioness in her three years of marriage produced two sons and was expecting a third on Tavistock's death, so for most of that time she must have been pregnant or recovering from child birth. The garrets were used for the extensive staff needed to maintain the family.

The importance of the inventory lies in its listing of furnishings that were almost certainly purchased in the years 1764–1767. The Marquis was well-off, well-travelled with a love of Italy and France and therefore likely to have been at the forefront of artistic fashion. Tavistock's furniture in the principal rooms was predominantly mahogany. In the drawing room, for example, was "a large Sofa with loose cusheons and 2 Bolsters covered with green mixt Damask brass nailed on a curved Mahogany frame". Also in mahogany were two elbow chairs to match the sofa, eight backstools, a lined card table, a lady's writing table with circular front wired round and backed with green silk and a spider leg table. Tavistock bought from Seiffert Alken "a mahogany bookcase with festoons of Music, War, Painting and Sculpture to the design of Sir William Chambers" in 1764.[20] Where this piece was in 1767 is unclear but it could have been in the library and not described as a fixture or it could have been the bookcase in the "Pea Green Dressing Room".

Tavistock also purchased two rectangular marquetry commodes mounted with rams heads (a reference to the Russell coat of arms) from Pierre Langlois and costing £140. It is possible that these two pieces are represented by "a Mahogany Night Table with Doors, a Ditto Commode with a writing Drawer and Slider", listed in what appears to be the principal bedroom, the cotton bedchamber.[21]

Other items reflecting Tavistock's continental interests are a lady's French writing table and a marble bust of Homer in the library. He purchased two scagliola slabs in Florence. He later added supporters "beribboned festoons of husks in ormolu". The references to festooned curtains shows a French influence.

Just occasionally an unusual wood is used, such as pear tree for inkstands and lime tree for a sideboard. Mr. Rawstorn, however, one of the estate officials, had a room entirely furnished in "wainscot" or oak.

Most of the inventories in this volume relate to the estates of middle-aged or elderly people without any young children. The equipment of the old and new nursery at Houghton House is therefore of some interest. In the new nursery were two wicker child's chairs and a basket. Next door was a small child's bed with ticken sides. The old nursery had a deal horse, more likely to be a rocking horse than a clothes horse, otherwise not mentioned in the inventory.

Tavistock like his father John, 4th Duke of Bedford, was interested in collecting china: Sevres, Chelsea, Dr. Wall period Worcester and, in the 1760s, Wedgwood. The inventory is unfortunately not specific about the type of china but mention is made of Japan fruit plates and various pieces of blue and white. Interestingly, a specific list is made of "Staffordshire or Cream Coloured Ware."

Houghton House after 1768

Lord Ossory, cousin of the Duke of Bedford, came to Houghton House around Michaelmas 1769, primarily to avoid the major building works he initiated at his own house of Ampthill Great Park. These were finished by 1771, and yet Lord Ossory kept on the lease until at least 1798. In 1784 the house was described as "a noble and venerable pile, furnished with great elegance with gardens laid out with taste and magnificence." This is echoed by Kimpton's drawings of the house of this date.[22]

In 1794 it was decided by the Duke of Bedford's advisers to build an impressive inn in Bedford to entertain both County and Borough voters on election day and to proclaim the political predominance of the Russells in the town. The easiest way to fit out the rebuilt Swan Inn was to gut Houghton House, no longer needed for Ossory to live in. The house was not sold as it was surrounded by the park, which Ossory still wished to rent. An account book entitled *Account of Swann Inn building, and pulling down Houghton House, putting by the old materials for the Inn and levelling ground for stables*[23] was kept. John Read was paid 15s 2d for watching the house for 13 days on Sundays before demolition began. Demolition therefore started in the summer of 1793. The last account in the book mentioning Houghton House is dated 15 February 1794. Demolition however continued well into the summer as the famous passage for May 1794 in the *Torrington Diaries*, written by the Honourable John Byng, later 5th Vicount Torrington,[24] reveals:

> But for thee – poor Houghton House – I must lament: herein were labourers employ'd to levell – thy strong build walls: – Down go the floors: Crash fall the rafters – ; the overseer – sent by his *Grace* the Duke of Bedford to oversee this havock, (at which let me suppose the last noble repairer – and inhabitant, the Marquis of T[avistock] to gaze with grief and astonishment) came forth to wonder at my overseeing – but he felt the delight of a butcher at killing a sheep. (Byng): So I see you are hard at work here? (Overseer): Yes Sir it is hard work for it is so strongly built; the materials were to have been sent to Bedford, but that I believe is given up now (B) Did you find anything curious? (O) Some coins Sir – and much painting upon

Plate 14: Houghton House: A view of the ruined west front.
(*Watercolour: c.1843*)

the wall when we ripped off the wainscot (B) That of course you attempted to preserve? And before that attempt the D of B had accurate drawings taken from them? (O) No They were beaten to pieces. (B) I remember a room wainscotted with cedar, what became of that? (O) Thrown amongst the other rubbish. (B) I see that his Grace is felling all the old timber as well upon the hill; as in the wood below. (O) Yes, his Grace is making a fine fall – ; and this avenue, – Sir, a mile in length – and which contains one thousand trees – will come down in the autumn. F. grinn'd anger, and comtempt.

Now why all this havock, and ruin? Only a job for the artful, perform'd by cunning stinginess. Shall I live to see all the noble old mansions of the Kingdom pull'd down, or deserted!! Why not have lent this to any relations, or friends who would inhabit it? Why not let it for a school! Why not permit Emigres to reside therein: putting up some useful furniture for them? Or why not establish some manufactory?

The park, including the ruins, remained in the tenancy of Lord Ossory till 1804. The Duke of Bedford exchanged the Houghton Park estate and manors of Ampthill and Milbrook with Lord Ossory, who gave the Lidlington estate, including the manors of Lidlington and Flitwick, in return[25]. On Lord Ossory's death in 1818 the Houghton Park estate along with the rest of the Ossory property reverted to his nephew Henry Richard, Lord Holland. Holland died in 1840 and in 1842 the Ossory inheritance was sold to the Duke of Bedford for £145,000.[26]

In 1877 portions of the south-west and north-east towers were in a dangerous condition and were removed under the superintendence of T.J. Jackson of Bedford, architect.[27] In 1918 the Bedford estate sold the Houghton Park estate.[28]

The recent history of Houghton House has been conveniently summarised by Mary George in her article on Houghton House in the *Bedfordshire Magazine* in 1948:[29] "For some years, when close inspection of the crumbling walls became dangerous, the ruins were enclosed by a fence. When, about twenty years ago, the Bedford Arts Club, at the instigation of Professor A.E. Richardson, initiated a fund to acquire and preserve the remains of the house from further deterioration, great interest was aroused. Many generous subscriptions were received and the ruins were purchased. Finally, the Ancient Monuments Department of the Ministry of Works took over the property and restoration was begun in 1936."

HOUGHTON HOUSE, AMPTHILL 1767

Inventory of Household Furniture, Linnen, China and other Effects of the late most Honble. Marquiss of Tavistock at his House at Houghton Park in Bedfordshire, taken April 27th etc. 1767.

Garrets.

No.1 Over my Lady's Apartment: a 4 post beach Bedstead, with blue and white check Furniture, a Check Mattrass, a feather Bed, Bolster and Pillow, 3 Blankets, a White Cotton Counterpane, a Check drawup Window Curtain, 4 Matted Chairs, an old Elbow Chair frame, an Old inlaid Table, green Bays Cover.

No.2 Footmans Room: Eight Beach 4 post Bedsteads with stained feet Posts, blue and White Check Furnitures, 8 Check Mattrasses, 12 Pair Blankets, 8 Bolsters, 8 Pillows and Linnen Quilts stuff Backs, 7 Deal Cloath Boxes, 3 Matted Chairs, 2 Camp Elbow Chairs Leather Seats.

No.3. Small Room and Closet: a Field Beach Bedstead, with scarlet Check thro'over Furniture, 2 Check Mattrasses, a Bolster and Pillow, 3 Blankets, a white Cotton Counterpane, a Deal Box as before, an Old Table, a ditto Chair and Stool, 5 Pairs of Old Tapestry.

No.4 Bedchamber following the last: a Field Beach Coloured Bedstead, Green Check Furniture, 2 Check Mattrasses, a Bolster and Pillow, 3 Blankets, a white Cotton Counterpane, a Check draw up Curtain, 2 Mahogony Backstools covered with Green Stuff Damask Brass Nailed, a Matted Chair, a floor Matt.

No.5 Bedchamber: A field Sloping Bedstead green Check Furniture, two Check Mattrasses, a Bolster and Pillow, 3 Blankets and a Counterpane, a Check draw up Window Curtain, 2 Chairs same as in the last Room, a Floor Matt, an Iron and a Tin Fender, Shovel tongs and Poker.

One pair of stairs floor.

No.6 New Nursery: a 4 Post Bedstead with Lath Bottoms, Mahogony feet Posts and Carved Cornish etc. compleat, a Green Stuff Damask Furniture to Ditto, 4 Check Mattrasses, a large Bolster and 2 Pillows, 4 large Blankets, a White Callico Quilt, 2 Mahogony Elbow Chairs covered with Damask and Brass Naild, 6 Back stools Ditto, 2 Green Damask Festoon Window Curtains, with Laths Lines etc. compleat, A Steel Grate Plain Molding Fender, Shovel Tongs Poker and Bellows, a Guard Iron, 2 Wicker Childs Chairs and a Basket, a Mahogy. Dressing Chest of Drawers with a Slider, a Ditto Night Table with Sliding Stool, a Ditto Chamber Table with a Drawer, a Glass in a Mahogy. Frame, a Mahogy. Bason Stand, a painted Floor Cloth.

No.7 Next Room: A Small 4 Post Bedstead with Red and White Check Furniture, 2 Check Mattrasses, 3 Blankets, a White Counterpane, a Bolster and Pillow, a Small Childs Bed with Ticken Sides and red

Check Furniture, a Check and a White Mattrass, a White fustian Pillow, 2 Bath Blankets bound, a Check Quilt same as the Bed, a Green Stuff Damask Window Curtain, a Mahogy. Chamber Table, a Ditto Bason Stand, a Dressing Glass, One Elbow Chair and 2 Backstools, a small Fender, Shovel, Tongs and Poker.

No.8 Library: Two Mahogy. Elbow Chairs carved feet and Elbows covered with red Morocco Leather brass Nailed, 12 Backstools to match, 2 Pair of Irons for burning Wood with Brass Pedestal Front and Brass Pierced Fender, Fire Shovel Tongs and Poker to each with Brass tops, a square Wainscot Table, An Oval ditto, a Ladys French Writing Table, a Marble Bust of Homer, 2 Pear tree Ink stands, 2 paintings in Miniature of Soldiers, a Mahogy. Library Table the Top Covered with Leather.

No.9 My Lords Dressing Room: One Red printed Cotton draw up Window Curtain lined, with Laths etc. Compleat and fringed at Bottom, 2 Bamboo Dressing Elbow Chairs, One Elbow Chair and 6 Backstools with Cotton Cases same as the Window Curtain, A mahogy. Dressing Chest of Drawers, a Large Chamber Table, a Dressing Glass in Mahogy. Frame, a Mahogy. Bason Stand with folding top, a pair of Irons for burning Wood with Brass Pedestals and brass feet, Fender, Shovel, Tongs, Poker and Tin Fender, Bellows and Brush.

No.10 Cotton Bedchamber: A 4 Post Bedstead with Lath Bottom, Mahogy. foot Posts, carved Cornishes and a red printed Cotton Furniture with a Drapery Head Cloth and the Valens fringed, 4 Check Mattrasses, a large Bolster and 4 Down Pillars, 4 large Blankets, a large Callico Quilt, One Elbow Chair and 5 Backstools with Cases same as the Bed, One Draw up Window Curtain Ditto lined, a Steel Grate with Brass Feet and pierced Border, a Brass feet fender with Shovel Tongs and Poker with Brass Tops and a Tin Fender, 2 Bedside Carpets, a mahogy. Night Table with Doors, a Ditto Commode with a Writing Drawer and Slider, a Dog Cushion and Green Check Cover, a Small draw up Window Curtain in the Closet same as the Bedchamber.

No.11 Ladys Dressing Room: 2 Red printed Cotton festoon Window Curtains lined as before, 4 Backstools with Cotton Cases, One Elbow Bamboo Ditto, a Ladys Mahogy. Secretary with a Book Shelf on it, a Small Writing Table with One Drawer, a Small Airing Linnen Horse, a Canvas Skreen on a Mahogy. Pillar and Claw, a Wainscot Toylet Table with a Flap and 2 Drawers, a Toylet Glass in a Japan Frame, a Grate Fender and Furniture same as in Bedchamber.

No.12 Blue Drawing Room: Two blue Moreen festoon Window Curtains fringed etc. compleat, a large Sofa with loose Back Cusheons and Bolsters on a Mahogy. Frame covered with blue Moreen and Brass Nailed, 10 Mahogy. Pembroke Elbow Chairs with Loose Seats covered with Lace, a Mahogy. Buroe Writing Table covered with Leather a

Ditto Card Table Lined, a Mahogy. Commerce Table on a Claw, a Ditto Breakfast Table, a Back Gammon Table with Boxes Dice and Men, 2 Small Pillar Skreens covered with blue Silk, a Dog Cusheon and Check Case a Pair of Doggs Fender and Furniture same as in Library, an Oval Glass in a Carved and Gilt Frame a pair of wrought double Brass Arms, a Small Tea Chest.

No.13 North Gallery: 6 Mahogy. Pembrooke Elbow Chairs, and 2 without Elbows the Seats covered with old Crimson Lace, a pair of doggs Fender and furniture same as in last Room, 2 small Globe Lamps on brass Hooks for burning Oil.

No.14 Blue and White Cotton Bedchamber: A 4 post Bedstead same as the last Bedchamber with a blue and White Cotton Furniture, 4 Check Mattrasses, 4 Blankets and a White Quilt, a Bolster and 2 Down Pillows, a Blue and White festoon Window Curtain same as the Bed, One Elbow Chair and 3 Backstools covered with Cotton, a Mahogy. Night Table with Doors, a Ditto Chamber Table with a Drawer, a Dressing Glass, a Mahogy. Bason Stand, a Mahogy. Dressing Chest of Drawers, One Bedside Carpet, a pair of Doggs brass Fender etc. as before, a Matt in the Closet.

No.15 Old Nursery: A 4 Post Bedstead red Check Furniture, 2 Check Mattrasses, a feather Bed Bolster and Pillow, 3 Blankets, a White Counterpane, a 4 Post Bedstead with Check Furniture and Bedding in every Respect the same as that in the Green Room next the new Nursery, a Draw up Check Window Curtain, a Small Ditto in the Closet on a Rod, 2 Wainscot Chests of Drawers, One square and One Round Table, 4 Matted Chairs and 2 Childrens Chairs, a Deal Horse, a Childs Bed with Check Furniture, 2 Mattrasses and a white Pillow, 2 Bath Blankets, a Check Quilt, a stove with Compass Front, fender and Furniture a pair of Bellows and a Tea Trivet.

Ground Floor

No.16 Sprigg Cotton Bedchamber and Closet: a 4 Post Bedstead with Lath Bottom and carved mahogy. foot Posts, carved Cornish and fine Spring Cotton Furniture lined, 4 Check Mattrasses, 4 large Blankets and a White Quilt, a Bolster and 4 White Down Pillows, The Hangings of the Rooms same as the Bed lined with Linnen, a festoon Window Curtain Ditto, One Elbow Chair, and 5 Backstools with Cotton Cases same as the Bed, a Mohogy. Ladys Dressing Table with proper Conveniences, a Ditto Night Table with 2 Doors, a Steel Molding Fender with Shovel Tongs Poker and Tin Fender 2 Bedside Carpets, a Mahogy. double Chest of Drawers, a Couch and Stool with 2 Pillows, and 3 Back Cusheons with Cotton Cases of a Decker Work pattern, 2 Bamboo Chairs with Cotton Cases, a Draw up Window Curtain the same Cotton.

No.17 Dressing Room to 16: Two draw up Cotton Window Curtains same Cotton of Bedchamber, One Elbow Chair and 6 Backstools with

Cotton Cases same as the Curtains, a Bamboo'd Elbow Chair Ditto, a pair of Dogs with Brass Ornaments, fender and Furniture, a Mahogy. fly Table, a Dressing Glass in a Mahogy. Frame.

No.18 Small Stone Hall: 2 Elbow Windsor Chairs and 4 Stools

No.19 Eating Room: a Crimson Moreen Festoon Window Curtain fringed etc. compleat, 2 Mahogy. Dining Tables to joyn, one with two, the other with one flap, a mahogy. Small Oval Table, a spider Leg ditto, a Ditto Dumb Waiter, a Ditto Tea Kettle Stand, a two leafd' Sliding Skreen, a Canvas Ditto on a Pillar, a Mahogy. Pedestal and a Pail with a pot Cupboard etc. in it, a Lime tree Side Board Table, a Stool for a Bottle Cistern, 12 Stained Matted Chairs, a large painted Floor Cloth, and 2 Small Ditto Ditto, 2 Doggs for Wood, 2 Brass Arms with One light each, a Dog Cusheon and Check Case.

No.20 Little Marble Hall: 2 Painted Windsor Chairs, a Mahogany Spider Leg Table.

No.21 Pea Green Dressing Room: 2 festoon Window Curtains of fine Sprig Cotton, One Elbow Chair, and Six Backstools with Cases of the same Cotton, a Bamboo Elbow Chair Ditto, A mahogy. Bookcase Bed Wired Doors and fine Sprig Cotton Furniture, 2 Mattrasses, a Bolster and Pillow, 3 Blankets, a White Counterpane, a Steel Grate pierced Fender Shovel Tongs and Poker, a Mahogy. Breakfast Table on Castors, a Ditto Spider Leg Table a Dressing Glass.

No.22 Bedchamber: a 4 post Bedstead, with Mahogy. Carved feet Posts on Castors etc. compleat and fine Sprig Cotton Furniture, 4 Mattrasses, a Bolster and 2 Down pillows 4 blankets, a White Callico Quilt, a festoon Window Curtain the same Cotton of the Bed, One Bamboo Elbow Chair Ditto, a mahogy. dressing Chest of Drawers with a Slider, a Ditto Night Table with Sliding Stool, a Ditto Spider Leg Table, One Elbow Chair, 5 Backstools with Cotton Cases same as the Bed, a Mahogy. Dressing Glass, a Deal Toylet Table with Green Stuff Cover and Silk Scarf, a Green Silk Window Blind in a Mahogy. Frame, a Cut Fender, Shovel, Tongs and Poker.

No.23 Drawing Room: Two Green mixed Damask Festoon Window Curtains fring'd etc. compleat, a Large Sofa with Loose Cusheons and 2 Bolsters covered with green mixt Damask brass Nailed on a Carved Mahogy. Frame and Check Cases, 2 Elbow Chairs to Match the Sofa, 8 Backstools Ditto, a Mahogy. Card Table lined, a Ditto Ladys Writing Table with Circular Front wired Round and backd with Green Silk, a Mahogy. Spider Leg Table, Two Small Green Silk Skreens on Pillars and Claws, a Ladys french Writing Table in laid, a Dogs Cushion, a Small Peartree Inkstand, an Oval Glass in a Carved and Gilt Frame, a Six leaf'd Map Skreen, a Steel Grate with fret Border and Fender, Shovel Tongs and Poker, a Pair Single wrought brass Arms, a Wilton Carpet.

No.24 Great Hall: 2 Wheel Barrow Garden Chairs, 2 Windsor Elbow

Ditto and 2 Stools, all painted Green, 2 Small Globes on Brass Hooks, a pair of old Fire Doggs, a large Case with Drawings etc. framed.

No.25 Stewards Dining Room: A large Wainscot Oval Dining Table, a small Ditto, an old Ditto, a Square Ditto, a painted floor Cloth, 12 Beach Chairs with black Leather Seats brass Nailed, Fender Shovel Tongs and Poker, a Water Tub and Stand.

No.26 Pantry: A Wainscot Oval Table, a Deal Painted Desk, 5 Chairs with Matted seats, a fender, Shovel, Tongs, and Poker, a Mahogy. Tea Kettle Stand lined with Tin, a Copper Plate Warmer, a Wainscot Tray with Partitions, a Ditto Knife Box, a Ditto Oval Tub, a Square Wicker Basket, a Ditto for Knives, a Ditto for China Plates, a Ditto for Coals lined with Tin, a Small Glass in Mahogy. frame, (the Plate broke) a Bread Bin with Partitions and Slider, 6 Mahogy. Bottle Boards, a Large Deal Chest in the Passage, a Copper Tea Kettle.

No.27 Blue and White Bedchamber opposite stewards Dining Room: a 4 post Bedstead on Castors with blue and white Cotton Furniture, a Check Mattrass, a feather Bed Bolster and White Down pillow, 4 Blankets, a White Counterpane, a Cotton draw up Window Curtain, a Mahogy. Chamber Table, 4 Mahogy. fan back Chairs with loose Seats, and blue and white Cotton Cases, a Moulded Fender, a Tin ditto, Shovel Tongs, Poker, Bellows and Brush, a Pendulum Clock on the first Landing of the Stair Case and a Pair of Steps.

No.28 Housekeepers Room and Closet: a Square Wainscot 2 flap Table, a Pillar and Claw Ditto, a Chamber Ditto with a Drawer, 8 Matted Chairs, a Moulding Fender Shovel Tongs and Poker Bellows and Brush, a painted Floor Cloth, a Mahogy. Butlers Tray, 2 Ditto round Tea Boards, 2 Ditto handboards, a Japan Tea Board, One Square and 4 round Birmingham Iron Japan'd Tea Waiters, a Copper Chocolate Pott, a Dutch Tea Boiler, 3 Ditto Coffee Potts, and 2 lamps, 1 Ditto Tea Kettle and Lamp, a fixt Coffee Mill and a Hand ditto, a Small red Check window Curtain, and A Green Stuff Damask draw up Window Curtain.

China: 2 Dozn. blue and white Scollopt Soup Plates, 21 Common Table ditto, 12 Japan Fruit Plates (2 of them cracked), 7 Blue and White Bowls of different Sizes, a blue and white Jug and a Mug, 4 Sauce Boats, 4 Small Cups with Covers, and 2 without, 2 Oval Butter Basons Covers and Plates, and 1 Round ditto, two Caudell Cups Covers and Saucers, 4 Tea Potts, 10 Cream ditto, 21 Small Sugar ana other Basons, 12 Tea Cups and Saucers Ribd, 15 Coffee and 11 Chocolate Cups and 12 Saucers, 6 large Scollopt Breakfast Cups and Saucers, 6 ditto, 6 ditto smaller, 6 Image handle Cups and Saucers, 12 small coffee and One Milk ditto, 6 Small Tea Cups, and 6 triangular Saucers, 2 brown Tea Potts, 4 large blue and White Handle Cups and 4 Saucers, 2 Spoon Boats. Staffordshire or Cream Coloured Ware: a Tea and a Coffee Pot with Stands, a Sugar Dish, a Cream Pott and Covers to ditto, a Slop

Bason and a Spoon Boat, 12 Handle Tea Cups and 12 Saucers, 12 Coffee Cups a Brown Tea Pott, 20 Jelly Glasses, 12 Small pieces Desert ditto.

No.29 Mr. Bridgmans Room: A Beach 4 post Bedstead with Crimson Check Furniture, a Check Mattrass, a Feather Bed, Bolster and Pillow, 3 Blankets, a White Cotton Counterpane, 3 Check draw up Window Curtains, a Wainscot Desk and Book Case, a Ditto Chamber Table, a Dressing Glass in a Mahogy. Frame, 4 Matted Chairs, an Iron and a tin Fender Shovel Tongs Poker and Brush, 27 Yards of Course 7/8 Cloth.

No.30 Housekeepers Bedchamber: 4 Post Bedstead, Crimson Check Furniture same as the last room, a Check mattrass, feather Bed Bolster and Pillow, 3 Blankets and a Counterpane, 2 Check Window Curtains, a Chamber Table, a Dressing Glass Ditto, 4 Matted Chairs, a Wainscot Single Chest of Drawers, One Iron and 1 Tin Fenders, Shovel Tongs and Poker, a Bamboo Elbow Chair in Linnen, an old Elbow Chair.

No.31 Lady's Maids Room: A 4 Post Bedstead red Check Furniture, Two mattrasses, a Bolster and Pillow, 3 Blankets, a Stuff back Quilt, 2 draw up Check Window Curtains, a Wainscot Single chest of drawers, a Ditto Table, a Dressing Glass Mahogy. Frame, 4 Matted Chairs, an Old Elbow Chair, an Iron and a Tin Fender, Shovel Tongs Poker and Brush.

No.32 Mr Rawstorn's Room: A 4 post Bedstead red Check Furniture, a Check Mattrass, feather Bed Bolster and Pillow, 3 Blankets, a White Counterpane, 2 Check Window Curtains, 4 Matted Chairs, a Wainscot Chamber Table, a Small Dressing Glass, an Iron Fender, One Iron and 1 Tin Shovel tongs and Poker, a Wainscot Chest of Drawers, a large Wainscot Writing Table with 3 Drawers, a Drawing in black and Gold frame, a French Fowling Piece, a Deal Table with one Flap in the Passage.

No.33 Housemaids Rooms: a Large Wainscot Table, a Small Deal Ditto, a fender Shovel Tongs and Poker, a pair of Bellows, a Tea Trivet, 2 Common ditto, 7 Matted Chairs, a Horse to brush Cloaths on, 2 Wig blocks, Maps Brooms and Brushes, a large old Chest.

No.34 Laundry: A Large Oak Mangle loaded with Lead, a large Hanging drying Horse with Jacks and Lines to ditto, 2 large Folding Drying Horses, 2 large and 1 small Deal Tables, 5 Wood Stools, 6 Matted Chairs, an Old Elbow Chair, 3 Piggons, 12 Flaskets of different Sizes, 11 Flat Irons, 1 Box Iron, 4 Heaters, 3 Stands, a hanging Iron, a fender, 2 Shovels, One Poker, a Small pair of Tongs, 4 Ironing Cloths, Coal Basket lined with Tin.

Laundry Maids Bedchamber: Two 4 Post Bedsteads blue and White Check Furniture, Two Feather Beds, 2 Bolsters, 1 Pillow, 6 Blankets, 2 Stuff back Quilts, 2 Old Tables, 7 Matted Chairs, 3 Old Cross Legged stools, an Old Table in the Passage, 2 small dressing Glasses.

Bedchamber over the last: A 4 Post Bedstead blue Check Furniture, 2 Mattrasses, 3 Blankets and a Quilt, a Bolster and Pillow, 2 Matted Chairs, an Old stool.

No.35 Housemaids Room: A 4 Post Bedstead with blue Check furniture, a feather Bed Bolster and Pillow, 3 Blankets and a Quilt, a Deal Chamber table, a Small Glass, a very old Chest of Drawers, One Elbow Chair, and One other Ditto, 2 Matted Chairs.

Kitchen Maids Room: 2 Bedsteads and Furnitures same as the last, One feather Bed Bolster and 2 pillows, 2 Mattrasses, a Bolster and 2 pillows, 6 Blankets, 2 Quilts, a very old nest of Drawers, an Old Elbow Chair and a Matted Ditto.

Farmers Room: a Bedstead and Furniture same as the last, 2 Mattrasses, a Bolster and Pillow Ditto, 3 Blankets and a Quilt, a Wainscot Desk, a Ditto Chamber Table, 2 Matted Chairs, a fender Shovel Tongs and Poker.

Cooks Room: a 4 Post Bedstead with Crimson Check Furniture, a Check Mattrass, a feather Bed Bolster and Pillow, 3 Blankets, a White Counterpane, 2 small Check Window Curtains, a Wainscot Chamber Table, a Small Glass, 3 Matted Chairs, an old Cane Couch, a fender Shovel Tongs Poker and Brush, a Tin Fender.

Store Room: A long Deal Table, 9 Stone Juggs of different Sizes, 40 Wood Trenchers, a Jack with a Multiplying wheel, Lead weight etcetera, another old Jack, 2[1/2] Dozen of White bone handle Knives and forks, 2 White Stone Tureens, 6 plates Ditto, 2 China Sauce Boats, 1 Butter Bason Cover and Saucer, 11 Egg Cups, 4 Sillabub Glasses.

No.36 Gardeners Room: A 4 Post Bedstead with blue Check Furniture, 2 Check Mattrasses, a Bolster and Pillow, 3 Blankets and a Quilt, a Wainscot Desk, a Ditto Table with 2 flaps, a Small dressing Glass, 2 Matted Chairs, 2 Old Elbow Ditto, Shovel Tongs Poker fender and Bellows and old Wainscot Cupboard.

No.37 Kitchen:

Iron: 4 Iron Wheel Spits and 2 Lark Ditto, 2 Double Gridirons, a Cinder Shovel, a Poker, a Coal Shovel, a Salimander, 5 Chaffing Dishes, 2 frying pans, 3 Candlesticks, a pan for Charcoal on feet, 8 Stove Trivets, 7 Pair snuffers, a Charcoal Shovel, 3 Cleavers, 3 Choppers, 2 pair Stake Tongs, 9 Iron Scuers 4 of them loaded, a Toasting fork, 2 Double Scuers.

Copper: 4 large Pottage Potts and Covers, 2 Brazing Pans, 1 large Turbot Pan Cover and plate, 2 Dobing Pans and Covers, 3 fish Kettles Covers and Plates, 1 Ditto without a plate, 2 Carp Pans and Covers, 2 Cullenders, 4 Stewing Potts and Covers, 9 large Stew pans and Covers, 20 Small Ditto and Ditto, 4 large and one Small Sauce pans with Covers, 4 ditto with Covers, 8 Baking Dishes, a pair Scales and Weights, 4 Baking Plates, a large Bottle Cistern, 3 Coal Skuttles, 4 Pottage Potts and Covers, 2 Smaller Ditto, a Boiler with a Cock, 6 Tea Kettles, 2 dripping pans on feet, 2 large drinking Potts, 2 lamps and Shades, 2 Basting and 5 Soup Ladles, 9 Slices, 7 Soup Spoons, 3 Warming Pans, a Drudger.

Brass: a Reading Candlestick, 2 High Candlesticks, 16 Common Table Ditto, 22 flat ditto, a Dish Kettle, a Bell Mettle Mortar Iron Pestle and Woodstand, a Dinner Bell.

Pewter: 35 Pewter Dishes, 77 Plates, 2 Cheese Plates, a Tureen and Cover, 3 Water Candlesticks, a Bed Pan.

20 Pieces of Tin Ware and Wood ditto, a large elm Dresser with drawers, a Marble Mortar Wood stand and Pestle, 2 Mahogy. Dish Trays, a Deal Table, a Form, a Choping Block, a Plate Rack, a Pair of Bellows, 4 old Elbow Chairs, a Basket lined with Tin.

Stone Ware: a Tureen and Cover, 2 Juggs and 2 Bottles, 28 round and Oval Dishes, 4 dozen Plates, 12 Flower Potts, 4 Egg Cups.

No.38 Servants Hall: a Long Deal Table, 5 Deal Forms, 1 Old Table, a Cupboard over ditto – a Garden Chair for a Child, a Large old Picture.

No.39 Dairy: 4 Milk Trays lined with Lead, a Deal Table and Stool, a Pickling Tub, 7 Round Tubbs, 1 large and 1 small Barrel Churn, 2 Bowls, 2 Trenchers, a Spoon, a Brass Scimmer, 5 Pails, a Beam and Scales, 4[1/2] hd. Weights, 1[1/4] ditto and a 14 lb. ditto, 5 Butter Baskets, a pair Butter Scales and Weights.

In the Bakehouse: 2 Peeles, 1 Rake, 30 trenchers, 1 Flower Tub, 8 Old Pails.

Washhouse: 4 Standing Wash Tubs, and 5 others, a Wrencing Tub, a Copper unset, Lead and Iron Work to ditto, 2 Wet Horses, 2 Pails, 1 Form and a Bowl.

No.40 Glass etcetera: 24 Decanters, 12 Carraffs, 7 Dozen Drinking Glasses, 12 Water Ditto and Saucers, 10 Salts, a Cruet frame with Glasses compleat, 2 Mugs, 7 Earth Ice Pails, 6 Punch Ladles.

No.41 Linnen: 3 pair and [1/2] of 3 Breadth Holland Sheets, 3 Pair of 2 Breadths Do., 18 pair fine Irish ditto, 21 pair Flaxen ditto, 20 pair of Hempen ditto, 14 Holland Pillow Cases, 71 Irish ditto, 5 Dozen and 9 fine Diaper Towels, 1 Dozen and 11 Coarser ditto, 6 dozen Huckaback Towells, 28 Damask Table Cloths, 12 Diaper Side Board ditto, 20 Huckaback Table Cloths, 1 Old ditto, 6 Diaper Breakfast Cloths, 13 Dozen and 11 Damask Table Napkins, 6 Dozen Breakfast ditto, 20 Glass Cloths marked P, 10 China ditto marked S, 1 Dozen of Housemaids Rubbers markd H, 1 Ps. [?piece] of new Cloth for 2 Dozen more, 1 Ps. Diaper for 1 Dozen, 6 Huckaback Table Cloths for Servants Hall, 22 long Towels.

Kitchen Linnen: 16 Table Cloths, 8 Fish Napkins, 3 Dozen and 7 Rubbers.

No.42 Stables: a Horse called Rigby; a brown Ditto Misley; a Dun

Colt, Trentham; A Grey Horse my Lady's; a Black Horse ditto; a Grey Ditto Northampton; a Poney,Cupid; a Horse called Crop; a Black Horse, Staffordshire; a Coach Horse, Punch; a Mare in foal by Romulus; a Bay Filley out of blossom by Newcombs Arabian; a Bay Colt out of Juliet by Duke of Bridgewaters Horse; a Bay Filley by ditto.

Two Feather Beds, 2 Bolsters, 5 Blankets and a Coverlid, 14 Horse Collars, 4 Wire Hanging Lanthorns, 6 Dung Forks, 3 Pails, 5 Saddles and Bridles, a Set of Regimental Horse Furniture, 2 Pair Harness for Travelling Coach, a Single Horse Chaise painted Green with Harness to ditto, a Crane Neck Phaeton and a pair of Harness to ditto, an old Post Chaise.

No.43 Cellars: 7 Butts of 4 Hogsheads each and 5 Pipes of Strong Beer, 5 Hogsheads ditto, One Empty ditto, 1 Empty Butt, 12 Pipes of Small Beer, 3 Empty Pipes, 7 Bearing Tubs for the Brewhouse, 2 Shovels, 2 Pokers, a Bowl, a Pail, a Funnell, 3 [?]Shoots, 2 Forms, a Small Cart.

Wine Cellar: 10 Dozen Claret in Bottles, 15 Dozen ditto (very bad), 8 Dozen Port, 5 Bottles Champaigne, 4 Dozen old Hock, 5 Bottles Rum, 13 Dozen Cyder, 4 Bottles Liquor

[No.44] Garden and Yards: 8 Cucumber Frames with 27 Glazed Lights, 25 Bell Glasses, 6 Watering Potts, 4 Spades, 3 Rakes, 3 Hoes and some other Tools, 6 Stone Rollers, two only with Iron Frames, 17 Wheel Barrows, 4 Standard Ladders, and a Number of Scaffolding Poles, 6 Stacks Billet Wood, a parcel of Charcoal, a parcel of loose Firewood, 4 large Iron Gates with Standards to ditto, a Quantity of Old lead and Iron in the Yards and Several Parts of the Building.

No.45 Apparel: 2 Scarlet Regimental Coats, One Waistcoat and 2 pair Breeches with Silver Cap'd Buttons, 2 light Coloured Cloth Coat and waistcoat with Gilt Buttons, a Duffle Coat Waistcoat and Breeches, a Dark Coloured Coat and buff Flannel Waistcoat, a Blue Cloth Coat, Buff Waistcoat and Breeches, a light Cloth Surtout Coat, an Indian Taffaty Quilted Banyan, a Green Camblet Coat Waistcoat and Breeches silver laced, a light Cloth colour Camblet Suit compleat with Gilt Buttons, a Buff Colour Cloth Waistcoat lapelld and laced with Gold, 2 Crimson Silk Military Sashes and a Silver'd Gorget, 2 Pair Coarse Linnen Breeches, 2 Pair Boots, 2 Pair Shoes, 2 Silver laced Hats and One with a Gold Loop and Band, a black Silk Cravat, 5 Hunting Whips, 6 thin Waistcoats, a Pair Scates, a Silver Basket hilted broad Sword, a Marking Hatchet.

[Farm, Stables and Dog Kennel at Woburn – Contents listed in detail]
Woburn Abbey

NOTES

1. Printed works on Houghton House include E. Curtis: *Life in the Palace Beautiful*. Elstow Moot Hall leaflet No.5, 1958 and her edition of the c.1725–1728 inventory in BHRS Vol.XXXVIII pp 97–104, 1958; M. George: 3 Articles in B.Mag Vol.I pp.169–174, 209–216, 261–265; Dr. A. Gomme *Notes on Houghton House*, May 1982 (CRT 130 Ampthill 34); M. Randall's *Houghton House*, unpublished thesis (available at BCRO Classification 130); VCH Vol.III pp.289, 291.
2. M. George, B.Mag Vol 1 p.169.
3. Gomme p.4.
4. 1793 Plans (R 1/1013).
5. Randall pp.9 and 16.
6. Randall p.14.
7. J. Gotch: *The English Home*, Batsford (1919) p.35. I am grateful to Andrew Underwood for the reference.
8. Gomme p.2.
9. Randall p.19.
10. A. Underwood: *Ampthill a Goodly Heritage*, Ampthill PCC (1976) pp.31 and 38; E. Curtis: *Life in Palace Beautiful*
11. Bedfordshire Hearth Tax for 1671, BHRS reprint 1990; Lord Cardigan: *The Life and Loyalties of Thomas Bruce* (1951)
12. BHRS Vol.XXXVIII p.98.
13. M. Girouard: *Life in an English Country House* (1979) Chapter 5, The Formal House 1630–1720
14. Russell Deed Books (photocopy available at BRO)
15. R 5/89.
16. P. Russell and O. Price: *England Displayed* (1769) quoted in Randall p.24.
17. Russell Box
18. Georgiana Blakiston: *Woburn and the Russells* (1980) pp.117, 139, 140, 143, 167.
19. See note 4 above
20. *Apollo* for June 1988 p.398 21. *Apollo* for June 1988 p.397.
22. Kimpton's drawings X 254/88/139.
23. R 5/594
24. C. Bruyn Andrews edition of *The Torrington Diaries*, Barnes and Noble Reprint (1970), Vol.IV pp.32–33.
25. Exchange of Houghton House RO 27/19
26. Sale of Houghton House 1842 RH 9/59
27. R 5/870
28. Sale Catalogue Z 155/15
29. M. George pp.173–174.

HOUGHTON MANOR HOUSE

Houghton Manor House up to 1740

Henry Brandreth, probably a wealthy City merchant, purchased the Manor of Sewell in the parish of Houghton Regis in 1652.[1] To this he added a couple of years later the main Manor of Houghton Regis, almost certainly including the site of the Manor House.[2] Two views of 1775[3] show the entrance and one side elevation to the house, which contained three storeys and had three gables. The entrance elevation had six sash windows on each of the two top floors. The ground floor had a pedimented front door with four sash windows. The side elevation illustrated had three sash windows on each floor but otherwise was plain. The other side elevation and the other main front were not included in the drawings, so we can not be sure what they looked like.

It is possible that Brandreth had the house built himself but it is more likely that he had an older house refenestrated and added the pediment to the front door to give the house a more modern, classical feel.

Other details from the views show that to the right of the main elevation was a long lower building, probably containing service rooms, and further on a dovehouse and some stables. In front of the main facade was a walled garden with a fine pair of late seventeenth/early

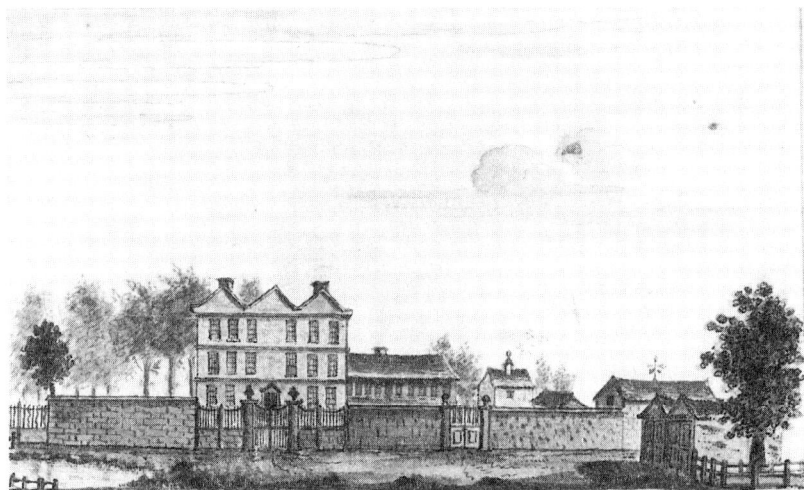

Plate 15: Houghton Manor: The building on the right was the coach house on the Green at Houghton Regis. (*Watercolour: c.1775*)

eighteenth-century gates. The house was sited opposite the north east end of the Green, on the north side of the High Street. The coach house was on the other side of the road, on the Green itself.

Henry Brandreth (1610–1672) had three children: Solomon, who was simple and so did not inherit Houghton, Nehemiah (1652–1719), who did, and Alice, who married Sir William Milard and built Houghton Hall by 1700. Nehemiah left a son Henry (1685–1739). Henry left a son, also called Henry (1723–1752), and three daughters. All were under age at their father's death. The inventory published below relates to the estate of Henry Brandreth (died 1739).[4]

The house, as it is described in the inventory, seems to have had its only entrance on the grander south side with the best parlour occupying the south-west corner of the house with two windows facing south and one window west. The common parlour occupied the south-east corner with a similar arrangement of windows. In between was probably one of the two halls mentioned, of which the white hall is more likely.

The richest room so far as contents are concerned was the withdrawing room, probably in the north-west corner of the house. Along much of the centre of the house seems to have lain the long hall. Room 11 and probably the kitchen lay in the north-east area with the service buildings lying east and north of that.

On the principal bedroom floor the best bedchamber was probably situated over the best parlour and room 6 over the common parlour.

Much of the fittings and furnishings belonging to Henry Brandreth were clearly old. Even in the second best bedroom is a "sacking bottom bedstead with old camblet furniture". Room No.7 had an old bedstead and three broken chairs. In the attic floor in the nursery was "an old fashion pair Chest of drawers". Although there is no indication of the type of wood of the furniture, there are a considerable number of cane chairs, fashionable in the late seventeenth century but looking out of date in 1740.

The numerous Indian pictures and Indian cabinet are a feature of the house at this time. Probably one of the Brandreths had links with the East India Company. In addition to the India pictures, Brandreth had four family pictures (portraits) and twenty eight prints, forming a modest collection of art. None, however, were put in the principal bedrooms.

His china consisted solely of cups and saucers, many of them "old" implying that they had been in use for some time. Where mentioned they are described as "blue and white", almost certainly at this date imported from China. He had two salvers in Tunbridge ware, a form of highly decorated marquetry work popular in the late seventeenth century. He had two clocks, one eight day and one thirty hour, as well as two old watches, one gold and one silver.

The inventory mentions three books, two from the 1630s and even in

1740 considered of sufficient value to be itemised. Clues as to Brandreth's leisure pursuits are given by the mention of fishing tackle and twelve shuffleboard pieces.

His wardrobe of waistcoats, breeches (one embroidered with silver), shirts and the ubiquitous wig give a good idea of the clothes of a modest country gentleman of his period; possibly slightly down at heel with his five old coats.

The inventory has a couple of interesting comments at the end. Henry's widow Mary had clearly taken out of the house "some plate, a Watch and Jewels". There was also a dispute over the non-payment of £1000 secured by a marriage trust.

Henry and Mary had in fact been sharing the Manor House with his mother Rebecca, who died in 1740.[5] She was called Rebecca Price and her cookery book has been published. In the back of the *Compleat Cook* is a transcript of her will. Clearly, many of the better pieces of furniture at Houghton Manor belonged to her and were therefore not listed in Henry's inventory. She owned the contents of the bed chamber and dressing room with six yellow stuff window curtains. She had six cane chairs, walnut pieces including a dressing table and a card table, as well as a small oak table and close stool of oak. She had had her own dining room, formerly a bedroom where her sons had slept. Furniture here included six cane chairs made out of cherrywood, japanned tea table and corner cupboard. Most of the silver listed in detail in the will belonged to her personally. She had a "Gold Strikeing Watch with the Amithyst Seale sett in Gold hanging". Although she had a tapestry hanging in her room, she also had a portrait of her father Roger Price "Set in Gold". Her rooms were probably on the principal bedroom floor.

Houghton Manor House: later history.

Henry Brandreth (1723–1752), heir to the property, had poor health and was not expected to live long. On 20 and 21 June 1750 he sold the whole estate "except the Messuage wherein he then dwelt with the Orchard & Close of Pasture adjoining containing 7 Acres with the Coach House on the Green and the Ground on which the said Coach house now stands with the Elm Tree by the Coach House". The purchaser was the Duke of Bedford and the price £12,005.[6]

Henry lived in the Manor House till 1752 and his wife Rebecca lived there till her death in 1779.[7] She was resident when the two drawings of the house were made in 1775. Henry's will,[8] proved 19 August 1752 gave his widow and his aunt Alice, life interests. The property was then entailed to his sisters Alice and Mary and his cousins Thomas, William and Nehemiah Brandreth (of the Houghton Hall side of the family).

The 1762 map of Houghton Regis[9] shows the house and outbuildings with the coach house on the Green opposite. The enclosure map of 1796 shows only the coach house remaining and the main house demolished and the fields thrown into the field called the Paddock.[10] The owner was Thomas Fossey, who probably bought the property from the Brandreths on Rebecca's death. A survey of 1797[11] shows that the Duke of Bedford now called another house the Mansion House. The lane to the east of the site is now called Drury Lane and part of the land attached to the Manor House is now occupied by the Memorial Hall.

HOUGHTON MANOR HOUSE, HOUGHTON REGIS, 1740

A true and Perfect Inventory of all and singular the goods, Chattels and hereditaments of Henry Brandreth late of the parish of Houghton Regis in the County of Bedford Esq., deceased which since his death have come to the hands, possession or knowledge of Richard Reddall and Thomas Beech Esquires, Curators lawfully assigned to Henry Brandreth the minor, the naturall and lawfull son of the said Deceased and Administrators for use and Benefit as well of the said minorities as of Ann, Alice and Mary Brandreth minors, the natural & lawful and only Children of the said deceased follows (to wit)

An Inventory of the household Goods, plate, Linnen and Wearing apparell of the said Henry Brandreth Esq., deceased which was taken, valued and appraised the twenty third day of May One Thousand Seven hundred and forty by John Smith and Ambrose Cooke follows (to wit)

Upper Story
In the Room No.1: One Sacking bottom bedstead with old Damask furniture; One Mattriss; One feather bed; one bolster and two Pillows; Three Blanketts, One Quilt; One Easey Chair and Cussion and Case; Six Chairs covered with Damask and Cases; Two Stools; Two Stands; One bass Chair; a pair Doggs; a pair Tongs; a fireshovell, a Brass fender; a pair Ears; Six India Pictures; Nine prints with Glass; a Corner Cupboard; a Two Leaved Leather Screen; a looking Glass; a pair Horse Pistles; a Cane fishing Rod with Silver head and Joynts, a Shagreen Case with fishing tackle; (China) Three cups, five saucers; One Boat, Two Plate; Two Candlesticks and some broken; Two Glass Salvers; a Plate Case with China Steps; a Iron Chimney back.   £12 2s 0d
In the Dressing Room No.2: A Couch bedstead with Green Cheney furniture and Squab; One Feather bed; One Bolster and one Pillow; Three Blankets; a Double Chest of Drawers; a Japan Table, a hanging Glass and Swing Glass; Two stands; Six Cane Chairs; seven India Pictures; Two pair of Window Curtains, Valance and Rods, Two Door Curtains, a Spring Bell.   £6 0s 6d
In the Nursery Room No.3: A Sacking bottom bedstead with old blew Harateen furniture; One Feather bed; One Bolster and Two Pillows, Three Blanketts; One Quilt; a press bedstead; a flock bed and bolster; One feather pillow; Two blanketts; One Quilt; an old fashion pair Chest

of Drawers, A hanging Glass and Swing Glass; Two square Tables; a Cloath press, Five old cane Chairs; Three India Prints; a fire shovell, Tongs & fender; Eight small Images; a Spring Bell; an Iron Chimney Back.   £5 13s 0d

In the Lobby and Clossetts, Middle Lobby Stair Case and Stair foot Passage. No.4:

(Clossetts) Two Warming pans, One Closestoole and Earthen pan; Two Boxes; One Leather Trunk; One hair Portmantua; one old Chair; six Small old boxes, a Parlour Cloth; Two Pott Cloths, four hand basens, Two Chamber Potts.

(Lobby) One Cloath press; One Chest; two broken Tables; a pair Tin Sconces, Eight and Twenty Prints; Ten pictures; Three books in folio videlicet Camden's History Dat. 1637, Gerard's Herboll Dat. 1636, Statutes Dat. 1661.

(Middle Lobby) One Square Table; a pair Tin Sconces, Two Prints.

(Stair Foot) Two Ovell Tables, a Back Gammon Table, boxes Dice and On a Dram Chest and Stand; a Table Leafe and side Table   £5 18s 6d

In the Best Chamber No.5: One Sacking bottom bedstead with Crimson silk Damask Curtains Basses Valences [– – –] head Cloth Tea[– – –]tar & Inner Valence, Crimson Silk Case & Curtains and Rods One Mattriss One feather bed One Bolster and Two pillows [– – –] and Cussion a fire hearth with a brass front, a brass fender, & Doggs fire Shovell, Tongs and a pair ears; a pair bellows and brush; Sixteen odd China Cupps and Saucers, a pair Candlesticks, Nine small peices, Stone and Earthen ware; Seven Small boxes; Two pair Brass Scales five pounds and Three Quarters, Brass Weights; 3 pair Sprigg'd window Curtains Valants & Rods; Two Salvers Tunbridge ware; one peice of Tapstrey.   £13

In the Room No.6: A Sacking bottom bedstead with Old Camblet furniture; One Case Rod; One feather bed; One bolster and two pillows; Three Blanketts; Two Quilts, Three Tables; Six Cane Chairs; a Closestoole Case and Earthen pan and a Quilted Cover; Two Cradle Mattresses; a Stone Grate, a pair Tongs, a fire Shovell; A Poker, pair ears, a pair bellows, Seven odd China Cups and Saucers; Three pair Window Curtains; Valants & Rods, an Iron Chimney back; One peece of Tapestry.   £7 1s 0d

In the Room No.7: One old bedstead and old furniture; One feather bed and bolster, four old Coverings; One old Table, Three broken Chairs, Two prints.   £1 10s 0d

In the Room No.8: A press bedstead; One feather bed; One bolster; Two Peices of Coverings, One old chest, One Wigg block; Two prints; one small Glass.   £1 5s 0d

In the Cheese Room No.9: One Looking Glass; Two tea tables; One still; Three old stove Grates; a pair Dogs; Nine broken boxes; Two

Casting Shovells; a Ratt trap; five old Chairs and Cheese Shelves.
£1 16s 0d

In the Laundrey No.10: One Long Table; Twelve Shoffellboard pieces;
Two Chests, one hair Trunk; a knapkin press; One Ironing horse, a pair
Iron Doggs; Three fire Nursery Irons; One broken Chair; five feather
pillows and two bolsters; an Ironing Stove.   £2 1s 0d

In the Room No.11: Two four Leaved Leather Screens; one old Trunk;
four old Chairs; a Thirty hour Clock and Case upon back stair case.
£2 10s 0d

In the Long Hall: One Eight Day Clock and Case; Two arm Six other
Cane Chairs and Eight Cussions; One Child's Arm Cane Chair; Twenty
Prints; five pair Tin Sconces (Clossett) Bottlebins.   £5 15s 0d

In the Comon Parlour: A Stove Grate, a fender, a fire Shovell; a pair
Tongs; a poker; a pair Bellows and Brush; Eight Cane Chairs; Eight
India Pictures; a weather Glass, a Claw Table and Stand, a Beaufetta
Tea Chest and hand Board; Three Brass wyer'd Cages; One Cane
Window blind; Three pair window Curtains, Valants and Rods; One
Square Table; Twelve odd China Cupps, five saucers; a Tea pot
Canister, a pier Glass; Three blew and white Dishes Six plates Two
punch bowles Three basons fifteen Small pieces white Stone ware; one
large Glass and Cover; One Quart Decanter; Thirty pieces of Small
Glass Ware.   £7 16s 0d

In the Withdrawing Room: One Indian Cabinett, six black arm Chairs
Seated with Velvett; Two Round Stools Ditto, One peir Glass; a Card
Table, Two family pictures; Eighteen China Cupps; One Sugar Dish; a
pair firescreens; three peices of Tapestry.   £20 9s 0d

In the best Parlour: A Brass fire hearth, Doggs, fender, fireshovell,
Tongs and Ears, a pair Bellows; a brush; a pair fire Screens; One peir
Glass; Two hanging Glasses with Glass Arms; a pair brass arms by the
Chimney; One Tea Table; Twelve Cane Chairs and Twelve Cushions,
Two family Pictures, three pair Window Curtains, Valents and Rods;
One Indian picture.   £10 18s 0d

In the White Hall: A Cane Couch; a Squabb and pillow; Two Corner
Cupboards; one small Ovell Table; One stand; One arm, Seven other
Cane Chairs, One Beauroe, Two pair Tin Sconces; a Glass Light, Six
prints and Maps, a stove Grate, a fireshovell, Tongs and Poker.
£3 6s 0d

In the Kitchen:
(Pewter) Thirty Seven Dishes, Seventy Nine Plates, Two Water plates,
One Pastry Pann; One Ditto plate; Seven Cheese Plates, Magarine and
waiters; One bason, Two Porringers; a plate Ring; One Chamber pott,
One Cistern and Cock and one bottle cistern.
(Copper) One boyler and Cover, One bottle Cistern, Three sause
pans, Two Tea Kittles; Two Drinking potts; One Chocolate Pott one
Coffee pott; Two preserving pans and one stew pan; Two Bellmettle

potts with brasse [– – –] lidds and Two [– – –] boyleing potts [– – –] One small pan; one Scimmer, a Pudding pan without a bottom, Eight Candlesticks; a Snuffer stand and pepper box.

(Iron) a Range of Grates, Cheeks keeper, fender, fire shovell Tongs and poker; One Iron back; Two pott hangers, one chaffin Dish; Ten Iron Scewers and frame; a hand Cleaver; a Chopping knife; a pigg iron; a pair standing Spitt Racks, a wind up Jack Compleat Three Spitts, Two bird Spitts & one frame; three Candle Sticks, one hussiff; a plate warmer, a pair snuffers; a flesh fork, a pair Bellows; Three boxirons; five pads & Two Rests, a pair Stilliards.

(Tin) A Candlebox, a bread Grater, a Dish & plate Covers, a Drudger, a half pint pott, Two sconces.

(Wood) a knapkin press; a Square Table; Six Chairs, one stool; a Bacon Rack; A Salt box, a marble Morter broke & wooden pestle; Eleven knives; Twelve forks, Ivory handles; Twelve odd knives & forks; One Kitchen knife; four pair window Curtains & Rods; Two payls; a plate rack, Three bowls; one flour tubb, nine trenchers & Dishes; a meat Screen. £22 4s 0d

In the Pastrey, Pantrey, Bacon Room & Lobb Hall:
(Pastrey) One large ovell Table, two Dough Troughs; two cupboards; Two Tosting Irons with tin pans; a Nurseing Candlestick & sausepan, a parcell Tin patty pans; a Pye peele; an Ironing board, a Cloath flaskett; Three basketts, one cage; Two voiders, one plate baskett, One Laun Sive.

(Pantrey) Three tin Cake hoops, One pudding pan, a Safe Cupboard, Two forms, One box, an old wyer scive.

(Bacon Room) Three sacks and Three Baggs with feathers; a parcell of Loose feathers in a Cupboard at stair head.

(Lobb Hall) A Tin kittle and Cover; a Double Cupboard; A Square Table, one form, Corner shelves and Some Earthen ware about the severall places. £2 7s 0d

In the Washhouse and Lauders: One Copper and Iron work only half belonging to the Estate; a wash stand; a kiver & one form, Two Cupboards; Two wooden Bottles; a powdering Tubb and cover, Two forms, a Chopping Block, a stone bottle; seven peices Red Earthen ware.£2 0s 6d

In the Brewhouse: A Copper and Iron work; an old Mash Tun and Under back, a Lead pump & Cistern from under back to copper; a Lead pipe from yard pump to Copper; one old Guile Tun; Two working tubbs; Two coolers; a Jett; a Mashridder, a Trunnell, a Pitch Kittle and marking Irons. £12 0s 0d

In the Cellars:
(Further Cellar) One hogs head, Three Beer Staleders, one stoole.
(Heither cellar) Two hogsheads, One kilderkin, Three firkins, three half Anchors, One two Gallon Bottle, three Drink Stalders, Two Brass Cocks.

(Small Beer Cellar) One hoggshead, One kilderkin, Two Tap tubbs; About thirty Dozen Quart Glass Bottles and one Dozen and a half pint bottles in several places and Lumber about the house.   £4 2s 6d

Linnin: Four pair Holland Sheets; Fourteen pair Flaxen Ditto; Three pair hempen Ditto and Three pair and a half Ditto very old; three Damask Table Cloths; Three side board cloths and Thirty four knapkins and Two new Damask Table Cloths (not made) Twelve Diaper Table Cloths Two and Twenty knapkins; Six Huckerback Table Cloths; Six very old Table Cloths; Fifteen Diaper Towells, Eight Flaken Ditto, three Round Ditto, Four pair holland pillow Beirs, Four pair Ditto very old, Six pair Flaxen.   £18 16s 0d

Wearing Apparell: One Light Coloured Cloth Coat waskett and pair of Britches Imbroidered with Silver; One brown Cloth Waskett & Britches, Five old Coats; Four Wasketts; Five pair of Britches, a Morning Gown, a Bed Gown, Four Hatts; One Cap, One wigg, Four pair Stockings, One pair Strapt Ditto Six Shirts; Six Neckcloths and two Cotton Capps.   £11 7s 6d

One Bridle and Sadle and Pistle holsters; Sadle and Pistle Housings Laced and Fringed with Silver; Five old Guns, Four old Swords and one sword Belt workt with Silver.   £3 10s

[*Detailed Inventory of Farm House & Buildings*]

Plate in the Mansion House: One Cupp, Two Salts, One Plate, one marrow Spoon; a Tobacco Box, Two Tobacco Stoppers, a pair Shoe buckles; one Stook buckle; Six Tea Spoons, one Strainer, one pair of Tongs; One half pint mug; One old Gold watch and studded case; One old Silver watch; One pint, One half pint muggs; One Strainer and punch Ladle plated.   £16 14s 6d

Ready money in the house   £34 12s

[*Detailed inventory of stock and crops*]   £85 4s 2¾d

These Exhibitants declare that They are informed Mary Brandreth the Relict of the deceased did possess herself of some plate, a Watch and Jewells which were in the deceased's house at his death the particulars of which they cannot set forth but declare that a Bill is filed for discovering the same. These Exhibitants do further declare that in and by the Marriage Settlement made between the deceased and the said Mary Brandreth and Charles Chibald Esq. the summ of one Thousand pounds was to be paid to the said deceased which summ as he is advised is still due to the Executors or Administrators of the said deceased's Estate and for which there is now a Contest.

These Exhibitants declare that no other goods Chattells and Credits of the said deceased have since his death come to their hands, possession or knowledge besides what are set forth in the above Inventory.

[*Note of Inventory being exhibited 14 April 1743*]

PRO: PROB 3/42/35

NOTES

1. Useful material on the Brandreths is to be found in the following sources: *The Family on the Green* by Rosemary Harris, 1985 (unpublished); *Introduction to Brandreth Archive*, BCRO (unpublished); *Brandreth Memoranda* (MIC 212) (unpublished manuscripts). On Houghton Regis VCH Volume II pages 389–393; *Royal Houghton*, 1986 and *Old Houghton*, 1988 both by Pat Lovering and published by The Book Castle, 12 Church Street, Dunstable, Beds. The main archives in BCRO relating to the Brandreths are found in B & X 689. Sewell Manor Sequestrations BCRO BW 1172.
2. Conveyance of Houghton Regis Manor 24–27 Dec 1669, BCRO B 1.
3. Views of Houghton Manor: *The South Front of Mrs. Brandreth's House at Houghton Regis, Bedfordshire* unsigned; *The Bowling Green front of Mrs. Brandreth's House at Houghton taken August 2, 1775* [blank] *fecit* BCRO Z 329/8; These items were part of sale at Sotheby's of *English Native and Provincial Art* on 22 July 1986
4. see R. Harris Chapter 3.
5. Madeleine Mason edit. *The Compleat Cook or the Secrets of a Seventeenth Century Housewife by Rebecca Price*, 1974 Routledge Kegan Paul. Rebecca Brandreth's will is on pages 344–348.
6. Russell Deeds Bundle 3 No.65
7. Will of Rebecca Brandreth, proved PCC 1779 (BS 1579)
8. Will of Henry Brandreth, proved PCC 1752 (BS 1578)
9. 1762 Map of Houghton Regis (B 553)
10. 1796 Enclosure Award and Map of Houghton Regis (X 21/386 and MA 842)
11. Survey of 1797.

ICKWELL BURY

Ickwell Bury to 1823

The Manor of Ickwell Bury in Northill, "late part of the possessions of the Hospital or Priory of St.John of Jerusalem now dissolved", was granted to John Barnardiston in 1543.[1] The estate stayed in the Barnardiston family till George sold it to John Harvey of the Inner Temple, London, for £3,250 in 1680. Included in this sale was the capital messuage or manor house called Ickwell Bury.[2]

It has been assumed previously that the house that was burned down in 1937 had been completely rebuilt for John Harvey (1631–1692). Modern photographs suggest that this is so.[3] Work was done in the 1680s. The mason's bill of Elisha Allen for £107, for work done in 1683 and 1684, includes six marble mantlepieces, 183 feet of window stones, "takeing up and new laying of 3 fire harths."[4] The stable block dates from 1683 and has a clock of that date, probably by Thomas Tompion.

Late seventeenth century detail in some of the rooms survived till the twentieth century.[5] This consistent picture of a late seventeenth century

Plate 16: Ickwell Bury: The Library. (*Photograph: c.1910*)

132

house being added to in the nineteenth century is questioned by the tiny illustration on Gordon's map of 1736.[6] This shows an irregular house with a prominent gabled door that is more likely to be early seventeenth century or earlier. The number of windows tally with later photographs of the east front. The drawing also suggests that the house had an irregular layout which included a mansard roof, that was subsequently remodelled. It would seem John Harvey remodelled the interior of Ickwell Bury and added the existing stable block.

By the time he made his will on 10 December 1691[7] he was clearly short of money. He made provision for the sale within a year of "the estate at Ickwell & the house called Ickwell Bury" to pay off debts and legacies of £4,700 to his younger children. Other estates were also included if the sale of Ickwell Bury raised insufficient money. In the event the estate was not sold and successive Harveys added to it. John, son of John Harvey (1631–1692), made ten purchases including the Rectory of Northill,[8] so that the financial problems may have been more imagined than real.

At some point during the middle to late eighteenth century the house was remodelled with sash windows and the gabled porch removed. The entrance at some point was put on the east side. During the nineteenth century various extensions were made on the front and a heavy colonnaded porch added over the new entrance. Exactly when these alterations took place is impossible to say as there is no mention of them in the letters and accounts, which only survive in full for brief periods.

The 1823 Inventory

On the death of another John Harvey (1772–1819), his widow Susannah decided to let Ickwell Bury. In 1823 a lease was drawn up with Richard Weyland of Wood Eaton, Oxfordshire, as tenant. Although a few rooms, such as the "Blue Parlour", one of the garrets in the gallery and the further wine cellar, were reserved for the use of the Harvey family, the accompanying inventory does give a good picture of the contents of the house at this date. Although they were probably not of the quality of the grander houses such as Southill and Colworth, various trends seen in other early nineteenth century houses are evident here. On the ground floor almost all the furniture was mahogany. In the dining room, for example, the twelve chairs, two elbow chairs, dining room table, sideboard and pole fire screens were all made out of mahogany. The dining room had a wine cooler and dumb waiter, probably also mahogany. The hall had a large oak table and a pair of painted flower stands, but here as elsewhere on the ground floor the majority of the furniture was mahogany.

The hall contained a number of weapons and pieces of armour, echoing perhaps the hall at Belvoir Castle, Leicestershire, remodelled between 1801 and 1820[9] to designs of James Wyatt and the Reverend

Plate 17: Ickwell Bury: An enlargement of a thumbnail sketch on William Gordon's county map of 1736. Note the irregular features of the 1690s house.

Plate 18: Ickwell Bury: The west and south fronts, with the stables in the background. This shows the house as it was at the time of the 1819 inventory.
(*Watercolour: Thomas Fisher, c.1820*)

James Thoroton, and used for the display of weapons and armour. The less important "Breakfast Parlour" had a walnut dining table and an oak sideboard.

The first floor also contained a considerable number of pieces of mahogany but also had painted furniture as well. The "Canopy Bedroom" had mahogany chest of drawers, dressing stand and one chair with a white cover but it also had six painted chairs. Although most of the beds were four-posters, more modern beds were found in the ladies' bedrooms. The "Canopy Bedstead with Pink Muslin Furniture", the tent bedsteads in Miss Harvey's room and the ladies' two bedded room were examples of types of beds fashionable around 1800. The last room mentioned had painted dressing tables, painted chairs and a painted airing horse as well as a mahogany bureau.

Up on the attic floor, which included a long gallery, a survival from the remodelling of Ickwell Bury in the time of John Harvey (1631–1692), is a greater assortment of furniture, no doubt banished to make way for the mahogany and painted furniture. The long gallery had twelve black chairs, either ebony or japanned. A number of the garrets had walnut chest of drawers and the middle garret had a walnut escritoire. The "Plaid Bed Garret" had an oak dressing table. Mrs. Hill's garret had three beech chairs.

All this evidence suggests that the contents of the house were changed within twenty or so years of John Harvey's death in 1819. Fashionable furniture was installed in all the principal rooms with the older pieces moved into the less important areas of the house.

The Harveys had a considerable collection of pictures and prints. These included portraits and one print of Macbeth; otherwise their subjects are not known. The upper drawing room contained "forty one prints framed and glazed" and "fourteen small and one large painting". There is no mention of any tapestry hangings. By this date they had been totally surpassed by pictures as fashionable wall decorations.

The carpeting in the house included Brussels and Turkey carpets but also ones of British make from Kidderminster and Wilton. The Brussels carpet in the library was fitted. The simpler styles of the 1800s extended even to curtains. None of those at Ickwell Bury were "Festooned".

Unusually, the Harveys left their china for the new tenant to use. The service seems to have been "Blue and White" and purchased probably fairly recently. The absence of cracked or broken items and the survival of full sets of two dozen table dishes and four dozen dinner plates suggests this. The glass listed by contrast seems to be less complete. The pair of quart decanters was described as faulty; the forty eight wine glasses were not all of the same pattern but the dozen cut glass tumblers were intact. As usual with inventories of leased property, the silver was not included.

Plate 19: Ickwell Bury: The east and south fronts, with the stables.
(*Photograph: c.1910*)

The kitchen and ancillary offices seem to have been fully equipped. The kitchen itself had the unusual addition of 57 stuffed birds. The equipment of the brewhouse is particularly detailed.

Ickwell Bury after 1823

Although Ickwell Bury was leased in 1823, by 1844 it was back in Harvey hands.[10] Unlike many of their contemporaries, it seems as if the family lived in their main property for the rest of the nineteenth century. By 1903, the house was leased out as a boys' preparatory school. In 1924 the Harveys sold the estate but the preparatory school, now called Horton House, continued to occupy the house till it was burnt down on 20 September 1937.[11]

The site was sold to Colonel H.G. Wells, who built a new house at the corner of the stable block, which survived the fire. The house, completed in 1940, was built to the designs of A.S.G. Butler, architect, who was the co-author of the memorial volumes of the late Sir Edward Lutyens. The new Ickwell Bury shows Butler's debt to Lutyens. The Wells family gave the house to Bedford School, who have leased it to the Yoga for Health Foundation.

ICKWELL BURY, NORTHILL 1823

8 November 1823/ Lease by Susannah Harvey of Ickwell Bury, widow, guardian of her son John Harvey, to Richard Weyland of Wood Eaton, Oxford, esq., at an annual rent of £350, of:
... all that capital messuage or mansion house called Ickwell   Bury House in the parish of Northill, together with certain land, outbuildings and sporting rights, with the use of the several household goods, furniture, books, pictures, articles and things in the schedule or inventory annext, excepting always:
a room on the ground floor of the mansion house called the Blue Parlour; one of the garrets in the Gallery; the furthest wine vault or cellar; the east end of the large barn in the Stable Yard; the Orchard (except for the fruit); the Granary in the occupation of Thomas Burton, and the lumber room over the old malting.

The Schedule or Inventory referred to in the before written Indenture:

Dairy: Two Milk Pails, two Butter Boards, wood Bowl, four Milk leads, twelve Milk pans, one Cream pot, two pickle Jars, four Pork or Egg pots, one Barrel Churn, Cheese Tub, one Butter Kimnel, Butter Scales, one one pound, one half pound and one fourteen pounds, Brass weights, Cheese press, two Butter pots, milk strainer and Tongs, one tin skimmer, one large meat jar (used as an ash pot).

Laundry: a grate and Ironing stove, Ironing stove and pipe, ten Flat Irons, Fender, One poker, one Shovel, one sifter, one hanger, one Box Iron, two heaters, two Resters, two italian Irons, two three leaved large folding drying horses, one airing Horse, a Bakers patent mangle, two Ironing Tables, four stools, two Chairs, A clothes Rack with lines compleat, one large deal Ironing table, two drawers, two long forms and two clothes Baskets.

Wash house: Two Coppers fixed, one lead Curb, two lye tubs, four good wash trays, seven old wash trays, two tub stands, two wash stools, one old table, two lye racks, one long table for wash trays, two iron trevets, one iron oven peel, one small tub and drying horse, a good dough trough, one pail, one Wood Bowl, one deal cupboard fixed,one folding drying horse.

Brew house: A Copper fixed with a Reservoir over the same, two pumps fixed, One under back, two Coolers leaded, a Mash Tun with a false bottom and Cover, two wood troughs from underback to the two Coolers, a step ladder and two forms, a mash rule, one Iron shovel, one hoe, one poker five hoes, two large working squares and a large working Tub, ten iron bound tubs of various sizes, one bearing tub, one small four wheel Truck, one large tub, one small tub, one bathing tray, a three wheel carriage, a Pan Rack in the Yard.

Small Beer Cellar: Six Beer pipes, three hogshead, four tap tubs, one pair of steps, a beer stall and a pair of barrel dogs.

Further Cellar: two pipes of ale, one bottling stand, cheese rack and Meat Jar.

Ale Cellar: twelve beer pipe, four full of ale and two pails.

Meat Cellar: two meat leads, one Chopping block, one long table, one Barrel stand, one round wire meat cover, one long form, one old Table, one trestle, twenty preserving bottles.

Servants Hall: A grate fixed, a dining Table and four forms, one round Table, one elbow and three other chairs, ten pair of pistol cases, seven odd pistol cases and three pair of Bucks Horns.

Room over Servants Hall: A grate fixed, one large grate not fixed with polished front for wood, one press bedstead, one old table, three old chairs, one high wire fire Guard, one Guard for a stove and three wood Coal hods.

House-keeper's Room: A small grate with a side oven, a polished fender and fire Irons, four Mahogany Chairs, two painted Elbow Chairs, a Kidderminster Carpet and hearth rug, one wool matt, one round walnut tree Table, small oval Glass (broke), eight prints framed and glazed, three pickle jars, two coarse pans (cracked).

Dining Room: A bright fronted grate for wood, a Polished fender and fire Irons, a wire fire Guard and Brush, twelve Mahogany Chairs and two Elbow Chairs with Morocco Seats and red cloth covers, one Mahogany Dining Table and Cloth, one Mahogany side Board with Drawer and brass rods, A pair of small square side boards, a Turkey Carpet eighteen feet by fourteen feet, A crimson Hearth rug, A piece of Baize about three yards by two yards and an half, one foot stool, A complete set of scarlet window Curtains embossed and fringed, A dumb waiter and wine Cooler, a pair of mahogany pole fire screens, a pair of fire shades, eight paintings and two prints in Gilt frames.

Study: A bright fronted Grate for Wood, a wire fender Brass Bead and feet and fire Irons, a pair of Mahogany pole fire screens on paw feet, Mahogany flower stand, Mahogany library Table, Green Cloth, four Mahogany Chairs Morocco seats Red Cloth Covers, A Brussels Carpet to fit the Room, a small hearth rug, one deal stool, one Mahogany covered Stool, A set of scarlet Moreen window curtains complete fringed, A painted Glass case with eight Drawers, a set of small Book Shelves, a pier Glass in shell frame, fifteen prints framed and Glazed and three paintings.

Library: A polished front grate Green wire fender Brass rim and Brass feet, fire Irons, one elbow and three other Chairs, a mahogany library Table, green Cloth, Brussels Carpet fitted, Round Table, A mahogany Book Case with glass doors (whole), A Mahogany Book stand, Two scarlet Moreen window Curtains fringed and four pins, four prints and one Map.

Hall: A Bright front grate for wood, a Hall Stove with plates and wire guard, A bright fender and fire Irons, A pair of Iron Dogs, four small pieces of Cannon, A set of Mahogany Dining Tables, One large Oak Table, eight Mahogany Hall Chairs with Crests, two old Chairs leather backs and seats, A piece of Marble coloured Floor Cloth from the front door to the stairs, two pieces of Floor Cloth side of the Stairs, two pieces of Matting, a Wool Matt and Cushion, A pair of painted flower stands, four old guns, three pistols, a Bow and a spear, one weather glass, nine Iron helmets, one other Helmet and nine pieces of Body armour, eleven large paintings, six small paintings, a case of arrows, a small Glass case, two Mahogany Card tables, four Maps, a spring seat and form, a Vase shape Hall lamp complete.

The Lower Drawing Room: A polished Register Stove and Fender, a set of fire Irons and Brush, a Brussels carpet to fit the Room, a floor Cloth and Hearth rug, eight Mahogany Chairs cane seats, A mahogany framed Sofa stuffed in Moreen, squab and cushions, two Mahogany settees to correspond with squab cushions and three linen Covers to the same, A complete set of Moreen window curtains with a linen Case and six pins complete, A pair of Book Stands, two Mahogany Pembroke tables, A Mahogany reading stand, A pair of elegant Pier Glasses, six prints in gilt frames and glazed, two paintings in Gilt frames, Chandelier and linen Cloth.

Passage near Garden Door: A piece of Matting, two Wool Matts, two Paintings, one print, one Bucks Head, one Weather Glass, and a Passage Lamp.

Breakfast Parlour: A polished Grate, fender, fire Irons and brush, four Mahogany Chairs with blue Covers, one Wood Elbow chair and leather Cushion, a Mahogany Bureau and Book Case, looking glass doors, A walnut tree Dining Table, Oak side board, a Harpsichord and Music Stand, a small Turkey Carpet and Hearth rug, two Mahogany Stools and fire screen, two blue Moreen window curtains, three Bucks Heads, and a print framed and glazed, six pair of gun loops.

Long Gallery: Twelve high Black Chairs, one easy Chair and a Couch, three Cane Back Chairs, four stools, two Mahogany Round back chairs stuffed with hair, a mahogany Chest of Drawers, one Camp Bedstead, six old Boxes and a pair of Stocks.

South West Garret: A Bedstead and Cotton Curtains, one straw mattress, Feather Bed, Bolster, two Pillows, three Blankets and Quilts, one piece of green ground Carpet, Bath Stove, high wire fender and fire irons, seven Black Chairs plaid and Back seat, one small mahogany chest of Drawers, one Walnut Tree Chest of Drawers with thirteen Drawers, A Black dressing Table and Box Glass, A painted Basin stand, Ewer, soap tray, one shelf and one Yellow Chambers Utensil, one Airing Horse, one Japanned fire skreen, one low canvas skreen and a Box of Moss, and a short Couch in a Cotton Case.

Garret on the North of the Last: A press Bedstead with White Curtains, A small Hair Mattress, Feather Bed Bolster and Pillows, three

Blankets, Marseilles Quilt, two Childrens Cribs, one Feather Bed, One Mattress two pillows, four Chairs White Covers, one small Mahogany Chest of Drawers, one Walnut Chest of Drawers on legs with ten Drawers, A walnut tree Dressing Table with box top, one Glass, one Dressing table, small Box Glass, one painted wash Table, Basin and Ewer, one Bottle, a Soap tray, one Chamber Utensil, one Airing Horse, two small Blankets and two pieces of green Carpet.

The Plaid Bed Garret: A Bedstead with plaid Curtains, one Wool Mattress, feather Bed, Bolster, two Pillows, three Blankets, a Counterpane, Bed round Carpet and Hearth rug, wire fender, shovel, poker and brush, Six Plaid Chairs, one stool, one oak dressing table one swing glass, one painted dressing table and Basin, one Bottle, one Glass, a soap tray and Chamber utensil, one walnut tree Chest of Drawers and wire fire guard.

Middle Garret East side of the House: A four post bedstead Needle Work Curtains, one Mattress in a Crankey Case, Feather Bed Bolster, one pillow, two elbow chairs, one other chair, an Oak Chest of Drawers, Walnut Escrutoire, A painted dressing-stand, white Basin and Ewer, one Bottle, soap tray, Walnut dressing table, pieces of Carpet, three Blankets, patch work Quilt, fender, shovel and tongs, one painting and Boot Jack.

Two Bedded Maids Room: Two Bedsteads and Green Curtains, one Mattress, two feather Beds, two Bolsters, three pillows, seven pieces of Bedside carpet, three Old Chairs, two stools, an Oak Dressing Table, an Oval Glass, one square swing Glass, one Oak Bureau, two low Chests of Drawers, a painted Basin stand, two Basins, one Mahogany Basin stand, Basin, Ewer and Tumbler.

Mrs. Hill's Garret: A four post Bedstead, Green Curtains, one Crankey Mattress, three Blankets, one Quilt, Feather Bed Bolster and two pillows, two pieces of Carpet, three Beech Chairs, one Night Chair and pan, one stool, a dressing table and a Walnut tree Box dressing Glass, A High Walnut tree chest of Drawers, a painted Dressing Table, White Basin, Ewer (cracked) and Saucer.

Back Upper Landing: An Old Chest of Drawers, Boot and Shoe stand.

Men Servants Two Garrets: Five Bedsteads and Curtains, five feather beds, four Bolsters, six Pillows, fifteen Blankets, five coloured quilts, nine old Chairs, one easy and one night chair, one walnut tree writing desk, five white chamber utensils, one basin, one ewer, one old chest of drawers, one night stool, two pewter pans, one old swing Glass, three Boxes, some broken Glass.

On Back Landing: Four Japanned foot pans, four Japanned lamps, four Japanned Candleshades, three tin mugs, one tin Candlestick, one yellow Decanter, one wood Bowl, two Copper coal scuttles, one eight day clock and candle box.

The Canopy Bed Room: A Canopy Bedstead with Pink Muslin

Furniture complete, window curtains to Correspond, Feather Bed Bolster and two pillows, three Blankets, one Marseilles Quilt, small floor Carpet, three pieces of Carpet, one Mahogany Chest of Drawers, a Mahogany Dressing Stand with looking glass, Basin, Ewer, Bottle Glass, tin mug & soap tray, six painted Chairs, one mahogany Chair white Covers, one Chimney Glass, a pair of stone candlesticks, Mahogany Wardrobe and a japanned box, Bath stove fire guard, fender, fire irons, Brush, Boot Jack, one print framed and glazed (Macbeth), two linen covers to Bed and Window Curtains, four curtain pins, two holland Blinds, small Mahogany Airing Horse.

Best Bed Room: A mahogany post Bedstead Muslin pink Hangings complete, a set of Window Curtains to correspond, two linen Covers to Bed and Window Curtains, A Straw Palliasse, one Wool Mattress, Large feather Bed, bolster, four pillows, three Blankets, a Marseilles Quilt, a wilton floor Carpet about five yards square, a six feet hearth rug, four pieces of carpet, one mahogany chest of drawers, a Mahogany Wardrobe, two Mahogany Dressing Tables, two large square Glasses, one high Glass in pillar frame, circular top Mahogany night Commode and pan, Corner Basin Stand, Coloured basin, Ewer, soap Brush tray, two Chamber Utensils, one tin mug, water Bottle and tumbler, six green painted Chairs and two stools, Mahogany Biddet and pan, Mahogany folding airing Horse, A Pantheon stove fixed, fender and fire Irons, Brush and Boot Jack, one large print framed and glazed, four curtain pins and three holland blinds.

Bedroom on the North of the last: A Mahogany Post Bedstead and striped Cotton Curtains lined, a folding Straw palliass, a Wool Mattress, Feather Bed Bolster, two pillows, three blankets, a Marseilles Quilt, A wilton floor Carpet five yards by four yards, two bed side and a Bird Hearth rug, two Mahogany Elbow Chairs, three other Chairs and cotton covers, one needle work Stool, biddet and pan, a pair of Satin wood pole fire screens, mahogany airing horse, Boot jack, Mahogany Bureau and Bookcase Glass doors, circular from chest of drawers, Mahogany Dressing table, Box dressing glass, two large paintings, painted Basin Stand, coloured Basin, Ewer, Soap and Brush tray, two Utensils, Bottle, Tumbler, Tin Mug, two Window Curtains to match the Bed, two linen Covers to Bed and Window curtains and two long Brass pins.

Best Landing: One square turn over Mahogany Table, two small Mahogany Tables, top table, a large Cabinet, four painted flower stands, two Mahogany flower stands, a small square Mahogany Table and one Battle piece painted.

Mrs. Harvey's Room: A Mahogany post Bedstead Dimity furniture, one straw palliasse, one crankey Mattress, Feather Bed Bolster two pillows, three Blankets and Counterpane, three pieces of Bed side Carpet, two painted chairs White covers, A painted Dressing stand, Coloured basin, soap dish, Bottle and Tumbler, a Mahogany Biddet and pan, small Mahogany Drawers, Mahogany night commode and pan, a high framed dressing glass, Hearth rug and stool with Needle work covers, an airing Horse, two Window Curtains to correspond with Bed, small Bath stove, fire guard, fire irons, Bellows and Brush.

White Tent Bed Room: Bath stove, high wire fender, fire Irons, Bellows and Brush, four pieces of Green Carpet, and old Hearth rug, a tent Bedstead with White Dimity furniture, A Crankey Mattress, Feather Bed, Bolster, two pillows, three Blankets and Counterpane, two dimity window curtains, A Mahogany Dressing Table Box and Glass, a Dressing stand Coloured Basin Ewer soap and Brush tray, Bottle, tumbler one utensil, Six Mahogany Chairs, airing horse and a walnut tree Bureau.

Dressing Room adjoining: A Mahogany Bureau, one Beach Chair, one Beach Stool, Airing Horse, deal dressing table, painted dressing table, Basin, Ewer, soap tray, one chamber Utensil, three pieces of Carpet, Dimity Window curtains, Mahogany Biddet stool and pan.

The Press Bed Room: A Mahogany Press Bedstead, White dimity Curtains to the same, one Hair Mattrass Feather Bed, Bolster, two pillows, small Wilton floor Carpet, two pieces of carpet and hearth rug, two Window Curtains, painted dressing Table and oval Box Glass, An Oak Chest of drawers, three Cane bottomed Chairs, one stool, oval pier Glass, Gilt frame Register Stove and fire guard, low wire fender, fire irons, Bellows and Brush, deal Basin stand coloured basin, Ewer, soap and brush tray, Bottle, tumbler, one Utensil, one Beer Jug, airing Horse, one print framed and glazed, Bird in a Case.

Yellow Room: A Mahogany Post Bedstead with Chocolate and Yellow furniture, two Window Curtains to match, one straw one wool mattress, feather Bed Bolster, two Pillows, three Blankets and Counterpane, Kidderminster Bed Round Carpet, one piece of the same and a mixed Hearth rug, Mahogany Chest of Drawers Circular front, two Mahogany pot Cupboards, Mahogany Biddet and Pan, three Cane bottom Chairs, one easy Chair, painted Basin Stand, Basin Ewer Bottle and Tumbler, two Chamber Utensils, one Yellow pitcher, two stools, airing horse, a painted dressing table, large square dressing glass, a bright grate, plain fender & fire Irons, a small Mahogany Table, one painted and one mahogany night stool and pan and painted airing Horse.

The upper Drawing Room: A Bright Grate and fender, fire Irons and Brush, A green Kidderminster Carpet fitted to the Room, Rug, one Chamber Organ, twelve Elbow Chairs, three settees to correspond, one sofa Table, one pillar and Claw oval Table, two Book stands, one boot [sic] rack, one small mahogany stand and a pair of pole fire skreens, a complete set of Window Curtains, Mahogany framed sofa, with squab, two Cushions, two pillows, two fire shades, forty one prints and portraits framed and glazed, fourteen small and one large painting and one small Mahogany Tea Chest.

Back Passage: One piece of matting.

Passage Room: A Grate, fire guard, plain Fender, fire Irons and Bellows, a Walnut tree Bureau, Book Case, One Double walnut Chest of drawers, a large plate Chest, a deal dining table, a floor carpet and an old Hearth Rug.

Small Tent Bed Room next Back Staircase: A tent Bedstead, neat Cotton hangings, A Wool Mattress, Feather Bed, Bolster and one Pillow, Blanket and Quilt, an Oak Chest of Drawers, swing Glass, painted Basin stand, Yellow Basin, Ewer, Bottle and Tumbler, one small oval pier Glass and two Stools.

Stiped Tent Back Room: A tent Bedstead with striped Cotton furniture, hair mattress, Feather Bed, Bolster, one Pillow, three Blankets and Counterpane, an Oak Chest of Drawers, Mahogany Pembroke table, oval Box Glass, Painted Basin Stand, Basin, Ewer and Tumbler, one Chair, one Stool and one piece of matting.

Dressing Room: Two Window Curtains, A Walnut tree set of Drawers, one chair, one stool, a painted dressing table, coloured Basin, Ewer, soap, cup, Bottle, Tumbler, one Yellow chamber utensil, one print and a small oval glass.

Miss Harvey's Room: A tent Bedstead and Dimity Curtains, one straw Mattress, one Crankey Mattress, Feather Bed, Bolster, one pillow, three Blankets, one counterpane, three painted chairs, two stools, two pieces of carpet, one small Mahogany Chest of Drawers, Oval Box Glass, three Blankets and Counterpane, A deal wash hand stand, Basin, Ewer, soap Brush tray, Glass and tumbler, one tin tea kettle, one Chamber utensil, one Window blind, one Green Window Curtain and small Book shelf.

The Ladies two Beded Room: A tent bedstead and dimity curtains, a straw mattress, one crankey Mattress and one Bolster, three Blankets, one counterpane, a Mahogany Bureau, A small set of drawers, two painted dressing tables, Yellow Basin, Ewer and Bottle, one decanter, one Glass Bottle, two painted Chairs, three stools and a painted airing Horse, a wilton floor carpet, one piece of floor Carpet, Bath stove, wire fender and fire Irons, two small cases, shelves, four prints framed and glazed and two green window curtains.

Small Dressing Room: One easy Chair, one Child's Chair, Mahogany Tea Table and a Mahogany Dwarf Wardrobe.

Kitchen: A grate fixed Crane and four pot Hooks, fender, tongs and poker, an Iron Horse, one trivet, a copper Tea Boiler with Tap, Wafer Irons, twenty one Iron skewers, one painted seat, fire skreen, one copper Boiler, one Turbot Kettle, two Copper Pots, one Cover, two Copper frying pans, one preserving pan, eight stewpans sorted and covers, one Tin Coffee pot, two pewter Salts, Beer Tray and small Bellows, one tin side Candlestick and sugar nippers, two Beer Jugs, one Basin, three pudding moulds (Bad), A Corner cupboard and Time piece, fifty seven cases of birds with glass fronts, fifteen tin dish Covers, one Coffee Mill, one

Hand Bell, one oak cupboard, dining table and two forms, one stool, five windsor Chairs, one elbow and one turnpinned Chair, one round Table and one Tea board.

Scullery: Two Coppers fixed, two Wood Covers, two old Shovels, one salamander, two Gridirons, five trivets, one hanging horse, eight iron saucepans and covers, five Copper sauce pans and three covers, one large brass slice, copper ladle, tin slice, one tin basting ladle, one water Tub, two Pails, one dish tub, two plate Racks, one wood and one Pewter Bowl, six pickling Jars, Iron Peel Coal Rake, Meat chopper, one pewter colander, tin dredge box and three Iron spoons.

Larder: A wire meat safe, marble pestle mortar and stand, one cradle spit, two common spits, one copper frying pan, one long spit, rack, dripping pan and stand, eight coarse pots and dishes, seven pickling Jars, six tin pans, fifteen small pieces of tin ware, six baking tins, one pair of copper scales, a seven pounds brass weight, two hair seives, three two gallon wood bottles, a copper still and a wood Jelly stand, one tin Turbot Kettle, one Chafing dish, one small plate rack, one mincing board, one chopper, two saws, chopping block, two wire covers, one small tub, one meat pot and stand, one salt and two flour Bins, one pair of steps and a square Table, two Iron Game Racks, five yellow dishes, twenty four plates, twelve small plates, fourteen small yellow preserving jars.

Store Room: twenty-four blue and white Table dishes, forty-eight dinner plates, twenty-four small and eleven small plates, four Vegetable dishes and covers, one sallad and one soup dish, Japanned Tea tray, eight Cups and saucers, Tea Pot and Basin, two Wood Candle Boxes, one pair of Sugar Nippers, one Mahogany tea Chest and one tin sugar canister.

Butler's Pantry: Seven Cups and Saucers, Tea board, Coffee Pot, two Basins, two pair Wine decanters, one water decanter, twelve cut tumblers, forty-eight wine Glasses various, one Japanned Tea Tray, one Cork screw, four nut crackers, one small ring glass, two bronze Tea urns plated Taps, one pair of Candlesticks, snuffer and tray, two oil cans and candle box, One pair of lemon squeezers, one pair of Quart Decanters (faulty), four Mahogany Butler's Trays, One Oak Butler's tray, one Plate Basket, two Mahogany tea boards, one Japanned tea board, three old oak Tables, three Chairs one Japanned plate warmer, one Napkin press, one set of fire Irons, fender and Trivet, a pair of deal steps, one Corner cupboard, five Maps, one shower Bath complete, five old green Clothes, one Boot Jack and six old urn Rugs.

Back Hall: One oak table, one pair of steps, two painted flower stands, one wood bowl and Butler's tray, one long house broom, two copper warming pans, one candle Box, five Japanned Candlesticks, one pair of brass Candlesticks, one glass side Lanthorn, two tin pails, one wood pail, one wool door Matt and one horn lanthorn.

Best Stair Case: four pieces of Kidderminster carpet for stairs, thirty wires, small carpet for landing, one Mahogany floor and Banister brush.

Passage to Drying Yard: One pair of large scale boards and beam four, fifty-six, one, twenty-eight and one fourteen pounds weights, a meat safe and lye Rack.

[Cow house, yards & garden contents listed in detail.]
8 November 1823

BCRO: HY 636

NOTES

1. The fullest published work on Ickwell Bury is found in Gordon Nares articles *Ickwell Bury, Bedfordshire*, CL Vol.117 pp.1174–1177 and 1234–1237 for 5 and 12 May 1955. VCH Vol III pp.242–246 is useful. The Harvey archive (HY) and its introduction are the main source for a history of the house. Letters patent of 1543 (HY 1).
2. Deed of 1680 (HY 9–10).
3. Z 50/16/116–119.
4. HY 839.
5. Z 50/16/120–128.
6. Gordon map (MC 2/8) and enlarged photographs of the sketch of Ickwell Bury (Z 50/14/222–223).
7. Will of John Harvey, made 10 December 1691, proved 20 April 1692 (HY 705).
8. Introduction to HY catalogue.
9. Colvin p.951; *Guide Book to Belvoir Castle*, 1978.
10. HY 637.
11. Nares, CL as above. For an account of the fire see *Bedfordshire Times* 24 September 1937 and for a photograph of the house after the fire see Z 50/84/47.

LEIGHTON BUZZARD PREBENDAL HOUSE

Leighton Buzzard Prebendal House up to 1749

The Leighs had inherited the lease of the Prebendal estate on the death of John Leigh's father-in-law, Christopher Hoddesdon, in 1610.[1]

The first detailed description of the Parsonage House on or near the site of the eighteenth century Prebendal House is in a lease of 1584. The property is described as the "Mansion House of the parsonage of Leighton Buzzard included the hall, the entry between the hall and the parlour, the buttery, the wool house, the wool house entry, the garner, the kitchen, the larder, the boulting house, the entry between the kitchen and the hall (the screens passage); three little houses adjoining the said entry, the steward's buttery, the Vergys house with lofts, chambers and lodges over them." The "Kill House" and a house late part of the malt

Plate 20: Leighton Buzzard: The Prebendal House and outbuildings from the south. (*Oil painting: —. Orme, 1797*)

146

house adjoined. There was a little court near the churchyard and the great garden significantly commonly called, the "New Garden".[2]

A dispute in 1620[3] indicates that the house had become decayed but by 1647, after repair and/or a partial rebuild, it could be described as "all that faire Prebend House in Leighton built partlie of stone, partly Brick and partlie Tymber being in very good repaire. Consisting of a Hall Parlour with Drawing Room, Kitchen, Pantrey, Brewhouse, Wash house and Two Cellars, and Porters Lodge, nyne lodging chambers with Six Closetts with one garrett and gallery".[4] There is a garden adjoining on the south wall. What is described is a typical seventeenth century house or earlier.

At the Sir John Soane's Museum is a list entitled "A short Account of Mr. James Gibbs, Architect And of Several things he built in England & After his return from Italy".[5] It records that Gibbs "built the House of the Honourable Charles Leigh in Bedfordshire; a very convenient building". Unfortunately, the author gives no date for this building and no accounts seem to have survived.

At least the document itself can be dated to 1709 or after, when Gibbs returned from Italy. The attribution to Gibbs[6] is at least a possible one, as the Ashmolean Museum holds a plan of a temple identical to the surviving Temple of Diana, that formed part of the estate.

Charles Leigh (1685–1749) second surviving son of Thomas Leigh of Stoneleigh, inherited the Prebendal estate from his uncle Charles in 1704. The younger Charles Leigh was a judge and in later life famed for his entertaining.[7] The site of the house in 1806 was partly on freehold and partly on leasehold. It is likely that the older part of the house was on the leased land, which lay on the east side of the site. This is confirmed by the references in the 1749 inventory to 'old' rooms all being in the east part of the house.

It would appear that Gibbs did not rebuild the house completely but enlarged and encased an earlier house. So skilfully was this masking done that it is impossible from the two surviving views of the exterior[8]to detect that this has happened.

The view of the north front shows a house on four floors, submerged basement, ground floor, first floor and attic. The house is divided into three bays, two wings with four windows each on the principal floors flanking a central bay with two windows and an entrance door on the ground floor and three windows above. This central bay is pedimented and slightly projecting. The roof of the entrance porch is supported by Ionic columns. The windows of the two principal floors are emphasised by lintels above and pronounced window sills below. The heads of the seven attic windows are alternately triangular and convex. There are three chimneys visible.

The southern or garden front was illustrated by Orme in 1797. Two projecting wings of two windows on the principal floors separate a central section of seven windows with the centre window accentuated by columns on either side. Drainpipes on either side of the middle three windows deliberately underline their importance.

Behind these windows was the saloon, used as a dining room. It was probably two storeys high. When her daughter took up the sub-lease of the house in 1779, Jemima Marchioness Grey recalled that she had been entertained there, probably in the 1740s, . She wrote, "I remember once to have dined at the House, an Age ago, with his Honour Leigh . . . of Famous Convivial Memory . . . & to have seen a very large Dining Room, which whatever related to good living, he was likely to have in perfection."[9]

This formed the principal room in Gibbs extension of the house to the west. Facing west was the new best drawing room which led off the saloon, forming a formal progression of rooms from the hall through the old drawing room through the saloon to the new drawing room.

The hall probably formed part of the extension, and the old hall of the pre-Gibbs house would then have been in the east part of the house, facing west with the kitchens looking out to Leighton Buzzard Church. Upstairs the new extensions provided at least two large bedrooms, the best chamber and the "Chamber over the New Drawing Room". The "Chamber over the Hall" and the "Bedroom over the Old Parlour" with "His Honour's Dressing Room" were all newly built or extensively re-modelled at this time.

To conclude, Gibbs appears to have extended an existing house to the west to provide formal rooms for entertaining on the ground floor and more extensive bedroom accommodation upstairs. He seems to have changed the axis of the house from east facing to south facing. Gibbs produced a restrained yet effective early eighteenth-century house in his later less Baroque style consistent with a date c.1730–1749.[10]

The 1749 Inventory

The 1749 inventory of the Prebendal House lists both room names and the value of the contents of each room. Comparison between the inventories of 1749 and 1774[11] and an undated but definitely eighteenth-century *Refferences to Plans of the First Floor & Atticks*[12] gives an indication of where rooms were located. Sadly the plans have not survived. While the tie-up is not exact, and a number of rooms on the *Refferences* must subsequently have become dressing rooms, a reasonably complete picture emerges.

On the ground floor the hall was in 1749 in the centre of the north front with a front door and a window flanking either side. Immediately to the east of the hall lay the old parlour with two windows. Behind it lay a passage and across it in the south-east part of the house lay the old drawing room. In the centre of the south facade was the saloon, probably two storeyed and definitely the most important room in the house. There was probably a central passage that separated it from the hall with the main staircase, made of mahogany somewhere in this area. In the south-west and west parts of the house lay the best drawing room. The western half of the north front was completed by the steward's parlour and room.

The eastern part of the house, as usual, contained the services side, including housekeeper's room, servants' hall, kitchen and butler's pantry (in the north-east corner, probably). In the north-east part of the house was the old or east stairs. In the courtyard were a number of other service buildings such as the laundry, brewhouse, coach house and old stables.

On the first floor above the pantry, at the top of the old stairs, was the green room (north-east corner bedroom) and dressing room, (possibly the east room in the *Refferences*). Between the last mentioned room and the room over the hall were the room over the old parlour and Charles Leigh's dressing room. The bedroom was the single most valuable room in the house and was almost certainly Charles Leigh's own. The room over the hall had only two window curtains while the hall occupied the equivalent of three windows. It is probable that the western two windows of the room over the hall were indeed above the hall, while the east window had the old parlour beneath it. On the western side of the room over the hall was probably the best chamber with the dressing room. In the *Refferences* there were three bedrooms in the west part of the house. These have not been able to be positively identified. Two of them at least must be the room over the best drawing room and its attendant dressing room. In the south-east corner of the house was the bedroom over the old drawing room, incorrectly marked in the inventory as dining room. Unusually, it had no dressing room attached. The area behind the backstairs in the inventory is difficult to tally with the *Refferences*. It could of course be the east bedroom but it could be just one part of the gallery that went down the centre of the house and connected up the two staircases. As I have suggested, a more probable use of the east bedroom is as either the green room or its dressing room. The *Refferences* state that there were seven closets on this floor. The sites of most of them are unknown.

The nearby east stairs led up to the attic floor of ten or eleven rooms. These were principally used for housing the servants but did include the steward. The housekeeper, butler, cook and two maids were accommodated there, as well as a large linen garret or store. Unspecified rooms included a Venetian garret and a green garret (probably directly above the green room on the first floor, as both were near to the east stairs). The footmen were banished to rooms over the old stables, no doubt to keep them as far away from the maids as possible!

The Prebendal House was probably refitted with furniture after the extensions attributed to Gibbs. No doubt some older pieces survived from the older, smaller house, such as the number of wainscot or oak pieces scattered over the house. The furniture dates from the transitional phase of the replacement of walnut by mahogany as the wood used for most pieces in the principal rooms of country houses. On the first floor there were few mahogany pieces: a mahogany claw table in the room over the hall and a dressing glass in a mahogany frame in the best chamber. "His Honour's Dressing Room" had no mahogany but included "a Black Cabinet and Stand" (probably japanned), a small walnut cabinet, a square table and a claw one, both wainscot, four gilt cane chairs and a large oak chest.

The best chamber showed a similar predominance of walnut and oak. Like many of the beds in the house, that in the best chamber was made out of walnut. It was accompanied by six walnut chairs; the dressing table was wainscot.

On the ground floor there were great contrasts, from the old drawing room being entirely furnished in walnut to the saloon next door being entirely furnished in mahogany, as was the hall. A more obviously transitional room was the old parlour where there were fourteen walnut chairs with two leather seats round a mahogany table. There was also a marble top sideboard.

The value given to the contents shows the importance of the room. Three rooms were valued at between £45 and £50. These were the best chamber and room over the old parlour on the north front of the first floor and the saloon on the ground floor of the south front. The contents of the kitchen were valued at £36. The best drawing room had the curiously low figure of £27. The only seating was provided by a settee. Did the footmen bring in chairs from different rooms when it was being used or had some furniture already been removed before the inventory was made?

Dwarfing the totals of individual rooms was that for the extensive china owned by Charles Leigh. This was valued at £67. For its date, 1749, it represents a fine collection. The blue and white and enamelled china mentioned in the inventory are almost certainly export ware direct from China. Although the trade was flourishing from the 1720s and 1730s, Charles Leigh had by contemporary standards a considerable collection with individual pieces of high quality, such as a "very fine scollop't bowl" and "Four Dozen of Good Plates with a crest".

The "Two Red Tea Pots with silver chains" were made of redware. Redware tea pots with chains were made at Burslem, Staffordshire, as early as 1690 by the Elers brothers.[13] They continued to be produced alongside the local Staffordshire pottery. The Staffordshire tea pot could have been of a number of sizes and designs, such was the versatility of their products in the 1740s.

On Leigh's death all his plate was brought from his houses at Brook

Street, London, Hoddesdon in Hertfordshire, and the Prebendal House. Although we can not now be sure which pieces came from which house, the list is certainly impressive. The gold teapot, cannister and cream pot with the gold cups and spoons, would have been eyecatching for Leigh's numerous guests. The number of gilt pieces would have reinforced this picture of opulence. Silver was used for conventional uses such as spoons and salts but also for more unusual ones such as a chafing dish, a warming pan and five chamber pots! Unfortunately, the items on this inventory were not priced, so we have no idea of the value of the silver in relation to the china.

One further inventory was made: of the pictures at the Prebendal House. Unfortunately, this is not priced, but from the descriptions of the individual pictures this formed a valuable collection, too. Only one of the artists is identified but he is an important one, Van Dyck. Is it a genuine attribution? Certainly Van Dyck painted portraits which included spaniels. His portrait of the children of Charles I, commissioned by Henrietta Maria for her sister, the Duchess of Savoy, includes a large red-brown spaniel. This picture was unlikely to have been extensively copied in England, as it was immediately despatched to Turin on completion. His portrait of the five elder children also includes a brown and white King Charles spaniel. Centre stage is a large mastiff, being patted by the future Charles II. Interestingly, on this inventory after Van Dyck's spaniel is a picture of a Dutch mastiff dog. Perhaps Leigh had two Van Dycks.[14]

As one would expect the collection contains a good number of portraits. The largest group of these are the family ones, including Sir Christopher Hoddesdon (d.1610), father of Ursula, wife of John Leigh, and hence ancestor of the Leighs of Stoneleigh and Leighton Buzzard. Christopher Hoddesdon first held the lease of the Prebendal Estate in 1584. Inevitably, there are portraits of Charles and Barbara Leigh and other members of the Leigh family. The Leighs were related to the Egertons and the Wentworths. So, in the collection are portraits of Thomas Egerton, (Lord Chancellor 1603–1617), Lord Strafford, (Charles I's unfortunate Lord Lieutenant of Ireland) and Lady Rockingham, feeding a lamb. The latter picture may well be an early example of the pastoral idyll that so captured the imaginations of French and British aristocracy, say, twenty years later, when to be a shepherdess was considered the height of bliss. Alternatively, Lady Rockingham may have had a pet lamb in the way that Jemima, Marchioness Grey, had a pet fawn at Wrest in the 1740s.[15]

Another group in the portraits are those of important political figures. Charles I heads the list with two portraits, appropriately, as the then head of the Leigh family, Sir Thomas Leigh, was a staunch Royalist. Two portraits are consistent with Charles Leigh's track record as a Tory MP who voted with the Whigs. *The Seven Bishops* shows his support for the Church of England's opposition to James II. His Toryism did not extend to Jacobitism. *The Elector of Hanover* was clearly purchased before George I came to the throne in 1714. He wished to make a political statement for the Protestant succession.

Charles Leigh's will[16] shows that he was a charitable man leaving money for setting up almshouses in Leighton Buzzard. He also endowed the chapel at Hoddesdon, which he had lately purchased. A number of his pictures reflect his religious interests. Apart from a picture of the Virgin and Child and another of the Holy Family, he liked a good story line to his religious painting: *The Tower of Babel, Moses in the Bulrushes* and *the Prodigal Son*. His pictures of *Bathsheba Bathing* and *Susannah and the Elders* no doubt appealed to secular tastes as well as religious. They could be compared with *Venus and her Attendants* in the parlour.

Charles Leigh evidently had a great love of the classics, nurtured by a Grand Tour visiting Rome and Venice. A number of his pictures refer to classical legends such as *Eneas carrying his father Anchises from the Flames of Troy*. Along with the legends, he purchased views of classical sites: *A Bridge over the River Tyber broken down* and *A Roman Amphitheatre*. A view of ruins shows the eighteenth-century passion for ruins, bred no doubt by what they saw on important Italian sites such as the Forum in Rome. Leigh bought four views each of Rome and Venice in addition to portraits of Pope Clement XI (Pope 1700–1721) and Signor Ficcorony, whom he must have met on his travels. Leigh had a few Dutch pieces including no doubt "three flower peices over the Stairs".

Prebendal House 1749–1774

Charles Leigh's widow Barbara continued to live in the house till her death in 1755. The estate should have passed to Charles's nephew Sir Thomas Leigh, 4th Baron, but he had died earlier in 1749. His son and heir was Edward Leigh (1742–1786), 5th Baron Leigh, and he inherited the Prebendal House as well. An attempt was made to lease the property in 1766 after repair work was done in the house by William White[17]. Whether this was successful or not is not clear but certainly the estate was still being run by John Franklin, the Leighs' bailiff, for whom correspondence from 1766 to 1769 survives.[18]

The 1774 Inventory

An inventory was taken in 1774[19] at the Prebendal House when Edward Leigh, 5th Lord Leigh, was declared a lunatic. Unlike the 1749 inventory, it is unpriced and the rooms are mostly referred to by number rather than name. However, a comparison of the rooms indicates that enough fittings correspond in the two inventories to be able to work out the room uses of the 1774 inventory. In the following list the room name indicates its 1749 use while the number indicates its place on the 1774 inventory. On the ground floor was the hall (1774: No.29), the old parlour (22), old drawing room (24), saloon (25), best drawing room (26), steward's parlour (27) and stewards room (28). The service wing, as before, lay on the east side of the house.

On the first floor over the hall was room 20 in 1774, room over the old parlour (13), His Honour's dressing room (part of 13), the green room and dressing room (22), room over the old drawing room (18) and room over the best drawing room (15). Somewhere in the west part of the house in 1774 was room 19. Its exact location cannot be determined but probably was a conversion of a dressing room. It could well be the bedroom G in the *Refferences*. On the north front lay the best chamber (21) and dressing room/closet.

Even some of the attic rooms can be identified: No.1 garret in 1774 was the green garret in 1749, the maids' garret in 1749 was probably No.2, Venetian garret (No.3), housekeeper's room (No.4). Then there was a passage mentioned in 1774. The cook's room was No.7, the cook's little room (No.8), steward's room (No.1). The additional rooms not identified possibly stood on the site of the great linen garret, so full in 1749 and dismantled by 1774.

As one would expect of a house rarely lived in by the owner since 1749, and probably mostly let to tenants, the furniture did not change greatly between 1749 and 1774. Much of the furniture remained in place with only a very few additions such as the pair of candlebranches in the best chamber and "Bustos" in the hall. The inventories show a remarkable uniformity, consistent with a house downgraded in importance and in slight decline. Even many of the curtains were still the same. The best chamber, for example, had crimson silk and worsted furnishings in both 1749 and 1774. The 1749 one tells us that the bedstead is made of walnut. In garret 7 three very old blankets seem to have survived from the 1749 inventory of the butler's pantry.

The pictures seem all to have remained in the house from 1749, although, as they are not identified, it is hard to be sure that the odd picture has not gone to Stoneleigh, London or the salerooms. The china and plate however seem to have entirely disappeared. Like the large linen garret there was no need to keep them in the house just for tenants and they would have gone straight to Stoneleigh or Leigh's London house.

Prebendal House 1774–1817

The Leighs continued to hold the lease of Prebendal House but did not actually live there, letting the house to tenants. The most prominent of these were Lord and Lady Polwarth, who lived there for a few months in 1779. In a letter of 21 March 1779[20] to her sister, Lady Polwarth wrote comparing the Prebendal House with her family home of Wrest Park: "I did believe that this house at Leighton was the very house where his Honour Lee used to invite the stage-coach company . . . It has a dining room big enough to dine half a dozen stage-coaches & drawing room scarce large enough for one, but hung with blue damask, not v. old & looking tolerably neat, spare bedchambers scanty in furniture, Offices good, Road to it from Woburn through sandy country, house stands v.little lower than the the village, at much the same distance from a meadow watered by running streams, as we are from the canal, but is much more raised above the level of the water than this house, all arched underneath; cellars seem dryer than usual!!"

By 1806 the Leigh estate was clearly trying to give up the lease of the Prebendal House. As a result, Christopher Hodgson, acting for the Prebend, commissioned the famous architect James Wyatt to survey the property for dilapidations. The house contained: "A Hall, Saloon, Dining, Breakfast, Drawing & Dressing Rooms, Steward, Housekeeper and Butler's Rooms, eight bed chambers, with Garrets over the whole, Kitchen, Servants Hall, Dairy & Cellars in the Basement Story. The outbuildings included the Brewhouse and Shrubbery, gardens & pleasure grounds added to the house, making a total of three and half acres. The tenant was John Dickinson and the House is in the most perfect order and neatness that I ever saw in a rented house."[21]

Despite this, in 1807 there was an acrimonious exchange of letters between Christopher Hodgson and the Leighs' solicitor over dilapidations and the liability of the Leigh estate to repair all the buildings.[22] The Prebend obtained possession in November 1806 by getting Mr. Dickenson to give up his tenancy "and allow tenant & pay Rent to him for the Prebendal Mansion". This legal dodge put the Prebend in a position to pursue the Leigh estate over the dilapidations issue. Unfortunately, the letters give no clue as to how the wrangle ended. Dickenson is listed in the land tax record up to and including 1809.[23] The "Mansion House Garden" is marked on Bevan's map of Leighton Buzzard of 1817, but *without* the house.[24] It is therefore likely the house was demolished between 1809 and 1817. Parts of the garden buildings including the Temple of Diana were later incorporated into the gardens of the Cedars School. Part of the site of the house is incorporated into the churchyard of All Saints, Leighton Buzzard.[25]

PREBENDAL HOUSE, LEIGHTON BUZZARD 1749

An Inventory of the Goods and Chattells of the late Honourable Charles Leigh Standing and being at his Seat and Manor House at Leighton in the County of Bedford as follows:

No.1 Green Garrett: A Stove Grate, Fire Shovel, Tongs, Poker, Fender, Bellows and Brush, A large Glass over the Chimney, A Bedstead with Green Camblet Furniture, One Bolster, Two Pillows,

Three Blankets, One Quilt, One Close Stool and Pewter Pan, Six black Chairs with Red Bottoms, A Cane Chair and Cushion, Two Round Stools, One Square Oak Table.   £7 10s.

No.2 In the Maids Garrett: Two Bedsteads with Blue China Furniture, Two Feather beds, Three Pillows, Two Bolsters, Six Blanketts, Two Quilts, One Square Table, One round Ditto, One Cane Chair, One Stool, A Small Glass, An Oak press with shelves.   £6 9s.

No.3 In the Venetian Garrett: A Bedstead with Work'd Furniture, One Feather Bed, One Bolster, Two Pillows, One Mattress, Three Blankets, One Quilt, Two Tables, One Glass, Three Black Chairs and one Gouty Ditto.   £6 5s.

No. 4 The Housekeeper's Room: A Bedstead with Yellow Furniture,a Feather Bed, One Bolster, One Pillow, Three Blanketts, One Quilt, a Fire Shovel, Tongs, A pair of Dogs and Fender, A Low Chest of Drawers, One Small Glass, A Stand, Two Matted Chairs, One Stool Ditto.   £4 14s.

No.5 In the Cook's Room: A Bedstead with Blue China Furniture, Two Feather Beds, One Bolster, Two Pillows, Three Blankets, One Quilt, A pair of Dogs, A Table, A Dressing Glass, Three Chairs.
                                                        £6 1s.

No.6 In the Cook's little Room: A Bedstead and Curtains, Two Feather beds, One Bolster, One pillow, Two Blanketts, A pair of Dogs, A Table, Three Cane Chairs, Two matted Ditto.   £3 2s 6d.

No.7 In the Blue Garrett: A Bedstead with Blue Camblet Furniture, One Feather bed, One Bolster, Two Pillows, Four Blankets, One Quilt, Two Tables, One Swinging Glass, One Close Stool with pewter pann, Two Cane Chairs, Two matted Ditto and One Bason Stand. £6 4s 6d.

No.8 In the Butler's Room: A Bedstead with Blue Furniture, One Feather Bed, One Bolster, One pillow, Three Blanketts, One Quilt, One Table, Two Chairs, One Stool.   £2 4s.

No.9 Stewards Room: A Bedstead and Furniture, One Feather bed, One Bolster, One Pillow, Five Blankets, One Quilt, A Stove Grate with Fire Shovel, Tongs, Poker and Fender, Three Tables, Five Cane Chairs, Two matted Ditto, One Stand, Two Bell Lights, One Oak Cloaths press, Two Cane Couches, One Squab.   £5 9s 6d.

No.10 Linnen Garrett: Two pair of Fine Holland Sheets, Five pair of Coarser and one odd Ditto, Two pair of new Holland Sheets, Four pair of Old Ditto, Three pair of new Osnaburgh Ditto and Eleven pair of Old Flaxen, Twenty pair of Servants Sheets, One odd Ditto and Six pair of Hempen, Three plain Callico Sheets and One Ditto Laced, Six pair of new Holland pillowbiers, Six pair of Old Ditto, One large Damask Table Cloth, One Small Ditto and Twelve Napkins, Four Spotted Diaper Table Cloths and two Dozen of Napkins, Five Leaf Damask Table Cloths, Three Dozen Napkins, One Damask Table Cloth and Six Napkins, One Damask Table Cloth and Twelve Napkins, Eleven

Damask Napkins, Two Dozen of Tea Ditto, Three Damask Table Cloths and Seventeen Napkins, Eight old Damask Table Cloths and Seven Dozen Napkins, Four Diaper Table Cloths and Three dozen and Ten Napkins, Four Spotted Diaper Table Cloths And Six Dozen Napkins, Five Diaper Table Cloths and four dozen Napkins, six new Diaper Table Cloths, four dozen diaper Napkins, Seven dozen and six Coarser Ditto of several Sorts, Nineteen Table Cloths of several Sorts, Six Huckaback Table Cloths, Three dozen of Damask Toweles, Three dozen of Diaper ditto, One Counterpane work'd, Two muslin Toileties, Five Dresser Cloths, Twelve Round Toweles, Four Servants Table Cloths and Eighteen Doyleys, One deal press, Three Boxes, Two Trunks and a pair of Dogs in the Chimney. £95 19s 6d.

No.1 One pair of Stairs: The Green Room and Dressing Room: A Bedstead with Green Camblet Furniture, One Feather bed, One Bolster, One Pillow, One Mattress, Four Blankets, One Quilt, One Counterpane, Four pair of Window Curtains and Rods, One Stove Grate and Fire shovel, Poker, Tongs, Bellows, One Iron Fender, One Tin Ditto, A Low Chest of Drawers, Two Dressing Tables, A Swinging Glass, Two Pier Glasses, Three Slip Sconces, One pair of Glass Arms, A Corner Cupboard, One Standard Ditto, An Easy Chair, Six Cane Chairs, Two Round Stools, One Square matted Ditto, One Round Close Stool and Earthen Pan. £20 11s 6d.

No.2 Over the Old Parlour: A Walnutt tree Bedstead with Crimson mix't Damask Furniture, A Counterpan Ditto, Two pair of Window Curtains Ditto with Pulleys, Rods and Lines, One Feather Bed and Bolster, Two Down pillows, One White Mattrass, One Check'd Ditto, Three Blankets, One White Quilt, One Dressing Table, One Glass Ditto, One Pier Glass, One India Cabinett and Frame, Six Chairs, One Elbow Ditto And Two Stools Covered with Crimson Damask and Check Cases, A Steel Stove with Shovel, Tongs, Poker, Fender and Brush, A Pair of Gilt Arms, A Close Stool and White Pan and a Claw Table. £49 11s 6d.

No.3 Over the Old Dining Room: A Bedstead with Blue Camblet Furniture, One Counterpane Ditto, Two pair of Window Curtains and Rods, One Feather Bed, One Bolster, Two Pillows, Two White Matresses, Five Blankets, One White Quilt, One Stove, Fire Shovel, Tongs, Poker, Fender and Bellows, A pair of brass Arms, A Chest with one Draw and Frame, One Wainscot Dressing Table, A Swing Glass, Two Stands, A Large Pier Glass in Black Frame, A Close Stool Chair and White Pann, Four matted Chairs, One Stool. £13 9s 6d.

No.4 Over the Best Drawing Room: One Bedstead with Blue Camblett Furniture, One Counterpane Ditto, Two pair of Window Curtains Ditto, One Feather Bed, Two Bolsters and Two Pillows, One White Matress, One Check Ditto, Three Blankets, One White Quilt, Iron Hearth and Brass Fender, Shovel and Tongs Ditto, A Small Stove

Grate, poker, A pair of small Dogs, A pair of Arms Brass, A Dressing Table, A pier Glass, Nine Walnutt Tree Chairs with Blue Camblet Seats, An old Easy Chair, A Close Stool and Earthen Pan, A Japan'd Box with four Small ones in it with Fish and Counters, A Fire Screen. **In the Dressing Room:** A Table, Bedstead, A Feather Bed, One Bolster, Three Blankets, One Quilt, One pair of Blue Window Curtains, One Wainscott Square Table, A Small India Cabinett and Frame, a Glass in a Black Frame, A Chimney Glass, a Stove Grate, Shovel, Tongs, Poker, Fender, Bellows and Brush. £19 14s.

No.5 His Honour's Dressing Room: A Stove Grate and Fender, Shovel, Tongs and Bellows, A Buroe, A Glass over it, A Black Cabinet and Stand, A Small Walnut Tree Cabinett, A Dressing Box, A Square Wainscot Table, One Claw Ditto, One Spring Clock, Four Gilt Cane Chairs, Two Elbow Ditto, A large Oak Chest, Two Deal Boxes, One Trunk, Four Festoon Curtains, One Pair of Double Barrell'd Pistols, mounted with Silver, One pair of Single Barrell'd Ditto, One pair of Double Barrell'd Steel mounted, Two pair of Single Barrell'd Ditto, Two pair Ditto Brass mounted. £21 8s

No.6 Behind the Back Stairs: A Small Stove, Shovel, Tongs, Poker, Fender Iron, One Tin Ditto, A Brush, A pair of Black Arms,One Round Table Ditto, A Walnutt Chest of Drawers, An Oak Table, One Chimney Glass, A pair of Window Curtains, Vallens and Rod, Three Matted Chairs, One Cane Stool. £3 17s

No.7 Over the Hall: A Bedstead with Wrought Furniture, A Feather Bed, One Bolster and Two Pillows, A White Mattress and One Check Ditto, Three Blankets and Two White Quilts, A Fire Shovel, Tongs, Poker and Fender, One Tinn Ditto, A pair of Bellows and Brush, Two Slip Sconces, A Walnutt tree Chest of Drawers and one Buroe, A Wainscot Dressing Table with one Silk and One Muslin Toilette, A Dressing Glass in Walnutt tree Frame, A pier glass in a black Frame, Two pair of Window Curtains, Valens and Rods, A Settee Bedstead Cover'd with Blue Camblett, One Feather bed, Two Blankets and One Quilt to Ditto, A Mahogany Claw Table, One Old Square Table, A Close Stool Chair and White Pann, An Arm'd Chair Cover'd with Blue Camblett and Cushion Ditto, Five Matted Chairs and one Stool, One Small Turkey Carpet. £19.

No.8 Best Chamber: A Walnutt Tree Bedstead with Crimson Mix't Damask Furniture, A Counterpane Ditto, Two Pair of Ditto Window Curtains with Pulley, Rods and Lines, One Feather Bed and Bolster, Two Down pillows, One White Mattress, One Check Ditto, Four Blankets, One White Quilt, A Steel Stove, Shovel, Tongs, poker, Fender and Brush, A pair of Gilt Arms, A Wainscot Dressing Table and Silk Toilette, A Dressing Glass in Mahogany Frame, A pier Glass with Tabernacle Frame, Six Walnutt tree Chairs Cover'd with Crimson Mix't Damask and Check'd Cases, Two Stools Ditto, A Close Stool &

White Pan. **In Dressing Room:** A Small Stove Grate, A Chimney Glass in Black Frame, A pair of India Silk Window Curtains, Rods and Lines, A Walnutt Tree Dressing Table with Drawers and Two Black Stands. £47 11s 6d.

No.9 Gallery: Three pair of Old Glass Sconces, One Pair of Glass Arms and Bell. 10s.

No.1 On the Ground Floor The Old Parlour: A large Stove Grate with Fender, Shovel, Tongs, Poker, Bellows and Brush, A pair of Brass Arms with Bells over them, A Mahogany Table, One Box Table, a Tea Chest Ditto, A Sconce in painted Frame, Two pair of Scarlet Window Curtains and Rods, Twelve Walnutt tree Chairs with Leather Seats, Two Elbow Ditto, A Two Leaved Fire Screen, A Marble Sideboard, A Japann'd Copper Cistern, A Mahogany Dumb Waiter, A Weather Glass, Two Black Stands, A large Matt for the Floor, A Tea Table and Brass Arm in the passage. £16 1s.

No.2 Old Drawing Room: A Stove Grate, Shovel, Tongs, poker and Brush, a Fender, A Chimney Glass in black Frame, One Ditto in the pier, A Walnutt tree Card Table, Two pair of Crimson Silk Window Curtains, Eight Walnutt tree Chairs with Strip'd Velvet Seats, One Arm'd Chair Covered with Blue flower'd Velvet, An old persian Carpet. £13 2s.

No.3 In the Saloon: A Stove Grate, Shovel, Tongs, poker and Brush and Fender, Three Gilt cups, one Cover, a Four Leav'd Gilt Leather Screen, A Mahogany Dining Table, One Claw Ditto,Two Bottle Boards, A Mahogany Cistern, A Higmegrig, A Large Marble Slab and Frame, Three Marble Blocks, One Chandelier, Silk Line and Ballance, Twelve Mahogany Chairs with Laced Seats, Two Smoking Chairs Ditto, One Arm'd Chair Covered with Buff Coloured Velvet, An old Turkey Carpet. £48 18s 6d.

No.4 In the best Drawing Room: A Steel Hearth, a pair of Dogs, Shovel, Tongs, Fender, Bellows and Brush, Two Spring Curtains, Two Green Silk Damask Festoon Curtains, A Marble Slab and Frame, A Sconce and painted Frame, A Mahogany Settee Cover'd with Green Silk Damask and a Squab Ditto, Eight Mahogany Chairs Cover'd with Green Silk Damask and Check Covers to them all, A Small Needle Work't Carpet, A Tea Table and Brass Arm in the Passage. £27.

No.5 Steward's Parlour: A pair of Dogs, Barr, Shovel, Tongs, Fender and Brush, Two Oak Oval Tables, One Square Ditto, Twelve Cane Chairs, Two Arm'd Ditto and Cushions, A Sconce in a Glass Frame, An Iron Plate Warmer, Seven Guns, two pair of Horse pistols and one Steel Bow. £3 5s 6d.

No.6 In the Steward's Room: A pair of Dogs, A Fender, Shovel, Tongs, Bellows and Brush, A Looking Glass, An oval Table, Two Chairs, A Small pair of Steps. 19s.

No.7 Hall and Passage: A large Grate and Fender, Shovel, Tongs and

Poker, Eighteen Mahogany Chairs, a large Square Table Ditto, Six Bell Lights & Sheds & Three Gilt Images.   £11 5s 0d.

No.8 Housekeeper's Room and Closett: A copper Lymbeck fix't, One Jelly pot, Two preserving pans, One Chocolate pot, One Coffee pot, Two large Tea Kettles, One Dutch Kettle and Lamp, A Coffee Mill, A Bell Metal Mortar and Two Iron pestles, Four Hair Scives, One Trevatt, A pair of Stake Tongs, A Shovel, An Iron Harth, A pair of Doggs, A Barr, A Shovel, Tongs, Bellows and Brush, A large Oak Dining Table, One Small Claw Ditto, A Mahogany Breakfast Board, A Looking Glass in black Frame, A Small Tea Table, Six Matted Bottom Chairs, Three pair of Short Window Curtains and rods, A pair of Brass Scales & Set of Brass Weights, Two Presses, Tin and Earthen Ware.   £5 16s 6d.

China:
Two large Blue and White Flower pots, One large Japann'd Jarr, One Small Blue & White Ditto, One Ditto & Cover with a Silver Cock, Twenty Enamell'd Dishes of Severall sorts and Sizes, Twelve Fine Enamell'd plates, Twelve Smaller Ditto, Seven Green Ditto, Two Scollop'd Ditto, Four fruit Ditto, one of them broke, Six Soop Ditto, Six Breakfast plates, One Scollop Ditto, Two Scollop't Bowls, One very fine Ditto, Four half pint Basons, Eight Blue and White Dishes of several Sizes, Two dozen of Meat Plates Ditto, Eleven Soop Ditto, Two Small Bowls, Two pint Basons, Two half pint Ditto, Six Chocolate Cups Enamell'd, Eight Coffee Cups Ditto, Two Red Tea Pots with Silver Chains, Three Blue and White Tea pots, One Red Ditto with Metal Handle, Six Custard Cups, Eight Saucers, Two large ditto, Two Blue and White Beakers, One large Bottle, One Mug and Cover, Twenty one odd Cups, Three Ribb'd Enamelled Saucers, Two Small Sugar dishes, Three White Cups And One Cover, Six Blue and White Cups, Three Saucers, One Spoon Boat.

On the Table next the old Parlour: Seven Blue & White Cups & Eight Saucers, Two Sugar dishes, One Slop Bason, One Boat, A large Saucer & Staffordshire Tea Pott.

On the Table in the Passage next the best Drawing Room: Eight Enamell'd Tea Cups, Ten Saucers Ditto, One Tea Pott, One Sugar Pott and Cover and Two Stands, A large Slop Bason, One Boat for Spoons.

In the Drawing Room over the Chimney: Two Enamell'd Jarrs and Covers, Two Blue & White Tankards, Two Birds and Stands, Two fine Enamell'd Bottles, Two Small Flower potts Ditto, A Handle Jugg and Cover, Three very small Blue & White Beakers, A parcell of Flint Glass of several Sorts.   £64 13s 6d.

No.9 Butler's Pantry: One long Table, One Square Ditto, A Napkin Press, A Higmegrig, A Copper Japan Cistern, Two Chairs, Two Stools, Two Knife Trays, A Glass Ditto, A pail, A parcel of White Flint Glass, Nine Quart and Six Pint Decanters, Fourteen Water Glasses and Two Dozen Saucers, Eighteen Wine and Water Glasses, Six Small Beer

Glasses, Six large Rummer Glasses, Six Champain Glasses, About Thirty Wine Glasses.   £3 12s 6d.

In the Kitchen: A large Range Compleat, An Ash Grate, A Crane and Three Hooks, A Smoak Jack Compleat, Two large Spit racks, One pair of Small Ditto, One Shovel, two pair of Tongs, A Fender, poker, Bellows, A Sallamander, Four lark Spits, Twelve Scewers, Two Beef forms, A Grid Iron, A Trevet, A pair of Stillards and Weights, Eleven large Spits, Three pair of pot hooks, A Dish Ring, A large Beam and pair of Wooden Scales, Three Bloom ½ hundred Weights, One odd Weight Ditto, Three Quarter Hundreds Lead Weights, One 14 pound, Two 7 Pound and five others amounting to £15. One Two pound and one pound Brass Weight, Five Stove Trevetts, Five flat Candlesticks, One Frying pan Copper & Brass, A Boyler with Two Brass Cocks Ironwork and Lead as fixed, Five Boyling pots and Covers made upright, Two other large potts with Necks and Lids, One large Boyler and Lid, a large Fish Kettle Plate and Lid, A large Gravy Pan and Cover, One Dish Kettle, One Dripping Pan, Thirteen Stew pans of several sorts and Sizes with Six Covers, A large Stewing Saucepan and Cover, Eleven Saucepans of different Sizes and Two Covers, One large Tea Kettle, Three Baking Pans with loose Bottoms, Thirty one Patty pans, One Melon Pudding Case, Two Warming Pans, Two Coal Trays, Two pails, Two Ladles, Two Scummers, Four flatt Candlesticks, Six High Ditto, A pair of Snuffers & Stand, A Drudger, a paper Box, A Skillet, A Bell Metal Pot, A Hand Dinner Bell, Thirty Eight pewter Dishes, One Fish Dish and plate, One old Dish, Four Cheese plates, three Salvers, One Cullinder, One hand Bason, Twelve Soop plates, Four dozen of Good Plates with a Crest, Three Dozen and Three Old Plates, One Fire Screen Tinn'd. One long Deal Table, One Oak Square Ditto, One Small Flat Ditto, A Chopping Block & Cleaver, A Marble Mortar and Wood Pestle, A Powdering Tub, Two Chairs, Six Stools, A Small pair of Steps, A Salt Box, A pepper Mill, A Brass Hog Pail, A Water pail, Tinn and Earthen Ware.   £36 8s.

Servants Hall: a Small Range and Fender, One long Table, Two long Forms, Two Leather Jacks, One Copper, Drinking Pots, A Clock & Two lights on the Stairs.   £4 14s.

Cellars:

Small Beer Cellar: Two Pipes Iron Bound, Two Butts and Thirteen Hogsheads Ditto, Eight Wine Hogsheads, Eight other vessels of different Sizes, Eight Stands and Two Brass Cocks.

In Dairy: A Table, a Brass Pan, A Cheese press, An Earthen Jurn and Panns.

In the old Cellar: Three Candle Chests About 15 dozen of Candles and Seventy Dozen of Glass Bottles.

In One Ale Cellar: Eleven Hogsheads Iron Bound, One Old Hogshead and Screw Hoop, Four Stands, Five Brass Cocks;

In the Other Ale Cellar: Fourteen Hogsheads Iron Bound, Four old Hogsheads, One half Hogshead Ditto and Two Small Casks, Six Stands and Two Brass Cocks. £38 7s.

In the Three Rooms over the Old Stables:

In the Wool Room: A Corded Bedstead with Blue Furniture, One Feather bed, Two Bolsters, Three Blankets, One Coverled, One Table Bedstead and Three Chairs.

In the footmen's Room: A Bedstead and Green Curtains, Two Feather beds, One Bolster, One Pillow, Three Blankets, One Coverled, One Square Table, Three Cane Chairs, One Wood Ditto and a Stool.

In the Game Keepers Room: A Corded Bedstead with Green Curtains, One Feather bed, One Bolster, Four Blankets, One Rugg, One table and a Chair.£5 15s.

The Coachman's Room: Two Corded Bedsteads and some Curtains, Two Feather beds, Two Bolsters, Five Blankets, A Cloaths Press, A Table, a Chair and Stool. £1 18s.

In New Building:

In the Room over the Coal Hole: One Bedstead and Bays Curtains, An old Press, A pair of Stepps, One Feather bed, One Bolster, One pillow, Three Blankets and a Quilt. £2 11s.

In the little Room over the Wood House: A Bedstead with Green Curtains, One Feather Bed, One Bolster, One pillow, Two old Matrasses, Three Blankets, One Quilt, A Fender, a Table, Two Chairs, Two Stools, Two Cushions and one pewter Chamber pott £1 13s.

In the Great Room over the Wood House: A Bedstead and Blue Linsey Furniture, One pair of Window Curtains & Rod, Two feather beds, One Bolster, One pillow, Three Blanketts, one Quilt, One Cane Chair, Two Stools, A Glass and a Stove. £4 19s.

In the Drying Room: A Mangle, A large Oak Chest, a Napkin Press, An old Couch, Two Oak Tables, One Deal Ditto, One Deal press, six brass Sconces and some Hair Cloaths' Lines. £3 2s.

In the Room over the Laundry: A Bedstead with Blue Linsey Furniture, One Feather Bed, Two Bolsters, One pillow, Four Blanketts, Two Quilts, A pair of Dogs, a pair of Tongs, poker, An old Square Table and Two Cane Chairs. £2 5s.

In the Laundry: A large Copper with Iron work and Lid as fixed, One Smaller Copper, One small Range and Cheeks, A pair of Tongs, Shovell & Bellows, A pothook, A Hanging Iron, Seven Flatt Irons, Two Stands, Two Box Irons, Three Heaters, a Jack with Multiplying Wheel and Lead Weight Compleat, A Large Skillet, A Tea Kettle, A Brass Sauce pan, An old pair of Scales Ditto, An old Cupboard, Two Tubbs, Two Covers, Two Wash tubbs, One pail, One Table, One Stool, One Chair, Five Cloaths Basketts, Five Drying Horses, Two Ironing Cloaths and Two Buck Cloths. £8 13s 6d.

In the Brewhouse: Two large Coppers with Lead and Iron Work, A large brass Kettle, A Scummer Ditto, A pot hook, An Iron fork and Rake, One Mash fatt, Two Coolers, Two working Vatts, One pump, Two Spouts, Three bearing Tubbs, One Funnell, Three Covers, One tubb, Two old Vatts, Two half Hogsheads Ironbound, One Hop Basket, One tap Whisp, One Mash Rule, One piggen and a pair of Steps. £26 8s.

In the Coach houses: One Coach, One Chariot, One Chaise Marine, A One Horse Chaise & Harness. £36 7s.

In the Gardens: One Iron Roll, Two Stone Ditto, Sixteen Wooden Chairs and a Marble Slab with Iron Brackets. £9 7s.

Total £716 13s

All the Goods mentioned in the Several Foregoing Pages were Valued and Appraised at Seven hundred and Sixteen pounds, thirteen Shillings from the Fifth to the Thirteenth of October 1749

An Inventory of the Pictures belonging to The Honourable Charles Leigh deceased and being in his late Dwelling House at Leighton in the County of Bedford

In the Parlour: Signor Ficcorony, A Bridge over the River Tyber broken down, The Tower of Babel, A Fountain and a Pot of Flowers over the Chimney, The Colossus of Rhodes, A Roman Amphitheatre, A Boy with a Litter of Whelps, Our Saviour and his Mother, Bathsheba bathing, Four prospects of Rome, The four Seasons, Venus and her Attendants and one other of the same Size.

In the Passage between the Parlour and Drawing Room: Lady Rockingham feeding a Lamb.

In the Old Drawing Room: King Charles the first, Thomas Lord Leigh, Lady Leigh, the Honourable Charles Leigh, Lady Barbara Leigh, The Honourable Mrs. Anne Leigh, Lady Leigh Holt, Lady Altham, a Lady in a small Gilt Frame, The like, A Landskip, Mrs. Lovett, Pope Clement the [blank], the Honourable Miss Verney, A Lady in a carved Gilt Frame over the Door going to the Saloon, Two Landskips in plain black frames.

All of small size and over the Pier Glass: A Gentleman in a Chair, A Lady playing on Musick, A Gentleman sitting, A Gentleman with a cane in his hand.

A Gentleman in a Gilt Frame, A Lady in Ditto, Pope Clement the 11th in a plain black Frame.

In the Salon: A Pyramid in an Arch, Two Fortune Tellers, A peice of Ruins.

In the little Room next the new Drawing Room: A Gentleman.

In the Stewards Room: Eddistone Lighthouse, A Map of Bedfordshire.

In the Housekeepers Room: A large Landskip over the Chimney, Two small India peices, Nine very small peices part-work'd.

On the Old Stair Case: Queen Eleanor and Fair Rosamund, St. George, A Landskip, A fruit peice, A White Hound with Spotted Ears, A Landskip, Lady Leigh, at length with her Grand daughter, A Spotted dog, Moses in the Bull Rushes, Three sisters named Wheelers, Eneas Carrying his Father Anchises from the Flames of Troy, Lord Strafford in a Gilt Frame In the best red Room

In the Green Room over the Pantry: The Honourable Mrs Verney in a Gilt Frame.

In the Closet: A Small Print of Robert Lord Brook.

Round the Mahogany Stair Case: Satyrs, A Gentleman, Three flower peices over the Stairs, The Month of Truth, Two Dutch peices, Spaniel Dog and Game, Cock and Hens, A peice of Birds and Gun.

On the other side: The Honble. Charles Leigh, The Holy Family, Dog and Hair and Gun.

In the Long Passage: Three Ladys in gilt Oval frames, Five Ladys in Square frames half Lengths, One Gentleman, An old Roman peice, Two of the Leighs half lengths, A Lady in an Oval Frame, A Lady in a Square frame half Length, Sir Christopher Hoddesdon, A Lady in a Square frame, half Length.

In the Batchelors Frame: King Charles the first and Son, Lord Chancellor Egerton.

In Lady Barbara's Dressing Room: [– – –] Leigh, Honourable Mrs Mary Leigh.

In Mr Leigh's Dressing Room: Four Views of Venice, Oronocko, A Lady with Deaths head, Two Philosophers, One pensive Lady, A Death's head, A Roman peice with Pen and Ink, The Honourable Charles Leigh – Mr. Leigh's Great Uncle, Painted Lady and Deaths head, A Lady in a Soldier's Arms, A Lady in an oval frame with a Bird in her hand, A Gentleman in a small black frame, A Lady in Red Drapery, Mrs Bowes, A black Lady, a brown Spaniel Dog, One Ditto done by Anton Van Dyke, A Dutch Mastiff Dog, Adolphus King of Sweden, The Elector of Hanover, A Lady, Ditto next the Dressing Room.

The Room Over the Stone Hall: The Right Honourable Countess of Leicester, The Seven Bishops.

On the Stair Case going to the Garretts: The Prodigal Son, Susannah and the two Elders, A Triton, A Landskip, Argalus and Carthenia, An Entertainment.

Shakespeare's Birthplace Trust: DR 18/31/903 (parts of)

NOTES

1. The chief archive relating to the Prebendal House are the Leigh Manuscripts held at the Shakespeare Birthplace Trust, Stratford and Kroyer Keilburg (KK) held at BCRO. Printed sources include Robert Richmond's *Leighton Buzzard and its Hamlets* 1928; VCH Vol.III p.408.

2. 1584 Lease (KK 91)
3. VCH Vol.III p.408; Chanc Proc (Ser 2) bundle 316 No.18
4. Terrier of 1647 (KK 799)
5. A Short Account of James Gibbs – see note in H.M. Colvin p.339 col.1.
6. Illustration of Doric Temple: Richmond *Leighton Buzzard* plate 7.
7. L 30/13/12/58.
8. Leighton Buzzard Church Prebendal House, undated c.1800 (P 91/28/39); Orme *Prebendal House* 1797 (P 91/28/40)
9. L 30/12/29/7
10. H.M. Colvin p.337–345; K. Downes *English Baroque Architecture* 1966
11. 1749 inventory SBT DR 18/31/903 and 1774 inventory SBT DR 18/4/42 (BCRO copy FAC 77/3)
12. *Refferences* KK 808.
13. John Fleming and Hugh Honour *Penguin Dictionary of Decorative Arts* (1977) p.266; R.J. Charleston and Donald Towner *English Ceramics* (1977) plates 107–8)
14. *Van Dyck in England* (1982) National Portrait Gallery, esp. pp.61–2, 71–2.
15. J. Godber *The Marchioness Grey of Wrest Park* BHRS Vol.XLVII p.30.
16. Charles Leigh's will: SBT ref. DR 18/13/9/22.
17. SBT Rent Book 901.
18. SBT ref. DR 18/18/3.
19. see note 11
20. Letter of 21 March 1779.
21. 1806 Survey KK 786
22. 1807 Correspondence, SBT.
23. QDL Leighton Buzzard
24. Bevan's Map
25. P. Fairbrother *The Cedars School, The First Twenty Five Years* (1946) p.4, H. Jackson & Co., Leighton Buzzard

MELCHBOURNE HOUSE

Melchbourne up to 1817

At the time of the Domesday Book, the manor of Melchbourne was held by the Bishop of Coutances. By the twelfth century it had passed to Alice de Clermont who gave it to the Knights Templars. They established a Preceptory at Melchbourne on a site near The Cottage.

The Victoria County History quotes John Leland's comment that Melchbourne House was built by Sir William Weston, last prior of the Templars, successors to the Knights Hospitallers. Be that as it may, the present house is thought to have started as a Jacobean house, and encased in the Georgian period.[1]

Following the Dissolution of the Monasteries, the manor was purchased by the Duke of Bedford in 1549. The Russells held it till 1604 when it was sold to Oliver St.John, the centre of whose estate was at nearby Bletsoe Castle. As a cousin of the Tudors through Margaret Beaufort, mother of Henry VII, royalty was received at Bletsoe Castle on at least seven occasions between 1605 and 1624. This was just at the time Melchbourne was supposed to have been built. It was probably built as an overflow house when royal visitors visited the area. It would mean that both king and queen could be entertained without one of them having to stay with what the St.Johns thought of as their inferior neighbours. They no doubt chose the site for the house at the centre of the park. James I would no doubt have loved it, as his great enthusiasm was for falconry and hunting. Much of the surviving correspondence of Oliver St.John with the King relates to hunting.

The house was substantial, having 33 hearths in 1671 as compared with 38 at Bletsoe.[2] Alternatively, the St.Johns may have found Bletsoe Castle uncomfortable. It would appear that about this time the family abandoned Bletsoe Castle in favour of the newly-built Melchbourne.

The only view of the house prior to its eighteenth century transformation is a thumb-nail sketch of the house on William Gordon's map of Bedfordshire of 1736.[3] Unlike the present house it seems to have been two storeys high with windows on the second floor only in the gables. The facade was dominated by an entrance porch/tower with a recessed bay of two windows on each side with two sets of gables outside them. It looks like a typical Jacobean house with a presence, making a considerable stamp on the local landscape. It lacks, however, the exuberance and arrogance of, say, Houghton House.

The surviving house still retains a number of seventeenth- century features, such as the steeply pitched roof, reused by the Georgians, and the gallery. A number of the 48 chimneys and some of the windows in the

Plate 21: Melchbourne Park: The main facade
(*Watercolour: Thomas Fisher, c.1820*)

top of the house date from this period. The only internal feature from the early seventeenth century to survive is a fireplace in the ballroom. More importantly the original 'H' plan has been retained.

In 1722 the senior branch of the St.John family died out and the title and estate passed to a cadet branch based at Woodford, Northamptonshire.[4] The estate was owned by minors till the accession in 1722 of John St.John (d.1757) as 10th Baron St.John of Bletsoe. In 1724 he married Elizabeth, daughter of Sir Ambrose Crowley of Greenwich, Alderman of the City of London. It was possibly the inheritance of a fortune on Ambrose's death that gave John sufficient money to contemplate the radical transformation of Melchbourne.

The drainpipes indicate that this took place in 1741. It was the south front that was more radically altered with the two bows giving an unusual south facade. The bows are true bows and not the semi-circular apses that would have been built, say, thirty years later. Melchbourne was built in red brick with yellow stone dressings. The unknown architect seems to have replaced the two gables at each end of the entrance facade with two bows each with three windows on each floor. The headers of the windows on the first floor are alternately triangular and semi-circular. The central block has five windows (except the ground floor which has an entrance door and four windows). The windows on the lower floors are large sashes while the attic has smaller ones, using no doubt the original seventeenth-century openings. The sash windows on the attic floor of the bows are larger than the central attics.

The garden front retained the seventeenth-century two light windows into the nineteenth century, as an undated illustration shows. The windows on the bottom two floors were converted to large sash. The spectacular seventeenth-century chimneys were retained.

The interiors were no doubt altered and modernised to mid-eighteenth-century taste. Unfortunately, no bills survive that give any clue as to what was done. The result of the alterations was an impressive mid-eighteenth-century house that retained a surprising amount of its original seventeenth-century features.

Although Melchbourne had been altered at considerable cost, the St. Johns still lived at least partly at their old home at Woodford in Northamptonshire. In 1771, for example, there was an advertisement of the house being to let placed in the *Northampton Mercury*[5] and Henry Beauchamp, John's grandson, rented Woodford from his mother from 1781 to 1786.

Henry Beauchamp St.John (1758–1805), 12th Baron, in 1780 married Emma Maria Elizabeth Whitbread, daughter of Samuel Whitbread I, the famous brewer and sister of Samuel Whitbread II, the Whig politician. With Emma came a fortune of £30,000 and a comprehensive reordering and redecorating of Melchbourne took place. Eventually, this involved the insertion of two Venetian windows in the garden front and possibly the addition of a classical entrance porch that looks an afterthought and is not integral to the overall design. Inside it would appear that a new ceiling was put in the long gallery at a lower height than the original one. At the same time no doubt, the classical carved pine overmantles were installed over the fireplaces. The strong classicism of the designs is not repeated in the exterior of the house apart from the entrance porch, which also appears to date from the 1780s.[6] The decoration corresponds with the ceiling of the Church, rebuilt at the same time by Samuel Whitbread. In the front stairs and hall gallery area a new staircase was installed and the ceiling decorated at this time.

The 1817 Inventory

The inventory of Melchbourne House of 1817 on the death of St.Andrew St.John, 13th Baron, shows a house filled with mahogany furniture. When this was installed is difficult to say. It is unlikely that it dates back to 1741. It could have been put in place in the major refit of the 1770s, but it is more likely that it had been bought comparatively recently, playing its part in the sizeable debts St.John left behind him (£16,739 and a further £18,000 on mortgage).[7] Melchbourne was furnished in a way befitting a Whig lord, allied to the wealthy Whitbread family. That the furniture was at least partly purchased fairly recently is hinted at by a small payment by Coutts Bank to Henry Tatham, well known upholsterer and furniture dealer.[8] Payments were made also to Messrs. Wedgwood, continuing a connection with the family since the

1780s when Josiah had made a black basalt font for Emma Lady
St.John for Melchbourne Church.

Melchbourne in 1817 had three principal rooms downstairs: the dining room (on the site of the later ballroom), the drawing room and the
library, as well as a number of other less important rooms such as "His
Lordship's Dressing Room" – old fashionedly on this floor – the buff
room, the brown room, and the usual service rooms. Interestingly, there
was no saloon and the rooms, although well equipped, were not
designed for the formal entertainment of large numbers of people. The
library had now become an important social room where the family's
visitors might gather to chat as well as to read. The Melchbourne library
was on the site of the later dining room.

On the first floor were five bedrooms, all with their dressing rooms.
There was also a nursery to accommodate the St.John's two young children. On the attic floor there were 11 rooms on the entrance side separated from the nine bedrooms on the garden side by the long gallery.

Most of the rooms in the house were furnished with mahogany with
some japanned items included. The only walnut was to be found in the
attic. In bedroom 8, for example was "a walnut chest of drawers, very
bad", perhaps a survival from the 1741 fittings. The only wainscot or
oak items were night stools, apart from the odd table. Chamber tables
for servants were made out of deal.

Quite how all pervasive mahogany was at Melchbourne is illustrated
by the buff bedroom, No.1 on the first floor. The following articles in
the room were mahogany: a low chest of drawers (top fitted up for writing and dressing), a two-leaf table, a card table (useful in a bedroom!),
airing horse (clothes horse), a stool bidet, pot cupboard and night table,
a tub and a swing glass. There were also japanned items and a cabriole
sofa and chairs.

Grander rooms such as "My Lady's Dressing Room" had a
mahogany commode and dressing table. It also contained the one substantial piece of satin wood in the house. "A large winged sattin wood
secretaire & book case" is mentioned in a list of 1920.[9] In the dining
room which was furnished in mahogany throughout was "a set of
Mahogany Dining Tables on sliding frames" with separate leaves. These
tables probably worked on a central spindle system, enabling the tables
to be larger or smaller as circumstances required.

The Library, whose books were sufficiently extensive to be listed in a
separate inventory, reveals its double purpose for relaxing socially and
for study. The mahogany bookcases lined the room. The lower parts of
the shelves were panelled and the upper, from the description, appear to
have been fretwork. The bookshelves were sliding and they could be
adjusted to accommodate different book sizes. There was a reading desk
on pillar and claw feet and no doubt the tables could be used for study.
However, alongside this are a number of quite comfortable chairs,

including a lounging chair. The globe made by Carey should be noticed. Over it all, inevitably, hung a print of Charles James Fox, the great Whig champion, as the presiding genius.

In Lord St.John's dressing room is an intriguing reference to a vapour bath. It was in a sarcophagus case with "copper boiler & flues complete." It sounds like a Turkish bath, an interesting piece of exoticism in out-of-the-way Melchbourne. Since Napoleon's invasion of Egypt in 1798 and his subsequent defeat by Nelson at the battle of the Nile, things Egyptian had become fashionable. The word sarcophagus appears a few times in this inventory.

The specialist rooms for children are noteworthy. They were still young at the time of their father's death. Andrew St.John only married when he was nearly 48. He and his wife Louisa (nee Rouse-Boughton) had two children, St.Andrew (1811–1874) later 15th Baron, and Louisa, who later married Norman Macleod of Macleod of Skye. The nursery on the first floor was used for one of the children to sleep in, as well as an accompanying nurse. The child slept in a crib bed and the nurse in a four-poster. There was a child's bamboo chair to sit on and a small swing glass for the children to see to brush their hair. The mahogany bookstand suggests that it could also have been used for doing lessons. Baby was in bedroom 6 in the attic, where there was a child's swing cot. A nurse maid slept in a four-foot field bed in the same room.

Despite their desire to be fashionable, the St.Johns wished to be warm. Every room had a register stove. These were designed to produce more efficient use of heat and may have involved elaborate pipe laying. With the growing interest of their menfolk in hunting, women were forced to spend a greater part of the winter in the country than had been customary, say, in the early eighteenth century. Keeping warm became a higher priority.

Turning to the moveable fittings, the St.Johns had a disappointing collection of pictures compared with most larger country houses of the period. The only room in which there are a reasonable number is the drawing room: one religious picture, *The Raising of Lazarus*; a Dutch sea piece; four portraits, including one of Elizabeth I; and three landscapes. An intriguing "Head by himself" is unfortunately left blank. About this time the two most valuable pictures in the house were commissioned portraits of Lady St.John by Hoppner and Sir Thomas Lawrence.

The St.Johns were well stocked with silver, with even the knives having silver blades. Sundry old pewter dishes and plates in bad condition were left neglected in the pantry. The St.Johns ate off blue and white Worcester. Their tea set was blue and gold edged. (A Derby dessert service of similar colouring was sold in 1913).[10] Some dishes were white and gold Worcester with the St.John crest on them. In the bow room there were three blue and white china ornaments on the mantlepiece. In the library there were also three chimney ornaments. These could have come from any number of factories but if they were purchased in the years of St.Andrew's marriage (1807–1817) they were most likely New Hall, which lasted till 1810. In the drawing room there were two very large china jars and covers, which were sold in 1913, described as "a pair of Nankin blue & white large vases and covers, painted with formal flowers & foliage." In the 1817 inventory other Nankeen porcelain is mentioned: soup basins and large breakfast cups. The description "Nankeen" is a general term describing some late eighteenth and nineteenth-century export ware from China and is called after the main port from which it came.

To accompany the fine porcelain plates and dishes was equally fine glass. Sets of cut glass wine glasses were supplied from pairs of cut glass quart decanters. The wine was kept cool in ten pairs of wine-coolers. (Two Sheraton wine-coolers were sold in 1913 for £94 10s. They were urns on pedestals.) The wine itself came from the seventeenth-century cellars. The wine stock itself was low but fortified wines were there in abundance. A staggering 337 bottles of port would have kept even the most bibulous follower of Charles James Fox happy.

A good list of the various types of linen listed separately indicates that the Scotch table linen, mostly napkins, had been bought in 1780, presumably for Henry Beauchamp St.John's marriage with Emma Whitbread. The damask table cloths and napkins were bought in the same year. A good investment this had proved as they were still in use nearly forty years later and there is no indication of any of them being worn. One wonders whether the date was embroidered on the napkins with the initials of the happy couple.

Melchbourne House after 1817
St.Andrew St.John (1811–1874), 14th Baron, was only five years old at his father's death. The long minority and the need by executors to sort out his father's considerable debts meant that there was little change to the house until the 1830s. St. Andrew married Eleanor Hussey in 1838. Sometime in the 1840s the drawing room was redecorated and the extension added to the north to house a magistrates' room. This was built after 1842 as it does not appear on the tithe map of that date.[11]

Eleanor and St.Andrew had five children, so the nursery would have been busy in the 1840s. By the 1860s they were all grown up. In her diary, Frederica St.John Rouse-Boughton, who married Richard Orlebar in 1861 and was a cousin of the St.Johns, describes a house party there in January 1861. Her small water colour sketches show the house being decorated for New Year and various members of the family skating on the lakes at Melchbourne. They put on a amateur dramatic display of a farce called *The Thumping Legacy*. A little sketch shows the curtain call at the end of the play.[12]

Plate 22: Melchbourne Park: The old School Room. Frederica St. John Orlebar's diaries provide useful details of life at Melchbourne.(*Watercolour: F. St.John Orlebar, 1861*)

St.Andrew's death in 1874 meant that the estate passed to his son also called St.Andrew, 15th Baron (1840–1887). Despite the onset of the agricultural depression, which hit landowners badly through reduced rent yield, St.Andrew pressed ahead with a thorough modernisation/ Victorianisation of the house in 1875. The *List of Buildings of Architectural and Historical Interest*[13] suggests that the plastered ceiling to the main staircase, pedimented doors, carved marble chimney pieces in the drawing room and coffered ceiling and panelling in the library all date from this period. It could be that the staircase to the second floor was put in at the same time.

On the death of St.Andrew St.John in 1887 without male issue the estate passed to Beauchamp Mowbray St.John who owned it from 1887 to his own death in 1912. He was a considerable local figure, being both Lord Lieutenant and Chairman of Quarter Sessions from 1891 to 1912. His death was the beginning of the end of the St.Johns' time at Melchbourne. To meet the death duties as well as the running sore of low agricultural rents, 1913 saw the sale of the most important contents of Melchbourne including the two portraits of Lady St.John by

Hoppner (fetched £4,830) and Sir Thomas Lawrence, as well as the Derby dessert service and the Sheraton wine-coolers. At a separate sale, the Victoria and Albert Museum bought the petit point panel, described by the enthusiastic auctioneer as "undoubtedly the finest of its kind that has ever been offered for sale". In his rapture he described it as "Elizabethan" and then mentioned its association with Elizabeth's great-grandmother Lady Margaret Beaufort (1443–1509)! The latter is plausible, as Oliver St.John of Bletsoe was Lady Margaret's stepfather[14].

Despite more sales in the 1920s, for a brief time Melchbourne became important in local politics when Maximilian Townley, married to the daughter of St.Andrew, the 15th Baron, became M.P. for Mid Bedfordshire from 1918 to 1922. He had been the steward of the estate since before the First World War. The last member of the St.John family left the house in 1939 when it was used for wartime accommodation, at one time 70 G.I.s sleeping in the long gallery. The house is now divided into separate dwellings.[15]

MELCHBOURNE 1817

Inventory of Fixtures, Furniture, China, Glass, Linen, Pictures, Books, Wine, Plate, Jewels and other effects – the property of the late Lord St.John at his residence Melchbourne, Bedfordshire taken the 24 October 1817.

Female Servants' Attics looking to Church: a 27 Inch grate; iron front as fix'd; a Wire fender, Shovel tongs & Poker; a Pair bellows; Iron window rod; Tammy Curtains; a 4 foot 2 four Post Bedstead & Cotton furniture; 2 small hair mattrasses; a feather bed & bolster; 2 matted seat Chairs, a Glass Plate broken.

Attic in Bow: a 4 foot 9 four Post Bedstead & Stripe Cotton furniture; A Mattrass in separate parts; a feather bed, bolster & 2 Pillows, 3 Blankets & Counterpane; An iron window rod & Curtain; a chest Walnut-tree drawers; a deal Chamber Table; 2 drawers; a square wash stand, basin & ewer; 3 Japan'd chairs stuff'd seats; 1 elbow Ditto; a black dressing Stool; a dressing Glass 14 x 10 (Silver off), 3 loose bedside carpets.

Right hand attic: A 4 foot 6 four Post Bedstead & furniture; a Crankey flock Mattrass; a feather bed, bolster and 2 pillows; 3 blankets and Counterpane; a low Walnut tree chest of drawers; a deal Chamber table with a drawer; a round Mahogany Washing Stand; a Wainscot night stool; 2 rush seat chairs & a dressing stool; a 10 x 8 Swing Glass (silver off).

Middle Attic: a 4 foot 9 four Post bedstead & Green stuff furniture; a Crankey flock Mattrass; a feather bed, bolster & 3 pillows; 3 blankets and a Quilt; a large deal Press with folding Doors and 8 Drawers; a deal Chamber Table; a Wainscot Night stool; 3 Chairs; a round Mahogany

Washing stand; a 10 x 8 Swing Glass; 3 loose bedside Carpets.

Left hand Attic: A 4 foot 6 four Post bedstead and Green harrateen Furniture; a Flock Mattrass in check case; a feather bed bolster & Pillow; 3 blankets and a rug; a Wainscot night stool; a Deal Chamber Table; 2 rush seat Chairs; a round Mahogany Wash-hand stand; a swing Glass (Plate broken).

Butler's Bed room: a 4 foot four Post bedstead and stripe furniture, old; a Crankey flock Mattrass; a feather bed bolster & Pillow; 3 blankets and quilt; a painted chest of drawers; a Deal Chamber Table; a Walnut Tree Night Table; 3 matted seat chairs; a square Wash hand stand, basin & ewer; a 5 x 8 hang up Glass; 3 loose bedside Carpets.

Attic in Bow (Men's side): a 5 foot Field Bedstead & buff stripe Furniture; a border'd flock mattrass in check case; a border'd feather bed bolster & 2 Pillows; 3 blankets & Essex quilt; a Deal Table with drawer; 3 odd chairs; a loose bedside Carpet, an 8 x 5 Glass; a basin ewer and Chamber utensil.

Attic No.2: Two 3 foot 6 four Post bedsteads & check furnitures; 2 feather beds, 2 bolsters & 2 pillows; 6 blankets & 2 quilts; an iron rod & Green curtain; 3 deal Tables with Drawer.

Attic No.3: A 3 foot 6 four post bedstead & Blue check Furniture; a flock Mattrass in hessen case, a feather bed bolster & Pillow; [*margin* in Attic No.2] a 3 foot 6 four post bedstead stript furniture, a feather bed, bolster & pillow, 3 Blankets and Quilt, 2 blankets & a rug; a 3 foot 6 four Post bedstead & Check furniture; a feather bed bolster & Pillow; 3 blankets & a rug; a deal Table with Drawer; 2 matted seat chairs; an 8 x 5 Glass[c].

Attic No.4: a 4 foot 6 Field bedstead; White dimity furniture; a feather bed, bolster & Pillow; 3 blankets & quilt; (a deal Table with drawer; an arm'd Windsor Chair; 4 old Mahogany knife cases & Green baize covers. Store Attic No.5)

Long Gallery: 2 flower Stages; 4 deal forms; a Shower Bath; a bed chair.

Pink Bedroom No.1: A four foot 6 four post bedstead & Cotton furniture; a Crankey flock Mattrass; a feather bed, bolster & Pillow; 3 blankets & Counterpane; a Walnut tree Chest of Drawers; a Wainscot Chamber Table; a painted Washing Table with drawer, basin & ewer; a 19 x 15 oval dressing Glass; 3 rush seat Chairs; a bedround carpet; a Window Curtain with pully lath to match bed.

Green Bedroom No.2: a 35 inch Register stove; iron front as fix'd; a Wire fender; Shovel tongs & Poker; a 4 foot Field bedstead, white dimity furniture; a feather bed, bolster & Pillow; 3 blankets & Counterpane; a Wainscot Chest of Drawers; a Mahogany Stool Bidet; 4 & 1 arm'd matted seat Chairs & a dressing stool; a Wainscot night stool; a White Dimity festoon Window Curtain, lath etc. 5 washing basins, 2 chipp'd.

Drab Bedroom No.3: A 27 inch Register Stove; cast iron front as fix'd;

a Wire fender; Shovel, tongs & Poker; a Pair Bellows; a 4 foot 6 four Post bedstead & Pink furniture; a Crankey flock Mattrass; a feather bed, bolster & Pillow, 3 blankets & Counterpane; a festoon Window Curtain & lath to match; a Walnut tree Bureau Chest of Drawers; a Wainscot two flap Table; a square Mahogany Wash hand stand, basin & ewer; a Mahogany pot cupboard; a bedround carpet; 2 arm'd & 1 single chairs; Dressing Stool Matted Seat; a box dressing Glass 18 x 14.

Bow Bedroom No.4: A 34 Inch Register stove; cast iron front; a Wire fender; Shovel, tongs & Poker; a 5 foot four Post bedstead with Dimity furniture; a border'd hair Mattrass; a border'd feather bed; bolster & 1 W. Pillow, 3 blankets & Counterpane; 3 festoon Window Curtains, Laths etc; a Wainscot 2 flap'd Table; a Mahogany Bureau Chest of Drawers; a Mahogany 3 corner Table; a Mahogany double night Table; a Mahogany Bidet; 4 & 2 arm'd Black chairs, matted seats; A Mahogany hearth broom, a painted Washing Table; 2 Basins.

Bed room No.5: a 4 foot four Post Bedstead and Cotton furniture; a border'd feather bed, bolster & Pillow; 3 blankets & Counterpane; a festoon Window Curtain, laths to match bed furniture; a wainscot Chest of Drawers; a Ditto Chamber Table; a Mahogany Wash hand stand, Basin, ewer & Pot; 4 Matted Chairs; Dressing Stool; a bedround Carpet; a swing dressing Glass.

Bedroom No.6: a 4 foot Field Bedstead; Cotton furniture; a feather bed; 3 blankets & Counterpane; a Crib bedstead; a child's swing cot; a Pillow; a double Wainscot Chest of Drawers; 4 matted seat chairs; a child wicker chair; a Japan'd foot tub; a festoon Window Curtain & Lath to match bed furniture.

Bed room No.7: A 4 foot Field bedstead & Cotton furniture, a flock Mattrass in Check Case; a feather bed & bolster, 3 blankets & Counterpane; a Mahogany Pembroke Table; 4 ditto chairs, stuff'd seats; a ditto Tambour-frame.

Bed room No.8: A 34 inch Register Stove, iron front; a fender; Shovel, tongs & Poker; a 5 foot four Post bedstead and furniture; a Crankey flock Mattrass; a feather bed, bolster & 2 Pillow; 3 blankets & Counterpane; 3 festoon Window Curtains to match; a Mahogany Chest of Drawers; night Table; a ditto fly leg Table; a Walnut tree bureau chest of drawers very bad; A Wainscot Chamber Table with drawer; 8 Mahogany Chairs stuff'd seats, covered with needlework; a Mahogany pole fire screen.

Bed room No.9: A 36 inch Pantheon Stove; a wire fender, Shovel, tongs & Poker; a 3 foot 6 four Post bedstead & Crimson Cloth furniture; a flock Mattrass; a feather bed, bolster & Pillow; 3 blankets & Counterpane; a Walnut tree Bureau Chest of Drawers; a pair bellows; 2 matted seat chairs; a Stool, basin & ewer; a hang up Glass; 2 bedside carpet.

Passage Rooms: a large linen Chest; 2 drawers under.

FIRST FLOOR

Buff Bedroom No.1: a 40 Inch Pantheon Stove; a Steel cut fender, Shovel, tongs & Poker; a 5 foot 6 four Post bedstead & Cotton furniture; a Crankey flock Mattrass; a White flock Ditto; a border'd feather bed bolster & 2 W. Pillows; 3 blankets & Counterpane; an eider down quilt; a festoon Window Curtain Lath etc. to match; a Wilton bed round Carpet; a hearth rug; a Mahogany low Chest of Drawers – top fitted up for Writing & dressing; a Mahogany 2 leaf Table; a Mahogany Card Table; a Mahogany airing horse; a Mahogany stool Bidet; a Mahogany pot Cupboard & night Table; a Mahogany tub; easy Chair, Cushion & Cases; 2 Cabriole elbow Chairs & Cases; 2 Black Chairs, matted seats; a dressing stool, ditto; A Mahogany swing Glass 13 x 12; an oval Glass over Chimney in Gilt frame 26 x 18; a Cabriole Sofa & case; a Japan'd Washing Table, 2 basins, 2 ewers & caraft; a tin Japan'd foot pan.

Dressing Room No.2: a festoon Window Curtain lath & line Tossell etc; a small Mahogany Chest of Drawers; a Wainscot Table; a Black chair & stool; a folding screen.

Canopy Bedroom: A 40 inch Pantheon Stove; a steel cut fender, Shovel tongs & Poker; a large size Canopy Couch bedstead; scroll and stuff'd lath bottom; iron rods to support the Canopy; White Dimity Furniture lin'd with White and border'd all round; A Crankey Hair Mattrass; a hair mattrass in White case; a border'd feather bed bolster & 2 Pillows; 3 blankets & Counterpane; a Druggett bedround border'd all round; 2 White Dimity Window Curtains, Laths, Tassells etc. complete; a Mahogany double Wardrobe; a Pair Mahogany Card Tables; a Mahogany Table inclosed under with Wire work; A Mahogany Bidet; a Mahogany airing horse; a Mahogany 18 by 14 Swing Glass, a Mahogany cir[cular?] Wash Stand, 2 basins & ewer; a Japan foot pan & tin can; a Mahogany double night Table & pot Cupboard; 3 arm'd Japan'd chairs; 3 Single ditto matted seats; a dressing stool; a Square Mahogany Pembroke Table.

Dressing Room No.4: a loose Grate on feet; a steel cut fender; Shovel, tongs & Poker; a White Dimity festoon Window Curtain; a 4 foot Field Bedstead & Dimity furniture; a flock Mattrass, Crankey case; a bordered feather bed, bolster & 2 White Pillows, 3 blankets & Counterpane; a bed-round Carpet; a small Mahogany Chest of Drawers with Secretaire top drawer; a Mahogany double night Table; a small Mahogany 2 flap'd Table with drawer; a large painted Chest of Drawers shap'd front, carv'd ornaments & handles; a 13 x 13 Swing Glass; a large Mahogany Chamber Table with a drawer; a Mahogany hanging bookshelf; a painted Washing Table, 2 basins, ewer etc; 8 Japan'd Chairs, matted seats; a Japan'd foot pan & Can.

Lady's Dressing Room: A 39 Inch half Register stove with japan'd front; a steel cut fender; Shovel, tongs & Poker; 2 White Holland roller blinds (bad), 3 Laths with brass pully rods; 3 Pair Cotton window curtains (very bad); The floor cover'd all over with Carpet; a Hearth Rug; a Square Sofa and cushions & set of Blue Cotton cases; 6 Cabriole arm'd Chairs & set of Blue Cotton cases; 2 dressing Stools; a large winged Sattin Wood Secretaire & book case, glas'd doors; a Mahogany Commode with Wire pannell'd doors, 2 drawers; a Mahogany Dressing Table with folding covers Glass to rise fitted up with bottles etc; a Mahogany Pembroke Table inlaid with Sattin wood; a Wainscot Pembroke Table with drawer; a box Dressing Glass 16 x 12; a Mahogany airing horse; a Japann'd tin foot pan & jug; an Oval Mermaid Glass.

Bed Room: A 35 Inch Register Stove japan'd front bright mouldings; a Steel cut fender; Shovel, tongs & Poker; a 5 foot six four Post bedstead, Mahogany feet Posts lath bottom, Japan'd Cornices; White Dimity furniture lin'd, Blue outside; Drapery Vallence fring'd; a flock Mattrass in Crankey; a Ditto in White case; a border'd feather bed, bolster & 2 White Pillows; 3 blankets & Counterpane; a bedround carpet; 2 Mahogany Pot Cupboards; a Capital 8 foot fine Mahogany Winged Wardrobe, Sliding Shelves in centre Part, 3 drawers under Wings with shelves for Dresses; a Wainscot Chamber Table; a Mahogany Bidet; 2 Japan'd Chairs; 1 arm'd Cabriole Chair.

Nursery: A half Register Stove; cut iron front; a high wire fender, brass top; Shovel, tongs & Poker; a Pair bellows; a 5 foot four Post bedstead with Dimity furniture; a flock Mattrass in Crankey; a feather bed bolster & 2 Pillows; 3 blankets & Counterpane;
[*marginal note* In passage opposite long Gallery *against* a large mahogany chair bed; a flock mattrass in crankey; a ditto ditto in White case;]
a feather bed, bolster & Pillow; 3 blankets & Counterpane; a Mahogany bureau Chest of Drawers; a Mahogany bookstand with 3 drawers, folding doors & 2 shelves over; a Mahogany knee hole dressing Table with drawer; a Crib bedstead & Dimity furniture; a Mattrass & Pillow; 3 blankets & a quilt; a Wainscot Pembroke Table; a Ditto Ditto; 6 black Chairs, matted seats; a Mahogany tea board; a child's bamboo chair; a small swing Glass; a Mahogany airing horse; a Copper Coal Scuttle.

Yellow Bedrom: a 42 inch Pantheon Stove; a Steel cut fender; Shovel, tongs & Poker; a Pair bellows and hearth brush; a 5 foot 6 four Post bedstead, Mahogany feet, Posts, Laths, bottom, Cornices etc; a White Dimity furniture; full Valance, Curtains lin'd with Yellow-Silk, Yellow-Silk fringe; a flock Mattrass in Cranky, a Ditto in White case; a border'd feather bed, bolster and 2 white Pillows; 3 blankets & a White Cotton Counterpane; a White holland roller blind; 2 Pully laths and White dimity Window Curtains border'd etc.; a Druggett bedround Carpet with yellow a la gree border; a Mahogany Chest of Drawers; a Mahogany double Night Table; a Mahogany dressing Table with folding cover, glass to rise; a Mahogany oval Pembroke Table; a Mahogany

Portrait Dressing glass, Plate 44 x 26; a Mahogany airing horse; a Japan'd Washing Table, 2 brown edg'd basins, Soap & brush trays; a Japan'd Stand for flowers; 6 Japan'd chairs, matted seats; a large Dressing Stool top cover'd with needlework; [a worked Carpet 18 feet by 5 *added in pencil*]

Yellow Dressing Room: a 34 inch Pantheon Stove; a wire fender; Shovel, tongs & Poker; a Callico roller blind; a 3 foot 3 single head Couch bedstead, Stuff'd head & seats and a set of Screw Posts & tester rails; a White Dimity furniture; a border'd feather bed & Pillow (excellent); a Window pully Lath; 4 Japan'd chairs; a Mahogany Chest of Drawers with Slider at top; a Pair bellows & hearth brush.

Green Bow Bedroom: A 36 inch Register Stove with bright Mouldings; a Steel cut fender; Shovel tongs & Poker; a Pair bellows & hearth brush; 3 White holland roller blinds; 3 Window laths brass pully Rods and Japan'd Cornices; 3 Pair White Dimity window Curtains border'd; a 5 foot 6 four Post bedstead Mahogany feet, Posts, Lath bottom, Japan'd cornices; White Dimity furniture with Drapery Valance fring'd; a flock Mattrass in Crankey; a Ditto Ditto in White case; a border'd feather bed, bolster & 2 Pillows; 3 blankets & Counterpane; a small single head Couch bolster & Pillow and white cotton cases; A 2 foot 9 Mahogany Chest of Drawers; a Pair Mahogany bed steps with caned sides; a Mahogany dressing Table with folding covers, Glass to rise, fitted up inside; A Mahogany Pembroke Table; an 18 x 14 reverse Swing Dressing Glass; 5 Japan'd arm'd chairs, can'd seats; a dressing Stool; a painted Washing Table, 2 brown edg'd basins & ewers, Soap and brush dishes; a painted flower stand; [Green worsted worked carpet about 7 feet by 13; Bedround Carpet *added in pencil*].

Green Dressing Room: a 36 inch Register Stove cast iron front; a steel cut fender; Shovel, tongs & Poker; a White Callico roller blind; a Window Lath Japan'd Cornice, brass pully rod; a Dimity Window Curtain; a 3 foot Mahogany Dressing Chest of drawers and slider; a 2 foot Mahogany Pembroke Table; a round Mahogany Wash hand stand; 2 blue China basins & ewers, 2 Soap dishes & covers; 4 Japan'd arm'd Chairs, caned Seats; a Pair bellows and hearth rug; a dressing Stool.

Staircase & Landing: An inlaid Table on Japan'd frame; 2 Vase Lamps with brass balance weights, Chains etc; an 8 day Clock by Gordon; a ½ circular flower stage.

Store Room 1st Floor: China taken further on.

GROUND FLOOR

His Lordship's Dressing Room: A 34 inch Bath stove; a large Vapour Bath in Sarcophagus case with Copper boiler & flues complete; a Mahogany Wardrobe with sliding Shelves & 4 drawers under; [*pencil note* in room above] a 3 foot 6 Mahogany Chest of 5 drawers, locks etc; a Mahogany Wash hand stand, folding covers, basins, ewers etc; a

Mahogany Pot cupboard; a Ditto boot & shoe horse; a Wainscot Stool top Bidet & Pan; 2 blacks chairs & stool; an 18 x 12 Dressing Glass, Silver damag'd.

Bow Room: a 38 inch half Register Stove; cast iron front; a Wire fender bright Mouldings & standards; Shovel, tongs & Poker; 3 White holland roller blinds; a piece Matting on floor; 3 Laths & wood pully rods & 3 Pair of dark Cotton Window Curtains; a Brusselles Carpet, old; a 4 foot Mahogany Tambour Writing Table, kneehole front, 5 drawers good locks & handles; a 4 foot plain Mahogany writing Table and long drawer, a gallery on top; an old Mahogany flap Table; 7 Mahogany chairs, hollow seat stuff'd and covered with Black Leather double nail'd; a 3 foot 6 Mahogany round Table on Pillar & Claw; a Chimney Glass in Bronze Frame 46 x 23; 3 blue & White China Chimney ornaments; a taper candlestick.

Dining Room: a 47 inch Register Stove, bright Mouldings; a Steel cut fender; Shovel tongs & Poker; 2 White Holland roller blinds; 2 Pair of Green worsted Damask rod Window Curtains and Drapery Laths etc. etc; 9 foot Mahogany sideboard Table on six legs; a Pair of Pedestals & vases with Plate racks, Celeret drawer etc.; a set of Mahogany dining Tables on sliding frames, 3 separate leaves, 6 screw legs together 13.0 x 4.8; a large Table Cloth, Green; an oil Cloth cover; a Mahogany oval Coper, brass hoop'd lin'd with lead; 2 round Mahogany Pails, brass hoops & handles; a Pair Mahogany 2 board dumb waiters; 3 Mahogany knife cases; 2 Square Mahogany Dining Tables, 5 foot by 4 foot 3 each; a round end Mahogany 2 flap Table 5 foot by 3 foot 9; 7 Single Mahogany Chairs with black leather Seats; 2 arm'd Ditto Ditto; A Mahogany Library Chair Caned all over etc. red leather back & seat cushion; a Brussells Carpet, old; a hearth rug; a Square Pair of Matting; 2 Chair backscreens covered with Scarlet Tammy; a black ewer & China basket; 2 biscuit ornaments.

Library: a 44 inch half Register Stove, bright grate & cast iron front bronz'd; a Steel cut fender; Shovel, tongs & Poker; a Pair bellows; The room fitted up with Mahogany Book Cases all round, the lower parts enclos'd by pannell'd doors; the upper Parts with doors and wire pannells, Sliding Shelves inside, good locks & keys; a Square Turkey Carpet; a hearth rug; 2 White holland roller blinds; 2 Festoon Window Curtains border'd & lin'd with white; a Square Mahogany Sofa cover'd with red leather, Ssquab, 3 back Cushions, 2 bolsters; 8 Mahogany arm'd chairs stuff'd backs & seat Cushions cover'd with red leather; a Mahogany elbow chair caned, seats & back Cushions cover'd with red leather; a lounging Chair with back & seat Cushion in red Cotton cases; 6 black matted seat chairs; a Pair of 21 inch Globes on Mahogany stands with Compasses under and leather covers by Carey; 2 small Mahogany hexagon Tables on Pillar & Claw; an oval Mahogany Pembroke Table; a Circular Mahogany Table on Pillar & Claw; a Green Cloth cover; a Reading Desk on Pillar & claw, top to rise with Horse; a Pair

Mahogany fire-screens on round bottoms; 2 foot stools; 3 Chimney China ornaments; a Print (Mr. Fox).

Drawing Room: A 44 inch Sarcophagus grate, metal paws and ornaments; a Steel fender to match; a set of fire irons; a Brussells Carpet to cover; a hearth rug; 5 White Holland roller blinds; 5 Pair of Green Stripe Silk Window Curtains with embossed cotton Drapery; Silk fringe Laths, rods and japan'd Cornices pins etc; 2 Cabriole Sofas, frames gilt, stuff'd & cover'd with Green Stripe Sattin; 12 arm'd Chairs to match; a Set of Blue Cotton loose cases for the 2 Sofas; 12 Ditto Ditto for chairs; a large lounging Chair back & seat Cushions and a set of red Cotton cases; a pier Table on Gilt Frame with Sattin Wood inlaid top & Damask leather cover; A Mahogany Sofa Table on Standards; 2 drawers; A Mahogany Pembroke Table with a drawer; a Mahogany Canterbury; a Mahogany stand for Portfolios; an oval air wood Pembroke Table inlaid & leather cover; a set of Mahogany trio Tables; a small Octagon Table; 6 black stain'd, matted seat chairs; a Ditto Stool; a Mahogany Screen Pole; 2 very large China blue Jars and covers; 2 blue & White Wedgwood flower Jars; a Pair of Gilt Girandoles for 2 lights each; [*added in pencil* Green Cloth to cover the Room].

Pictures: Raising of Lazarus; a Dutch Sea Piece; a Landscape; Portrait of Queen Elizabeth; Margaret Countess of Derby; Head of [*blank*] by himself; Portrait old Man & boy; 2 small Landscapes; a Drawing fram'd & Glaz'd; 2 small Drawings fram'd & Glaz'd; a Ditto Ditto Sea Coast; Ivory Model of Ship in a Glass case.

Brown Room: A Standard Grate; a fender; a set of fire irons; a Mahogany Bureau book case with Plate silver'd Glass doors each 34 x 16; a Square Mahogany Table with 2 drawers top cover'd with Black Leather; a Mahogany reading Desk to rise out of Pillar; a smaller Ditto Ditto; 2 Mahogany Chairs, seats cover'd with Black Leather; a Wainscot Chamber Table.

Entrance Hall: a large Register Stove bright front etc; a Steel cut fender; Shovel, tongs & Poker; a Pair of Yew Tree Circular Card Tables, leather covers; a Mahogany Table with drawer, top cover'd with Green Cloth; An oval Pembroke Table; 2 Pair low 4 leaf Screens, sliding Pannells, cover'd with Tammy; 2 Japan'd Pedestals with glass Vases for lamps; 12 Japan'd Hall Chairs with Crest & Coronet in back; A Mahogany Tro Madame Table; 2 earthenware Pedestal Chimney ornaments for flowers; 2 smaller Ditto Ditto; 3 family Portraits in gilt frames; a length of matting; 2 smaller pieces.

Butler's Pantry: A Grate as fix'd; fender & fire irons; an arm'd Windsor Chair; 2 matted bottom Ditto; a Wainscot Table with drawer; A Linin Press with Ditto; a large Deal Table; a beating horse; 2 Mahogany Butler's trays.

Glass: 3 Pair Quart cut Decanters; 1 Pair Ditto Ditto; 3 Pair Plain Water Crafts; 18 Plain finger Glasses; 10 Plain Wine coolers; 12 cut ½

Pint Tumblers; 6 Plain Ditto Ditto; 12 Plain ale glasses; 4 Ditto Ditto; 12 large cut Wine Glasses; 12 small Ditto Ditto; 12 Ditto cut Ditto; 24 Ditto plain Ditto. Sundry oddments: a cut Sugar glass & cover; a Ditto Pepper Ditto.

Silver: A Tureen Dish & Cover; 6 Sauce Dishes & Covers and Ladles; 2 Ladles for Soup; 2 16 inch Salvers; 2 12 inch Salvers; 2 8 inch Ditto; a bread basket, 6 Salt Tureens & Spoons; a Sugar Caster & spoon; a Pepper Ditto & Ditto; a Mustard Ditto Ditto, a boat to contain the three; a Tea urn; 2 Pair high Candlesticks; 2 Pair small Candlesticks; a Coffee Pot; a Tea Pot; a sugar basket; a Cream basket; stand for oil & vinegar; a Coffee urn; 2 Tea Pots; 4 high Candlesticks; 6 Salts & Spoons; a Cruet stand; a Pair snuffers & stand; a Tea Caddy; 4 Chamber candlesticks & extinguishers; a round cruet stand; a Cheese toaster; 3 Saucepans; 4 Salts & 4 spoons; Asparagus tongs; 3 Scallop Shells; a Muffinere; 8 Gravy Spoons; a Sallad fork; 36 beaded large forks; 6 skewers; 12 beaded large spoons; 2 pap Boats; 2 sauce ladles, Apostle Spoon; Nutmeg grater; a Cream ladle; 12 Coffee Spoons; 12 large beaded forks; 24 small Ditto Ditto; 36 large Ditto Spoons; 24 desert beaded Spoons; 24 beaded tea Ditto, 3 pair Sugar tongs; 1 Fish Slice; 1 Marrow Spoon; 10 Plain Desert Spoons with Crest; 24 odd table Spoons; 3 odd desert Spoons; 1 marrow Spoon; 8 Wine Labels; 12 odd tea spoons; An inkstand with 3 glasses in Library; 4 Carvers & Forks with Silver handles; 4 dozen large bead knives; 3 dozen small bead knives; 11 small knives with round end handles; 21 large knives with round handles and forks; 12 Desert knives with Silver blades, ivory handles; 12 Desert Forks; 2 Butter knives Ditto [ivory handles]; 4 Bottle stands; 5 inch diameter with Silver & wood bottoms; a Wine strainer; a toasting Fork, wood handle.

Plated Articles: An egg stand with six cups & spoons and Salt cup on the top; a Ditto Ditto not so modern; An Epergne with 4 branches & glass Cups; 6 bottle stands; a Copper Biggin & Lamp; An Argyle for sauce; 2 horns lined; a Chamber Candlestick; a Ditto for a lamp; a Taper Stand; 3 flat Candlesticks; a Toast rack.

Servants Hall: A Grate as fix'd; a fender and fire-irons; a long Deal Table; 3 long Forms; 2 Short Ditto; 3 Wood bottom chairs; A Pair of high Steps; a Pair of low Ditto; a Turk head Broom; 24 leather Water buckets; 2 low 2 leaf Cloaths' horses.

Kitchen: A large Range with Drop bar swing trivets, Spit racks & crane; A Smoke Jack complete with multiplying wheel; a wrought iron oven, set in brick; a Copper boiler set; 2 cocks; a range of Charcoal Stoves; a large iron fender; Shovel, tongs & Poker; a large Meat screen lined with tin; a large Elm Table on cross legs 11 feet by 3 feet 4; an oval 2 flap Wainscot Table; a round corner Ditto Ditto; a Wainscot Chamber Table; very old Ditto; a Chopping Block; 6 x 2 arm'd Windsor Chairs; a Marble morter on stand; an iron footman.

Coppers: A large Fish kettle & cover; A large Stock pot & cover; 2 Smaller Pots & covers; a frying pan, a Turbot kettle & cover; 2 oval Fish Kettles & covers; 3 frying Pans black; 9 stew Pans & covers; 14 Saucepans & covers; 2 Coffee pots; 1 Chocolate Ditto; 4 Tea Kettles; 3 beer cans; a brass Skillet & cover; 2 Warming pans; a dripping pan; 3 Soup ladles (NB Coppers very old).

Tins: A Dutch oven; 2 pudding pans; a Soup Tureen; 3 dish covers; a bread grater; a cheese toaster; a Spice box; a Drudger, 2 Pepper boxes.

Irons: 2 Spits; 3 Grid irons [*pencil note* only 2]; 3 Cook holds; 2 Meat saws; 2 meat Choppers; 1 Suet Chopper; 1 beef fork; a set of Skewers & frame; 2 Salamanders; 3 trevets; a Pair of Steak Tongs.

Scullery: A Copper set in brick; 2 plate racks; 2 dish Tubs; 4 Pails.

Pewter: Sundry old Pewter Dishes and Plates in bad condition.

Larder: fitted up with rails and hooks & shelves all round; a large Bacon trough lin'd with lead & cover; a Circular Meat tub lin'd with lead & cover, a Ditto Ditto smaller; A bread tub & cover; 6 Milk Pans; 4 red Pans various; a wood bowl; a low Pair of Steps; a Table lin'd with lead; a Ditto with Marble Slab; A Pair of plank Scales and 8 weights; a large flour Tub; 2 small oval Tubs; 2 Sieves; a honey Sieve.

House keeper's Room: a 38 inch half Register Stove with cast iron front; a wire fender; Shovel, tongs & Poker; a large Deal Press upper & lower part enclos'd by 2 Pair of doors, inside fitted up with Shelves etc; a large Press with wings pannell'd doors all the way up, Shelves inside Locks & key; 3 Pully Window Laths (no Curtains); a Sloping writing Table with drawer painted; a round Mahogany Table on Pillar & Claw; a Square Wainscot 2 flap Dining Table; 8 x 2 arm'd Mahogany Chairs, seats cover'd with hair Cloth; A Wainscot Chamber Table with drawer; a round tub & cover; a hang up Glass 11 x 14 (silver damag'd); a piece of Square matting; a Copper coal scuttle; an iron footman; A Sugar knife & mallet.

Still Room: a Jelly Stand; 2 Clay's tea boards; 1 Mahogany tea board; Sundry jugs and basins, blue & white dishes, Tureen and oddments.

China Closet:

Glass: A Jelly Stand and 24 cut glasses for jellies; 4 very handsome cut glass cups with scollop'd edges & dishes to match; a large cut Glass Cream bowl and 4 cups to match for Sweetmeats belonging to an Epergne; 15 cut Lemonade Glasses with handles; 2 oval cut Dishes; 5 cut Egg cups; a Sugar Glass & Cruet; 2 butter Dishes & covers cut; 1 Honey Ditto Ditto; 2 cream Jugs and covers; 4 plain Water Crafts; a Globe for Fish; 5 Plain wine coolers.

China: Indian Breakfast Service with arms; a very large bowl; a smaller bowl; 2 Butter Cups and Stands; a sugar basin; 12 Coffee Cups & Saucers; 24 tea cups and saucers; 12 large Plates; 24 smaller plates.

Nankeen: 4 Soup basins, covers and stands, 6 small ½ pint basins; 6 Ditto ?int Ditto, 6 Ditto Ditto Ditto; 12 large breakfast cups &

Saucers; 8 smaller Ditto Ditto.

Blue and Gold edge: A Tea Pot and Cover; a Tea Caddy; A Slop basin; a Sugar basin & cover; a Cream jug and cover; 12 Coffee Cups and Saucers; 15 Tea Cups and Saucers; 1 bread & butter plate.

White & Gold Worcester with Crest: 16 Dishes in sizes; 5 dozen plates.

Sundries: 2 blue and Gold Scent Jars; Sundry oddments of Cups, Saucers, Tea Pots, Dishes Plates etc; an Ivory inlaid Backgammon Table; an Ivory engrav'd Tea Caddy; 2 hang up Glasses; Print of Rt. Honourable C.J. Fox fram'd & glaz'd; 8 Drawings fram'd & glaz'd; a Copper tea urn; 26 brass 40 inch Stair wires.

Blue & White Worcester in Housekeeper's room: 21 dishes various; 6 Vegetables & covers; 2 Tureens and covers; 4 Sauce Tureens covers and stands; 4 Ice pails with covers; 18 Soup Plates; 5 dozen large Plates.

Laundry: 34 inch Copper set in brick with lead curb; 32 inch Ditto Ditto; 20 inch Ditto Ditto; a range of five troughs with cocks for hot and Cold Water; a Deal Press, folding doors; A 12 foot deal Table on Strong frame; a common Mangle; 2 cloaths Horses; an ironing Stove and Pipe.

Bake House: a kneeding trough; a Deal Table.

Brewhouse, Coach house, Gardener's House: [*Contents listed in detail*].

Ale Cellar: 5 Hogsheads Ale; 5 Ditto small beer; 18 Pipe Barrells empty, 8 Hogsheads empty, 4 half Ditto empty, a large vat empty.

Wine: 332 bottles Port, 111 Ditto Sherry; 2 Ditto Mountain, 1 Ditto Barsach, 55 Ditto Madiera, 3 Ditto Burgundy; 2 Ditto Champagne; 4 Ditto Brandy; 97 Ditto Syracuse, 61 Cape Wine in Pints, 7 Syracuse, 4 Ditto Rum, 4 Ditto Cape Madiera, 5 Ditto Orange, 12 Ditto Elder. A Hogshead of Claret   £80.

Linen:

Damask: 1 large Table Cloth, 18 Napkins to match; 1 Table Cloth, 11 Napkins to match; 2 Table Cloths, 24 Ditto Ditto; 1 Table Cloth, 18 Ditto Ditto; 1 Table Cloth, 12 Ditto Ditto; 5 small breakfast cloths, 24 Napkins to match; 1 Table Cloth, 10 Napkins Ditto; All   in   the year 1780.

1 Table Cloth, 12 Napkins; 1 Table Cloth, 12 Napkins; 1 Table Cloth, 12 Napkins; 1 small Table Cloth, 12 breakfast Napkins; 1 very large Cloth; 1 small Table Cloth; 12 Napkins, 1 Table Cloth; 1 Table Cloth; 2 Table Cloths; 7 small Table Cloths   All very much worn.

Indian Diaper: 2 large Table Cloths, 12 Napkins to match; 17 Napkins.

Scotch Table Linen: 2 large Cloths, 22 Napkins; 4 large Cloths, 12 & 8 Napkins; 3 lay over, 17 Napkins to match; 11 Birdseye Napkins, 8 Napkins, 6 Birdseye Tea Napkins All in the year 1780.

Scotch & Huckaback: 13 Cotton Huckaback; 4 Ditto Table Cloths; 1 Table Cloth very fine, 12 Napkins for Ditto; 24 Huckaback Napkins; 23 Ditto Ditto; 2 Scotch Table Cloths; 1 Ditto Spotted pattern; 12 Scotch Napkins; 4 Scotch Napkins; 8 Scotch Table Cloths; 6 Small

Table Cloths; 1 large Table Cloth; 6 Napkins; 1 Huckaback Table Cloth; 2 Old Fish Napkins; 1 large Diaper Table Cloth; 1 large strip'd Table Cloth; 1 small Table Ditto; 1 Ditto Ditto very course & old.

Bed Linen: 4 Pair Holland Sheets, 6 Pair Ditto Pillow cases; 8 Pair Irish Sheets; 10 Pair Irish Sheets; 22 Irish Pillow cases, 10 Pillow cases; 1 Pair fine Holland Sheets, 1 Pair Holland Crib Ditto, 1 Pair Irish Ditto Ditto, 1 Pair Russia small Ditto, 1 Pair Ditto Ditto, 1 Pair Ditto Ditto; 1 odd Callico Sheet; 6 fine Holland Pillow cases; 5 Ditto Ditto very small Ditto; 9 Pair Irish sheets; 2 Pair fine Pillow cases.

Servants: 4 Pair Sheets; 3 Pair Ditto Ditto; 1 Pair sheets; 4 Pillow cases; 2 Pair sheets, 2 pillow cases; 3 Pair Sheets; 11 Pair Sheets good; 4 Pair small Ditto; 14 Pillow cases; 1 Pair Sheets.

Table Linen for Servants: 2 large Huckaback Table Cloths; 4 small Ditto Ditto, 7 round Towels, 2 Table Cloths; 12 round Towels; 6 Oyster Cloths.

Scotch Towels: 29 Towels, 24 Ditto, 24 Huckaback Ditto; 12 Huckaback Towels; 34 Ditto Ditto; 33 Ditto Ditto, 24 fine Ditto, 12 Ditto large Ditto.

Doylies: 24 blue Border'd, 61 white; 12 blue Ditto, 12 red Ditto (very old), 12 White, 12 Pink Border'd.

[*Farm House rooms listed in detail, including a table clock by King and a fowling piece by Grierson. Also list of books in Library 1817, signed Thomas Turner*]

Bedford Library: L 942/565 MEL

NOTES

1. The J. and St.J. Archives at BCRO relate to the St.Johns and Melchbourne. Hugh de B. Lawson Johnston's unpublished essay *St.Johns of Bletsoe 19.9* is available there (L J4). Printed works include C. Hussey's article on Melchbourne in *Country Life* Vol.76 pp.168–172 (1934). Harvey's Hundred of Willey, *VCH Bedfordshire Vol III*, pp.142–3. Short Guide to the House, n.d., CRT 130 Melchbourne 8. Pevsner p.124.
2. *1671 Hearth Tax*, BHRS Vol.XVI p.69 (reprinted 1990).
3. Gordon's Map, 1736 (MC 2/8). An enlarged photograph of his sketch of Melchbourne is found at Z 50/143/218.
4. Introduction to ST catalogue.
5. *Northampton Mercury* 5 August 1771.
6. *Guide to Melchbourne* p.2.
7. SJ 482.
8. SJ 497–582, dated 1817–1820.
9. SJ 1272.
10. SJ 1075.
11. Melchbourne Tithe Award, valued 1841, apportioned 1847 (AT and MAT 32).
12. Frederica Orlebar's Diary 1861: OR 2244/5a for 1861.
13. *List of Buildings of Architectural Interest.*
14. SJ 1075 and SJ 1263. Article on petit point carpet: Betty Chambers, Two Bedfordshire Carpets *Beds. Mag. II* p.317–20 (1969). 15. *Short Guide to Melchbourne* p.2; Sale Catalogue Z 449/1

NORTHILL MANOR

Northill Manor before 1731

On 12 and 13 July 1652 Thomas Ellis conveyed the Manor of Northill including the Capital Messuage in Northill to Thomas Bromsall, grandfather of Owen Thomas Bromsall, whose inventory is transcribed below.[1] It was undoubtedly an ancient site and almost certainly moated, as the deeds of 1653 mention one in the vicinity. It is impossible to say if the house was rebuilt by the Bromsalls. The only illustration of the house is a small conventionalised sketch on Thomas Jeffreys's map of Bedfordshire,[2] dated 1765. The picture shows a rectangular house such as could have been built any time from say the 1680s onward.

If the house had been rebuilt the most likely Bromsall to have done it would have been Ralph, who died 1693.[3] After laying out "severall great Sumes of moneys in the repairing and building" of his house at Moggerhanger, he moved to Northill Manor House on the death of his father in 1682. He could well have rebuilt or altered the house in the period 1682–1693.

Owen Thomas Bromsall's death in 1731 led to a Chancery case and the inventory below comes from Chancery records, held at the Public Record Office. An identical copy is kept among the Prerogative Court of Canterbury Archives and originally accompanied his will.[4]

Northill Manor Inventory 1731

The inventory itself does not greatly help us with dating the house. It contains at one and the same time a possible traditional hall and screens passage as well as signs of the formal arrangement of apartments that was such a feature of early eighteenth-century houses. It looks therefore like a sixteenth/seventeenth century house adapted before 1731 to meet the new fashions of the period. The formal end of the house, probably the south, saw a progression from the east facing hall through the drawing room to the best parlour. The servants' hall was close to the best parlour and probably also had a door through to the main hall, so that orders could be attended to promptly.

This formality is mirrored on the first floor where the main staircase led to a suite of rooms probably above the drawing room and best parlour which included the ante-chamber, dressing room, "Blew Room" and "Blew Chamber Closet".

The less formal side of the house is more difficult to unravel and what follows is just one possible hypothesis. From the back of the hall ran a passage to the little parlour, which seems likely to have been used as the dining room. This probably lay in the north-east corner of the house.

Between it and the hall would have been the smoking room. Possibly the two rooms were once combined. On the far side of the passage lay the kitchen and a numerous array of ancillary rooms and maybe even detached separate buildings providing the service end of the house. Proliferation of specialised service buildings is supposed to be a feature of nineteenth-century houses. It was happening in Northill in the early eighteenth.

Between the kitchen and the best parlour was the pantry and the servants' hall, probably separated from the main hall by the remains of the screens and the main staircase. Upstairs, above the little parlour, smoking room and hall, and possibly the kitchen, were four rooms: the "Damask Chamber", hall chamber, "Yellow Room" and new room. These were probably grouped round the northern side of the main staircase. The new room was clearly incomplete at Bromsall's death and indicates that alterations were still taking place.

Slightly out on a limb was the chamber over the servants' hall. It was probably close to the west side of the main staircase for easy access.

The attic level of the house contained numerous garrets used partly for storage of apples and malt. It included a powder garret with a barber's block. Bromsall was clearly fashion conscious and determined his wig should look just right. Across the garret gallery was an area which included the nursery and the maids' garret.

Owen Bromsall was obviously a wealthy man. His extensive collection of china, which would have been mostly imported from China itself, and his ivory handled and agate handled silver cutlery underline this. His principal pieces of furniture were walnut with no mahogany mentioned, which can be explained if the house had been furnished some years before. He had a walnut escritoire, as well as a walnut card table to amuse himself with. A pair of draught tables indicates another game that was played in the house.

His picture collection was of modest size in comparison with John Bullock (died 1764).[5] Twelve pictures are mentioned in the inventory but subjects of none of them are given. The two major pictures surrounded by their gilt frames were above the chimney pieces of the best parlour and the drawing room. For so prominent a local family it is curious there are no portraits mentioned.

Unusually among inventories there is a list of Bromsall's complete wardrobe and its value. Twenty two shirts were valued at £8 5s, a brocade waistcoat £1 1s and four pair of dimity splatterdashes and one pair of worsted were valued at a shilling. Splatterdashes were long gaiters or leggings.

Miscellaneous items of interest include a clock with a japanned case in the ante-chamber and an eight day clock in the little parlour. Unfortunately, the maker is not given but with Tompion coming from nearby Ickwell it is possible they were by him. In the pantry were two mouse traps which were essential with so much food available. One is surprised they were not to be found up in the apple and malt garrets!

Northill Manor after 1731

Owen Bromsall left the Northill Manor Estate to his wife Elizabeth.[6] She held it till her death when it passed to Bromsall's nephew, John Robinson of Denston Hall in Suffolk. He never lived in the house and in 1767 it was let to John Franklyn Esquire[7]

He was to prove its last tenant but a map of 1781[8] shows the house still standing. By 1802 when the Robinsons sold the estate, the house had been pulled down. The sale catalogue[9] lists for sale: "The site of Ground, on which the Mansion formerly stood, with a Large Garden walled all round, Yards and Buildings (excepting the Old Brick Stable, which hath been recently dispensed of". The estate was sold to John Harvey but the large garden walls of the house still survive.[10]

NORTHILL MANOR 1731

A true and perfect Inventory of all and singular the Goods Chattells and Credits of Owen Thomas Bromsall late of Northill in the County of Bedford Esqr. deceased taken valued and appraised the eleventh, twelfth and thirteenth, fifteenth and Sixteenth days of March Anno Domini One Thousand seven hundred and Thirty at the Deceased's late Dwelling house at Northill aforesaid by Bromsall Throckmorton, John Sellis, Gabriel Johnston, Thomas Manning, George Fitzjohn and Thomas Love Commissioners named in a Commission of Appraisement issued forth under the seal of the Prerogative Court of Canterbury for the inspecting valueing and takeing an Inventory thereof – follows videlict.

[Farm produce listed in detail.]

Item in the Garrett over the Hall Chamber: One Bedstead with Camlett Furniture £1; One Feather Bed, two Bolsters and one Pillow £2 10s; Six old Blanketts and two Quilts 12s; Three Chairs 1s 6d; One Cradle with a Mattress and Counterpane £1; A parcell of Shelves with two doors and a pair of Doggs 4s.

Item in the Apple Chamber: Two Coffers 7s 6d; Nine stands 6s; A parcell of Lumber 5s.

Item in the Malt Garret: One Table Bedstead 6s; a Bedstead Curtains and Counterpane 10s 6d; One Feather Bed, two Bolsters and one Pillow £1 10s; One Coffer and a square Table 4s.

Item in the Green Garret: A Bedstead with green Furniture 8s; One Feather Bed and Bolster and a Flock Mattress 15s; One Form and a pair of Dogs 1s.

Item in the Powder Garret: Two Screens 8s; One Trunk and a Barber's Block 2s; Two Buff Coats and a parcell of Lumber 7s.

Item in the Garret Gallery: Three pictures 10s 6d; One large Coffer and a Square Table 5s; Two Hides of Tann Leather and one Hide of white Leather 2s 10d; A Table Bedstead and a parcell of old Curtains 10s 6d; One side Saddle and a Trunk 2s.

Item in the Damask Chamber: One Bedstead with Damask Furniture £1; One Feather Bed, Bolster and Pillow £3; Four Blanketts, One Quilt £1; One broken Looking Glass, a Table and stand 5s; Eight Cane Chairs 8s; An Iron Hearth, two pair of Iron Dogs, a Blower, a Brush and a Pair of Curtain Rods 10s 6d.

Item in the Hall Chamber: One Bedstead with Crimson Mohair Furniture lined with silk, a Case Compass Rodd with stuff Curtains and a Counterpane of the same with the Lining £6 6s; One Feather Bed, One Bolster and One Pillow £2 5s; Four Blanketts, one Quilt 9s; seven chairs lined with Silk and Mohair with Cases to them £1 1s; Two pieces of Hangings £1 1s; One large Looking Glass, One Swing Glass and a Table £2 2s; An Iron Hearth, a pair of brass Dogs, a pair of Iron Dogs, brass Fire Shovell and Tongs, a pair of Bellows and Brush 15s.

Item in the Yellow Room: One Bedstead with yellow Camlet Furniture £8; Two Feather Beds, one Bolster £4; Four Blankets, One Silk Quilt 10s; One Walnuttree Chest of Drawers 10s; Two Square Tables 3s; A pair of Linnen Window Curtains 2s 6d; Four Chane Chairs 2s 6d.

Item in the New Room: A leathern Screen 10s; A parcell of Deal Lath 14s; a parcell of Boards £1.

Item in the Stair Case: Six Cane Chairs 6s.

Item in the blew Room: One Bedstead with blew Furniture 10s 6d; One Feather Bed and two Pillows 15s; Three Blanketts and an old Quilt 9s; A Chest of Drawers 5s; A Square Table and Cover and a Glass 10s 6d; Three Cane Chairs 3s; Two pair of Iron Dogs, Tongs, Bellows, Fire Shovel, Brush and Blower 10s; Two pair of Linnen window Curtains 5s; One Close stool and Pan 5s.

Item in the blew Chamber Closet: One glass Case £1; a Square Table 3s; Three Cane Chairs and a Stool 4s; a Picture 1s.

Item in the Dressing Room: One large Cabinett £2 2s; One Dressing Table and Glass £1 1s; a large Looking Glass 15s; Two Pair of Window Curtains 5s; Four matted Chairs 16s; Two cane stools and one Cane Chair 6s; A Stove Compleat 6s; A Box lined with green Bays 2s; Two Baskets and a stool covered with green 1s; A small square Table 1s 6d.

In the Closet: One Walnuttree Escritoire £2 5s; One Oval Table 2s; Three Chairs lined with Velvet 7s 6d; One pair of Window Curtains 5s; A Chints Quilt in the Drawer of the Escritore 15s.

In the Anti chamber: One Clock with a Jappann'd Case £3 3s; The Front of a Press with Shelves 8s; Two Cane Chairs 1s 6d; A pair of Linnen Window Curtains and Rod 4s; a small Looking Glass, a Picture and Brush 1s; A pair of brass Doggs 2s; A Baskett Matt and scrubbing Brush 1s.

In the Nursery: One Bedstead with three Curtain Rods 5s; One Feather Bed, One Bolster and two Pillows £3 3s; Four Blanketts, one Coverlid 8s; A Wainscot Chest of Drawers 8s; One Square Table 3s; One Oval Table 2s; One Oblong Table 1s; A Looking Glass with a black Frame 1s; Five Chairs and a Stand 5s; A Linnen Press 10s; A Grate, brass Fender, pair of Bellows, Tongs, Fire-shovell and Brush 5s.

In the Store Room: One Spanish table 1s 6d; Seven new Mops and one hairbrush 4s 6d; Two pair of winding Blades and a pair of Scales 1s 6d; A Close Stool and brass pan 2s 6d; Eight old Boxes 2s; an old leather Cloke Bagg 1s; A Stool and four Basketts 1s.

In the Maid's Garrett: Two old corded Bedsteads 2s 6d; One Feather Bed Bolster and pillow on the red Bed £1; Three Blanketts and a Coverlid on the same Bed 5s; One other Feather Bed and a Bolster and a Flock Bolster 17s 6d; One Blankett and Coverlid 1s; One Chest of Drawers and one Table 1s 6d; Three Flasketts 3s; A parcell of old Lumber 1s.

Item in the Room over the Servants Hall: One Corded Bedstead with green Curtains 2s 6d; One Feather Bed, Bolster and two Pillows £1; Four Blanketts and a Coverlid 2s 6d; One Coffer 2s; A Bell 2s; A Square Table and a Chair 1s 6d; A pair of Ropes 1s 6d.

Item in the Pantry: Two Tables 1s 6d; A Napkin Press 1s 6d; One Japann'd Bowl and a leaden Cistern 7s 6d; Ten knives and ten forks with Ivory handles 3s; Two chairs and one Form 1s 6d; Twelve Agate handled knives and forks with a Box 5s; Twelve Ivory handled knives and forks with a Box 6s; A large Copper Cistern 10s 6d; A parcell of old Setting Nets and Lines 5s; A Copper Shaving pott 6d; A Tobacco Sieve 6d.

Item in the Servants Hall: Two Tables and two Forms 4s; Some Matting and two Plate Basketts 3s; Two old warming pans and Iron Crove 3s.

Item in the best Parlour: One large Looking Glass Japann'd and a Table of the same £2 2s; A large Picture over the Chimney peice with a gilt Frame £2 2s; One little Table, One Tea Table and a Tea Board 5s; Twelve Cane Chairs £1 10s; A pair of brass Dogs, Shovel, Tongs, Bellows and Brush 4s; Forty one blew China Plates £1 0s 6d; Twenty one blew China Plates £1 1s; Twelve Plates of burnt china 12s; Four Jappann'd Flash Basons 12s; Three large blew China Dishes 15s; seven small blew China Dishes 14s; seven large blew China Saucers 3s; Nine large Saucers of burnt China 6s 6d; A large blew China Bowl and cover 10s 6d; A blew China Jarr and Cover 5s; Five blew China Coffee Cupps 1s; Six Saucers of burnt China eight square 2s; Two sugar Dishes and Covers of burnt China 3s; A pair of White China Cupps 4s; Five Dram Cupps 1s; A White Sugar Dish and Cover and a Saucer of white China 4s; a Tea Pott of burnt China 2s; Two Images of White China 2s 6d; Two Jappann'd China Images 2s 6d; a blew China Tea Pott and Thirty

Six Cups and Saucers 8s; Ten small China Bottles and Two China Lyons 3s 4d; Three China Chocolate Cups 1s 6d; Six Basons and two small Sugar Dish Covers 6s; A red China Tea Pott 1s; Three China Candlesticks 1s; Glass Whole and broken 10s; Delpht Ware and China Ware 5s; Nine Tin Canisters and two Glass Jarrs 2s.

Item in the Drawing Room: A large Chimney Glass with a gilt frame and a pair of gilt Sconces £2 12s 6d; A large Picture with a gilt Frame £1 11s 6d; A Wallnutt tree Card Table 8s; An India Tea Table 10s 6d; A Walnut tree corner'd Cupboard with a Glass Case £1; Ten Walnut tree cane Chairs £2 2s; Two pair of Window Curtains, Vallants, Rods and Squobbs of sprigg'd Callico £2 2s; Two pair of Dogs, Tongs, Shovell, Bellows and Brush 10s; One large blew China Punch Bowl 15s; Eight Cupps of Burnt China, Saucers Ditto and Tea Pott, Sugar Dish and Cover, Slop Bason, Milk Pott and Boat for Spoons 10s 6d; a Moon 5s.

Item in the Hall: One large Oval Table 12s 6d; Two Square Tables 5s; Seven Cane Chairs 14s; A Barometer 10s 6d; Two pair of Dogs 4s.

Item in the Passage: One large Oval Table 7s; One lesser Ditto 7s 6d; A pair of Draught Tables 2s; A Quilting Frame and two Tresseles 1s.

Item in the little Parlour: One large Oval Table 5s; One lesser Ditto 2s 6d; An Eight day Clock in a Black Case £3 3s; One large Looking Glass 10s 6d; One lesser Glass with Glass Sconces and brass Nozells 10s 6d; Two Pictures with Gilt Frames, One Ditto with a black Frame [*no valuation*]; Seven Cane Chairs 14s; A Painted Floor Cloth 5s; A Stove compleat with brass Fender, Bellows, and Brush £1 1s; A pair of brass Arms 2s; Two pair of Cullgee Window Curtains, Vallants and Rods 7s 6d.

Item in the Smoaking Room: One Wainscot desk and Book Case £1 5s; One pair of Globes with Covers £1 1s; Two silver hilted swords £1 11s 6d; One Mourning Sword and two militia swords 2s; One small Oval Table 2s; A pair of pistolls with brass Barrells 15s; A Blunderbuss 10s 6d; A Fowling peice £1 11s 6d; A pair of Iron Dogs, Shovel, Poker, Tongs and Fender 2s 6d; Four Musketts £3; A Walnuttree Buroe, Claim'd by Mr. Bromsall Crouch [*no valuation*]; A large Looking Glass with a black Frame 10s 6d; Furniture trimm'd with Silver compleat £7.

Item in the Kitchen: Four pair of high brass Candlesticks 8s; Five flat Ditto 2s; Four Iron Candlesticks 6d; Six Spitts 7s; One Iron Jack with Chain Lines, Pulleys and Weights 10s 6d; Six Pikes and fourteen peices of old plated Armour 8s; Seven old leather Bucketts 7s; Two Forms 1s; Thirty eight Pewter Dishes weight one hundred and fourty pounds at seven pence per pound £4 1s 8d; Three dozen of Pewter Plates at Nine Shillings per dozen £1 7s; Six dozen ditto at seven shillings and six pence per dozen £2 5s; Two dozen and nine ditto much batter'd at six shillings per dozen 16s 6d; Two Water Plates 4s; A Pewter Cullender, two salts, a Cheese Plate and a peice of old Pewter 3s; Two Iron Spit Racks 10s;

Six Iron Scewers 6d; One Iron Horse and Fender 1s 6d; A pair of Tongs, Fire-Shovel and Poker and Cinder Shovel 3s; Two pair of Stilliards 6s; An Iron Grate of five Barrs with Cheeks and Cinder Grate 15s; Five Box Irons with Stands and Pads 5s; A Warming Pan 3s; Six pair of Bowls amd Six Walletts 12s; Two Copper Tea Kettles 5s; Three Stools, one Bacon Rack, one Salt Box and one Chair 4s; Two Iron Rings and Three Trevetts 1s 6d; An Iron Plate Rack 2s 6d; One brass Tinder Box and a small Chafing Dish 2s; One Copper Chocolate Pott 2s; a Hand Bell 3s; A Copper Pan to carry Coals with 6s; Three Copper Potts 6s 6d; An Iron Pigg, One Iron Blower and an hanging candlestick 3s.

Item in the Kitchen Closet: One Sweet Meat Cupboard 5s; One Chair, one Tea Board and two Tables 3s; A Coffee Mill and a pair of brass Scales and Weights 2s; Five Tea Potts, four Cups and saucers and a parcell of Earthen Ware 1s.

Item in the Scullery: One large Pottage Pott, weight sixteen pounds 13s 4d; One lesser Ditto eleven pounds 9s 2d; One Bell mettle Pott, ten pounds 4s; One Fish-Kettle and Plate, thirteen pounds 15s; One old Boiler, twenty four pounds 12s; Two brass Dish kettles twenty one pounds 12s; Four Stew Pans ten pounds 10s; seven sauce pans 8s; Three brass Skilletts, one Bell mettle Skillet 8s; Two brass Ladles, a Slice and a Skimmer 1s 6d; Two tin Covers, two tin dripping pans and a small Cullender 1s; Two Chopping Knives and a Chopping Block [*no valuation*]; Two Gridirons 2s 6d; Two Rack Spitts 4s; Two brass frying Pans 6s; A wooden Mortar and Iron Pestle 1s; A Plate Rack and a Fire Screen 4s; A wooden Maid [*no valuation*]; Sixteen Patty Pans 1s 6d; One hand bowl and two Pails 1s; A Water Tubb, two Trevets, A Chafing Dish and Peel 2s; A brass Cullender and lid of a Warming Pan 2s; A pair of Wafer Tongs 1s 6d; Two Iron Beef Forks and a broiling Iron 1s 6d; A parcell of Earthen Ware [*no valuation*]; A Mustard Bowl and two leaden Weights 3s.

Item in the Pastry: A large Marble Mortar 10s 6d; One Flower Bing 4s; A Flower Tubb 1s 6d; A hanging Shelf 1s; Three tin cake Hoops and an Apple roaster 6d; A Copper Stew Pan, One Copper Pastry Pan 6s 6d; A pair of brass Scales and four Weights 6s; Five Stone Jarrs 2s 6d; One Peck, a parcell of Earthen Ware and two mouse Trapps 1s 6d; One Tubb, One Chair, one Table and a large Bowl 1s 6d.

Item in the Laundry: One wooden Horse 4s; Two Tables 2s; Three Cane Chairs [*no valuation*]; A leaden Weight one hundred Weight 9s; Four Ironing Cloths 1s; A pair of Iron Dogs, Fire Shovel, Tongs and Bellows 1s; An Iron Tread, an Earthen Pott, a Form and a Leaden Weight with a Ring on it 4s.

Item in the Washhouse: One Copper Weight fifty three pounds and a Grate £2 5s; One lesser Copper weight thirty pounds 17s 6d; Five Tubbs, four Tap tubbs £1 5s; An old batter'd brass kettle 2s; A peice of Sheet Lead 1s 6d; Two Stands, two Pails, a Battledore and Block and two

Barrell Tubbs 6s 6d.

Item in the Drying Chamber: A Still and Trevett weight fifteen pounds 11s 6d; An old Coffer, a lye leach and several hair lines 3s; Two Garden Seats 5s; a parcell of Lumber.

Item in the Scalding House: One Copper weight seventeen pounds 11s 3d; A Barrel Churn 6s; a Cheese Press, a pail and a Bowl 3s.

Item in the Dairy: A Cheese Press 6s; Nine Cheese Fatts and a suitor 2s 6d; One Stand and two Kimnells 2s 6d; a kneading-trough, a stand and Form 4s; Five pails 4s.

Item in the Lardry: Three powdering Tubbs, two large Earthen Jarrs 15s; A Chopping Block, Cleaver, Kimnel and two Drinkstalls 4s.

Item in the small Beer Cellar: Nineteen Hogsheads and four Drinkstalls, two tubbs, two Kimnells and a Tunnell £3 15s.

Item in the Strong Beer Cellar: Nine Butts £2 14s; sixteen Hogsheads £2 8s; Six Drinkstalls 15s; Four brass Cocks 2s 6d.

Item in the Brewhouse: One Copper £8; A Mash Fatt £5; A Working Fatt £3; A small working Fatt 14s; Two Coolers £1 7s 6d; One Tubb 7s 6d; A Hop Sieve 2s; An Underback £1 13s 9d; A leaden Pump £1 2s 6d; A Grate £1; A bearing Tubb 2s; Eight Tap Tubbs 8s; Two little Barrells 1s 6d; A Malt Mill 15s; Three Hoggsheads 15s; Two Mash Rules, two Troughs and a Jett 5s; One Pail 1s 4d; Six Tubbs and a Kimnell 9s; A leaden Cistern and Pipes £2 12s.

Item in the Coach house: [*Contents listed including a coach and a chaise*]

Item Plate in the House: Five hundred and four Ounces at Five shillings and six pence per Ounce £138 12s; Twelve large Silver handle knives £1 16s; Twenty four Desert Knives and Forks with Silver Handles £2 8s; a Gold Watch, seals and Chain £12 12s; Two Enamel'd Gold Rings 10s 6d; Two pair of Christal Buttons set in Silver 3s; A peice of French Silver 2s; A Case of Instruments 15s; Two Lancetts in a case 3s; A peice of yellow Mettle, query if Gold [*no valuation*]; A Black Stand belonging to the Tea Kettle and Lamp having a Silver Nutt 6s; A Silver Shoe Buckle put into the Book Case 2s; A Studded Box in the same place 7s 6d.

Wearing Apparel and Linnen of Mr Bromsall: Twenty two shirts £8 5s; Fifteen handkerchiefs and one stock 7s 6d; Five Ditto 2s 6d; Fourteen Shirts £2 2s; Fifteen Stocks 5s; Twelve Night Caps 2s; Five pair of Silk Stockings £1; Twelve pair of Thread Stockings 6s; Four pair of Dimity Splatterdashes and one pair of Worsted Ditto 1s; A Suit of light coloured Cloth trimmed with Silver £4; Ditto White Cloth plain £1 11s 6d; Ditto black Cloth £2 2s; Ditto Cinamon colour'd Cloth £1 5s; Two Scarlet Rugg Coats and two pair of Breeches Ditto £1 10s; A Brocade Wastcoat £1 1s; Six Dimity White Wastcoats, one Holland Ditto £1 8s; A flower'd Damask Banyan and Cap £1 6s; Three Tye Wiggs and two Bob Wiggs £1 1s; Two pair of Shoes and two pair of

Boots, and three pair of Slippers 10s; A pair of Leather Splatterdashes 2s 6d.

Item House Linnen: Fine Flaxen Sheets, eight pair £5;, Two pair Ditto £1; Twenty five pair of middling sheets £6 5s; Ten Damask Table Cloths £2 5s; Sixteen Huckaback Table Cloths £1 12s; Twenty one Diaper Table Cloths £2 5s; Thirty seven Damask Napkins £1 4s; Thirty eight Diaper Napkins and one Side Board Cloth 12s 6d; Twenty four Pillowbiers 14s; Eight coarse Table Cloaths 8s; Forty one Towells and a parcell of old rubbers 10s 6d.

[*Contents of the numerous yards, barns, outbuildings and grounds listed in detail including* "A Bell on the House Top"]

Item in the Bottle House: Fifty five dozen and an half of Glass Bottles £3 14s.

Item in the Cellar: Two dozen of Glass Bottles 2s 8d.

Item in the Wash House: Thirteen Flasks and sixteen Glass Bottles 2s 6d.

Item in the Chamber over the Wash House: Four hundred and fifty new Dutch Tiles £1 17s 8d.

Item in the Hall Passage: A glass Lanthorn 3s.

At Thomas Brotherton's of Biggleswade, as appears by Information Twenty dozen of Glass Bottles valued at £1 6s 8d.
Exhibited 17 April 1731.

PRO: C 107/145
[second copy PRO: PROB 3/30/60]

NOTES

1. Undoubtedly the best account of Northill Manor is given in Miss P. Bell's *Northill Manor*, CRT 130 Northill. Conveyance of 1652 see AD 1622, VCH Vol III p.243.
2. Thomas Jeffreys Map of Bedfordshire, fully described in BHRS Vol.62. An edition with notes published by BHRS.
3. Ralph Bromsall's will proved 1693, (F 499).
4. Chancery proceedings relating to O.T. Bromsall found in C 107/145. The reference to the will in PCC is PROB 3/30/60. Both are held at the PRO. Abstract of Decree and proceedings in Chancery 1738–1754 [HY 62]
5. See Sharnbrook House Inventory of 1768.
6. Will of O.T. Bromsall, proved PCC 1731 (BS 11).
7. Marriage Settlement 1767 (BS 15).
8. Map of Northill 1781 (X 1/87).
9. Sale Catalogue (HY 74).
10. Conveyance to John Harvey of whole estate for £10,291 (HY 85–86).

OAKLEY HOUSE

Oakley House to 1772

The Manor of Oakley Reynes was purchased by the Duke of Bedford from William Levinz Junior in 1737.[1] Included in the sale was the Mansion House later called the Burystead. This house was situated to the south-east of the present house and is marked on a map of 1737.[2] The present house was added to the map at a later date in a different ink. It was in a field called Odells Upper Hullands.

The present house was therefore built entirely after 1737 and is not a late seventeenth-century house. It was probable that the Duke always intended to build himself a hunting lodge there.

The admittedly incomplete vouchers of the Russell estate suggest that the house was built between 1748 and 1750. At exactly the same time Woburn Abbey was being transformed by Henry Flitcroft. In the steward's correspondence there are a number of mentions of Flitcroft's involvement with Woburn, never any with Oakley. A voucher presented by Thomas Moore shows that he drew up unspecified plans for Oakley on 6 December 1747.[3] He was the equivalent of clerk of works at both houses and it seems as if Oakley was considered to be of less importance than Woburn and could be left to Moore to both design and oversee.

In a building lease of 1751, granted by the Duke of Bedford to allow him to build a house in King Street on the Russell's Bloomsbury estate, Moore is described as a bricklayer of Ilford, Essex. By 1763 his widow had taken on the lease.[4]

Through the vouchers it is possible to find out who the individual craftsmen were who worked on the house. Jones and Matthews provided much of the metal work from a large neat brass knocker on the front door for 10s 6d to a large "Kitchen Range & cheeks" for £6 3s 11d.[5] The same firm fitted most of the hearth equipment. The library, for example, had "A neat Steel Hearth Plate cutt & vailed with bright O.Gs & large Dutch Back for Do vailed weight 1lb 1qrs 14lb, a Pair neat Steel Globe head Dogs, a pair neat Steel Globe head Tongs and Shovel", all valued at £7 6s 0d.

Their bill lists most of the rooms of the house: the library, china room behind it, dressing room, "Lady Duchess's Bedchamber", its dressing room, dining parlour, room behind it, steward's parlour, butler's pantry, servants' hall and kitchen. There is no mention of a great parlour or withdrawing room.

Carpentry work done by John Phillips[6] included a frame over the chimney in the dining room. Much of the carving work was done by William Linnell, who worked at Woburn as well.[7] He carved a chimney

193

piece including marble frames over both dining room and library; all "by drawing", i.e. from a predetermined illustration, provided presumably by Thomas Moore. He was paid £6 15s 0d "To Carving a Cornish for the Bed chamber below, 3 members to Ditto Carvd as pair of Trusses and a frieze with festoons of fruit & flowers to Ditto." Linnell was helping give the house a rococo feel. Another marble architrave chimney piece was provided by Thomas Stephens.[8]

As no views predate Holland's alterations it is difficult to say what the exterior looked like. It possibly looked much as today but without the verandah and Holland's drawing room. It had at least 31 sash windows and a circular one for the staircase. William Burge supplied them in August 1748 to Bedford House in Bloomsbury, from where they came to Oakley by cart.[9]

By the same method, 4,400 best slates came from the Russells' Tavistock estate to Bedford House and then to Oakley.[10] By the beginning of 1749 carpenters were providing panelling for some of the rooms.[11] In April 1749 Robert and Matthew Huntley supplied 63 yards of printed cotton[12] and in July William and Joseph Harris, mercers, supplied 501¼ yards of yellow damask for curtains and bed fittings.[13] Yellow damask rooms were a feature of all three of the Russell houses in Bedfordshire.

Many of the suppliers and craftsmen were no doubt London based but occasionally local people were employed such as Thomas Berrill, living at Bozeat, "now employed for his Grace of Bedford at Oakeley".[14] Berrill was a stonemason and it was suggested that pressure be brought to bear on him to vote for the candidate the Duke supported in the forthcoming election.

It must have been at the end of 1749 or the beginning of 1750 that the Duke was able to enjoy his new hunting lodge.

The 1772 Inventory

The Inventory of 1772 of Oakley House was prepared to accompany a lease to Lord Trevor following the 4th Duke's death. It does not give the floor each room is on, but there is mention of at least two footmen's garrets, indicating that the dormer windows in the attic floor predate Henry Holland's alterations of 1787–1792. Three other chambers are probably on that floor.

On the main floor seem to have been only two principal bedrooms and the "Duchess's Dressing Room". It may be that there are empty rooms unaccounted for in the inventory, as they had been completely cleared before the lease was drawn up.

Downstairs were a study, dining parlour with a parlour adjoining, the yellow bedchamber with a yellow parlour adjoining. A passage led to the service wings in a separate block behind the main body of the house. This included the butler's pantry, steward's room and servants' hall. It

Plate 23: Oakley House: This view shows the house after Holland's alterations. (*Engraving: J.P. Neale, 1820s*)

omits the kitchen, which must have been cleared completely.

The ground plan suggests a compact house with the family and the service functions kept separate. It is not a house designed for overnight visits except by the Duke and his immediate family with perhaps one guest. It was intended to be a pied-à-terre for him to spend the night after a hard day's hunting locally with the precursor of the Oakley Hounds.

Most of the pre-1787 fittings and furnishings for Oakley were swept away by Henry Holland. The inventory when compared with contemporary changes at Woburn can yield some idea of what the house was like.

Geoffrey Beard and Helena Hayward when commenting on the mantlepieces at Woburn stated: "The Fourth Duke seemed to prefer the contrast between a carved wood overmantel and a chimney piece in statuary marble".[15] At Oakley the contrast was the same but the roles reversed, so that the overmantels were marble or Portland stone and the chimney pieces wooden. In the yellow bedchamber was a Portland stone mantle-slab with a wood chimney piece "& ovolos richly carv'd". The study and the dining parlour had marble ones. The wood work for the

Woburn overmantels seem to have been carved by William Linnell as well as the chimney pieces at Oakley.

The number of yellow rooms at Oakley is very significant with the yellow bedchamber containing the most furniture of any in the house, as well as being unusually for its date situated on the ground floor. At Woburn there is a "Yellow Drawing Room" with gilt rococo plasterwork. As a result of his embassy in France in 1763, the 4th Duke became a more ardent Francophile.[16] At Woburn the yellow flock paper was taken down and replaced by damask hangings of the same colour. At Oakley in 1772, 90 yards of yellow mixed Damask were used in the yellow bedroom and 70 in the yellow parlour adjoining. The curtains were "festooned", again a French idea. In the "Yellow Bedchamber" there were "Four Walnut tree French Elbow Chairs on Castors".

The Duke had created a room at Oakley straight out of Paris. Another possibly rococo piece is the "Pier Glass in a carved and gilt frame 37½ by 26½" which may well have been similar to the carved and gilt pier glasses supplied to the Duke in 1760 by Samuel Norman.

Many of the pieces can not be pictured readily because of their brief descriptions. As one would expect of a house furnished fashionably in the 1750s–1760s much of the furniture was in mahogany. In the study were a commode chest of drawers, a corner table, a square pillar and claw table on castors, a two- flap dining table and a tea kettle stand, all made out of mahogany. Walnut was not totally eclipsed as the chairs in most rooms were made out of walnut. In the dining parlour were nine walnut tree fan back chairs "cover'd with leather and brass nail'd". Both Duke and Duchess looked at themselves in oak framed mirrors.

As the inventory is attached to a lease no porcelain is mentioned. Eight cut glass water glasses and six decanters were left for the new tenant Lord Trevor, who for some reason either felt Bromham Hall was out of date or needed extra accommodation not too far away.

Oakley House after 1772

For the years of the 5th Duke's minority the furniture and fittings at Oakley would have remained unchanged. In 1787 the Duke started on the radical alteration of Woburn Abbey and Oakley House. His fondness of hunting and his need for a bolt-hole from the endless building work at Woburn Abbey meant that Oakley was completed first in 1792. Henry Holland, architect on both projects, transformed the rooms into a dignified Louis XVI French style rather than the more exotic rococo of his patron's grandfather.[17]

The "Hanging Book Case . . . Japann'd Pink and Gold in 3 Compartments Shaped front and circular top carved & gilt Bracket carved Partitions" fits oddly with this but Simon Houfe is convinced this is very much a piece of the 1790s. His detailed examination of pieces known to have been at Oakley shows how many of them stayed there until the sale of 1935.[18] Photographs of the 1920s show the Holland furniture in the drawing room in situ.

Much of the furniture was French inspired and a number of the pieces were painted.

Being a less important house, the furniture and decorations were not changed as each new owner sought to make their mark; a succession of elder sons and dowagers who lived in the house did not feel the need for radical change. After the tenancy, from 1898 to 1918, of Rowland Prothero, Lord Ernle, agent to the Duke and famous historian of agriculture,[19] the estate was sold to the Duke's cousin Lord Ampthill.[20] It was only in 1935 that the house passed from the Russell family and the contents dispersed.

OAKLEY HOUSE 1772

The Inventory referred to in a certain indenture of Lease bearing Date the 20th day of March 1772 made Between The Dutchess of Bedford Dutchess of Marlborough and Robert Palmer of the one Part And Robert Lord Trevor of the other Part, contained in Eleven Pages or Folios.
[signatures] Gertrude Bedford, C. Marlborough, Trevor, Robt. Palmer.
witnesses: Don: Murray, Danl. Beaumont.

An Inventory of the Furniture at Oakley House in the County of Bedford.

No.1 Footman's Garret: A 4 Post sacking bottom Bedstead with Green Cheney Furniture to ditto, A Feather Bed, Bolster and Pillow, Three Blankets and an old Stuff Back Quilt, A stump Bedstead and ½ Canopy, Laths and blue Cheney Furniture to ditto, a feather Bed & Bolster, three Blankets & a stuff back Quilt, A Wainscot Table with a Drawer, an old Linnen Chest, two matted Chairs and one stuff'd ditto, Four Rolls of Matting and some Hair Lines, Two short green Window Curtains and Rods, A wainscot Tray and a dry Rubber.

No.2 Footman's Garret: A 4 Post Bedstead and green Cheney Furniture to ditto, a Feather Bed and Bolster, two Blankets, Four matted Chairs, a green Cheney Window Curtain & Rod, & a wainscot Tray.

No.3 Mrs. Farrow's Chamber: A 4 Post Bedstead with a workt Dimity Furniture lin'd to ditto, A feather Bed and Bolster, Five Blankets & a white tufted Counterpane, A check Mattrass fill'd with Flocks, a Couch with a single Headpost & Laths & yellow throw over check Furniture to ditto, A check Mattrass and two Pillows, Three Blankets and a white tufted counterpane to ditto, A yellow and white check Case for Couch and Pillow, Two short cotton Window Curtains lined and Rods to ditto, Three matted Chairs, a Rope Ladder, a small dressing Glass in a Walnut tree frame, a tin Fender, a wainscot Table with a Drawer and a piece of matting.

No.4 Mrs. Gale's chamber: A 4 Post Bedstead and green Cheney

Furniture to ditto, A Feather Bed Bolster and one Pillow to ditto, Four Blankets and an old stuff back Quilt, A Horse Bedstead, a Flock Mattrass, two Blankets & a Coverlid, & a flock Bolster, Two green short cheney Window Curtains and Rods, A wainscot Table with a Drawer, a matted Chair & a stuff bottom ditto, and a pair of Steps for a Trap Door.

No.5 Mr. Branson's Chamber: A 4 Post Bedstead and green Cheney Furniture to ditto, Two check Mattrasses filled with Flocks, Three Pillows two Blankets and a stuff back Quilt, A Deal Case Two Check Mattrasses filled with Flocks, and two Blankets, Three matted chairs, One stuff Bottom ditto, a Wainscot Close Stool and Stone Pan, a Wainscot Table with a Drawer, Two green Cheney Window Curtains and Rods, A small Dressing Glass and two Tin Boxes.

No.6 Dutchess's Bedchamber: A steel Stove Fender, Shovel Tongs Poker Bellows and Brush, A wainscot lath bottom Bedstead with Mahogany Feet Posts, with a flower'd Cotton Furniture lined to ditto, Three check Mattrasses and one white ditto filled with Flocks, A feather Bolster and two Pillows, Three Blankets, A flower'd Cotton quilt lined with white, Two flower'd Cotton Festoon Window Curtains lined, Laths Lines and Tassells compleat, Six Walnut tree stuff back Chairs with flowerd Cotton Cases lined, Two Mahogany Night Tables, A Mahogany Commode Chest of Drawers, A Ditto Spider Leg Table, A Wainscot dressing Table, Two dressing Glasses in Mahogany Frames, A matted bottom Elbow Chair, A Mahogany Bason Stand, a Rope Ladder, About 76 Yards flower'd Cotton in Hangings for the Room.

No.7 Dutchess's Dressing Room: A Steel Stove Fender Shovel Tongs & Poker, A Walnut tree Couch frame with a single head, Posts and Laths, and a yellow & white throw over check Furniture to ditto, A flower'd Cotton Case for a Couch lined, a check Mattrass filled with Flocks and a feather Bolster, Three Blankets and a white tufted Counterpane, Two flowered Cotton Festoon Window Curtains lined, Laths Lines and Tassels compleat, Five Walnut tree stuff back Chairs stuft in Linnen with flowerd Cotton Cases lined to ditto, a Wainscot dressing Table with a Drawer, and a dressing Glass in a Walnut tree frame, About 50 Yards flower'd Cotton in Hangings round the Room.

No.8 Duke's Bedchamber: A steel Stove Fender Shovel Tongs Poker Bellows and Brush, A Wainscot Bedstead with a lath Bottom, Mahogany feet Posts 6 feet wide and 8 feet 6 Inches high with a flower'd Cotton Furniture lined to ditto, A borderd Bed tick & Bolster, Four down Pillows & two small Bolsters, A check Mattrass filled with Flocks, Four Blankets, A flower'd Cotton Quilt lined with white, Two Cotton Festoon Window Curtains lined, Laths Lines & Tassells compleat, Five Walnut tree stuff back Chairs cover'd with Linnen and flowerd Cotton Cases lined to ditto, A wainscot dressing Table and a Drawer and a ditto Glass, A Wainscot Close Stool and stone Pan, About 50 Yards flower'd Cotton in Hangings round the Room.

No.9 Study: A pair of steel Dogs Shovel & Tongs, A Landscape and Figures in a rich carv'd & painted Frame, A Pier Glass in a carv'd and gilt Frame 37½ by 26½, three yellow Camblet Festoon Window Curtains, Laths Lines and Tassels compleat, A Mahogany Commode chest of Drawers and green Cloth Cover, A Mahogany Corner Table lined, A Mahogany square Pillar & Claw Table on Castors, a small Mahogany two flap Dining Table, Eight Walnut tree fan back Chairs cover'd with black Leather and brass nail'd, A Mahogany Tea kettle Stand.

No.10 Dining Parlor: A steel Stove compleat, Three yellow Festoon Window Curtains Laths Lines and Tassels, A two flap oval Mahogany dining Table, Two Mahogany one flap dining Tables to join, a Mahogany Pillar and Claw reading Table on Castors, Nine Walnut tree fan back Chairs coverd with Leather and brass nail'd, a Landscape & Figures in a rich carv'd and painted frame, A Piece of Oil Cloth.

No.11 Parlor adjoining: A steel Stove Shovel Tongs Poker and Fender, Two yellow silk and worsted damask Festoon Window Curtains lin'd, Laths Lines and Tassels compleat, Five Walnut tree stuff back Chairs cover'd with yellow mixt Damask, brass nail'd and check Cases to ditto, One Elbow ditto, A Wainscot Table with a Drawer and a ditto Pot Cupboard, About 70 Yards of yellow mixt Damask to the Hangings round the Room.

No.12 Yellow Bedchamber: A steel Stove Shovel Tongs Poker Fender and Bellows, A Wainscot Bedsted with a Lath Bottom 6 feet wide and 8 feet 6 Inches high the feet post Mahogany with a yellow silk and worsted Damask Furniture and Cornices to ditto, Four check Mattrasses filled with Flocks, Two white ditto fill'd with Flocks, A feather Bolster and two Down Pillows, Four Blankets, a white Callico Quilt, A yellow mixt damask Counterpane lin'd with Stuff for the Bed, Two yellow mixt Damask Festoon Window Curtains lined, Laths Lines &c, Four Walnut tree French Elbow Chairs on Castors, stuft in Linnen and check Cases to ditto, Four Walnut tree stuff back Chairs cover'd with yellow mixt Damask brass nail'd and check Cases to ditto, A small Mahogany Spider leg Table, A Mahogany Night Table and Stone Pan, A wainscot dressing Table, a Dressing Glass in a Mahogany Frame, Two Elbow Chairs & matted Seats, About 90 Yards of yellow mixt Damask in the Hangings round the Room.

No.13 Yellow Parlor adjoining: A steel Stove Fender Shovel Tongs and Poker, Two yellow silk & worsted Damask Festoon Window Curtains, Laths Lines and Tassels compleat, Five Walnut tree stuff back Chairs cover'd with yellow mixt Damask, brass nail'd and check Cases to ditto, An Elbow ditto, a wainscot Table & a dressing Glass in a Walnut tree frame, About 70 Yards of yellow mixt Damask in the Hangings round the Room.

No.14 Passage: A brass Lantern frame glaz'd with Crown Glass and glass Shade, Two Camp Stools with painted Frames, a wainscot two flap oval Dining Table, An Umbrella and a piece of Matting.

No.15 Butler's Pantry: An Iron Stove with Cheeks Fender Shovel Tongs and Poker, Two wainscot Oval dining Tables, A wainscot Table with a Drawer and 5 old matted Chairs, Two Copper warming Pans, a Chocolate Pot & Quart Mug, Six pair of high brass Candlesticks and Eleven flat ditto, An Iron plate Warmer, Two Sets of Shovels Tongs and Pokers, Ten Iron high Candlesticks, one flat ditto and 4 pair of Snuffers, A small Bell Metal Pestle & Mortar & a Pewter Ink Stand.

No.16 Steward's Room: An Iron Stove Shovel Tongs Poker & Fender, A wainscot Bureau, A ditto long Table with two Flaps and a Drawer to ditto, A wainscot Pillar amd Claw Table, Five old matted Chairs & a Tin Sugar Box, Eight cut Water Glasses, and Saucers, Four Salts, Six Decanters and Stoppers, Twenty Pieces of Glass Ware and one Dozen Bone Handle Knives & Forks.

No.17 Servant's Hall: A Fender Shovel Tongs Poker & Trivet, Six flat Irons and two Stands, A Gridiron and a Dripping Pan Stand, Two Copper Tea Kettles and a frying Pan with an Iron handle, A Deal Table 12 feet long 3 feet wide with two Drawers, & a ditto 7 feet long with one Drawer, Three Forms, a small Deal Table, A Plate Rack, Three Cloaths Horses, A pair of Bellows, two old matted Chairs and six Wood Pails, Six Pewter Water Candlesticks.

Farm House

No.1: An old Bedstead & Curtains, A feather Bed & Bolster, Two Blankets and a Rug.

No.2 Garret: A four post Bedstead with Linnen Furniture lin'd A feather Bed & Bolster, Two Blankets & a Rug

No.3 Garret: A Bedstead & blue Stuff Furniture, A feather Bed and Bolster two Blankets and an old Rug.

[**No.4 Lumber Garret:** Six old Stump Bedsteads, Four ditto; Forty two old Blankets and three Rugs, Six flock Bolsters and a flock Mattrass, Ten Canvasses for flock Beds, Four Close stools, A Cloaths Horse and two deal Chests, Forty Earthen Pots, A tin Fender, two Iron shovels and four Pokers, Twenty four pair of coarse sheets. *entry deleted*]

No.5 Bedchamber: A four Post Bedstead and old green Furniture, A Feather Bed, A small Bolster and a Pillow, Three Blankets and an old stuff back Quilt, An old Chair, A Table and a Tin fender.

No.6 Bedchamber: A four Post Bedstead & old yellow Furniture to ditto, a feather Bed and Bolster, Three Blankets & a Coverlid, An old chair & a Tin fender.

No.7 Ground Floor Bedchamber: A four post Bedstead with an old blue Furniture fring'd, A feather Bed and Bolster, An old Blanket and a Quilt, An old Chest of Drawers, An old Table, Two old Chairs and a tin fender.

No.8 Bedchamber: A four post Bedstead with old blue Stuff Furniture to ditto, A feather Bed, Bolster and Pillow, Three Blankets and a Rug, A half Canopy Bed with old blue stuff Furniture to ditto, A feather Bed, Bolster and Pillow, A white Mattrass, Three Blankets and an old stuff back Quilt, Two dressing Glasses in black Frames, An old Chair and a Tin fender.

No.9 Kitchen: A large Range Cheeks Keeper and Iron back, A pair of standing Racks Hooks and Pins, A large fender Shovel and Poker, Two Spits and five Stove Trivets, Three Beef Forks Cleaver and Chopper and some Iron Skewers, A wind up Jack with a lead Weight. Copper: A Porridge Pot and Cover, A dripping Pan, Two oblong Stew pots and Covers, Three large stewing Pots and two Covers, Four small ditto and 3 Covers, Eleven Stew pans and Covers various, Two square and two round Pudding Pans, Two Octagon Dishes and two oval Ditto, Two Saucepans, A Cheese toaster, A Dredger and Jelly Pan, A Grater, A Spice Box, A round Pan and odd Cover, A Gallon drinking Pot, A Quart ditto, three Ladles and four Skimmers. Pewter: Two Tureens and Covers, 4 round Dishes, 20 Oval ditto, 7 Dish Covers, A Fish plate, A Water ditto, 13 Soup plates, 2 Doz. and ½ Plates, A Cullender, A Wash hand Bason. Brass: A large Dish kettle. Wooden Ware: Two old Tables, A chopping Block and Form, A Meat Screen lin'd with Tin, a marble Mortar, A Trough lin'd with Lead and 4 Wash Tubs.

[*Nos. 10–19: detailed list of contents of outbuildings.*]

Schedule of Fixtures

No.1 Footman's Garret: Two Sashes with Crown Glass & Iron hooks to Ditto, A deal Nest of Drawers, A deal Front to a Press Lock & Key, An Iron Lock and Key to the Door.

No.2 Footman's Garret: A Sash with Crown Glass Iron Hook to Ditto & an Iron Lock to the Door.

No.3 Mrs. Farrow's Chamber: Two Sashes with Crown Glass & Iron Hooks to ditto, Iron Bars & Brackets for a Rope Ladder, A Deal Press back lined Lock & Key, A Deal Nest of Drawers, a small Range & Iron rim Lock & Key to the Door.

No.4 Mrs. Gale's Chamber: Two Sashes with Crown Glass & Iron Fastning's to Ditto, A Deal Nest of Drawers, A Front to a Press, Lock & Key, An Iron Lock & key to the Room Door.

No.5 Mr. Branson's Chamber: Two Sashes with Crown Glass & Iron Fastnings to ditto, A Deal Nest of painted Drawers, A Front to a Press Lock & Key, An Iron Lock & Key to the Room Door.

No.6 Dutchess's Bedchamber: A Portland Stone Chimney Piece & Slab with chimney Piece and Ovolos richly carv'd, Two Sashes with Crown Glass, inside cut Shutters, Iron cross Fastnings to Ditto, a Cove plaister'd Cornice, Deal Lining from Ditto to Skirting, and 2 Mortice Locks & Keys to the Door.

No.7 Dressing Room: A Portland Stone Mantle & Slab, A Chimney Piece & Ovolos in Wood, Two Sashes with Crown Glass, Cut Shutters & Iron Bars to Ditto, Plaister Cornice, Deal Lining from Ditto to Skirting, & two Mortice Locks & Keys to the Door.

No.8 Duke's Bedchamber: A Portland Stone Mantle & Slab, A Chimney piece & Ovolos in Wood, Two Sashes & Crown Glass, inside Shutters & Iron fastnings to ditto, A plaister block Cornice, Deal Lining from Cornice to Skirting, A Closet with two Shelves, Two Mortice Locks and Keys to the Doors.

No.9 Study: A marble Mantle Slips & Slab, A wood Chimney Piece and Tresses richly carv'd, Three Sashes with Crown Glass, inside cut Shutters and Iron Fastnings to ditto, Two Mahogany Book Cases with Shelves & Drawers & gilt Edges, A plaister'd Cieling in Compartments, Plaister block Cornice, Wainscotted from Cornice to Skirting, And Lock & Key to the Door.

No.10 Passage: A Sash with Crown Glass, inside Shutters & Iron Fastnings to ditto, Wainscotted Dado & a Plaister block Cornice.

No.11 Dining Parlor: A Marble Mantle Slips & Slab, A Wood Chimney piece and Ovolos carvd, Three Sashes with Crown Glass, inside cut Shutters, & Iron cross Bars to ditto, Wainscotted from Cornice to Base, & two Mortice Locks & Keys to the Door.

No.12 Parlor adjoining: A Portland Chimney Piece & Slab, A wood Chimney piece and Ovolos, Two Sashes with Crown Glass, inside cut Shutters & Iron cross Bars to ditto, A plaister'd Cornice, Wainscotted Dado, Deal Lining from Cornice to ditto, And 2 Mortice Locks and Keys to the Doors.

No.13 Yellow Bedchamber: A Portland Stone Mantle & Slab, Wood Chimney piece, & ovolos richly carv'd, Two Sashes with Crown Glass, inside cut Shutters & Iron cross Bars to ditto, A plaisterd Cornice, Wainscot Dado, Deal Lining from Cornice to Ditto, & 2 Mortice Locks & Keys to the Door.

No.14. Yellow Parlor adjoining: A Portland Stone Mantle & Slab, Wood Chimney piece & Ovolo, Two Sashes & Crown Glass, Inside cut Shutters & Iron Bars to ditto, A plaister Cornice, Wainscot Dado, Deal Lining from Cornice to Dado, & 2 Mortice Locks & Keys to the Doors.

No.15 Stair Case & Passage: a Venetian Window Crown Glass, Inside Shutters Cross Iron Bars to ditto, Wainscot Dado & plaisterd to Cornice, a Block Cornice with Arch on Columns & Festoons of Flowers in the Passage, A large Iron with Bolts to the Front Door, & three Bells with Pulls to the several Rooms.

No.16 Butler's Pantry: A Portland Stone Mantle & Slab, The Front of a Deal Press with Shelves, A Corner Cupboard with folding Doors, Two pair of Window Shutters & Lock & Key to the Door.

No.17 Steward's Room: A Portland Stone Mantle & Slab, The Front of a Deal Press with Shelves, Two pair of Window Shutters & Iron Lock & Key to the Door.

No.18 Servants Hall: A Portland Mantle, A Range as fixt, A brass Kettle with Brick Iron & Lead Work, A lead Pump, A large Trough lin'd with Lead, A Cupboard with Shelves, Pav'd with Pavingham Stone & Lock & Key to the Door.

No.19 Larder: A deal Dresser with Shelves, A hanging Shelf, A Deal Cupboard, An Iron Lock & Key & Latch to the Door.

No.20 Cellars: Ten Wood Bins, Two Locks & Keys to the Doors, A Bottle Rack in the Passage.

Farm House

No. 1, 2 & 3: Three Latches to the Doors.

No.5: A small Range, 2 pr. Window Shutters, & a Lock & Key to the Door.

No.6: A small Range, 2 pr. Window Shutters, & a Lock & Key to the Door.

No.7: A small Range, 2 pr. of Window Shutters, & a Lock & Key to the Door.

No.8: A small Range, a Wood Mantle, & a Lock & Key.

No.9 Kitchen: A Copper with Iron & Brick work, Three stewing Stoves & Stone Top, & some Deal Shelves.

No.10 Larder: A deal Dresser with Drawers, A Safe with a Partition & a Lock & Key to the Door.

[Nos. 11–14: detailed list of fixtures of outbuildings]

BCRO: Russell Box 252

NOTES

1. Russell Box 188 Bundle cc 1 No.55; Russell Deeds Register Vol.1, No.225.
2. R 1/57.
3. Russell Box 762 Bill No.333 for July 1749
4. NC 1341 lease of building land in King St., Bloomsbury, to Thomas Moore of Ilford, Essex, Bricklayer, 1752. His widow held a similar lease in 1763. He died in 1760. He was the father-in-law of Richard How II of Aspley Guise. (HW Catalogue)
5. Russell Box 762 Bill No.58 incurred July-August 1749, paid 9 February 1749 [1750]
6. Russell Box 762 Bill No 56 receipted 26 January 1750 [1751]
7. Russell Box 762 Bill No.617, December 1749
8. Russell Box 763 Bill No.189, March 1750
9. Russell Box 762 Bill No.137, May 1749
10. Butcher Correspondence 3/49 19 July 1748
11. Butcher Correspondence 5/48 19 January 1748 [1749]
12. Russell Box 762 Bill No.133, 6 April 1749

13. Russell Box 762 Bill No.321, July 1749
14. Butcher Correspondence 2/16 27 March 1748
15. Geoffrey Beard and Helena Hayward's article in *Apollo* Vol. CXXVII No.316 p.394 (June 1988)
16. Beard etc. p.397
17. Simon Houfe's article *Furniture for a Hunting Box* in CL Vol.CLXXXV No.11 pp.54–56
18. Simon Houfe *Furniture* etc. p.56
19. Lord Ernle: *English Farming Past and Present*, 1912 (new edition of 1961 with Introductions by G.E. Fussell and O.R. Macgregor)
20. Simon Houfe *Furniture* . . . p.54; Oakley House Sale Catalogues of 1918 (X 65/103) and 1935 (X 67/411)

SHARNBROOK HOUSE

Sharnbrook House and Estate up to 1768

Long before the present Sharnbrook House was built, the site was occupied by the mansion house for the manor of Parentines. There was probably a house here in mediaeval times but certainly by 1563 it was the "chief messuage" of the joint manor of Langtons and Parentines when it was bought by Thomas Cobb. His family owned the house, latterly called Broadgates Hall, till 1694 when the last male Cobb died.[1]

An inventory of the house was made on 13 September 1675 on the death of William Cobb.[2] While useful in listing the stock of his farm buildings, the inventory does not describe the house room-by-room and so it is difficult to get an accurate picture of the lay out of the house. Like most of the houses of the Tudor and Stuart period in Sharnbrook it was probably built out of stone. It was surrounded by a number of farm buildings such as the "greate barn", "the barley, pease and oate hovel" and the "wheate hovell".

The only room that is named in the inventory is the "Kitchen Chamber", i.e. the room over the kitchen. The contents valued at £18 were: "one bedstead, one trundle bedstead, 2 feather beds with beding, Trunke chest and chest of drawers, close stoole, chaires, two stooles, Tooles, 2 stands, 1 Looking glass, 1 pair of bras rads (rods), one brasse fire shovell and tongs, 1 pair of bellowes and the hanginge of the same." Cobb possessed a number of silver items.

In 1700 the manor of Langtons and Parentines was split between three sisters, including Anne Aspin.[3] She lived at Sharnbrook House till 1724 and had the splendid gates cast, which now have been moved to a different site closer to Sharnbrook Church.[4] By 1740 John Bullock held all the mortgages on the estate and on 23 and 24 May 1740 he bought the freehold of the Sharnbrook estate, which consisted of the mansion of Langton and Paretines, Home Farm and Upper Farm.[5]

In addition to the mortgages for £2,579 he paid out an additional £3,180 to purchase the freehold. It was probably during the early years of his time at Sharnbrook that he had the modest red brick Sharnbrook House built. The drainpipes are dated 1749, consistent with his having decided to rebuild as soon as he purchased the estate. Thomas Fisher's watercolour of the house, dated c.1820, shows the entrance or west front of the house.[6]

John Bullock died in 1764 and the estate passed to his eldest son John, who assigned the estate to the executors of the last will of George Welson of the City of London for £2,200.[7] He took the unusual step of including the contents of the house in a mortgage, probably to pay off

Plate 24: Sharnbrook House: This view shows the house as it would have
looked at the time of the 1766 inventory.
(*Watercolour: Thomas Fisher, c.1820*)

his father's creditors and meet the legacies left by his will. It seems
unlikely it was caused by severe financial pressure because it was not
until 1791 that another son of John Bullock, senior, sold the Sharnbrook
estate to the Gibbards, by which time the Bullocks had long ceased to
reside at Sharnbrook House. The last entry in the parish register is of the
burial of Mary, wife of John Bullock, junior. Even Sarah, John senior's
widow, is not recorded there. They probably returned to London.

Sharnbrook House Inventory of 1768
The inventory almost certainly represents the furnishings, fittings and
pictures collected by John Bullock, senior.
The inventory lists 17 rooms and shows a house with six on the
ground floor, six or seven on the first floor and three or four on the
attic/garret floor. Absolute certainty in reconstituting the plan is difficult because of the mention of a chamber over the dining room and yet
there being no dining room listed in the inventory. A large mahogany
oval dining table is mentioned in the inventory of the hall with eight
walnut tree chairs. It could well be that the dining room led off the hall
behind the main staircase which would have come down into the hall.
If this is correct the inventory seems to have been taken in room
order. This would mean that the west or street front contained the common parlour (probably at the south-west corner of the house) the hall
and the stone parlour in the north-west. Next to the common parlour
in the south and probably south-east part of the house lay the best par-

lour. Next to it and possibly adjoining the hall but definitely in the east part of the house were the study and closet. The kitchen was adjacent to the stone parlour and probably occupied the north-east part of the house. As the stone parlour had two sideboards it is likely that it inter-connected with the dining room as did the kitchen.

A similar pattern emerges on the first floor. The west front contained the "Green Damask Chamber", the hall chamber and the "Blue Damask Chamber". It is probable that the "Green Damask Chamber" lay in the south-west and the "Blue Damask" in the north. Behind them there could well have been a landing with a window looking out to the south. The east side seems to have contained the new chamber and the chamber over the dining room. The name new chamber could possibly indicate new building between 1749–1768. A more likely solution is that the new chamber and the chamber over the dining room were divided into two. The cabinet was next to the "Blue Damask Room". The exact whereabouts of the nursery is difficult to determine. It was either in the north-east part of the house on the first floor or in the more usual posi-tion on the attic floor, which contained two maids' garrets and a men's garret.

The house was probably fitted out in the late 1740s or early 1750s. The furniture shows an interesting mixture of walnut and mahogany, both being found in the principal rooms. Walnut was now becoming less usual in prominent positions as it gave way to the fashion for mahogany. In Sharnbrook House, however, both were given equal weight. In the dining part of the hall the large oval dining table was accompanied by eight walnut chairs. In the best parlour two mahogany card tables were near eight walnut chairs.

John Bullock was clearly a serious collector of pictures. Unusually for a smaller Bedfordshire country house of this period, he had a consider-able number of pictures: 66 in total. The number of religious pictures, probably mainly from Italy, is immediately noteworthy: "The Wisemen's Offering", "Our Saviour in the Garden", "His Holy Family", and "The Samaritan". In Sharnbrook Church is a long and eloquent elegy to John Bullock on a monument in the chancel.[8] Maybe looking at the Samaritan in the hall chamber had a good effect.

The collection includes a number of Dutch pictures such as *Dutch Kitchen*, *Dutch Wakes*, and *Dutch Nursery*, as well as others that are likely to be Dutch such as the two *Landscapes with Cows* (school of Cuyp?) and the *Interior of a Church*. The number of seascapes noted could well be Dutch, though *India Fort with Shipping* could well be by a British artist. The *Flower pictures* are likely to be Dutch also, as they were the pioneers in this field.

In the hall he tried to create a consciously classical feel with a paint-ing of "Venus and Cupid", a black marble table on iron brackets, two alabaster figures and eleven plaster of paris busts and vases. This would have echoed the plain classical pediment over the hall door on the exterior.

The common parlour was reserved for the family "pictures", no doubt portraits of himself, his wife and his father-in-law, Thomas Edwards. They were deliberately put in the common parlour, where the family could see them most often.

Some of Bullock's intellectual interests are given by the inventory. He had a barometer and a compass. His study had over one hundred books of different sorts and a couch and pillow for him to recline on if the strain of study got too much! This collection was quite small in comparison with Elizabeth Kingsley's of Hasells Hall (died 1761) and John Orlebar of Hinwick House's (died 1765).[9]

Although china was replacing pewter almost entirely in fashionable houses, there was still plenty of pewter in Sharnbrook House in 1768. The best plates mentioned we must assume to be china but nowhere it is stated that they are. Unlike his exact contemporary Richard Antonie at nearby Colworth, Bullock seems to have collected virtually no china. The only reference to china in the inventory is to "a china stand with old China" in the "Blue Damask Chamber" and "two china chamber pots" in the closet.

Bullock, however, was well in advance of his contemporaries with his bell system for summoning servants. Such systems were only being installed in large houses at this date. No doubt a compact house like Sharnbrook House made setting up such a system easier.

On John Bullock junior's death the estate passed to his brother William. He sold it in 1791 to the Reverend John Gibbard.[10] His brother William Gibbard of the Grange in Sharnbrook lent John £1,565 17s. William's son, another John, inherited it. On the failure of male heirs, the estate ultimately passed to Leonard Stileman, who assumed the name Gibbard. Stileman-Gibbard sold the house to Esme Arkwright, from Harrold and the Master of Foxhounds of the Oakley Hunt. In 1912 Arkwright employed Clyde Young of Lancaster Place, London to double the house to its present size.[11] The onset of World War I meant that the role of Sharnbrook House as a grand country house in which to entertain smart friends down from London for a spot of hunting was seen as inappropriate.

As soon as peace was declared, Sharnbrook House was auctioned. From 1919–1950 the house was owned by the Gawens. On 20 May 1950 the house was again auctioned and purchased by the Women's Royal Voluntary Service, who after initial wholesale repair have maintained the house and its "beautifully laid out grounds" ever since, as a home for elderly people.[12]

SHARNBROOK 1768

The Schedule to which the above Deed refers:

In the Men's Garret: Two Bedsteads with half Canopy Furniture, Two Feather Beds, Two Bolsters, One Pillow, Three Blankets, One Quilt, One Rug, a large cradle pillow.

Maids Front Garret: a Four post Bedstead, Green Furniture, Feather Bed Bolster, One Blanket, One Coverlid.

Maids Back Garret: a Four post Bedstead, Red Furniture, Feather Bed Bolster, Three Blankets, One coverlid, Two Chairs.

In the Nursery: a Four post Bedstead, Serge Furniture, a Feather Bed, Bolster, Two pillows, a Mattress, Two Blankets, One Quilt, One small Bedstead and Feather Bed, Bolster, Two pillows, Two Blankets, One Quilt, One low Walnut Tree Chest of Drawers, Six Chairs Leather Bottoms, a Tea Table, a Cinder Shovell, a Compass Fire Iron.

In the Chamber over the Dining Room: a Four post Bedstead with Red Furniture, a Feather Bed, Bolster, One pillow, Three Blankets, a mattress, a White Quilt, a low Walnut Tree Chest of Drawers, a Dressing Table and Swing Glass, Two Mahogany Chairs, Tongs, Fire Shovel, poker and Fender, a Drapery Checked Window Curtain.

In the New Chamber: a Four post Bedstead, Green Furniture, a Feather Bed, Bolster, Two pillows, Three blankets, a White Quilt, a Walnut Tree Bureau, a large Looking Glass, a Chimney Glass, an India print, a picture of Three Ships, a Cloaths press, Three Ewe Tree Chairs, a night Elbow Chair Compleat, a large Checked window Curtain and Rod, Tongs, Fire Shovel, Fender and Brush, a new Riding Saddle and Girts, an Oval Dressing Table with Drawers.

In the Green Damask Chamber: a Four post Bedstead, Mahogany posts, Green Damask Furniture, a Feather Bed, Bolster, Two pillows, Three Blankets and Mattress, a white Counterpane, Four Needle work window curtains, Four Chairs needle work seats, Four stools Ditto, a Mahogony dressing table, a large Looking Glass Gilt Frame, a Picture of inside of a Church, a Landskip of Cattle etc., Bason and Stand, Dog Irons, Fire Shovel and Brush; in the Closet a Night Stool and Oval Looking Glass.

In the Hall Chamber: a Four post Bedstead, Mahogony posts, White Camblet peeling Furniture, a Feather Bed, Bolster, Two pillows, Three Blanketts, a Mattress, a Quilt, a Mahogany Bureau Dressing Table, large Looking Glass Gilt Frame, a large Swing Glass, Two pair yellow Silk Damask Window Curtains, Five Chairs Ditto Seats and Cases, an Elbow Chair with Work Seat, The picture of The Samaritan, a large Landskip, Two Dog Irons, Tongs, Fire Shovel, Fender and Washing Stand.

In the Blue Damask Chamber: a Four post Bedstead, Blue Damask Furniture, a Fether Bed, Bolster, Two pillows and mattress, Four Blankets, One Quilt, Two Sets Blue Window Curtains and Rods, Cherry Tree [?Dressing] Table Seven Drawers, Four Walnut Tree Chairs Blue Damask Seats, One Elbow Chair, Needle work Seat, a large Walnut

Tree cabinet, a China stand with old China, a small mahogany Dining Table, a large Landskip of Cattle, A compass Fire Iron and Stove, Grate, Tongs, Fire Shovel, poker and Fender, a hand Brush.

In the Cabinet Drawers: One large curious worked white Quilt, One Flowered Quilt, One white Counterpane, One pair of Needle Work Window Curtains, Nine pieces of Needle work, One piece piece [*sic*] of needle work.

In the Closet: One large Box with papers, a Window Blind, a Basket, Two Old Curtains and Rod, Two China Chamber pots, a Green Silk Umbrello.

In the Study: Two large Book Cases with Glass Doors and upwards of One Hundred Books of different sorts, a Couch and pillow, One Mahogany Chair, One Smoaking Chair, One pair of Dog Irons.

In the best Parlour: Brass Hearth Dogs, Shovel, Tongs and Iron Back, a Chimney Glass in a Glass Frame, a Landskip in painted Frame, The Wisemen's Offerings, our Saviour in the Garden, and the Holy Family, Two Flower pieces, and India Fort with Shipping, a Frost piece and Dutch Kitchen, a Sea piece with a Ship on Fire, a Dutch Nursery, Two old pictures, Seven Landskips, a Candle Light peice, a picture of Ruins, a Ditto in Crayons, Two Coats Arms, Two Sets Window Curtains, Two Sconce Glasses in Frames, Two Mahogany Card Tables, eight Walnut Tree Chairs and Cases, One Brass Lock, and Key and Pull to Bell.

In the Common Parlour: a Compass Stove, Fender, poker, Tongs, Shovell, a Chimney glass in a painted Frame, the Picture of the Holy Family in a Frame, a Head in Ditto, a piece of Shipping, Six Family pictures, Charles First and Corella, a Sconce Glass, Glass Arms, a Barometer, Three Setts yellow Silk Damask Window Curtains, a Table, Three Window Blinds, a Mahogany Tea Table, a Ditto Oval Table, an English Carpet, Six Walnut Tree Chairs, Three Cloak Pinns, Three Bottle Boards, a Tea Chest, a Copper Coal Skuttle, a Brass Lock and Key and Pull to Bell.

In the Hall: Two Dog Irons, a Shovel and Tongs, a picture of Venus and Cupid, Two Water Peices, Two Dutch Wakes, a Stags Head, a Glass Gilt Frame, a Black marble Table on Two Iron Bracketts, Two Alabaster figures, Eleven plaister of paris Busts and Vases, a large Mahogany Oval Dining Table, a Claw Table, Eight Walnut Tree Chairs, Two pieces of Floor Cloth, a Large Copper, Four Hat pins, a Pull to Bell.

In the Stone Parlour: a Compass Grate as fixt, a Fender, poker, Tongs and Shovell, Two Hooks, a Chimney Glass in a Gilt frame, a Landskip, a piece of still life, a Fruit Peice, Two side Boards, Two Sconce Glass Gilt Frames, nineteen pictures, a Mahogany Table, six Cherry tree Chairs, Two Claw Ditto, Door Curtain as fixt, a Brass Lock, pull to Bell and a spud.

In the Kitchen: A Smoak Jack and Chain, Iron Racks, a Crane and

Hooks, Dog Irons, a large Iron Grate and Wings, Keepers, Tongs, Fire Shovel, poker and Fender, One Cradle Spit, Three Common Spits, One Cinder Shovel, a large meat Screen, Three Gridirons, a Clever and Choping Knife, Four Box Irons and Heaters, Four flat Irons, Two pair Stilyards and Weights, One Salt Box, One pair Bellows, a Copper Coal Skuttle, Seven Saucepans, Three Tea Kettles, Three Stewpans, One Coffee pot, Two Fish Kettles and Covers, a Chocolate pot, One Quart Copper Bottom of Warming Pan, a Warming pan, Two Cheese Toasters, Six upright Brass Candlesticks, Three flat Ditto Ditto, five upright Iron Candlesticks, Four flat Ditto Ditto, Two pair of Steel Snuffers, Two small pudding pans, Two Two leav'd Dining Tables, Two Tea Tables, a Candle Box, One Deal Dresser and pewter Frame, Nineteen pewter Dishes, Nine water-plates, Eleven Soup plates, Fifteen best plates, Forty Common plates, a Cullinder, a Fish Strainer, a Bed pan, Five small pewter wine measures, One small Ditto Tunning Dish, One Case of Shelves for Earthenware, Two large Elbow Winsor Chairs, Four small Winsor Chairs, Three old Leather Chairs, One Umbela, a child's lofty Cane Dinner Chair, Four pottage potts and Covers, One .Kettle, One Bell mettal pot, One Brass Laddle, One Brass Simmer, Two Tin Dripping pans, One Lead Sink in Scullery, Three Iron hoop'd barrells in passage, One marble morter and pestle, One Wooden Ditto Ditto, One Trivet and Footman, One Bottle Rack and Six Dozen Bottles.

In the Wash House: Two Stills and Worm, a Japan Cistern and cock, a pickling Tub and Cover, a Washing Furnace and Iron Bar and an Iron Oven Door, a Salimander.

In the Stable: Two Mares and One Colt.

21 Dec 1768

BCRO: AD 324

NOTES

1. See my unpublished notes *The History of Sharnbrook House* CRT 130 Sharnbrook 14. W.M. Harvey's *Hundred of Willey* p.465. 1563 Conveyance see VCH Vol.III p.91.
2. William Cobb's Inventory of 1675 PRO ref. PROB 4/2118.
3. GA 769.
4. Joan Anderson *Family Story*, B. Mag Vol.7 pp.59–65 on the Gibbards. On p.64 is a photograph of Anne Aspin's gates.
5. GA 825–827.
6. Slide 861. Shuttleworth Collection.
7. AD 324.
8. Monument in Sharnbrook Church, Harvey pp.472–473.
9. Compare inventories of Hasells 1761 and Hinwick House 1766.
10. GA 2565.
11. Stileman-Gibbard still owned Sharnbrook House estate at the time of the so-called Domesday Survey of 1910 but by 1911 had sold it to Esme Arkwright. Clyde Young's plans have the reference RDBP 1/162.
12. Sale Catalogue – copy at CRT 130 Sharnbrook 14.

SOUTHILL PARK HOUSE

Southill till 1779

In the years after the Civil War, Sir John, later Chief Justice Kelyng, bought up property in Southill. Among his purchases was a capital messuage "formerly occupied by Sir Henry Massingberd and lying a little to the north-west of the church".[1] In 1693 it was sold to Admiral Sir George Byng[2] (created Lord Torrington in 1721). It was a comfortable house with six reception rooms on the ground floor and the kitchen quarters to one side and reached by a colonnade.[3] Byng lived there and in his son's marriage settlement, dated 1724, he gave his wife a life interest in the house he then lived in.[4]

Yet by his will and a further settlement in 1732[5] he specifically gave his wife a life interest in his capital messuage "newly erected at some distance from the old one pulled down." He wanted to build a grand house with grand gardens and canal to emphasise his and his family's importance. His grandson John Byng, the diarist, commented in 1793: "My grandfather ... built Southill House in an open field; and had to plant trees, to dig canals, to make mounts, and to throw money away in vile taste."[6]

This evidence suggests a date for the building of the core of the present house between 1724 and 1732 indicating that Southill is not a seventeenth-century house. A sketch on Gordon's map of 1736[7] and one by Thomas Badeslade c.1740[8] show a central block connected to two square pavilions by open arcades. The central block contained a basement and two principal floors of five windows across. Only above the central three windows was another storey of bedrooms and above that attics with dormer windows. The entrance porch was columned with a pediment above carrying what appear to be the Byng coat of arms. Steps lead up to the front door on the piano nobile. The pavilions had Venetian windows. What is illustrated by these views is substantially what the first Lord Torrington built. As the time span in which he could have built the house was so short, it is unlikely that it was built in two stages.

Isaac Ware has been consistently referred to as having a major hand in the building of the pre-Holland Southill. There is little evidence for his working as an architect until the mid- 1740s, i.e. after the main part of the building had been erected. He did remodel Chicksands Priory in 1750 and it is possible he put in a new main staircase at Southill then. It is difficult to see what else he might have done to Southill, as a view of 1782[9] of the same facade as Badeslade shows no exterior change from c.1740, apart from the filling in of the arcades and turning them into rooms.

TORRINGTON. *BARON of* Southill *REAR* ... *ADMIRAL of* GREAT BRITAIN, *ADMIRAL and COMMANDER in C*

Plate 25: Southill Park: An early view of the house as it would have looked at
the time of the 1779 inventory.
(*Engraving: Thomas Badeslade, c.1740*)

The 2nd Lord Torrington in the late 1770s decided to add a new service wing but mounting debts forced him to leave the country.[10] In 1779
the house was let to Lord Polwarth and his wife Amabel, daughter of
Marchioness Grey of Wrest Park. While the Polwarths were still considering taking the house she wrote to her mother on 6 May 1779
describing Southill: "There is an apartment of large rooms below stairs,
& a bedchamber with 2 dressingrooms, good & convenient excepting in
the want of a closet to the lady's apartment. Over this are 8 v.g. rooms,
4 bedchambers, & 4 dressingrooms, only they do not lie so conveniently
to each other. On the 3rd story are 4 bedchambers with small closets,
these served for nurseries in Lord Torrington's time, & 4 garrets are
overhead. Most of the servants then lay in the underground floor, but
there are 3 or 4 rooms near the kitchen that would do for our upper servants at least. The most curious part is a new range of low offices that
were scarcely finished when Lord T. left England, & are almost as pretty
& complete as anything at Holcomb, a confectionery, a stillroom, a
bakehouse, & a laundry, & washhouse. You never saw anything neater
than the last, with its range of 7 troughs, with 2 cocks for hot or cold
water in each; you would think the ladies of the family intended to wash
sometimes for their own amusement. There is also an unfinished bath
where the workmen seem to have been sent away at a minute's warning, for the very mortar is lying ready to join some tottering bricks. . . .

Nothing is wanting for any family but linen & china. . . . Most of the pictures are gone, but the lady's dressingroom is hung round with Worlidge's gems & Bartolozzi's red prints."[11]

The 1779 Inventory

The inventory of Southill prepared in 1779 accompanied the lease of the house fully furnished to Lord Polwarth and his wife Amabel.

The inventory starts in the garrets in the central block where there were four rooms and a landing. On the nursery floor, again in the centre, were Miss Byng's bed chamber, dressing room and closet, the nursery, the room of Mrs Ganycliff the head nurse maid and a landing. The inventory then goes to the next floor called the best bedchamber floor. It took in the whole of the central block which had four bedrooms with their dressing rooms and a landing. Down the staircase the inventory finally arrives at the piano nobile level where were the principal rooms. To the left hand side of the great hall were the library, eating room, ante-room and ball room as on Holland's plan of Southill of 1795, drawn before rebuilding. Similarly, behind the hall was the drawing room with Lady Torrington's dressing room, Lord Torrington's bedchamber and dressing room as on that plan. The small room adjoining Lord Torrington's dressing room was called the powder room. The lady's maid's room was opposite. Holland's small hall and hall parlour must be represented by the vestibule and hall bed chamber.

The kitchen was in the east pavilion. Underneath in the basement were the various "Caves" in the inventory, providing bedrooms for servants. They were called caves because they were domed. They included an early gentlemen's water closet, where they could weigh themselves on the "neat Beam & Scales" as well. Elsewhere there was a bathing room. There were as usual a number of auxiliary service buildings, some of which were no doubt in the basement and some near the kitchen. Below the basement were extensive cellars for ale and wine. In the grounds were the garden house and the menagery. The list for the menagery ends with an extensive list of gardening tools.

The house was let fully furnished but there was no silver, china or glass included, so the Polwarths would have to have brought their own. The furniture of all the principal rooms is almost exclusively mahogany, some of which survived to the Whitbreads' ownership of the house. The chairs in the hall had an earl's coronet on them and the round table in the eating parlour had a "border of different wood" as an inlay. The great dining table had a central winding system so that further pieces could be inserted. In 1779 two square pieces were in the ante- room.

The inventory shows that the Byngs were beginning to introduce new equipment into the house. Bath stoves were scattered over the house but in none of the principal rooms. They appear in the hall bed room, in Miss Byng's nursery and in the small chintz bedroom and dressing room. The one in the lady's maid's room was removed to my lord's dressing room.

The long distance between kitchen and eating chamber meant that there was a good chance of the food getting cold. In the oak parlour was a "wainscot Plate Warmer lin'd Tin and Iron Heater". In the hall was a "Mahogany Breakfast Oven Lin'd with Tin".

Many of the curtains were made out of Manchester, i.e. cotton, replacing the heavier damasks of a few years earlier. The Byngs clearly favoured striped fabrics. A detailed list of carpets shows that most of the principal rooms had their own carpets and in one instance there was colour co-ordination with the large blue carpet going to the large blue dressing room. There were four carpets to go round beds.

Although no china or silver was left behind, there was some very fine pewter in the kitchen, much of it marked with a "T" or a crest and coronet. The only china items mentioned were one large blue and white Delft and five Queen's ware (light earthenware Wedgwood) hand basins.

There were a considerable number of pictures, including one Chinese, family portraits and prints. Lady Torrington's dressing room contained 53 pictures, in 18 of which there are several small ones within the outside frame.

Southill since 1779

On 19 and 20 June 1795 the Southill estate was sold to Samuel Whitbread, the famous brewer, for £85,000.[12] Whitbread came from a Bedfordshire family who had already built up a sizeable estate in nearby Cardington. Unfortunately, he only lived for just under a year at Southill, dying on 8 June 1796.

He had, however, made the important decision to remodel Southill with Henry Holland as his architect. By December 1795, Holland had prepared plans of the existing house[13] and by 1796 building work had started. It is almost certain Whitbread's son, Samuel Whitbread II, was consulted over Holland's appointment. As a friend of the Prince Regent and a close political ally of the Duke of Bedford he knew Holland's

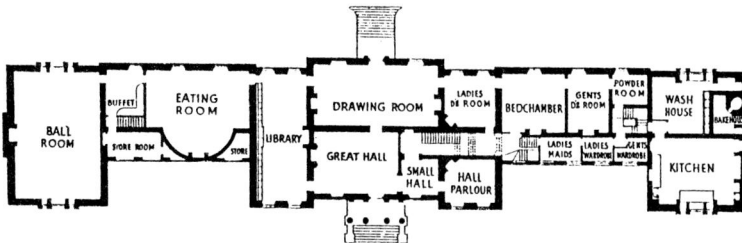

Plate 26: Southill Park: Ground plan of the house before alterations in 1795

work at Woburn and Oakley, undertaken from 1787 to 1802, and more importantly Carlton House. Samuel Whitbread I's death did not interrupt the work, as £3,250 was paid to Holland for work done in 1796. The full project took from 1796 to 1803 with the bulk done between 1796 and 1802, costing £54,188 16s 10d.[14] Samuel Whitbread's own accounts show substantial payments on furniture. It is therefore probable that the money paid to Holland related mainly to building and decorating work.

What did Holland intend to achieve at Southill and what did he actually do? His final plans for the project are dated 1800 but it is clear that the broad outlines were fixed from the start.[15] He wanted to convert the existing house rather than totally demolish it. He wished to rearrange the principal rooms to give a formal French progression of rooms in the centre of the house. The east pavilion was to be a domestic family area with the west pavilion housing a billiard room and breakfast room. The kitchens were to be banished to the basement. The principal rooms were to be decorated in a style influenced by French designs but "whose ultimate effect was wholly English"[16] as Professor Richardson justly remarks. Some of the furniture was designed by Holland himself. The rest of the furniture installed during his period as architect was bought from a few main craftsmen with the specific intention of complementing and enhancing his overall scheme. In short, exterior was intended to complement interior, ceilings to offset furniture, room to harmonise with room. Unified yet subtly different, all was to be executed to the highest level of craftsmanship. Although Southill has been rightly described as "the only completely intact monument to his style as an architect and an interior decorator and shows his style at its most mature phase",[17] recent restoration work has revealed the important changes to Holland's colour schemes made by his assistant C.H. Tatham in the years after his death.

To create the formal progress of rooms Holland decided to make an entrance on the north side, rather than the south where it had been previously. He put this off-centre so he could retain the former drawing room as a dining room. To this he added a bay window so that a good view could be obtained of the park and lake to the north. On the south, a colonnade was added and the old great hall converted into the dining room.

The new hall had displaced the library, which was moved into a new room. In the old west pavilion area had been a ball room. This was now occupied by a billiard and breakfast room. The corresponding east pavilion now contained the nursery and Mrs. Whitbread's room, displacing the kitchen. Although no doubt an improvement so far as the principal rooms were concerned, the banishment of the kitchens to the basement meant difficulties for the domestic staff. In 1927 a rating assessor commented: "Kitchen and Domestic Offices in Basement, From

Kitchen to Dining Room 15 yards up 8 steps, 29 yards to lift, up lift, 10 yards to Dining Room door".[18]

To give a greater harmony and consistency to the exterior Holland had the old brick house encased in Totternhoe clunch and Portland stone. The work on the exterior was in full swing by 1797 when George Garrard made his watercolour sketch of workmen unloading stone near the north front, which is encased in scaffolding. It was subsequently made up with interesting differences into an oil painting entitled *The Building of Southill*.[19] Unfortunately, Holland's small use of Totternhoe clunch was unwise, as it has not weathered well and let in water, causing rot. The major restoration of the 1990s has been required to solve the problem.

In addition Holland raised the two sides of the central block of the house to attic level and crowned it with a classical pediment. Whether he totally rebuilt the two pavilions and their connecting sections to the main part of the house or merely remodelled them is unclear.

The house was occupied by the Whitbreads by April 1800. What did

Plate 27: Southill Park: The hall. Some of the furniture belonged to the Byngs and may therefore be included in the 1779 inventory.
(*Photograph: c.1930*)

the rooms look like? Clues are given by the paint scrapings made during the recent restoration and by the 1816 inventory taken on the death of Samuel Whitbread II.[20] Not all the furniture that was there in 1816 was there in 1800, and as we shall see the decoration in some rooms was very different.

It is likely that the Whitbreads bought some of the existing furniture from Lord Torrington. Between Midsummer and Christmas 1796, £553 was spent on furniture and this may well represent purchases from the Byngs.[21] Christopher Hussey reckons that some of the mahogany furniture listed in the 1816 inventory and illustrated in his *Country Life* article came from the Byngs.[22] Unfortunately, it is not clear which pieces these were in the 1779 inventory. The two large marble tables with gilt frames in the drawing room in 1779 could well be the "two Kilkenny marble slabs on large carved painted frames with Scrole legs." The mahogany doors upstairs remained in position and were used in the Holland alterations.

The vast majority of the pieces were purchased from cabinet makers and dealers, rather than from the Byngs. In 1797 over £1,000 was spent on furniture and only in 1807 did it fall below that figure up to 1813. High expenditure included £5,704 in 1798 and £5,495 in 1802. In 1811 after a lower figure it rose to over £2,000 where it remained for 1812 and 1813. Some of the pieces were to Holland's own design such as the commode book case in the library and the decoration of the pier glass above it.

Holland used cabinet makers and upholsterers who had worked at Carlton House, Woburn, Oakley and later Colworth. Holland knew his craftsmen well and could trust their skills to make furniture to his exacting standards of excellence. As F.J.B. Watson remarked: "But the character of much of the furniture is so marked by Gallic idioms that it is impossible to suppose that he kept a merely supervisory eye on what furnishings purchased by others. The stamp of his taste is too firmly imprinted on much of the furniture . . . and it seems reasonable to suppose that he had a hand in the design of at least the most important of the principal rooms".[23] The furniture from the Byngs was placed principally in the entrance hall, a deliberately understated room, where slightly out-of-date furniture could be tolerated.

The dining room was described by the Reverend Samuel Johnes in April 1800 when he visited Southill as "rather a gloomy room and too low. It is green with white stucco and dark green curtains".[24]

The furniture in 1816 was all mahogany. The severe rectilinear design of the twenty four chairs echoed what is described by F.J.B. Watson as "the rather severely Roman character of the room".[25] The design of the five mahogany sideboards on "curved Chimera legs" is close to ones reproduced in the book *Fragments*, 1806 by C.H. Tatham, Holland's assistant.

The drawing room and ante-room were in Holland's original scheme "Covered with Green Paper". In the ante-room the handsome kingwood writing table mentioned in the 1816 inventory was covered with green velvet. The cushions of the small chairs were also covered in green velvet. The carpet was rose and green embossed. The large ottoman had a carved and gilt frame "and decorated with Ormolu Ornaments on green velvet Ground . . .". Similar pieces of furniture covered with green velvet were found in the drawing room.

The interrelationship of the furniture at Southill and that at Colworth was highlighted in an exhibition at the Royal Pavilion in 1951 where the two were intermingled. The Southill arm chairs with bolt heads dating from 1796 to 1799 being contrasted with those from Hartwell (where the Colworth furniture had gone[26]). The "round Kingwood Table with Lions' Heads on the gilt rim, on a large Pillar and triangular bottom very richly carved & Gilt etc. in the best manner" is of similar design, though not shape, to the octagonal library table at Colworth.[27]

The library at Southill contains bookcases designed by Holland himself. Although housing an important collection of books, added to regularly at a cost of several hundred pounds a year up to 1813,[28] it was becoming a more general reception room. This foreshadows the library at Wrest Park, which Earl de Grey designed to be the largest room in the house. At Southill were numerous chairs, a Pembroke table (able to be converted into a backgammon board), drafts, ivory chess men, dice and a "Pope Joan board". The splendid Louis XVI clock and barometer were originally in the room. They were both made by Frenchmen with the cases by German emigres to Paris.

In the east section of the house the boudoir next to Mrs. Whitbread's room contained in 1816 a painted panel over the chimney glass and two fire screens were painted by Louis Andre Delabriere, painter, of Tenterden Street, London. In Mrs. Whitbread's room were pieces clearly French inspired such as the writing desk. The gilt frames were supplied by March, partner of Tatham, who supplied much of the furniture at Colworth. Both rooms were furnished by April 1800. The house was probably completed by 1802 including many of the important collection of pictures and Garrard and Gilpin's plaster casts over the doorways. On 17 June 1806 Henry Holland died.[29]

Surprisingly, in the years 1808 to 1813 subtle changes to Holland's designs were made, probably by his assistant C.H. Tatham. Gervase Jackson-Stops[30] sees these changes as paralleled by the redecoration of Carlton House by Walsh Porter and Thomas Hopper in a more opulent style. He detects a "sea change at Southill" about 1808. The dining room was painted in a darker green about 1809. At this time, no doubt were added the narrow panels with vine leaves intermingled with grasshoppers and snails depicted to give more appearance of height to the room

Johnes described as "too low" in 1800. They also help give the room a less severe feel.

More dramatic was the conversion of the drawing room and ante-room from green paper to "Geranium Red". Jackson-Stops comments, "The flamboyance and femininity of the ante-room and drawing room . . . are in a new late Regency vocabulary that might well haver left him cold." The paper was supplied in 1808 by Robson and Hale, paper hangers to the Prince of Wales. The "Red Sarsnet Curtains" mentioned in the 1816 inventory repeats the new colour scheme but some of the furniture, as we have seen, survived from the Holland scheme.

The astonishing feature of Southill is that so little of the fittings and decoration scheme has changed since 1816. In many great houses, major alterations occur every generation or so. The Whitbread family are now celebrating two hundred years of owning the Southill estate and have preserved Southill as unchanged as possible. In the years immediately after Samuel Whitbread II's death they had no choice as retrenchment was necessary following his extravagance.[31]

Thereafter it has been a matter of choice. Successive generations have grown up there, been busy as M.P.s, chairmen of Whitbread's Brewery, county councillors and lords lieutenant. They have been happy to leave the house undisturbed.

In 1989, however, major decisions had to be made as a result of the rot brought about by the deterioration. Characteristically, after careful paint scrapes had been taken the Whitbreads decided to return the dining room to the colour scheme of 1806 and the drawing room to the appearance in 1816. As Jackson-Stops commented: "After a three year restoration programme Southill has re-emerged as the archetypal Regency house".

SOUTHILL HOUSE 1779

Inventory of Furniture in Southill House as taken the 28th & 29th Days of May 1779.

Landing Place Garrett: 3 Cott Bedsteads with Furniture to each like that in the north Stript Garrett.[32]

North Stript Garrett: 1 Bedstead Stript Cotton Curtains, 1 Feather Bed, 1 Boltster, 1 Pillow, 1 Matrass, 3 Blanquetts, 1 Quilt, 1 Crimson Velvet Arm Chair, 1 Old Black Chair, 1 Old Blue & White Settee, 1 Ditto Chair, 1 Chest, 1 Large Old Chest, 2 Old Gilt Tables, 1 Square Table with 2 Drawers, 1 Picture, 1 Old Crimson Damask Chair, 1 Small Grate, Shovel, Tongs, Poker. 1 Cott Bedstead, 1 Matrass, 1 Bolster, 3 Blanquetts, 1 Quilt.

White Garrett: 2 India Japan'd Screens, 1 Paper Ditto, 2 Maps Ditto, 1 Old Chest with a Sett of Canvas Curtains and a Green Cloth for the Drawing Room Floor, 1 Picture, 2 Prints. 2 Mahogany Biddys Delf pans, 1 Old Chest of Drawers, A Small Grate, Shovel, Tongs, & Poker,

1 Long Chest Lockt up the Key not to be found.

House Maids Garrett: Old Bedstead with White Dimity Curtains and Beding Belonging to the White Garrett, 1 Bedstead Stript Curtains, 1 Feather Bed, 1 Matrass, 1 Boltster, 1 Pillow, 3 Blanquetts, 1 Quilt, 1 Alarm Clock, 2 Blue & White Chairs, 1 Japan'd Table.

Garrett North of the House Maids: 4 Small Matrasses, 2 Boltsters, 5 Blanquetts bound with Ferritting, 1 White Quilt, 3 Setts of Green and Check Curtains, The above Furniture is all for Childrens Beds. 3 Crimson Chairs, 1 Wicker Stool, 1 Black Table, 1 Chest of Drawers, 9 Small Prints.

Miss Byngs Bed Chamber: 1 Four post Bedstead Yellow Curtains, 1 Feather Bed, 1 Matrass, 1 Boltster, 2 Pillows, 3 Blanquetts, 1 Counterpane, 1 Check Window Curtain, 2 Rush Chairs, 1 Mahogany Table with Drawers, 1 Wash hand Stand, 1 Wallnut Tree Writing Desk, 1 Chest of Drawers, 1 Cloaths Press, 1 Small nest of Drawers, 1 Fire Screen, 1 Picture in a Gilt Frame, 1 Grate, 1 Tin Fender, Shovell, Tongs, Poker & Brush.

The Nursery: 1 Four Post Bedstead Red Damask Curtains, 1 Feather Bed, 1 Matrass, 1 Bolster, 1 Pillow, 3 Blanquetts, 1 Quilt, 1 Blue & White Window Curtain, 1 Oak Chest with a Drawer, 1 Old Bureau with a Glass Front, 1 Mahogany Claw Table, 1 Childs Chair, 1 Ditto Stool both Mahogany with Covers, 1 Mahogany Cloaths Horse, 4 Rush Chairs, 1 Small Oak Box, 1 Picture Gilt Frame, 2 Prints, 1 Old Fire Screen, 1 Stove, Grate, Fender, Shovel, Poker, Tongs, Brush.

Mrs. Ganycliffs Room: 1 Bedstead Blue and White Stript Curtains, 1 Feather Bed, 1 Matrass, 1 Boltster, 1 Pillow, 3 Blanquetts, 1 Counterpane, 1 Blue and White Window Curtain, 4 Rush Chairs with Blue & White Seats and Backs, 1 Mahogany Table with a Drawer, 1 Ladys Wash hand Stand, 1 Chest of Drawers, 1 Glass over the Chimney, 1 Grate, Fender, Shovel, Tongs, Poker, Brush, Bellows.

Miss Byngs Dressing Room: 1 Small Tent Bedstead & Curtains, 1 Feather Bed, 1 Matrass, 1 Boltster, 1 Pillow, 3 Blanquetts, 1 Counterpane, 4 Rush Arm Chairs, 2 Small Ditto, 1 Fire Screen, 1 Mahogany Claw Table, 1 Square Ditto, 1 Round Ditto, 4 Book Cases Ditto, 1 Small Scotch Carpett, 1 Small Settee, 1 Bolster for Ditto, 1 Blue & White Window Curtain, 1 Green Window Blind, 1 Picture Gilt Frame, A Bath Stove, Fender, Tongs, Poker, Shovel, Bellows and Brush.

Closett to Miss Byngs Dressing Room: 3 Rush Chairs, 1 Small Bureau with Glass Front, 1 Corner Sett of Drawers, 1 Ladys Wash hand Stand, 1 Square Table with a Drawer, 1 Blue & White Window Curtain

Landing Place Nursery Floor: A Bell Glass Mahogany Frame and Bottom, A Small hand organ, A Small Marble Mortar & Pestle (the above things in a Cupboard), 1 Large Oak Chest, A Rope Ladder in a Cupboard by the Old Water Closett Door.

Landing Place on the Best Bed Chamber Floor: 1 Large Chest in which is 2 Pillows, 3 Old Floor Carpetts, 6 Bedside Ditto and Nine moveing Dressing Glasses, 4 Family Pictures Gilt Frames, 1 Ditto without a Frame.

Small Chintz Bed Chamber: 1 Four Post Mahogany Bedstead Chintz Curtains, 1 Feather Bed, 2 Matrasses, 1 Boltster, 1 Pillow, 3 Blanquetts, 1 Quilt, 1 Counterpane, 2 Stript Cotton Window Curtains, 4 Chairs, 1 Stool, 1 Ladys Wash hand Stand, 1 Small Table with Drawers, 2 Small Chests of Drawers, 1 Horse, 1 Screen, those all Mahogany, 1 Ditto night Table, 1 Glass Gilt Frame, 1 Picture Gilt Frame, a Bath Stove, Fender, Shovel, Tongs, Poker and Brush.

Dressing Room to Ditto: 1 Mahogany Turnup Bedstead Green & White Furniture, 1 Feather Bed, 1 Boltster, 1 Pillow, 1 Matrass, 3 Blanquetts, 1 Quilt, 3 Chairs, 1 Stool, 1 Fly Table, 1 Gent. Wash hand Stand, 1 Stript Cotton Window Curtain, 1 Glass over the Chimney, 1 Picture Gilt Frame, 1 Horse, 1 Fire Screen both Mahogany, a Bath Stove, Fender, Poker, Tongs, Shovel, Brush and Bellows.

Yellow Bed Chamber: 1 Mahogany Four post Bedstead, Yellow Damask Curtains, 1 Feather Bed, 2 Matrasses, 1 Boltster, 2 Pillows, 3 Blanquetts, 1 Manchester Quilt, 1 Horse, 2 night Tables, 1 Commode Table, 1 Ladys Wash hand Stand, all Mahogany, 2 Stript Window Curtains, 1 Arm Chair, 5 Small Ditto, 1 Coverd Stool, 1 Picture Gilt Frame, 1 Steel Grate, Fender, Tongs, Shovel, Poker, Brush, 1 large Pier Glass[33]

Yellow Dressing Room: 1 Cloaths Press, 1 Glass over the Chimney, 1 Couch Consisting of 1 Feather, 2 Boltsters, 2 Pillows, 3 Blanquetts with Green and White Check Curtains and Yellow & White Cover to the Couch, 1 Writeing Table and Drawer, 1 Gent. wash hand Stand, 2 small Chairs, 2 Arm Ditto, 1 Stool those all Coverd with Yellow and White, 1 Ditto Window Curtain, 1 Horse, 1 Screen, 1 Picture Gilt Frame, 1 Steel Grate, Fender, Tongs, Shovel, Poker, Brush and Bellows, Bath Stove.[34]

Blue Bed Chamber: 1 Mahogany Four post Bedstead Blue Damask Curtains, 1 Featherbed, 3 Matrasses, 1 Boltster, 2 Pillows, 3 Blanquettes, 1 Manchester Quilt, 1 Night Table, 1 Ladys Wash hand Stand, 1 Commode Table, 1 Pembroke Ditto, all Mahogany, 2 Arm Chairs, 4 Small Ditto, 1 Dressing Stool, 1 Peir Glass, 1 Ditto over the Chimney, 1 Picture in a Gilt Frame, 2 Window Curtains Blue Damask, 1 Screen, 1 Horse, 1 Steel Grate, Fender, Tongs, Shovel, Poker, Bellows and Brush.

Blue Dressing Room: 1 Peir Glass, 1 Ditto over the Chimney, 1 Commode Dressing Table, 1 Fly Table (broke), 1 Fire Screen, 1 Horse, 1 Dressing Stool, 1 Gent. Wash hand Stand, 2 Stript Blue & White Window Curtains, 1 Arm and Seven Small Chairs Coverd with Ditto, 1 Sofa Cover'd with Ditto with 1 Bed, 1 Back, 1 Pillow,

2 Boltsters, 3 Blanquetts and Green and White Curtains to Ditto, 4 Pictures in Gilt Frames, 1 Mahogany Cloaths Press, 1 Grate, Fender, Poker, Shovel, Tongs and Brush.

Great Chintz Bed Chamber: 1 Mahogany Four Post Bedstead with Chintz Curtains Lin'd with Blue Sattin, 1 Feather Bed, 3 Matrasses, 1 Boltster, 3 Pillows, 4 Blanquetts, 1 Quilt, 2 night Tables, 1 Horse, 1 Fire Screen, 1 Cloaths Press, 1 Commode Table, all Mahogany, 2 Chintz Window Curtains, 1 Ladys Wash hand Stand, 1 Arm Chair, 2 Small Ditto, 1 Stool all Blue & White Manchester Coverings, 1 Large Glass, 1 Picture Gilt Frame, 1 Steel Grate, Fender, Shovel, Tongs, Poker, Brush and Bellows.

Dressing Room to Ditto: 1 Mahogany Turnup Bedstead Blue & White Furniture, 1 Feather Bed, 1 Matrass, 1 Boltster, 1 Pillow, 3 Blanquette, 1 Bureau with Glass Front, 1 White & Gold Framed Glass over the Chimney, 1 Blue & White Stript Window Curtain, 4 small and 2 Arm Chairs Cover'd with Ditto, 1 Dressing Stool, 1 Screen, 1 Horse, 1 Gent. Wash hand Stand, all Mahogany, 2 Pictures, 24 Prints, 1 Steel Grate, Fender, Shovel, Tongs, Poker & Brush, & Bellows.

Stair Case and Passages: 6 Globe Lamps and Shades, 5 Glass Lanthorns, A White Cabinet with the Modell of a Ship.

The Great Hall: 6 Jermes with Lamps, 2 Lamps over the Chimney (note three of the lamps are broke), 1 Marble Statute on the Chimney Piece, 1 Large Mahogany Side Board, 1 Ditto Settee and 6 Ditto Chairs with the Crest and Coronet, 1 Mahogany Breakfast Oven Lin'd with Tin, 1 Steel Stove Grate, Fender, Shovel, Tongs, Poker and Bellows.

Vestibule to the Hall: 1 Hanging Lamp, 1 Marble Bason.

The Hall Bed Room: 1 Sofa Bed Green and White Stript Manchester Furniture, 1 Feather Bed, 2 Matrasses, 1 Boltster, 1 Pillow, 3 Blanquetts, 1 Counterpane, 1 Glass in a Gilt Frame, 1 Table & Drawers, 1 Gent. Dressing Table, 1 Night Table, 1 Screen, 1 Horse, all Mahogany, 3 Rush Chairs, 2 Green Silk and Worsted Damask Window Curtains, 17 Pictures Gilt Frames, 1 Bath Stove, Fender, Tongs, Poker, Shovel, Brush and Bellows.

Library: 2 Pier Glasses in Gilt Frames, 1 Glazed Print (N.B. glass gone), 1 Picture White and Gold Frame, 4 Window Curtains Green & White, Brocaded Manchester, 12 Small Green and White Cain Chairs, 2 Arm Ditto with Cushions, 2 Peach Mortelo's, 2 Beds, 1 Boltster, 1 Pillow to each, 1 Sofa, 2 Beds and Boltsters to Ditto, those all Cover'd with the same Stuff to the Window Curtains, 1 Breakfast Table, 2 Card Ditto, 2 Reading Desks, 2 Arm Chairs, 1 Stool, 1 Small Square Table, 1 Stand, those all Mahogany, 1 Small Stool Cover'd with Red Leather, 1 Square Oak Dineing Table, 1 Black Ink Stand and Glasses, 1 Harpsicord, 1 Musick Stand, 1 Small Green Leather Couch and Cover same to the Window Curtains, 1 Steel Grate, Fender, Shovel, Tongs, Poker, Bellows and Brush.

Eateing Parlour: 1 Steel Stove Grate, Fender, Shovel, Tongs, Poker, and Brush, 18 Mahogany Chairs Black Leather Seats, 1 Round Mahogany Table with a Border of Different Wood, 1 Large Dineing Table, 2 Side Boards, 1 Claw Table, 2 Bottle Stands, all Mahogany, 1 Large Marble Side Board and Cistern, 2 Canvas fire Screens, 1 Wainscott Plate Warmer Lin'd with Tin and Iron Heater, 2 Green Damask Window Curtains, 7 Pictures, 1 Large Tarpaulin for the Floor, 2 Small Pieces of Ditto.

Anti Room: 1 Mahogany Cupboard, 1 Ditto, Cellarett with Brass Hoops, 2 Round Ends and 2 Square Peices of the Great Dineing Table Mahogany, 1 Hanging Globe.

Ball Room: 1 Shuffle Board, 1 Small Billiard Table, 1 Iron Madon Table, 1 Loo Table Cover'd with Green Cloth, 1 Oak round Table Cover'd with Ditto & a Brass Candlestick in Ditto, 1 Pembrook Table, 1 Small Ditto with a Drawer, 1 Stool, 2 Candle Stands All Mahogany, a Devill and Taylors and two peices of Mahogany for some kind of amusement, 2 Settees coverd with Leather, 6 Leather Arm Chairs, 4 Rush Ditto, 3 Cain Ditto, 2 Red Velvett Ditto, 6 Green & White Check Cushions, 3 Chandeliers, 1 Large Round Mahogany Writeing Table Cover'd with Green Cloth and Drawers, 1 Steel Stove Grate, Fender, Tongs, Shovel and Poker, 2 Canvas Screens, 6 Globes, 2 Draught Boxes.

Small Room at the Top of the Eateing Parlour Stairs: 1 Deal Table, 1 Old Chair, A Sett of Bed Curtain Rods, A Sett of Bed Laths for Bed Valances, A Parcell of Marble Busts, Slabs etc. in a Closett.

Drawing Room: 12 Arm Chairs with Red & White Stript Manchester Covers, 2 Sofas, 6 Cushions & 2 Boltsters to Each, 2 Peach Mortelo's, 2 Beds 1 Boltster and 1 Pillow to each all with Covers the same as those upon the Chairs, 2 Large Pier Glasses Gilt Frames, 2 Large Marble Tables with Gilt Frames, 1 Macarone Table, 1 Small Ditto with Leaves, 2 Candle Stands, 2 Small Ditto, 2 Square Ditto those all Mahogany, 4 Crimson Silk fire Screens, 2 Yellow Wood Candle Stands, 3 Crimson Damask Window Curtains, 2 Steel Grates, 2 Fenders, 2 Pair Tongs, 2 Pokers, 2 Shovels, 1 Brush, 1 pair Bellows.

Lady Torringtons Dressing Room: 1 Large Square Glass, 1 Ditto over the Chimney both Gilt Frames, 2 Green Lutestring Window Curtains, 4 Arm Chairs, 2 Small Ditto, 1 Sofa, 1 Bed, 1 Pillow, 2 Boltsters to Ditto the above all cover'd with Green and White Stript Manchester, 1 inlaid Yellow Wood Secretory, 1 Ditto fire Screen with a Shelf and Cover'd with Green Silk, 1 Flower Stand lin'd with Tin, 2 Flower Stands painted Green and White, 1 Mahogany Horse, 1 Steel Grate, Fender, Shovel, Tongs, Poker and Brush, 53 Pictures in 18 of which there are several small ones whitin the outside Frame.

Lord Torringtons Bed Chamber: 1 Large Mahogany Fourpost Bedstead with Flowerd Cotton Furniture, 1 Feather Bed, 3 Matrasses,

1 Boltster, 3 Pillows, 5 Blanquetts, 1 Quilt, 2 Great Arm Chairs, 4 Small arm Ditto 2 Small Ditto without arms, 1 Small Dressing Ditto, all with Green and White Stript Manchester Covers; 1 Mahogany moveing Wardrobe, 1 Ditto Horse, one inlaid Dressing Table, 1 Mahogany Night Table, 1 Yellow Wood Fire Screen and Shelf Coverd with Green Silk, 1 Green Lutestring Window Curtain, 1 Steel Grate, Fender, Shovel, Tongs, Poker, Bellows and Brush, 1 Inlaid Chest.

Lord Torringtons Dressing Room: 1 Large Mahogany Gent. Dressing Table with Folding Top, Drawer &c., 4 Rush Chairs, 1 Mahogany Arm Ditto, 1 Couch with a Matrass, 1 Boltster & 2 Pillows, all with Covers of Green & White Stript Manchester, 1 Green Lutestring Window Curtain, 1 Cloaths Horse, 1 Claw Table, 1 Square Ditto with a Drawer, 2 Book Cases, 1 Large Moveing Secretory, All these Mahogany, 1 Fire Screen, 2 Pictures in Gilt Frames, 2 Green and White Flower Stands, 1 Steel Grate, Fender, Shovel, Tongs, Poker, Brush and Bellows.

Small Room Adjoyning Ld. Torringtons Dressing Room: 1 Looking Glass, 1 Leather Arm Chair, 1 pair of Mahogany Steps, 3 Maps of Bedfordshire.

Ladys Maids Room and Closett: 1 Turnup Bedstead Yellow and White Check Curtains, 1 Feather Bed, 1 Matrass, 1 Boltster, 1 Pillow, 3 Blanquetts, 1 Quilt very old & much Worn, 1 Yellow & white Window Curtain, 1 Green and White Ditto, 1 Arm Chair Yellow & White Cover, 3 Small Chairs, 1 Wainscot Spider Table, 1 Deal Table with a Drawer, 1 Old Japan'd Chest of Drawers, 2 Wainscot Cloaths Presses Lin'd with Green, 1 Small Bath Stove, Fender, Poker, Shovel, Tongs, and Brush, 2 Pictures, 4 Prints.

Small Room adjoyning the Kitchen: 1 Turnup Bedstead, Yellow and White Check Curtains, 1 Feather Bed, 1 Matrass, 1 Boltster, 2 Pillows, 3 Blanquetts, 1 Quilt, 1 Green and White Check Window Curtain, 1 Chair, 1 Stool, 1 Chest of Drawers, 2 Prints, 1 Small Bath Stove,[35] Shovel, Tongs and Poker.

The Bathing Room: 1 Large Oblong Copper, 1 Bath Stove.[36] **The First Cave:** 1 Tent Bedstead Green & White Check Curtains (no Beding to it), 2 Yellow Stuff Window Curtains, 2 Ditto Window Seat Cusheons, 1 Looking Glass, 1 Chest of Drawers, 1 Oak Table, 1 Ditto Claw Table, 1 Wash hand Stand, 2 Chairs, 1 Picture Gilt Frame, 2 Prints, 2 Queens Ware Vases, 1 Grate, Fender, Shovel, Tongs, Poker & Brush.

Stewards Room: 8 Chairs, 1 Large Oak Table, 1 Mahogany Dumb Waiter, 2 Large Pictures Gilt Frames, 2 Ditto without Frames, 1 Chinese Painting over the Chimney, 6 Prints, 1 Large Glass, 1 Grate, Fender, Tongs, Poker, Shovel, 1 Iron Plate Warmer.

Housekeepers Room: 5 Chairs, 1 Long Sett of Wainscot Drawers & Cupboards, 2 Linen Presses, 1 Marble Cistern, 1 Wire Safe, 1 Coffee Mill, 1 Spice Ditto, 1 Large Tin Box with 6 Divisions, 2 Large Square Tin Canisters, 3 Round Ditto, 2 Ditto Long Ones with Partitions,

1 Large Marble Mortar and Wood Stand, 2 Small old Japan'd Trays, 4 Black Writeing Stands two only compleat with Glasses, 12 old Blue and White Linen Covers for the Drawing Room Chairs, 6 Small Glass Decanters and Covers for the Upper Rooms, 6 Tumblers with Covers for Ditto, 1 Small Mahogany Tea Board, 5 Queens Ware Wash hand Basons, 2 Water Decanters, 6 Ditto Chamber Potts, 1 Large Blue & White Delf Wash hand Bason, 1 Small Japan'd Biscuit Rack, 6 Tin Lamp Stands with small Glass Globes & Cotton Tins for the Lanthorns in the Passages, 1 Small White Glass Lamp, 1 Grate Fender, Shovel, Poker, Tongs, Brush, 2 Footmen, 1 Trivitt, 1 Toasting Fork, 1 Chestnut Roaster.

The Slop Room: 9 Hair Sceives of Different Sizes, 1 Wood Sugar Tray, 1 Brass Candle Box, 1 Single Flap Oak Table, 1 Small Mahogany Dinner Tray.

Butlers Pantry: 3 Iron Straining Hoops, 1 Ditto Large Needle, 3 Small Cranes for Racking Wines &c., 2 Bottle Basketts one with 9 Divisions the other with six, 11 Green Handle Knives, 11 Ditto four prong'd forks, 1 Ditto Carveing Knife, 1 Ditto fork – all much worn, 1 Tin Baskett to hold Materials for Dressing Lamps.

The Second Cave: 1 Four post Bedstead yellow Stuff Curtains, 1 Feather Bed, 2 Matrasses, 1 Boltster, 1 Pillow, 3 Blanquetts, 1 Quilt, 1 Desk with Drawers under the Window, 1 Table with a Drawer, 1 Wainscot Bureau, 1 Large Chest, 2 Chairs, 1 Wicker Stool, 11 Prints, 2 Brace of Pistols, 1 Lock Gun, 1 Fowling Peice, 1 Blunderbuss, 1 Grate, Fender, Shovel, Tongs, Poker and Brush.

The Third Cave: 1 Tent Bedstead Green & White Curtains (no beding to it), 1 Turnup Bedstead Yellow and White Curtains, 1 Feather Bed, 1 Matrass, 1 Boltster, 2 Pillows, 3 Blanquetts, 1 Quilt, 2 Marble Slabs, 1 Large Looking Glass, 3 Crimson Velvet Chairs, 1 Ditto Stool, 2 Velvett Cusheons for the Window Seats, 1 Cain Chair, 1 Ditto Stool, 1 Oak Chest with a Drawer, 1 Chest of Drawers, 1 Small Japan'd Table, 2 Pictures Gilt Frames, 2 Ditto without Frames, 25 Prints, 2 Chinesse Paintings, 1 Mahogany Table & Drawer, a Bath Stove, Fender, Poker, Shovel, Tongs and Brush.

The Fourth Cave: 1 Wainscott Cloaths Press, 1 Grate, Fender, Shovel, Tongs, Poker and Brush.

The Fifth Cave: 1 Four Post Bedstead with Crankey Curtains, 1 Bedstead Blue Stuff Curtains, 2 Feather Beds, 1 Matrass, 2 Boltsters, 2 Pillows, 2 Ruggs, 6 Blanquetts, 1 Small Turnup Bedstead with a Feather Bed, Matrass, Boltster, 3 Blanquetts, 1 old Quilt and Old Stuff Curtains to Ditto, 2 Pictures in Gilt Frames, 2 Prints, 2 Coach Seats, 19 Bowles and 2 Jacks for the Bowling Green.

The Sixth Cave: 2 Four Post Bedsteads with Blue & White Coffoy Curtains, 2 Feather Beds, 1 Matrass, 2 Boltsters, 4 Pillows, 6 Blanquetts, 2 Counterpanes same stuff as the Curtains, 1 Sofa and 4 Chairs of the same, 1 Picture Gilt Frame, 1 Deal Table with a Drawer, 1 Grate, Fender, Shovel, Tongs, Poker, Brush.

The Seventh Cave: 1 Four Post Bedstead with Crankey Curtains, 1 Feather Bed, 1 Matrass, 1 Boltster, 2 Pillows, 3 Blanquetts, 1 Rugg, 1 Small Bedstead Blue and White Check Curtains 1 Feather Bed, 1 Matrass, 1 Boltster, 1 Pillow, 3 Blanquetts, 1 Counterpane the same to the Curtains, 1 Arm Leather Chair, 1 Old Deal Table.

The Eighth Cave: 1 Four Post Bedstead with Green Stuff Curtains, 1 Feather Bed, 1 Matrass, 1 Boltster, 2 Pillows, 4 Blanquetts, 1 Quilt, 1 Mahogany Table with 2 Drawers, 1 Chest of Drawers, 3 Old Chairs, 1 Stool, 2 Brown Silk Window Curtains, 1 Grate, Fender, Tongs, Shovel, Poker.

Gentlemans Water Closett: A neat Beam and Scales, Nine Large Lead Weights to Ditto of Different Sizes, A nest of Small Weights to Ditto, Eight in Number.

Servants Hall: 2 Tables, 2 Forms, 1 Grate, Fender, Shovel, Tongs & Poker, A Deal Cupboard.

The Wett Larder: 1 Ham Tubb and Cover, 1 small Salting Tubb and Cover, 1 Large Red Salting Jarr, 1 Large Cleaver, 1 Beam and Scales and 12 Lead Weights of Different Sizes.

Shoe Room: 1 Large Iron Brazier and Stand, 1 Large Marble Cistern, 1 Large Salting Jarr, 1 Large Candle Chest, 1 Old Chair.

The Old Wash House: 1 Small Choping Block, 1 pair Large Double Steps, 1 pair of Small Ditto, 1 Small four Step Ladder, 1 Large Scouring Brush, 1 Good Drye Rubbing Brush Leaded, 1 Old Ditto, Leaded, 3 Old Long House Brooms, 2 Ditto New, 1 New Turks Head Broom, 5 Hand Brooms, 1 Dust Pan, 2 Door Feet Brushes (one Quite New), 4 Wood Pails.

The Kitchen:

Pewter Viz: 18 Long Dishes Different Sizes mark't with a T., 1 Ditto Ditto markt with the Arms in a Diamond, Corronet, 2 Ditto Ditto markt with the Crest and Corronet, 13 Round Dishes Different Sizes markt with the Crest & Corronet, 1 Ditto Ditto markt with the Crest only, 5 Ditto Ditto Different Sizes markt with the Arms in a Diamond and Corronet, 1 Ditto Ditto very Large markt with a Cypher, 1 Ditto Ditto without a mark, 3 Ditto Bakeing Dishes without marks, 1 Ditto Ditto markt with the Crest and Corronet, 24 Water Plates markt with the Arms in full (19 only Compleat), 8 Soup Plates markt with the Crest and Corronet, 24 Common Plates markt with the Crest and Corronet, 78 Ditto Ditto markt with a T, 15 Oblong Plain Covers of Different Sizes markt with the Arms in full, 11 Ditto Scollopt Different Sizes markt the Same, 6 Round Plain Covers markt with the Arms in Full, 4 Ditto – Scollopt markt the Same, 4 Square Cornerd and Scollopt Ditto markt the Same, 4 Sauce Boats without Marks, 1 Salt without a mark, 4 Freezeing Potts without marks, 4 Fluted Ice Moulds (one incomplete),

24 Fruit Ditto Ditto of Different Sorts, 1 Bed Pan.

Copper: 1 Large Double Boiler with Covers, 1 Large Pottage Pott & Cover, 1 Small Pottage Pott without a Cover, 1 Large Soup Pott & Cover, 3 Small Ditto with Covers, 1 Small Ditto without a Cover, 1 Large Brazeing Pan and Cover, 1 Oblong Ditto and Cover, 2 Round Fish Potts and one Plate, 2 Long Ditto Ditto Different Sizes with Covers and one Plate, 4 Large Sauce Pans, 3 small Ditto all without Covers, 1 Small Ditto and Cover for Melting Butter, 3 Odd Sauce pan Covers, 16 Stew Pans Different Sizes with Covers Compleat, 2 Ditto Ditto without Covers, 3 Odd Covers for Stew Pans, 3 Round Pudding Pans, 1 Oblong Ditto, 2 Preserveing Pans, one Ditto Spoon, 3 Cake Pans Different Sizes, 1 Large Flatt Cullender, 1 small Round Ditto, 4 Bakeing Sheets, 1 Cheese Toaster, 2 Coffee Potts, 1 Chocolate Pott, 1 two Quart Drinking Pott, 40 Aspect Moulds Scollopt Different Sizes, 2 Oblong Plain Ditto, 3 Round Plain Ditto, 13 Small Plain Ditto of Different Shapes, 1 Boat and Bridge Aspect Mould, 2 Parting Shapes, 5 Scollopt Paste Moulds, 1 Spice Box, 1 Large Driping Pan and Basteing Ladle, 4 Large Ladles, 2 Large Spoons, 2 Large Strainer Spoons, 2 Large Skimmers, 2 Small Skimmers, 1 Tea Kitchen, 5 Tea Kettles Different Sizes, 2 Warming Pans, 2 Large Coal Scuttles, 2 Fryeing Pans, 1 Chafeing Dish, Large Double Lamp for the Stoves, 7 Pattee Pans, 4 Pattee tins.[37]

Brass: 1 Stand with a Heater, 1 Ladle, 1 Dredger, 15 Flatt Candlesticks, 1 Pair of Pillar Ditto, 2 Large Pails and Covers, 1 Pair Scales with a Nest of Weights but not Compleat, 1 Cake Pricker, 1 Scillit, 1 Large Pillar Lamp Stand.

Tin: 1 Compleat Double Bread Grater, 2 Large Round Sugar Canisters, 1 Small Ditto, 1 Square Ditto with a Partition, 12 Pint Potts, 1 two Quart Ditto 1 two Quart Japan'd Ditto, 15 Peices of Moulds and Landscapes, 5 Claws for Cow Heel, 1 Large Dredgeing Box, 1 Round Grater, 1 Sauce Pan Cover, 1 Foul Plate Baskett, 2 Knife Trays, 1 Slice, 1 Ladle, 2 Flatt Candlesticks, 2 Tinder Boxes Compleat.

Iron: A Large Wind up Range with Checks and Back, 1 Large Poker, 1 Ditto Shovel, 1 pair Tongs, 1 Trivit, 1 pair Bellows, 2 Large Racks, 1 Crane and 4 Pott Hooks, 1 Smoke Jack and two Chains, 1 Pigg Plate, 1 Salamander, 1 Role Rasp, 1 Grid Iron, 1 Fryeing, 7 Small Stove Trivitts, 1 Ditto for the Broiling Stove, 1 Cuckhold and Balance Sckewer, 4 Large Spitts, 3 Lark Spitts, 1 Large Sckewer, 3 Small Ditto, 2 Beef Forks, 1 Iron for Drawing Poultrey, 2 Pair Stake Tongs, 1 Cleaver, 3 Chopers, 2 Coal Scutles, 6 Pillar Candlesticks, 6 Pair Snuffers, 1 Whetting Steel, 1 Peper Mill Fixt.

Other Kind of Furniture in the Kitchen: 1 Very Large Long Oak Table, 2 Oak Flap Tables (incompleat), 1 Small Deal Table with a Drawer, 1 Small Form, 1 Choping Block, 1 Suett Tray, 1 Large Marble Mortar on a Wood Stand with a Large Wood Beater, 1 Wicker Meat Baskett,

1 Large Meat Screen Lin'd with Tin, 2 Large Green Stuff Window Curtains, 1 Large Dial by Perrin, 4 Large Redd Earthen Potts.

The Old Bake House: 1 Large Chest with 2 Drawers, 1 Large Bran Box, 1 Large Salt Box, 1 Choping Stand, 1 Small Dresser.

Scullery: 1 Copper and Cover as Fixt, 1 Lead Rinseing Cistern, 1 Plate Rack, 1 Swill Tubb, 1 Large Tubb, 1 Small Ditto, 2 Flatt Wood Bowles, 1 Deep Ditto, 2 Freezeing Tubbs, 2 Piggons, 4 Hair Sceives, 7 Trenchers, 1 Turnip Squeezer, 1 Choping Board, 13 Large Wood Spoons, 1 Large Iron Shovel.

The Old Laundry: 1 Turnup Bedstead old White Dimity Curtains, 1 Feather Bed, 1 Matrass, 1 Boltster, 2 Pillows, 3 Blanquetts, 1 Quilt, 1 Four Post Bedstead with Old White Dimity Curtains, 1 Four Post Bedstead Blue and White Stript Cotton Curtains, 2 Feather Beds, 2 Boltsters, 1 Matrass, 6 Blanquetts, 2 Quilts, 1 Small Old Chest of Drawers, 1 old Chair, 2 Stools, 1 Old Mangle, 1 Linen Press, 2 Window Seats one in Blue and White and one in Green and White Check Cases.

The Maids Room: 1 Bedstead Blue Stuff Curtains, 1 Feather Bed, 1 Matrass, 1 Boltster, 1 Pillow, 3 Blanquetts, 1 Quilt, 1 Old Chest of Drawers, 2 Old Chairs, 1 Deal Table, 1 Old Painting in a Black Frame, 1 pair Doggs, 1 pair Tongs.

The Cooks Room: 1 Four Post Bedstead Blue & White Check Curtains, 1 Feather Bed, 1 Matrass, 1 Boltster, 1 Pillow, 4 Blanquetts, 1 Quilt, 1 Wainscott Bureau, 2 Leather Chairs, 1 Deal Table with a Drawer, 1 Glass, 3 Pictures Gilt Frames, 10 Prints, 1 Grate, Brush and Bellows.

Carpetts: 1 Large Turkey Carpett for the Eateing Parlour mark't E, 1 Carpett to Cover the Drawing Room markt on the underside Drawing Room, 1 Ditto markt Ladys Dressing Room, 1 Ditto to Bedchamber markt 13, 1 Ditto for Lords Dressing Room markt Ld. T. room, 1 Ditto Small markt 22 for the Hall Bed Room, 1 Ditto For the great Chintz. Dressing Room which Covers the Room no mark to it, 1 Large blue Ditto markt 19 Large Blue Dressing Room, 1 Square Ditto markt 21 1 Square Ditto markt 23 belonging to Library, 4 Carpetts to go Round Beds.

Lower Ale Cellar: Good Oak Drink Stalls all round the Cellar, 1 Bell Cask of between 2 & 3 Hogsheads, 1 Two Hogshead Tun Shaped Cask, 1 pair Steps, 2 Wood Filters.

Lower Wine Cellar: 1 Small Drink Stall, 1 Hanging Shelf.

Blue Ale Cellar: Good Oak Drink Stalls on both Sides the Cellar, 1 pair Steps, 1 Hanging Yeas[t] Trough, 1 Large Wood Tunnel, 1 70 Gallon Bell Cask, 9 Large Tun Shaped Casks painted Blue markt and number'd 1.2.3.4.5.6.7.8.9..

Upper Wine Cellar: 1 Small Drink Stall.

Servants Hall Ale Cellar: Oak Drink Stalls all round the Cellar, 4 two Hogshead Tun Shaped Casks.

Best Small Beer Cellar: 3 Oak Drink Stalls, 4 Tap Tubbs, 1 pair Dogs, 6 Two Hogshead Tun Shaped Casks.

Cellar Opposite the Last: 1 Oak Drink Stall, 2 164 Gallon Tun Shaped Casks, 5 Ditto two Hogshead Casks.

Common Small Beer Cellar: Good Oak Drink Stalls all round the Cellars, 3 Two Hundred Gallon Tun Shaped Casks, 8 Ditto two Hogshead Casks, 1 Large Vessell for Carrying Beer with a Long Leather Pipe belonging to it.

[*omitted:* Furniture at the Farm House; Lower Kitchen; Upper Kitchen; Cellars]

[*These items crossed through on original*]

The Pastery Physick and Still Room: 25 Stone Jars of Different Sizes, 1 Stone Pitcher, 5 Dozen Sweet Meat Potts of Different Sizes, 1 Deal Table, 1 Small Mahogany Table, 1 Pair Wafers Irons, 2 Glass Retorts and one Receiver for the Sand heat Still, 1 Copper Still and Worm Tubb, 1 Chair.

The Bake House: A Copper as Fixt Compleat, 1 Fine Brass Wire Sceive, A Large Dough Trough with Bread Hoe, Roll Rasp, and Flour Shovel, A Meal Binn in four Divisions.

The New Wash House: 1 Large Mangle with Lead Weights and Mahogany Rolls – Compleat, 2 Large Coppers Fixt, 1 Copper Sauce pan and Cover, 1 Large Rinseing Tubb, 6 Washing Tubbs, 2 Small Ditto, 1 Pail, 1 Piggen, 1 Hand Bowl, 1 Stool, 2 Tables for the Mangle, 1 Hanging Horse with Pulleys, 1 Standing Cloaths Horse.

The New Laundry: 3 Long Cloaths Basketts, 4 Round Ditto, 2 Arm Red Leather Chairs, 1 Old Oak Table, 2 Deal Ironing Stools, 2 Old Drawers Loose, 4 Ironing Stands, 1 Old Tea Kettle, 1 Iron Scutle, 1 Shovel, 1 Poker, 1 Raker for the Stove, 2 Dozen Flatt Irons, 1 pair Steps, 2 Hanging Horses with Pulleys, 3 Folding Cloaths Horses.]

[*Omitted:* Furniture in the Different Rooms at the Stables: The Grooms Room, The Boys Room, Saddle Room, Coachmans Room, In the Boiling Houses at the Kennell.]

Furniture at the Menagerie

In the Parlour: A Mahogany Camp Tea Table with Tea Board and Drawers (but no China), A Mahogany Pembrook Table with a Drawer, A Mahogany Book Case and Cupboard, 2 Beech and Cain Slideing Settees with four Cusheons to Each in old Green and White Stript Covers, 4 Small Beech and Cain Chairs, A Scotch Carpett for the floor, A Steel Fender, 2 Yellow Canvas Blinds with Springs.

In the Kitchen: 8 Ash Tent Chairs

In a Room up Stairs: 1 Old Night Stool Coverd with Crimson Velvett and a White Pan.

In the Avery: 2 Stands for Bird Seeds with Divisions, 2 Range of Bird Nests, 2 Small Stove Grates.

Furniture in the Garden House
 Bed Room: 1 Bedstead Blue Stuff Curtains, 1 Feather Bed, 1 Matrass, 1 Boltster, 1 Pillow, 3 Blanquetts, 1 Quilt, 1 Wallnut Tree Table with 4 Drawers, 1 Ditto Chair Red Damask Seat and Check Cover, 2 Blue & White Stript Window Curtains, 1 Small Glass, 12 Prints two of them Glazed, 1 small Grate, A Cloaths Press and Drawers with Blue Stuff Front, 3 Flannell Curtains Belonging to the Green House, 1 Wainscott Writeing Desk.
 Parlour: 1 Japan'd Tea Table, 5 Wallnutt Tree Chairs Red Damask Seats and Check Covers, 1 Small Bath Stove and Fender.
 Kitchen: 1 Large Cupboard and Drawer, 2 Old Tables, 1 Grate, 1 Fender, 1 Fowleing Piece, 2 Old Chairs.
 Shed By the Hott Houses: 1 Small very old Bedstead, 1 Feather Bed and Boltster to Ditto.

Inventory of Garden Tools: 1 Four Light Frame, 4 Three Light Frames, 1 One Light Frame with 17 Sash Square Lights for them, 80 Large Cup Glasses, 5 Small Ditto, 9 Small Bells Ditto, 1 Horse Gravell Hoe, 1 Ditto Harrow, 2 Wheel Barrows, 1 Hand Ditto, 2 Large Tubbs in the Shed of the Hott Houses, 1 Ditto under a Spout of the Green House, 1 Grindstone Frame Iron and Wood Compleat, 6 Scythes and Snaiths, 3 Iron Rakes, 2 Wood Grass Rakes, 6 Dutch Hoes, 5 Small Drag Hoes, 4 Large Tan Forks, 1 Small Hand Ditto, 3 Dung Ditto, 2 Pitching Ditto, 1 Grass Edgeing Iron, 3 Garden Reels with two Old Lines, 1 Pair Garden Shears, 1 Pair Fumigateing Bellows, 2 Trowells, 2 Hammers, 3 Old Watering Potts, 2 Large Flatt Basketts, 2 Large Cradle Ditto, 1 Peck Ditto, 7 Small Fruit Ditto, 1 old Spade, 2 Small Ladders, 2 Frame Steps, 2 Pair Horse Boots, 10 Peices Large and Small Netting in General very much Worn, 1 Mettle Horse Roll, 1 Stone Hand Ditto, 3 New Double Garden Seats with Wheels, 1 Ditto Single with Wheels, 1 Old Seat, 2 Green House Stands, 3 Bee Hives Stockt with Bees.

The Above Inventory Taken by us Paul Walker, John Gough

Augst 28th 80. Taken out of Southill House by Permission of the Duke of Portland and Lord Polwarth a Harpsicord from the Library to send to Lord Torrington. Paul Walker, John Gough

Account of Furniture Sav'd From the Fire in the Offices December 27th 1780.

 In the Scullery all the Articles as particularis'd in this Inventory.
 In the Pastery Physick and Still Room's the Copper Still, 1 Deal Table, 4 Stone Jares, 10 Sweet Meat Potts.
 The new Bake House: the Copper now at Menagery.
 The New Wash House: 2 Coppers, 1 Copper sauce pan and Cover, a

Hanging Horse, a standing Cloath Horse, 2 Small Washing Tubs, 2 Long Cloaths Basketts, 1 Table belonging to Mangle.

The new Laundry: Three Folding Cloaths Horses, 24 flat Irons, Shovel poker, Coal Scuttle, Tea Kettle.

The Above Taken the 29 Day of December 1780 By Paul Walker, John Gough

BCRO: L 31/190

NOTES

1. For the earlier part of this introduction I am grateful to Miss P. Bell for showing me her notes. See Introduction to Part II of the catalogue of the Whitbread Archive (BCRO).
2. W 1319–1321 and 1398.
3. Plan at Southill Park entitled *Ground Plan of The Old House at Southill about the year 1700 which stood near where a pond now is in the shrubbery – An adjacent Pear Tree grew against the Kitchen Wall.*
4. W 2132.
5. W 2134 and 2317.
6. Torrington Diaries Volume III pp.318–319.
7. MC 2/8. Small sketch of house on magnified photograph: Z 50/143/238.
8. AD 1589.
9. Z 49/172.
10. W 2199 etc.
11. letter (L 30/9/60/195) Details of later tenants in Southill Poor Book (P 69/5/3)
12. W 2200.
13. Various authors including Albert Richardson *Southill: A Regency House*, 1951, p.2 fig.1.
14. *Southill A Regency House* p.66. The best studies of Samuel Whitbread II are Dean Rapp *Samuel Whitbread: A Social and Political Study*, Garland Publishing Inc., 1987; Roger Fulford *Samuel Whitbread 1764–1815 A study in opposition*, 1966.
15. *Southill: A Regency House* p.3 fig.2
16. *Southill: A Regency House* p.9
17. *Southill: A Regency House* p.41.
18. DV 1/R/47 pp 16–23
19. Illustrated in Gervase Jackson Stops's article *Southill Park, Bedfordshire*, CL for 29 April 1994 pp.62–67. It is discussed in S. Deuchar *Politics & Porter: Samuel Whitbread and British Art* 1984, pp.66–67.
20. Original at Southill, typed transcript by Marita Prendy available at BCRO, classification 130 Southill.
21. R. Fulford p.310.
22. Christopher Hussey's article *Southill Park: the seat of Samuel Howard Whitbread* CL 68: (1) 42–8, (2) 80–86, (3) 108–114, published 1930 especially p.81 pl.2.
23. *Southill: A Regency House* p.20.
24. G. Jackson-Stops p.63.
25. *Southill: A Regency House* p.34.
26. Clifford Musgrave plate 5.
27. *Southill: A Regency House* p.30.
28. R. Fulford pp 310 and 311.
29. For Holland's career see Colvin pp.423–426. Dorothy Stroud *Henry Holland His Life and Architecture* 1966.
30. G. Jackson-Stops's article *Southill Park, Bedfordshire* CL for 29 April 1994 pp.62–67.

31. Z 575 including introduction.
32. A number of pencil additions to rooms on the Garret Floor to furniture "Supposed to be in Old Laundry".
33. Pier Glass added in pencil.
34. Bath Stove added in pencil.
35. Small Bath Stove; note added in pencil "Now at Menagery".
36. Bath Stove; note added in pencil "now in Lord Torrington's Dressing Room".
37. Note added in pencil "1 Tea Kettle wanting".

TODDINGTON MANOR HOUSE

Toddington Manor to 1719

In 1528 Sir Thomas Cheney (c.1485–1559), of an ancient Hertford-shire family, married Anne Broughton, heiress of Toddington Manor. Cheney was in the royal service and managed to increase his estate in Toddington and Harlington as a result of the dissolution of the monasteries. In c.1545 he built Toddington Manor House. From a drawing on a map of Toddington of 1581 it appears that the house was built round four sides of an inner court. It was three storeys high with turrets on the four corners. Opposite the great court was the central gatehouse. On the other side of the inner court was a lesser gatehouse leading into the back court which had a number of domestic buildings round the outside.[1]

It is described accurately by J.H. Blundell as "Cheney's Palace". It certainly has the effect of one, even if it was never actually called it. In 1671 it had 45 hearths, the fifth largest house in Bedfordshire. It was visited twice by Elizabeth I and once by James I. The 1644 inventory contains two rooms called the Queen's Room and Leicester's Room (after Elizabeth's favourite).[2] Cheney had clearly intended to build a house large and impressive enough to entertain royalty.

Henry, Lord Cheney, Thomas and Alice's son, held Toddington till his death in 1587, when it passed to his widow Lady Jane. In 1614 the house passed to Thomas Wentworth, her great nephew. In 1626 he was made Earl of Cleveland and, because of the expense of life at Court, got heavily into debt. An order was made for their payment.

The Wentworths were Royalists. The Earl was imprisoned 1642–1648 and both father and sons were exiles with Charles II in 1650. Inevitably, the Parliamentarians seized their estates. Most of the furniture at Toddington was confiscated, taken up to London and "sold for the use of the State". An inventory was made of the rest of the goods, valued at £64 11s 2d. Because so little had been left, the Countess of Cleveland was allowed to keep them and did not have to pay for their value.

A number of rooms had only been left with the bedsteads. Lady Cleveland's own room was left mainly intact, partly because most of the fittings were so old. It was hung with five pieces of old arras. Round the bed was "a vallance and Curtaines of old damask". The dining room was reduced to "a table, a carpet of old green bayes, cupboard and leather carpet, two old Turkey worke Chaires & ten old or turkey worke stooles".

234

The inventory provides useful information as to the ground plan of the house. Near the hall was the steward's room which was next to the dining room. Another little group of rooms close by were the chapel, great parlour and green room. On the first floor was another dining room over the steward's room (probably the later great dining room). The great chamber was over the parlour. The nearby "Queen's Chamber" was connected to "Leicester's Chamber" (at end of the picture gallery) by the "Green Gallery". This room was probably at a corner of the house. At the service/north end of the house was the "Square Chamber over the Pantry" and "the Chamber at the end of the [Real] Tennis Court". There were two chambers over and one in the wash house. There were chambers for a falconer and a huntsman.

The Restoration of 1660 saw the return of the Wentworth males to Toddington but the estate's income had to be used to pay off the Earl's debts estimated at £100,000 in 1650. Royalty however were again entertained at Toddington. The Duke of Monmouth, illegitimate son of Charles II, had a love affair with Henrietta Maria, Baroness Wentworth. They carved their names on the famous oak tree in the grounds. Unfortunately, Monmouth was executed after his failed Rebellion in 1685. The estate eventually passed to Anne Johnson, whose marriage in 1711 to Thomas Wentworth, 1st Earl of Strafford, a cousin of the Toddington Wentworths, brought Toddington back to the family.

The 1719 Inventory

By the time Anne, Lady Wentworth, commissioned a survey of the house in 1719, the house was in a terrible state of repair. Most of the upper rooms had either no plaster remaining, or plaster on the verge of collapse. Many of the windows had broken glass. More serious structural problems were found in a number of rooms. In the north gallery it was found: "the Brickwork in the Front and the Foundation of the Stone Collumn, being Crush'd & tore to pieces, the Railes and Bannisters between the Collumns being rotten and part gone, the two beams of the Gallery being shor'd". The round tower at the north west corner was lying "open and part covered, the Timbers are Rotten and Tumbling down, the Floors and Cieling the same". The main wall of the house, near the chapel and overlooking the tennis court, had a dangerous bulge. The battlements and stone coping "being very much decayed and part fallen down". Even the "new" laundry roof had to be shored up and the front was "ready to tumble out". The "Purloyn being broke" could only be repaired by taking the roof off. Given a pardonable desire to tout for business by painting as black a picture as possible, Joseph Stallwood, bricklayer, and Matthew Lowndes, carpenter, were surely right in seeing Toddington Manor as in an appalling state of repair with

Plate 28: Toddington Manor: The old kitchen. (*Sketch: 1843*)

sections of it about to collapse. It had been brought about by years of neglect and was likely to get worse as the lead piping on the roofs was so defective.

The inventory does not list the contents of the rooms, as everything of value had been removed long before. It is included in the volume because it gives good details of the layout of the rooms of a major Bedfordshire country house.

In the south front were two cupolas, presumably forming part of the gatehouse in the 1581 drawing. On this front were ten upper rooms on the second storey, the long gallery on the first floor and the marble gallery on the ground. This last mentioned could well have been refurbished in the 1670s or 1680s, as it is not mentioned in the 1644 inventory.

The west front, looking out to the garden, contained the great state room with ante-rooms between it and the long gallery and great staircase. In this area were the great parlour and a back staircase.

The east front contained ten upper rooms on the second storey. On the first floor were the long passage and the common passage. Senior household officials seem to have lived at this end of the house. The chapel was in this area near to the real tennis court. In the north floor were the north gallery and the great dining room on the first floor with the servants' hall and two rooms opposite the great hall.

Toddington Manor after 1719

What Lady Wentworth did about the gloomy report is not known. On her husband's death in 1739 the house passed to William, Lord Strafford (1722–1791). If the house was still in as bad a condition in 1739 as in 1719, it is understandable that he decided to demolish the major part of the house. The Toddington ballad "If Lord Strafford had never been born . . . The Old Manor House would have always stood" is surely unfair. Even without him, the house would have collapsed from neglect but he did demolish much of the Tudor house. Surprisingly, he kept the old kitchen which had been in poor repair itself in 1719, possibly because the chimneys were too massive to knock down easily. The kitchen was later converted into the dining hall. The adjoining turret and one stable were also retained.

No doubt using materials from the demolished house Strafford built the present house for his steward. It is three storeys high with three windows on the top two floors of the main facade. On the ground floor the front door and Victorian entrance porch are on the left. The original entrance porch was probably in the centre to achieve greater symmetry.

Not all the fittings of Toddington Manor were broken up when the major demolition occured in 1745. J.H. Blundell in his *Annals of Toddington* traces the subsequent history of the carvings of Apollo and the Muses from Toddington Manor to Hockliffe and back again. Carvings of birds and flowers, supposedly by Grinling Gibbons, were according to Blundell "recently over the doors at Toddington Manor".[3] Carvings dated 1566 from Toddington were at the White Horse Inn, Hockliffe.[4]

William, Lord Strafford's death in 1791 meant that his sister Lady Anne Conolly inherited Toddington. Her son, Thomas, sold it in 1806 to John Cooper. His daughter, Elizabeth, married her second cousin, William Cooper (later Cooper-Cooper). Three generations of Cooper-Cooper lived there till 1905 when it descended to Mrs. Elizabeth Warner Vernon.

TODDINGTON MANOR HOUSE 1719

A Survey of the Several Defects and other Reparations that are wanting to be done at the Mannor House, etc. of Teddington in the County of Bedford belonging to the Right Honourable the Lady Wentworth Surveyed by her Ladyships Order December 29, 30, 31, 1719 by us Joseph Stallwood Bricklayer and Matthew Lowndes Carpenter who have subscribed our Names to this and the five following pages.

Imprimis The 2 Cupaloes in the South Front, the Cantls some are boarded up and some ly open and exposed to the Weather without any Doors to the same and the Plaistering and Floor of the Room under the Cupaloes is in a great Measure Destroyed.

Plate 29: Toddington Manor: All that remained of this once substantial mansion by the opening years of the nineteenth century.
(*Watercolour: c.1806*)

The heads of Eight Stacks of Chimneys being perished and part broke down by the Extremity of Weather.

The Tileing over the Stewards Room wants new Ripping and the Brickwork of the Gable End and Copeing are very much broke and Damaged.

The 10 Upper Rooms in the South front of the House remains Unfinished as to Floors and Plaistering.

The long Gallery under the same Room in the South Front remains Unfinished as to the Plaistering, the Cielings and Brick Wall bare.

The Marble Gallery in the same Front on the Ground Floor the Marble not made good before the Chimney the Front and one End Room remain unplaistered and half the Wainscott of the other Front next the Inner Court being Wanting and Without a Door and Case to the same.

The Room opposite to the Stone Gallery being full of Old Stone & Intirely Unfinished without Floor, Plaistering or Door.

The 3 Rooms adjoining on the Ground Floor remain unfinished as to Floors & plaistering.

To 6 Sash Windows and Glass wanting in the same Front and 4 Windows Stopt up in the 2 Towers.

The frontespiece not finished, the Stone Pediment not being put on with other Ornaments that are wanting.

The West Front next the Garden

The Garret or upper Rooms in the same Front remain intirely Unfurnished as to some without plaistering and some part of the Floors unboarded and most part of the same Rooms without Doors. The back Stair Case the Beam that carrys the Lanthorn being broke and ready to fall the Plaistering in great part rotten and broke down.

The Great State Room floor not boarded and no Wainscot upon the Walls above the lower Pannel.

The Room between the State Room and Long Gallery the greatest part of the Wainscot wanting and a Window to the Stair Case wanting.

The Room from the great Stair Case to the State Room fronting the Inner Court no Door nor Wainscot in the front.

The two Rooms fronting the Garden by the great Stair Case the Wainscott & Doors broke in Several places.

The Round Tower at the N.W. corner of the House lying open & part uncovered the Timbers are Rotten and Tumbling down the Floors and Cieling the same.

The Great Stair Case the Wainscot broke in Several places as also pannels Wanting the plaistering & Lathing Wanting the Sashes & Glass of the Lanthorn over the Stairs being very much broke & rotten.

The Great Parlour the Door lynings and suffets & the Door into the Inner Court are wanting.

The East Front

The 10 Upper Rooms, the Lathing, Plastering & Cieling and boarding in Several places Wanting a purloin broke & shor'd and A beam likewise and several Beam Ends partly rotten.

The Long Passage at the Head of the Little Back Stairs the Cieling Joyst & plaistering wanting.

The Comon Passage to Mr Norris's Room the Lathing & Plaistering in some places wanting & the Front piers not plaistered.

In Mr Alstone's Room & Closet the Cieling broke in several places.

The Tennis Court: The brick Work of the Main House next the Chapple being Defective & bulg'd out in the Middle the battlements & Stone Coping being very much decayed & part fallen down. The Fence Wall that Incloses the Court being part fallen down and wants New Copeing. Part of the Tyling next to the Tennis Court wants new ripping and no lead pipes in the Court to bring the Water down. Two lengths of Lead Pipes at the South East Tower and one Length Ditto at the other Tower on the same Side being all that remains to carry the Water from the Top of the House all the Lower parts of the two Stacks of Pipes being gone.

The North Front

The Rooms over the North Gallery the Main Timbers being Shor'd and Plaistering and Boarding in several places Wanting.

The Garret over the Great Dining Room the plaistering of one side being wanting and part of the Floor being Unboarded and the next Room being in the same Condition.

The Room at the West Corner of the North Front the Girder being broke and Sunk and the Floor not Boarded great Settlements in the Stack of Chimneys in the same Room and another in the Front.

The Back Stairs at the same Corner Lathing & Plaistering wanting & a Window at the Top of the Stair Case & a great Settlement in the Wall by the Stone Door Case at the head of the Stairs.

The Room and Closet at the West End of the North Gallery and a great Settlement in the Middle Wall and part of the Cieling broke.

In the North Gallery

The Brickwork in the Front and the Foundation of the Stone Collumns being Crush'd & tore to pieces, the Railes and Bannisters between the Collumns being rotten and part gone the two beams of the Gallery being Shor'd.

No paving nor Flooring against the Collumns and the rest of the Boarding of the Gallery being half rotten and wanting.

The Wall at the North East Corner of the Gallery being Crush'd and Defective and the Wainscott of the same being Broke and gone in several places.

Ground Story:

The two Rooms Opposite to the Great Hall the Window Jambs not plaistered, the Floor under the Lead, Sink rotten, part of the Cieling being broke and part of the Brickwork to the Windows being not Workt up the Stone Door Case to the back Stairs from the Hall being very much Settled.

The Servants Hall the Lathing and Plaistering being broke Down in Several places.

The Room over the Servants Hall the Floor not boarded and only Wainscotted Surbace High.

The Inner Court   The Finishing on the Fronts being broke off in Several places and much Damaged A Stone Compartment pannel under the Long Gallery Windows being left out and not finished.

A Stack of Lead Pipes wanting on each Side of the Hall Door and 4 Lengths wanting to 4 other Stacks of Pipes in the same Court to bring down the Water from the Top of the House.

The North front next to the Woodyard. The Stone copeing and the Brick Work under it being in great part Perished and Decayed.

Three Lengths of Lead Pipes to three Stacks of Pipes and one Length to another Stack of Pipes being all that remains and all the lower parts of the same being wanting.

The Front next the Garden The Coving Cornish of the two round Towers being not Lath'd nor Plaistered the stone Copeing over the Sun Dial being Broke and Decayed the Stone Cornish over the three Windows the same and the Stone Window Stools several of them being broke.

To 24 Square of Crown Glass in Sashes in the fronts being broke. To 8 Squares of Castle Glass in Sashes broke besides several Window Lights and Casements being wanting about the House.

The Old Wash house and Room adjoining The Stone Paving very much broke and Destroyed and the Tops of the Chimneys Broke and Decayed.

In the Kitchen The Door and Case wanting into the Poultrey Court and the Tops of the Chimneys broke and Decayed and the Paving of the Court being all worn out the Boarding of the said five Rooms for the Servants the most part of the same being Rotten and Gone.

The Old Stable: The Lathing and Plaistering of the Cieling being broke and gone in Several places the Collums and Arches being broke in Several places and part of the Tyling wants new riping.

The New Office

The two first Rooms only Carcased in without Boarding Plaistering or Glazing.

The 7 Horse Stable adjoining no Boarding on the Floor or Plaistering under it.

The three Coachhouses the Floor not Boarded nor Plaistered underneath no Door to the same.

The new Laundry Roof Shor'd and the Front ready to Tumble out the Purloyn being broke which cannot be mended without taking off the Roof.

The Garden Walls

The 2 Dwarff Walls each side the Garden on the West side of the House the Tops being Decay'd and Tumbling down in several Places.

The Back Wall at the White Gates next the Town the Copeing all being Decay'd and gone.

The Opposite Wall next the Park part of the Copeing being Decay'd and down.

The Brick Wall about the Pond in the Wood Yard the Top being Broke in several places and the Tyling of the two little Houses wants Mending.

Half the Pailing round the Park is out of Order and wants new Setting as also the Pales round the Mount.

Several Rooms about the House Sealed up as could not be seen.

[*signatures*]Joseph Stallwood: Mathew Lowndes

December 29th 1719

BCRO: P 8/28/10

NOTES

1. The best published material on Toddington Manor is found in Joseph Hight Blundell's *Toddington Its Annals and People*, 1925, and Allan Fea's *The Loyal Wentworths*, 1928. VCH Vol.III pp.440–441 is also useful. The 1581 Map is reproduced in Blundell opposite p.49. The Toddington Scrapbook (P 8/28/10) includes illustrations of the house, as well as the 1719 inventory.
2. Blundell p.49; BM Add Ms 5494, published in BHRS Vol.65 pp.144–149.
3. Blundell p.50.
4. Blundell p.77.`

WREST PARK

Wrest Park up to 1740

The ancestors of the Grey family held the manor of Silsoe, including the site of the future Wrest Park in 1086.[1] Quite when a house was built at Wrest is not clear but by 1308 there was a capital messuage, a dovecote and a substantial amount of land.[2] A highway case of 1330 reveals that as early as 1315 there was a park, probably carved out of ancient woodland.[3] In 1344 Roger de Grey claimed free warren in his demesne lands of his manor of Wrest and had his claim for a park there confirmed.[4]

Edmund Grey, Roger's great-great-grandson, bought Ampthill Castle in 1454 and from then till 1508 Wrest ceased to be the chief residence of the Grey family.[5] As a result of a judicious change of sides at the battle of Northampton and his marriage to Edward IV's sister-in-law, Edmund (1416–1490) was created Earl of Kent in 1465 and became Lord Treasurer of England in 1463. His grandson Richard, however, was a waster and gambled away his money and in 1507 he was forced to sell Wrest to Sir Henry Wyatt.[6] To prevent it being pulled down for its scrap value, Richard's half-brother Henry bought Wrest in 1512. A law suit records that "for as muche as the seyd Sir Henry Grey had then no house of hys owne convenyent for hym to dwellyn and allso for petye he hadde that the seyd house wheryn dyverse and many off his aunces-tres had dwellyd schould be so utterly dysstroyed, he offered to bye off the seyd Sir Henry Wyat the seyd manour of Wreste and other landes and tenementes in the seyd countye nygh unto the seyd manour."[7]

Sir Henry claimed he was too poor to be able to use the title of Earl of Kent, yet he slowly bought back parts of the Greys' former estate and fought protracted legal cases over some of the remainder. By the death of his grandson Reynold, 4th Earl of Kent, in 1573, Wrest was a substantial house that had been expanded from its mediaeval core of great hall, great staircase, great chamber and kitchen. The drawing by Buckler of the east front in 1831 shows the window of the old chapel, which looks Perpendicular.[8] Whether that was mediaeval, there certainly was a chapel by 17 April 1534, when the Blunham rectory accounts record "delivered to the fremason that mayd my maisteres chapel at Wrast by a redytoken of a quarter off malt."[9]

The 1573 inventory[10] lists in addition to the above rooms, nineteen chambers, as well as a store house, porter's lodge, buttery and "Low Parlour next the Chapel." The house was built round a courtyard with an entrance gate at the porter's lodge. This basic ground plan was to remain, despite rebuilding at various periods until the demolition of the house in 1839. The kitchen was in the west part of the house and the great hall in the south. It was built of lath and plaster, which probably indicates that the additions to the smaller mediaeval house were made probably before 1550 rather than later when brick would have been more usual for so large a house.

The 1573 inventory shows a house only partly lived in with some principal rooms virtually empty of contents. The kitchen contained "3 plankes and 2 shelves (valued at 2s), a short troughe (10d), a dresser boorde without (6d)". In the "low Parlour next the Chapel" were stored various beds and bed fittings. However, there was a Venice Carpet. Some mediaeval fittings seem to have survived to this date. In the "Chamber next the Storehouse" was a "covering of Imagery very oulde, 20d." In the "Chapel Chamber" was a cushion with the ragged staves and dolphins of the Grey coat of arms.

A poem of c.1639 by Thomas Carew[11] shows that the then Earl of Kent was still entertaining in the great hall. Those "of better note / Whom wealth, parts, office, or the herald's coat, / Have sever'd from the Common, freely sit / At the Lord's table . . . " Most country houses had given up such hospitality by this date with the owner of the house eating separately in a dining room even on festive occasions such as Carew describes.

The next inventory of 1667[12] shows little change in the basic structure of the house since 1573. The fittings of the rooms had been altered considerably, however. The dining chamber, for example, contained "6 peeces of Hanging Tapestry of the Story of the Apostles, 2 Tables with 2 Turkey Work Carpettes, 2 black standes, 1 great Chaire, 16 high backe chairs, 2 low back Chaires, and one little stoole all of fugered Velvett. 3 long red window Curtens of bayes lined with red stuff with iron roddes and a Chymney board and my Lady Eliz's picture, and in the staires to the Dyninge Roome were 4 great pictures the stories of Rosamond, David Ahasuerus and the Angells appearing to the Sheppardes. 14 flower glasses and 14 Iron Crowns guilded to hold them. 4 guilded blazws to hold Candles. 6 Wooden Chaires painted and guilt and a Chaire to carry Ladies Inn."

The 1670s saw the first major change to Wrest since the Tudors. Amabel, the Good Countess (1607–1698), was widow of Henry, 10th Earl, and had inherited a fortune from her father, Sir Anthony Benn. In 1663 her son Anthony, 11th Earl, married another potential heiress Mary Lucas, (later Baroness in her own right), shortly afterwards. Mary came into her money in 1671. The family's combined wealth was used in purchasing land to the north and west of the house and on rebuilding part of the house. The purchase of the Cainho estate with an extensive warren, a building later called the Stand (south of the present drive to Gravenhurst) and the bowling green house was intended to be the showpiece of a grand entrance to the house.

Plate 30: Wrest Park: A view showing the new north front of the 1670s.
(*Engraving: J. Rocque, 1735*)

In 1672 it was the east side that was remodelled. The chapel chamber
was to be raised to 13 feet high, two windows added and the old window to be arched "and put in the Maid's Chapel. It was to be refloored
and a rise of 4 inches high added for the bed to stand in."[13] The whole
of Lord Lucas's apartments were to be demolished and replaced by
twelve rooms on a front 44 feet long and 37 feet wide.

To complement the east facade was built the splendid north front of
212 feet long with a return on the west end of 24 feet long. It cost £3,227
and was supervised by Thomas Hooper, Steward to the Greys.[14] No
architect is known but it is possible Hooper and his patrons designed
the building themselves using practical guides to country house building
that were now appearing, such as Hugh May's translation of Freart's
Parallels of Architecture of 1665. At least three architectural books produced in the 1660s and 1670s were in the Wrest library in 1740.

The result was a classical facade, typically post- Restoration, as Pratt
might have built himself. The front was three storeys high with two projecting wings and a slightly projecting entrance gateway, surmounted by
a pediment and balustrade. To crown this was a turret, which gave the
building added height and majesty, as well as screening the higher roofs
of the older building behind.[15]

In 1684 the work began on the planting of the great north park to be
viewed from the north facade. In 1689 the walled great garden was
extended.[16] It was probably at this time that the existing fish ponds, part
perhaps of the original double moat, were formalised into canals, the
largest of which is the surviving great canal.

In 1702 the estate was inherited by Henry, 12th Earl and future Duke
of Kent (1671–1740), an important figure at court. He had been on the
grand tour in 1690 and had gained a great love of things classical. His

overriding interest was in the development of the gardens to the south of the house. This took place with many alterations and changes of plan from 1702–1740.[17] The exact details of these need not trouble us but so that he could enjoy the gardens, various buildings were erected. The chief of these was the Baroque pavilion by Thomas Archer,[18] built between 1709 and 1711, described unsympathetically by Horace Walpole, probably in the 1770s, as "a frightfull Temple, designed by Mr. Archer, the groom porter".[19] The smaller viewing house on Cain Hill to the east of the gardens is probably also by Archer.[20] Other buildings included a Temple of Diana and two "Halfway Houses". The buildings were placed at the end of vistas so that the gardens could be appreciated to the maximum advantage.

In 1715 the Duke decided to rebuild the house on a site approximately where the present house is and asked Giacomo Leoni, the well known Italian architect, to prepare the surviving plans. They show that the north front was to be kept, including a chapel and a smoking room. Behind it was to be a rebuilt house arranged round two courtyards with principal rooms, including a saloon and a vestibule. These plans were shown by the Duke's sons on their Grand Tour to leading Italian architects, including Juvarra.[21] The collapse of the South Sea Bubble and the death of the two sons that survived to adulthood deterred the Duke from embarking on the rebuilding. By the 1730s the project was clearly abandoned with Batty Langley remodelling the dining room in 1736. He also refronted the Bowling Green House and built the greenhouse. His influence is detected in the creation of the "Serpentine Water" and the adding of informal paths to the main gardens.

The 1740 Inventory

Despite all the alterations to the landscape in which the house was set, the house was substantially the same in 1740 as it had been in 1680 after Hooper's alterations. Even with a couple of plans prepared by Earl de Grey conjecturing what the house would have looked like in 1740 and 1797,[22] it is still difficult to establish the exact location of all the rooms at the time of the 1740 inventory.

The house was entered by an arch in the north front with a porter's lodge on the right. The rest of the ground floor was filled with rooms of officials and servants of the house, including Mr. Sobière, perhaps a French chef. At the west end of this front was a bakehouse and meal house. The first floor contained the library in the most prominent central position with the green room and Lady Mary Grey's (1719–1761) bedchamber and dressing room to the right and the billiard room and Lady Portland's (d.1751) room, with her maid's room, over the bakehouse. Rooms of further officials lay to the left of that. Attics filled the entire second floor of this front. There were at least three staircases

Plate 31: Wrest Park: The library which was in the north part
of the house added in the 1670s.
(*Drawing: J.C. Buckler, 1831*)

between ground and first floor but their location is difficult to determine
as the plans prepared by Leoni and Earl de Grey differ.

The centre of the north front was connected to the older part of the
house by a block containing at ground floor the steward's parlour (presumably next to the steward's room mentioned earlier in the inventory)
and the servants' hall. Above these were a series of rooms serving the
Duke himself. His bedchamber was over the steward's parlour and his
valet's – Mr. Bonafos – room and his dressing room were presumably
over the servants' hall.

The west side of the old part of the house contained the service wing
with kitchen and attendant specialist rooms, such as the pastry room
over which was the housekeeper's room. Beyond the servants' hall was
the passage between the kitchen and the hall which had Lord
Ashburnham's (1724–1812) room over it. Next to the passage was the
butler's room and probably on the site of the later south drawing room
were the parlour and little drawing room. The Duke's wife and his
daughter, Sophia (1730–1780), had their apartments on the first floor
over these rooms.

In the centre of the old house was the great hall. Out of it led
the "Great Staircase", almost certainly later described as the "South
Staircase". The next room is the great dining room. Its exact position is
unclear but could have formed part of the east side of the house and

been on the first floor. Access to it would have been difficult from the kitchen block and no doubt the great parlour was used more for day-to-day meals. Next door was the great drawing room described by Horace Walpole, "Like the State Bedchamber: Round the hangings are spotted velvet fluted Ionic pillars with a freeze of devices in patchwork . . . entwined with festoons between the columns."[23] It is described as being in "the Garden Front". This could also include the east front. The "Crimson velvet rooms" adjoined it, probably in the south-east corner of the house. The long gallery was at the top of the great staircase. In the same south-east corner of the house were "the Spangle Rooms", all on the first floor.

Underneath it is probable that there were a series of rooms connected with the chapels. Both of de Grey's plans and the earlier inventories suggest that the chapel was near the great hall. Leoni's plans for the rebuilding of Wrest do show the chapel in the north front of the existing house in the east side. It is possible that for a period the chapel was moved, returning to its original position later in the eighteenth century. It is more likely that the chapel remained in the same position from Tudor times till its demolition in the 1830s.

While it is impossible to be sure that the above ground plan is correct, with its inconsistencies and question marks it remains the most plausible suggestion.

Wrest fittings in 1740 show a house that has not been refurnished for some time. A number of rooms have tapestry hangings, some of them "very good" and one depicting the story of Marcus Aurelius. These would have given a late seventeenth/ early eighteenth century feel to the house. A number of rooms had old furniture and linen. "Lady Mary's Bedchamber", for example, had an "old walnut escritoire, six old matted chairs and two old strip'd muslin Window curtains". Her dressing room was just as old-fashioned.

In the principal rooms, such as the great parlour, the odd small pieces of mahogany appear such as the stand, tea chest and tea table. The room contains furniture of a mixture of styles: "a side board with a large marble slab", "an old walnut tree card table" and a "wainscot table with two oval dining tables". Everywhere there was a substantial amount of caned furniture that would have been old fashioned by 1740. In the Duchess's room was a splendid "ebony cabinet enlaid with tortoiseshell with brass carved capitals upon Pillasters." Such a piece was unusual at Wrest rather than the general rule.

The house was filled with pictures, mainly portraits, but also some "Landskips" and at least one "History piece". The portraits were principally of the Greys and their relations, the Crews, the Benns, and the Evelyns. There are a number of portraits of royalty and two of workmen on the estate. The Van Dycks mentioned by Horace Walpole were purchased by Philip Yorke and his wife Jemima, Marchioness Grey, after the death of Sir Robert Walpole in 1745.[24]

The Duke possessed a considerable amount of blue and white china, probably Chinese export at this date. He had one or two pieces of Delft. The amount of plate he owned was prodigious, on a suitably ducal scale.

The contents of the garden buildings are included in the inventory. In the Hill House on Cain Hill, looking down over the gardens, was a "Prospect of Versailles", a conscious comparison. Also listed was a portrait of the head of "Mr. Archer", to whom the building has been attributed.

Wrest 1740–1839

The new owners of Wrest Park were Philip Yorke, later 2nd Earl of Hardwicke, and Jemima, Marchioness Grey, the Duke of Kent's granddaughter (1722–1797). They imposed their own taste on the gardens. At various stages a root house and a pagan altar were established. Between 1758 and 1760 the gardens were conservatively "improved" by Capability Brown. The house itself saw changes, too. The building of a replacement to the dining chamber was the first priority and a new one was built between the south staircase and the parlour in 1760, supervised by Henry Flitcroft, who remodelled Woburn Abbey.[25] Its chief feature was the bay window, projecting deliberately to give an off-centre focal point to the south front. In 1763 John Smith, Clerk of Works to Kensington Palace (1761–1783), turned the old "Great Parlour" into the new "South Drawing Room" for an estimated £429.[26]

Considerable repairs were undertaken in 1769, mainly for the roofs of the north front, the "Old Dining Room" and "Chapel chamber" as well as the chapel roof. The chapel itself was refitted and on the 22 April 1769, the Vicar of Flitton could write to Lord Hardwicke: "We likewise visited the New chapel on Tuesday last; the floors, pews, pulpits, desk etc. almost finished. A very neat and commodious oratory."[27] It is possible that Edward Stevens, who designed the Bath House at Wrest in 1770, was the architect involved. It is probable that by this date the turret in the centre of the north front had been removed.[28]

The main architectural weakness of Wrest was the result of the piecemeal development which caused none of the fronts to match; particularly glaring in contrast to the formality of the landscape in which it was placed. Major alterations, estimated at £4,888, were undertaken under the supervision of John Woolfe (d.1793), Examining Clerk in the Office of Works and architect of the 1770s wings at Colworth.[29] The central link between north and south front was reroofed and a large "Chinese Drawing Room" and passage were added to the east of the existing block. The gap at the south-east corner of the house was filled up with a breakfast room and the "Spangle Room" filled the gap between the south drawing room and the kitchen block. The east block known as

Plate 32: Wrest Park: View from the south east during the demolition
of the old house.
(*Watercolour: J. Buckler 1838*)

Queen Anne's was pulled down. The rooms had been fitted up for a visit
she never made. The remainder was harmonised and for the first time
Wrest looked from the exterior to have a unity its intricate ground plan
belied.

Jemima's daughter, Amabel, and grandson, Earl de Grey, did little to
the house apart from routine repairs. In the gardens the root house and
Cain Hill had to be demolished. In his *History of Wrest House* Earl de
Grey wrote: "It was quite clear to us all, many years before the place
came to me, that something upon rather a grand scale must be done, if
at all. The old house, with its cracked walls and its long passages, and
its windows that annually become less capable of being closely shut
down was evidently incapable of any essential repair and improvement."[30] De Grey employed John Shaw (1766–1832) in 1818 to draw up
plans for a stage-by-stage replacement of the house on the existing site.[31]
By degrees de Grey felt that Shaw's plans would not do. From 1822 he
had become fascinated by French art and decided that Wrest should
have a French chateau to replace the old house. He decided to build on
a site further away from the canal, roughly where the Duke of Kent had
intended to build. When de Grey finally inherited the estate in 1833 he
decided to put his plans into execution and demolish the old house.
"For many years before [1833] . . . I had felt the utter impossibility of

doing anything to or with the old house. It was very old, but it had nei-
ther antiquarian or architectural value. It was not essentially out of
repaiur, but it was of very bad construction (much of it nothing but lath
and plaster), very extensive without a possibility of concentration,
utterly impossible to warm, and with no suite of apartments upon any
floor."[32] Elsewhere he commented on the damp mist which so frequently
rises in that part, more remote from the pieces of water, and "the clouds
of gnats which used to eat us up."[33]

Between 1834–1838 detailed sketches were made by Buckler and Earl
de Grey himself of the house during the various stages of demolition.
The last walls were taken down on 30 January 1840. The present house
for which the foundation stone had been laid on 12 February 1834 was
ready for occupation in October 1839.[34]

WREST PARK, SILSOE 1740

An Inventory of the Furniture, Linnen, Plate and other Goods
belonging to the Most Noble Henry Duke of Kent late deceased at Rest
House in the Parish of Silsoe in the County of Bedford taken the 19th,
20th, 21st, 23rd of June 1740 by us whose Names are hereunder written.

In the Old Lodge on the right hand coming into the Court North Front:
Twenty one Boxes for Bees, Three Fishing Nets and a Parcell of old
Lumber, Four Iron Coal Scuttles, Four Fire Brushes.

In the Passage: A Fire Engine and Leather Pipes.

**In the first Room to the left hand of the said Passage called the
Steward's Room:** A Sacking Bottom Bedstead with Green China
Furniture & Counterpane, A Feather Bed, Bolster, two Pillows, a
check'd Matress, three Blankets & a Quilt, The Tapestry to the Room
of Forrest Work, Four old Chairs, Two old Tables, A Small Dressing
Glass, Fire Shovel & Tongs, Poker and Fender very old, Three very old
Mapps, A large Chest for Plate, Three Iron Locks & Bolts.

In the Closet to the said Room: A Close Stool and Earthen Pann.

In the Area, Library and Stair Case: Four Wooden Cases containing
Parcells of carved Figures in Wood, Two Canvas painted Chimney
Blinds and an Old Indian Picture.

In the Room beyond the Stair Case, called Mr. Mallet's Room: A
Sacking bottom Bedstead with old purple course Cloth Furniture, A
Feather Bed Bolster & Pillow, three Blankets & a Quilt, two chequer'd
Linnen Matresses, Five very old Cane Chairs, an old Deal Table, The
Tapestry Hangings very old, An ordinary old Red Bays Curtain and
Rod, A green Bays Door Curtain & Rod, an Iron Grate fix'd and a
Fender.

**In the Room beyond the back Stair-case In the North Front called Mrs.
Sobiere's Room:** A Sacking Bottom Bedstead with white Dimity
Furniture, lined with white Callicoe, a Feather Bed, Bolster & three

Pillows, Four Blankets, one Quilt, one chequer'd Linnen Matress, one white Holland matress very old, Old Tapestry Hangings to the Room, two pieces pretty good, An old large hanging Glass in a Walnut Tree Frame 2 feet by 2 feet 8 inches, A Walnut Tree Table and Drawer, An old Leather Easy Chair and Cushion, An old Deal Table, Six Cane Chairs & an Iron Grate fix'd, Tongs Poker & Iron Fender, An old Crimson Velvet Close Stool, An old Screen, 4 Leaved blue Linsey. In the Closet to the said Room: A Small Walnut Tree Table.

Upon the Great Stair-case to the Library: An old large Glass Lustre, Crimson Silk Tossel and Pullies Ditto.

In the Room to the left hand of the said Stair-Case called Lady Mary's Dressing Room on the Second Floor: The Tapestry Hangings to the Room pretty good, Three sets of Green China Window Curtains lin'd with green Tammy, Pullies and Laths, Six Matted Chairs and one cane Chair, An old Table with a Dressing Glass with Drawers, A large Glass in a Walnut Tree frame 2 feet 8 inches by 2 feet, A Steel Grate with Furniture complete, An old Deal Table and Stool Ditto, One old Cushion, an old Fire Screen, an old Indian Tea Table, Five Tea Cups & Saucers of blue and white China, Seven handled Chocolate Cups Ditto, A Tea Pot & Saucer in raised Figures & Colours, One blue & white China Slop Bason, Five Portrait Pictures, One Ditto Small, Two eight Inch brass Locks, One old Lock upon the Doors.

In the Closet: The paper Hangings to the Closet, A Small Walnut Tree Bureau, One green China Window Curtain Lines and Pullies.

In the Room beyond the Back Stairs called Lady Mary's Bedchamber: A Lath bottom Bedstead with wrought worked Dimity Furniture lined with glazed Callicoe, A Down Bed & Bolster, Two Pillows, Two Blankets, A large white Holland Quilt, One chequer'd Matress, One white Holland Ditto, Two pieces of good Tapestry Hangings, A Glass three feet two [Inches^c] by two feet three Inches fineer'd with Rose Wood, A Table Ditto, A Small Dressing Glass, A Cafoy Easy Chair and Cushion, A Chimney Glass in a black Frame, An ordinary Landskip over the Chimney, Two large cane Stools, One old Crimson Mohair Stool & Cushion, Six old Matted Chairs, A large Indian Chest for Cloaths, An old Walnut Tree Escritore, Two old strip'd Muslin Window Curtains & Rods, Two old Deal Tables, An Iron Grate fix'd Furniture complete.

In the Closet to the said Chamber: A Deal Table, Two Chairs, A green Worsted Damask Window Curtain & Rod, A Small Picture of a Judge.

In the room to the Right hand of the great Stair Case next to the Library called The Green Room: Green Worsted Damask Hangings, Four green Damask Chairs and an Easy Chair Ditto, Two Walnut Tree Card Tables with Leather Covers, A Picture over the Chimney, Thirty large and small Prints, Twelve with black frames and gold Beads, the other all plain black, A Weather Glass and Thermometer, A large Oval

Indian Table, Eight blue and white Tea Cups and Saucers, Six handled Coffee Cups Ditto, A Tea Pot and Stand Ditto, a Spoon Boat Ditto, A large Slop Bason Ditto, One less Ditto, Three odd Basons, A Sugar Dish Ditto, A white China wrought Sugar Dish & Cover, A Nutmeg Box Ditto, A Steel Stove with Furniture complete, A painted Canvas frame to the Chimney; A Commode Table with a green Cloth Cover.

In the Library: A large Mahogany Bureau Table, Six Stools Ditto, Two Arm'd Chairs cover'd with worsted Caffoy, Two old black flower'd Velvet Chairs, One old Easy Chair and Cushion, A large Carpet, A pair of Globes with Leather Covers, Six Matted Chairs, Six Square Stools, A Mahogany Reading Stand, A Steel Grate and Furniture Complete, A painted Blind for the Chimney, A pair of Steps, Two large brass locks upon the Doors, A Small Mahogany Desk for a Book.

In the Billiard Room: A large Billiard Table & Rods with a Leather Cover, A Settee and Cushion cover'd with a yellow Mohair, two old Yellow Stools and Cushions, Six Matted Chairs, A Grate & Furniture complete, A Canvas Blind for the Chimney, The Duke of Kent's Picture.

In the Room next to the Billiard Room called Lady Portland's Room: A Lath bottom'd Bedstead with Strip'd Callimanco Furniture, A Down Bed & Bolster, A Chequer'd Linnen Matress, Two white Holland Matresses pretty good, Tapestry Hangings to the Room, An Indian Chest for Cloaths, a Wainscot Corner Cupboard, Four yellow Caffoy Chairs, Two yellow round Stools Ditto, A large White Holland Quilt, Two large Blankets, A Yellow Silk Quilt, Two Setts of Yellow Caffoy Window Curtains, A Small Table Grate and Furniture complete, A large Glass two feet eight inches by two feet, A Table and a pair of Stands, A large four leav'd Map Screen & a two leav'd Screen Ditto, two eight inch brass Locks.

In the Closet to the said Room: The worsted Damask Hangings, & a Set of Window Curtains & Lines; An old Yellow silk round Stool and a Close Stool.

In the Room over the Bakehouse, called Lady Portland's Maid's Room: A Settee Bedstead with strip'd Stuff Furniture, A Feather Bed, Bolster, one Pillow, four Blankets, A Quilt, One chequer'd Linnen Matress, Four Old Stuft Chairs, An old Wainscot Chest of Drawers, A Wainscot Table, Two Setts of Strip'd Window Curtains, A three leav'd Screen, An Iron Grate Fender and Bellows, A Glass, A black Japan'd Table, Tapestry Hangings pretty good.

In the Room over the Meal House called Mr. Skinner's Room: An old Sacking Bottom Bedstead with old ragged Furniture, A Featherbed, Bolster & Pillow, four Blankets & Quilt, Two pair of old green Window Curtains, two odd Curtains, Tapestry Hangings, Three old Chairs and two Tables, An Iron Grate fix'd Furniture Complete.

In the Room over the Still Room called Mr. Cornaby's Room: A Sacking bottom Bedstead with white Dimity Furniture, A Feather Bed,

Bolster & Pillow, Three Blankets, a chequer'd Linnen Matress, One old white Matress, A Strip'd India Quilt, An old red Silk Quilt, Tapestry Hangings old, Four Matted Chairs and a Table, An Iron Grate fix'd Furniture complete.

In the Garret over Mr. Cornaby's Room: A Corded Bedstead with green Linsey Furniture, Two Feather Beds, One Bolster, one Pillow, An old Matress, Three Blankets & a Quilt, four old Chairs, Two Tables, A pair of Dogs & Fander, The Hangings red Linsey, Two old blue Window Curtains, A Small Glass and an old Close Stool.

In the Garret over My Lady Portland's Maid's Room: A Corded Bedstead with green Linsey Furniture, A Feather Bed, Bolster & Pillow, four blankets, a Quilt & a Red Rugg, an Old Matress, Five old Chairs, A Stool, An old Table, An old Grate and Iron Fender, Two Window Curtains & Rods.

In the Garret over Lady Portland's Room called Mr. Pferinger's Room: A Sacking Bottom Bedstead with green Linsey Furniture, Two Pillows, Three very old Blankets, Three old Chairs, A Table, An old Iron Grate, A Bell to the Room, A pair of old Bellows, An old Cushion.

In the garret over the Billiard Room: A Sacking Bottom Bedstead with very old Crimson Velvet Furniture, A Feather Bed, two Bolsters, one old Blanket, Two Chairs, A Stool, and a pair of Dogs.

In the Garret over the Green Room next to the Library: A Corded Bedstead with very old Cloth Furniture, A Feather Bed & Bolster.

In the Garret over Lady Mary's Dressing Room: A Corded Bedstead with green Linsey Furniture, A Feather Bed, Bolster, Three Blankets & a Rugg, A Table, Three old Chairs, Four Feather'd Ticken Stools, A Deal Table, An old Curtain and Rod, A Small Glass Sconce.

In the next Garret over Lady Mary's Dressing Room: A Sacking Bottom Bedstead with green Linsey Furniture, A Feather Bed & Bolster, one Pillow, three Blankets & a Quilt, A Wainscot Table, Two Chairs and Window Curtains, A Grate fix'd & a Fender, A Close Stool & the Hangings.

In the Garret over Lady Mary's Bedchamber: A Sacking Bottom Bedstead with green Linsey Furniture, A Feather Bed, Bolster & two Pillows, Three blankets and a Quilt, Six old Chairs and a Table, The Tapestry Hangings to the Room, An Iron Grate and Shovell, One Stool & a Close Stool, A Pair of Iron Dogs.

In the Steward's Parlour: Twenty matted Chairs, A long Table, Two small Tables, The Tapestry Hangings to the Room, Two large Maps of the City of Rome, Seven Prints of the Battles of Alexander by Le Brun, Two old Linnen Window Curtains, Three Rods, A pair of Iron Dogs, Fender & Tongs, An old Cupboard, A Backgammon Table, A Print of the City of Prague, A Deal Tea Table.

In the Servants Hall: A long Table, Three Forms, Two Small Tables, An old Broken Chair, Two old Partridge Nets.

In the Butler's Pantry: Two large Copper Cisterns, an old Deal Table, Three old broken Chairs, Three Wooden Trays, A Napkin Press, A large Cupboard, Five Pitchers, six White Decanters, Six Glass Decanters, Five Dozen of Drinking Glasses, One Dozen of Water Glasses, One Dozen of Vinegar Cruets, One Dozen of Jelly Glasses, Ten China Saucers, Six Lignum Vitae Plates for Bottles, A Copper Toaster for Cheese, Four large wooden Trays, A Lignum Vitae Mortar and Pestle, A Tin Scuttle, A Grate fix'd.

In the Anti-Room to the Great Parlour: Eight Cane Chairs, A Glass Lanthorn, A Thermometer.

In the Confectionary adjoining to the said Anti-Room: Two Old Deal Tables, Two old Chairs, a large wooden Bowl, Four midling China blue & white Dishes, Five Ditto of a less Size, Twenty one Syllabub & Jelly Glasses, Eleven ordinary blue & white China Plates, A wooden Tray, Thirty Seven China Plates. In the Cupboard Eight China Dishes of a Small Size, A China Strainer, A Dozen small Earthen Cake pans, A Glass Salver for Jelly Glasses.

In the Great Parlour: Three Setts of Crimson Damask Window Curtains & Rods, Three worsted Damask Cushions & three Crimson Silk Cushions, Thirteen large Prints, Forty five lesser Prints Ditto being Views of Noblemen's & Gentlemen's Seats all with black Frames and gold Beads, A large Diagonal Weather Glass, A Landskip over the Chimney, A Side Board Table with a large Marble Slab, An old Walnut Tree Card Table, A Small Wainscot Table, Two Wainscot Oval Dining Tables, A Mahogony Tea Table, A Mahogony Stand for the Tea Kettle lin'd with Copper, Six large ordinary Tea Cups & Saucers, One brown Cup Ditto, 5 handled Coffee Cups Ditto, Three Chocolate Cups Ditto, One Slop Bason, One China Boat for Spoons, One Small China Cup, A Mahogony Tea Chest, Twenty four Cane Chairs, Three old Elbow Chairs, A brown China Tea Pot & Sugar Dish, The Old Grate and Furniture complete, Two pieces of Green Cloth for the Dining Table, A brass Lock upon the Door.

In the Little Drawing Room: Tapestry Hangings very good, A Picture half length of Queen Anne, Another Ditto of Lord Godolphin, Two large Walnut Tree Corner Cupboards with Indian Pictures, Two Indian Paper Fire Screens, Two Small Walnut Tree Stands, A Mahogony Card Table, A Wainscot Table, Two setts of yellow Damask worsted Window Curtains, Valents & Rods, the Curtains lined with yellow Tammy, Eight matted Chairs, Two Stools, Eight Damask Cushions for the Chairs, Two Damask Cushions for the Stools, A Glass over the Chimney, A pair of glass Sconces, A Settee cover'd with yellow Silk Damask, and a Silk Cushion with a loose Cover, An old Iron Grate and Iron back fix'd, A pair of Bellows, A large Glass two feet four Inches by three feet Six Inches, A Table of Rose Wood Ditto, A Small old Tea Table, An old brass Lock upon the Door, A Map of Bedfordshire.

In the Great Hall: Three Wooden Frames with three large Marble Slabs for Side Boards, Twenty one Cane Chairs, A large Glass Sconce with three Arms, A pair of large Sconces, Three Small Sconces, The Grate & Furniture Complete, Three old red Cushions, A Picture of King James the 1st at length, Another of his Queen Ditto, Prince Henry Ditto, A Copy of Cornaro Family, A large Piece over the Door going into the Garden, The Mother of Mary Queen of Scots in full length, Ditto of Mary Queen of Scots Ditto, A Plan of the Gardens at Rest, Two Glass Lanthorns with Bell Glasses over them.

Garden Front.
In the Room beyond the Area of the Great Stair Case, going out of the Hall, called the Long Gallery. Twelve Cane Chairs, A half Length Picture of the Countess of Shrewsbury, Ditto Countess of Derby, Ditto Sir Randolph Crew, Ditto of Mary Mother of Anthony Benn, A Head of Sir Eustace Hart, Ditto Elizabeth Smith, Ditto of John Evelyn, A half Length of Elizabeth Lady Maynard when a Child, Eleven old Maps, An old Table Frame with a Stone Slab, A whole Length Picture of John Duel, Gardiner; Ditto William Milward, Wood-Cutter Ditto; A large Mahogany Leaf Table, wainscot Frame with folding Joynts, One curious Garden Chair with Springs, One ordinary Ditto, A Child's Coach, Four large Windsor Chairs, Four small Ditto, Three Glass Lanthorns, An Iron Beam, Scales & Weights; Four half hundred Bloom Weights, One Quarter Ditto, two fourteen pounds Ditto, Three seven pounds Ditto, Two four pounds, One two pounds Ditto, Three single pounds, four half pounds brass Weights, A large Marble black & yellow Slab & an old Frame, One old red Cushion.
In the first Room upon the Right hand next to the said Long Gallery called the Spangle Room: A Sacking bottom Bedstead with a wrought Dimity Furniture worked with red worsted and Spangles, A Feather Bed, Bolster & Pillow, three Blankets and a Counterpane the same of the Curtains, Nine Cushions of Needle work Ditto, the Hangings to the Room Ditto, A Chequered Matress, an old White Holland Ditto, Two Setts of very ordinary Stuff Window Curtains, Valens & Rods; Nine old Cane Chairs & Couch Ditto; An old Walnut Tree Table & a pair of Stands Ditto; A Glass two feet seven Inches by one foot eleven in a Walnut Tree frame, An old Grate & Furniture complete, An old Close Stool.
In the next Room beyond the Spangle Room, called Mr. Bartlett's Room: A Sacking bottom Bedstead with crimson & green flower'd silk Damask lined with white Indian Peeling work'd; A White Flower'd Silk Quilt, A Feather Bed, Bolster & 1 Pillow; Three Blankets, One chequer'd Linnen Matress the bottom Leather; One white Holland Ditto, Three Silk Damask Chairs Ditto, Two arm'd Chairs Ditto, The Tapestry Hangings of ordinary Forest work, Two Setts of Silk Strip'd

Cotton Window Curtains & Rods, A Picture being the Head of Amabell Benn, Ditto of Elizabeth Hartop, An old Walnut Tree Table, A pair of Stands Ditto, A Glass Two feet eight Inches by two feet, A broken Deal Table, An old Grate etc. & Close Stool, A pair of Bellows.

In the End Room to the Gallery call'd the Little Spangle Room: A Sacking Bottom Bedstead with wrought Furniture Spangled, A Feather Bed, Bolster, one Pillow, three Blankets, One old Holland Matress, an old Red Rugg, One white Dimity Window Curtain & Rod, Six old Cane Chairs, An old Walnut Tree Table, An old Grate Shovel & Tongs, A half Length Picture, A Bell.

In the Area of the Great Stair Case, going out of the Hall: A Large Wainscot Oval Table, An old Glass Lustre with crimson Silk Tossel, Lines and Pully.

Round the Sides of the said Staircase: A whole Length of Anthony Earl of Kent, Mary Countess of Kent Ditto, [Henry Earl of Kent Ditto'] Jemima Countess of Kent Ditto, Sophia Duchess of Kent at Length, Henry Earl of Kent Ditto, Amabella Second wife of Henry Earl of Kent Ditto, Anthony Grey Rector of Burbage Earl of Kent Ditto, Magdalen Countess of Kent half Length, Elizabeth Countess of Kent at Length, Henry Earl of Kent Son of Charles at Length.

In the Great Dining Room: Crimson Camblet Hangings, Two sets of Crimson Window Curtains & Rods, Sixteen Crimson flower'd velvet Chairs, One armed Chair Ditto, Two Square Stools Ditto, Two Marble Slabs vein'd upon two old Walnut Tree frames, An old Wainscot Table & Stool, A pair of large brass Chimney Dogs, Hand Iron Shovel & Tongs Ditto, A pair of small Iron Dogs and an Iron back fix'd; A small Indian Fire Screen on a Walnut Tree Stand; a whole Length Picture of Lady Ann Cavendish, Ditto of Jemima Countess of Ashburnham, Ditto of Amabella Lady Glenorchy, Ditto Countess of Harold, Ditto Anthony Earl of Harold, Ditto Lady Harper, Ditto Thomas Lord Crew, A half Length of Jemima Duchess of Kent, Ditto of [Blank], Ditto over the Door, A large Family Piece of Henrietta, Ann & Jane Daughters of Henry Duke of Kent when Children.

In the Room next to the Great Dining Room, Garden Front called the Drawing Room: Crimson Velvet Hangings with Velvet Pilasters & Needle work Festoons, Two Setts of crimson flower'd Ditto Window Curtains & Rods, Eight blue yellow & White Needlework'd Chairbacks & Seats alike and Covers, An old Glass Lustre crimson Tossel, A Landskip over the Chimney with Figures, A pair of Glass Sconces, A whole length of Jemima Duchess of Kent with Lady Mary a Child, An Indian Tea Table, Eight Square red & white Tea Cups & Saucers, A Slop Bason, Tea Pot & Plate Ditto, A Small white China Sugar Dish & Cover, An old Walnut Tree Table & a pair of Stands Ditto, A large Pier Glass two feet three Inches wide in three Lengths, A black Japan'd Card Table.

In the Room next to the Drawing Room Called the Crimson Velvet Room: A Lath bottom Bedstead with crimson Velvet Furniture lined with crimson Persian, A crimson Silk Quilt, One pair of large Blankets, A Down Bed & Bolster, two Pillows Ditto, A white Holland Matress, A chequerd Linnen Matress, Six crimson Velvet Chairs backs & Seats alike, Two Elbow Chairs Ditto with loose Covers, Two Setts of flower'd Velvet Window Curtains Valens & Rods, A Landskip over the Chimney, The Figure of a Statue, Two blue & white Incense China Bottles armed with Silver, Two Ditto with Silver Tops, Three Ditto Plain, Three China Cups upon Stands, A six leaved Screen cover'd with India paper, eight feet high; A black Japann'd India Cabinet, A large Jarr & Cover & two Beakers enamelled with Divers Colours, An old Walnut Tree Table and a pair of Stands Ditto, A large Glass three feet one Inch by two feet four Inches, Four pieces of Fine Tapestry Hangings containing the Story of Marcus Aurelius, an old Grate and Furniture complete, a Round Stool.

In the first Room on the right Hand, coming up the back Stairs at the end of the Long Gallery called a Dressing Room to the Crimson Velvet Room: The old Tapestry Hangings to the Room, A Mahogany Night Table, A Walnut Tree Chest with a Drawer, A pair of Walnut Tree Stands, A Glass two feet by one foot eight Inches with a broad frame of wrought brass intermixed with Glass, Four matted Chairs & a Close Stool, A white Damask Linnen Window Curtain & a Rod.

Garden Front.

In the Room next to the Crimson Velvet Room called The Crimson and white Velvet Room: A Lath bottom Bedstead with crimson and white flower'd Velvet, lined with green & white Strip'd thread Sattin, A Counterpane Ditto, A Feather Bed, Bolster, two Down Pillows & two Blankets, A White Holland Matress, A chequer'd Ditto, Eight Crimson and white flower'd Velvet Chairs, Backs and Seats alike, Two Setts of crimson flower'd Velvet Window Curtains lined with crimson Serge & Rods, Fine Tapestry Hangings to the Room containing the Story of Marcus Aurelius continued, A Glass over the Chimney, A pair of small Sconces, A Picture over the Chimney of an old Man & an Angel, A Landskip over the Door with Statues & Fountains, A Green Velvet Easy Chair, An old Velvet Stool, a five leav'd Screen Canvas painted with Trees, A Walnut Tree Table inlaid, A pair of Stands Ditto, A Glass Ditto 3 feet by 2 feet 2 inches, a Scritore inlaid & Dressing Glass Ditto, An India Fire Screen upon a Walnut Tree Stand, An Old Grate with Furniture Complete.

In the Dressing Room adjoyning to the Crimson and white Velvet Room: Brown Stuff Hangings wrought in Pannels, A Glass in a black Frame eighteen Inches by twenty two, A two leaved Screen cover'd with Cloth paper flower'd with Silver, A two leaved Indian Screen, Six old Matted

Chairs, One old Cushion, A round Stuft Stool, An old Walnut tree Table, One white Damask Linnen Window Curtain & Rod, A Picture over the Chimney being a History Piece, A pair of Ordinary Sconces, Four Japan'd Beakers, Four small Japan'd Pieces, Three Flint Beakers, A Grate Complete, A Close Stool and a Seven Inch brass Lock upon the Door.

In the Garret over the Crimson Velvet Room: A Corded Bedstead and Matt with Strip'd Camblet Furniture, A Feather Bed, Bolster, & one Pillow, Three Blankets, A Plad Counterpane, Six old Ticken feather'd Cushions with red Serge Covers, Green Linsey Hangings to the Room, Two old Window Curtains & Rods, An old Table, A Stove Grate and Furniture complete, A Bell, A Close Stool, A piece of a Settee Bedstead.

In the Garret over the Crimson and white Flowerd Velvet Room: A Corded Bedstead with a green Cloth Serge Furniture lined with a Bengal, A Feather Bed, Bolster and Pillows, Three Blankets & a Quilt, Two white old Holland Matresses, Six old Cane Chairs the bottoms stuft and coverd with green Cloth Serge Ditto, An old Table, Two old Yellow China Curtains & Rods, A Grate complete, Two old Chairs, A pair of Andirons and a Bell & a Close Stool.

Upon the Back Stair Case at the end of the Long Gallery: A Picture at length of Henry the 4th of France, A Glass Lanthorn.

In the Chapel: The Communion Table and old Crimson Velvet Cover, An old Pulpit Cushion and Cloth Ditto, Two Seat Cloths Ditto, A long red Plush Cushion, Six old Chairs and Seven old Cushions, A Desk Cloth Ditto, Four Folio Common Prayer Books & Bibles, Six large Octavo Common Prayer Books, 12 Small Common Prayer Books.

In the Bed Chamber next to the Chappel: A Sacking Bottom Bedstead with brown camblet furniture lined with Silk, A feather Bed, Bolster & Pillow, three Blankets, One other Feather Bed, an old Silk Quilt, two setts of blue Harrateen Window Curtains & Rods, The Tapestry Hangings of ordinary Forest Work, A small glass Sconce, five old Chairs, An old Table, An ordinary Picture over the Chimney, Two Gordons Maps of Huntingdonshire, A Grate, Fender, Tongs & Shovel.

In the Smoking Room: Sixteen Cane Chairs, Eleven Maps, Thirteen Small prints of Several Towns, An oval Table, A Marble Slab upon an old Frame, A pair of brass headed Dogs, An Iron Back to the Chimney fix'd.

In the Bed Chamber on the left hand of the Smoaking Room: A Sacking bottom Bedstead with old yellow and blue silk damask Furniture, An old Silk Quilt, A Feather Bed, Bolster and one Pillow, Four old Blankets, A white Holland Matress, Five old Chairs & an old Couch, A Walnut tree Table, a Close Stool, A Window Curtain & Rod, Old Tapestry Hangings, An ordinary Picture over the Chimney, A pair of Iron Dogs, Tongs & Fender.

In the Chappel Room: The Green worsted Damask Hangings, Three Setts of Damask Window Curtains, two Valens & three Rods, Three Settees of flower'd Tapestry & green Serge Covers, One Elbow Chair and Cover Ditto, Six Chairs backs & Seats alike with Covers Ditto, Six Green Damask Cushions Ditto, Four plad Cushions, Three old Tapestry Cushions, A Glass over the Chimney, Two small Sconces, A Steel Hearth complete for to burn Wood, A black Japan'd Table, Two Arms Ditto, A Pier Glass in three Pieces two feet wide, A Carpet, Eleven Common Prayer Books 8vo, A Folio Bible bound in Turkey Leather & Gilt.

Pictures:

Lady Amabella Grey Sister to Henry Earl of Kent at full Length, Ditto of Anthony Earl of Kent, Ditto of Banister Lord Maynard, A half Length of Mary Lucas Sister to John Lord Lucas, Ditto of Lady Jane Grey, Ditto Elizabeth Daughter of Gilbert Earl of Shrewsbury, Ditto of Anthony Grey Rector of Burbage, Ditto of Mary Countess of Kent, Ditto of Elizabeth Lady Maynard, Ditto of Amabella Countess of Kent, The Head of Ann Nevill, Ditto of Henry Earl of Kent, Ditto of Sir Anthony Benn, Ditto of Jane Evelyn.

In the Passage beyond the said Room: A Whole Length of Henry Duke of Kent 1723 [*marginal note* gone to the Duchess of Kent], Ditto of Ditto 1718, A Copy of a half Length of Lady Susan Longueville, A Head of Henry Earl of Kent, son of Charles Earl of Kent, A half Length of Sir Charles Lucas.

In the Anti Chamber to the Alcove Room: Blue Camblet Hangings with Velvet Pillasters & Borders, A Set of Window Curtains Valens & Rod, Eight Chairs – backs & Seats alike Ditto, A Walnut Tree Table & a pair of Stands, A Glass in a Walnut Tree Frame two feet three Inches by three feet one Inch, A pair of small sconces 1 broke, An Iron back to the Chimney, A Picture over the Chimney, A half Length Picture of Sir Randal Crew Lord Chief Justice of England, Ditto Nathanael Lord Crew Bishop of Durham, Ditto Sir Thomas Crew Speaker, A Family Piece of Jemima Duchess of Kent & her Sisters Armine & Elizabeth when Children, half length John Lord Crew, Ditto Jemima Mother of Jemima Dutchess of Kent, Ditto of [*blank*] Ditto of [*blank*]

In the Closet to the Antichamber: The Plad Hangings and a Close Stool.

In the Alcove Room: A Sacking bottom Bedstead with purple Velvet Furniture pannel'd with needle work and lined with yellow Sattin, A Quilt Ditto with Silk Fringe, A Down Bed and Bolster, Three Blankets & a white Holland Matress, A chequer'd Ditto, Six Squar'd Velvet Stools with needle work Ditto, two Arm'd Chairs Ditto, Six square Stools of Yellow Silk Damask and Covers, Two arm'd Chairs & Covers Ditto, Two pair of Yellow Mohair Curtains Valens Lines & Rods, the Curtains lin'd with Silk, A pair of Sconces Silver'd, A black Table edged with Looking Glass & cover'd with wrought brass, A pair of Stands Ditto, A Glass Ditto Nineteen Inches by twenty four Inches, Five pieces of Fine figur'd Tapestry Hangings, A Curious Landskip over the Chimney, A pair of Steel Dogs and an Iron back, The floor of the Alcove cover'd over with a Barbary Matt.

Under the back stairs that goes out of the Anti-Room to the Great Parlour: About one Dozen of old Frames for Pictures, the Head of Sir Randal Crew, & eight more unknown, all without frames, Five half Lengths unknown without Frames, An old Map.

In the Room over the Great Parlour called Lady Duchess's Room: Five Pieces of Fine Tapestry Hangings, Six Chairs cover'd with blue Velvet, One Arm'd Chair Ditto, Two blue Mohair Stools, A large Ebony Cabinet inlaid with Tortoise Shell with brass carved Capitals upon the Pillasters, Two Tables Ditto, Two Glasses Ditto two feet four Inches by one foot ten Inches & an half each, Two setts of blue Caffoy Window Curtains, Valens & Rods, A Walnut Tree Chest with a Drawer upon a Frame, A Mahogony Card Table, A large Turkey Carpet, A Grate fix'd & Furniture complete, An eight inch brass Lock upon the Door, A Curious Landskip over the Chimney with Figures, A large Map of all the Towns in England.

In the little Closet: A corner Cupboard & Close Stool.

In the Closet next to the Duchess's Room called Lady Sophia's Closet: A Wainscot Tea Table, A Wainscot Square Table Ditto, Two Chairs cover'd with Crimson Velvet flower'd, Four Square Stools cover'd with Chints, Two green Silk Door Curtains, The Paper Hangings.

In the Room in the Passage next to Lady Duchess's Room, called Mrs Perkins's Room: A Sacking bottom Bedstead with blue Harrateen Furniture & Counterpane, One Window Curtain Ditto and Rod, A Feather Bed, Bolster and two down pillows, Three Blankets, an old Holland Matress, A chequer'd Linnen Matress, The Tapestry Hangings very old, Two old Tables and a broken Dressing Glass, a Bell, Six old Chairs, A Grate fix'd with Furniture complete. In the Closet a Chest of Drawers, 3 old Chairs & an old Stool.

In the Room over the Butler's Room called Lady Sophia's Room: A Sacking bottom Bedstead with old Crimson Mohair Furniture & Counterpane, a Down Bed, Bolster & two Pillows Ditto, three Blankets, one Check'd Matress, one Sett of very old Mohair Window Curtains Valens & Rods, Two old Mohair Stools, two Cushions, two old Cane Stools, Three matted Chairs, Three strip'd Stuff Cushions, Two old Cane Chairs, A Wainscot Chest of Drawers, A Walnut Tree Table & A broken Glass very old, Tapestry Hangings to the Room, An Iron Grate fix'd, Furniture complete, A Field Bedstead with a Lath bottom, A Yellow and white flower'd Silk Drugget Furniture & Counterpane Ditto, A Down Bed, Bolster & Pillow, three Blankets, A white Holland Matress, A Chequer'd one Ditto, A Callicoe Quilt.

In the Gallery, looking to the Hall: Two Persian foot Carpets, Two long seats cover'd with needlework, An old Couch and Squab, Two Pillows, One small four leav'd Screen, One large four leav'd old Screen, Two old Indian Pictures, A Small Canvas Fire Screen, A large Matt, Some old Lumber.

In the Room over the Passage between the Hall and Kitchen Called Lord Ashburnham's Room: A Sacking Bottom Bedstead with Yellow Harrateen Furniture, the Curtains lin'd with Harrateen, a Down Bed, Bolster & Pillow, Four Blankets & a Quilt, A white Holland Matress, a chequer'd Ditto, A Horse Bedstead with strip'd Single Camblet Furniture, A Feather Bed, Bolster, Three Blankets & a Quilt, Two Yellow Stuff Window Curtains and Rods, Two small Tables, six Old Chairs, Tapistry Hangings to the Room very old, A Wainscot Cupboard with Shelves, A Grate fix'd, Furniture complete.

In the Room next to Lord Duke's Dressing Room, called Mr. Bonafos's Room: A Corded Bedstead with Brown Cloth Furniture, A Feather Bed, Bolster and Pillow, Four Blankets and a ragged Rugg, One other Feather Bed, Old Tapestry Hangings to the Room, Three old Chairs, A Table & Stool, A Close Stool, A Sett of Curtain Rods, An old Curtain & Rod, An old Chest, A large Bell.

In my Lord Duke's Dressing Room: A Clock in a Walnut Tree Case, A Walnut Tree Table & Drawer, A pair of Stands, A Glass in a Walnut Tree frame 20 inches by 2 feet 6 inches, A Copper Tea Kitchin & stand, A Corner Cupboard with an Indian Picture, The Tapistry Hangings to the Room, A Set of blue & white Window Curtains and Rod, A Walnut Tree Table, Bureau & Drawers, A Mahogony Night Table, A two leav'd paper Screen, A three leav'd Leather Screen, Two old Chairs, Lady Glenorchy's Picture when a Child, Henry 2^d Son to the Duke of Kent when a Boy, Lord Harold when a Boy, The Duke of Kent when a Boy, Two Draughts of the Gardens, Two old Cushions, a large Map, A Picture of Rest Gardens in a black frame & gold Bead, A Print of Newmarket Horse Races in a black frame & gold Bead.

In the Duke's Bed chamber over the Steward's Parlour: A boarded Bedstead with blue Velvet Furniture, Counterpane Ditto, Two Blankets, A White Quilt, A Thick Matress, A Down Bed, Bolster and three Pillows, Two White Holland Matresses, A Carpet, Tapestry Hangings to the Room, A large Indian Chest, A Walnut Tree Table & A Glass two feet three Inches wide, three feet five Inches long, A pair of Stands, four Crimson flower'd Velvet Chairs, Four arm'd Chairs Ditto, An old Caffoy Easy Chair, A Picture of Nine French Prints in one Frame over the Chimney in a black Frame and gold Bead, A Print of Cardinal de Fleury & two of Admiral Howard in black Frames & gold Beads, A Print over the Closet Door, A black Japan'd Writing Box, A Picture, A View of Rest House & Gardens, Gordon's Map of Bedfordshire, A Small Wainscot Table, A Sett of Caffoy Window

Curtains, Three Door Curtains Ditto & Rods, A Grate & Furniture complete, Two brass Locks on the Doors, A Pistol Tinder Box and a Close Stool.

In the Great Closet to the Duke's Room: A large Walnutt Tree Buroe, A Walnut Tree Book Case with Glass Doors, Tapestry Hangings to the Room, Four Crimson Velvet Chairs, A Box with Brass Scales & Silver Troy Weights, A Small Fire Screen, An old blue Fire Screen, A Turky Scymiter mounted with Silver.

In the Lumber Garret over Lady Duchess's Apartment: An eight Foot Six leav'd Indian Screen, Two Glasses in black Frames Eighteen Inches Square each, A Blind for a Chimney, Two old Globes Sixteen Inches Diameter, A Spanish Table, Some old Chairs, Sashes, Boxes & other Lumber.

In the Closet to the left hand in the Lumber Garret: Twelve Square Stools with gilt Frames cover'd with crimson silk Damask, Nine cushions Ditto with Covers to them, Four round Stools Ditto, three old Square Stools & four round Ditto very old, one gilt Sconce in a gold Frame pretty good, Eight old Sconces, some of them broke, A Parcell of old Picture Frames.

In the Great Wardrobe Garret over my Lord Duke's Apartment: A Leather Squab fill'd with Down for a Settee, A Leather Bag for an easy chair fill'd with Down, Three Feather Bags for Cushions, Four small Pillows, One Feather Bed & Bolster narrow Strip'd Ticking, Five old Feather Beds, Four Bolsters, Three old Squabs for Window Seats, Two large Stools cover'd with yellow Stuff, Two old Cradles & a Child's Chair, Two small cane Chairs for Children, An old Bedstead, two old Trunks, A Needle work'd Couch, the Frame broke & yellow Cover, Two old Cushions, Four very old Chairs with Stuft backs, two Wainscot Small Tables, Two Matted Chairs, A Pallet Bedstead, An old Bedstead, A Copper Tea Kitchin, A Parcell of old Curtain Rods, A Feather Bed & Bolster, One other Feather Bed and Bolster, A Barrel Churn, A chequer'd Matress, One white Ditto, Four very old Blankets & a Coverlid, An old Yellow Silk Quilt, A Strip'd Quilt, an old Carpet, A pair of Stands, two large Chests, One Trunk, A Parcell of Old broken Cornishes, Boxes, Stands, A Chimney Glass in a black Frame, One Sconce Ditto, A New Pewter Close Stool pan.

In the First Bed Room on the Kitchin Stair Case on the right hand, called Robert Channon's: A Sacking bottom Bedstead with green Linsey furniture, A Feather Bed, Bolster, three Blankets & a Quilt, one old Table, two Chairs.

In the next Room called the Butler's Room: A Sacking bottom Bedstead with blue Serge Furniture, Two Feather Beds, one Bolster, two Pillows, Four Blankets & a red Rugg, all very old, Two old Tables, Four old Chairs, one old Window Curtain & Rod, A pair of old Iron Dogs.

In the room over the Scullery: A Corded Bedstead, Two Feather Beds, a Bolster, Two very old Blankets & a Quilt, three old Chairs and a Table.

In the Footmen's Garret: A Corded Bedstead with green Linsey Furniture, A Feather Bed, Bolster, Four old Blankets, 2 Ruggs, A Sacking bottom Bedstead with green Linsey Furniture, A Feather Bed, Bolster, one Pillow, Three old Blankets, and a Coverlid, Two old Tables, Two old Window Curtains & Rods.

In the Garret next the Footmen's Room: A corded Bedstead with old Torn Curtains, A Feather Bed, Bolster, one Pillow, three old Blankets & a Rugg, An old Table, A Small Glass, two old Chairs, a Window Curtain & Rod, A Table.

In the Room over the Pastry called The Housekeeper's Room: A corded Bedstead with Strip'd Camblet Furniture lin'd with blue & white Drugget, Two Feather Beds, A Bolster, two Pillows, three Blankets and an old Quilt, Two Window Curtains & Rods, An old Couch, a Deal Table, Four old Chairs, Some old brown Hangings, A Door Curtain & Rod, A broken Glass.

In the Garret over the Housekeeper's Room: A Corded Bedstead, with old blue Curtains, A feather Bed, Bolster & two Pillows, Four old Blankets & a Coverlid, Five old broken Chairs & a Deal Table.

In the Kitchin: The Coal Grate, Two large Iron Racks, Two Cranes, Shovel, Tongs, Poker, Fender, Cinder Grate, Three Pot Irons, Bellows, Two Plate Heaters, Two Chopping Knives, Two Cleavers, A Wind up Jack, Chain, Lines, with a Multiplying Wheel, A large Leaden Weight, Seven large and small Spits, Seven Lark Spits, Ten Iron Scuers, Two long Kitchin Tables, The Servants Bell, Twenty Small and great Stewpans, Four large round Copper Fish pans and Covers Ditto, Six Copper Pudding pans, A wooden Salt Box, Four Copper & brass Strainers, Fifteen Saucepans, Two large Iron Racks for the other Chimney, A large Iron Cinder Shovel, Two large Chopping Blocks, Twenty Seven Copper and Brass Covers for Saucepans, Stewpans & potts, Two small Copper Stew Potts, eight Copper and Brass Porridge Potts, A large Copper Dripping pan, A basting ladle, Three large Ladles, A small brass Ladle, two small brass Skimmers, Two Copper Spoons, Seven Irons in Stoves, A Beef Fork, Three large Copper Drinking Potts, A large Copper Tea Kettle, A Chocolate Pott Ditto, 2 Coffee Potts, 2 Small Tea Kettles, A Spice Box, Two Tin Nutmeg Graters, A Bell Mettle Mortar & Pestle, A Marble Mortar & Pestle, 4 Pewter Bedpans, four Pewter Close Stool pans, Two Gridirons, A Parcell of old Hair Seives, An Iron Rasp for Bread, Five large Brass Patty pans, Twelve Copper Oval Ditto, Eleven round Ditto, Five large Pewter Dishes, seven Ditto 2nd Size, Eleven Ditto 3rd Size, Five Ditto 4th Size, Three Ditto of the least Size, four new dishes of the 3rd Size, Four Ditto of the 4th Size, Four Ditto of the 5th Size, Four Ditto of the least Size, 5 Dozen of old Plates, Two Tereans & Covers, A Cheese

Plate Ditto , One Water Plate, One Pewter Stew Box with a Cover
Screw'd on, Seven Pewter Chamber Potts, Pewter Salts, A large Copper
Dutch Oven and Cover, A large Firescreen, Two Kimnels, A Butter
Tub, A large Tin Drudge Box, Ten large brass hand Candlesticks, One
brass hand Tinder box, Seven brass Small Ditto, Three Iron Ditto, Two
Tin Tinder Boxes, A pair of brass Candlesticks amd Snuffers, One small
Copper Chocolate Pott & Mill, Three Tins to burn Rush Lights, Five
old Chairs, Four Copper Warming pans, Two parcells of Iron Hoops.

In the Boiling House: A Large Copper and brass Cock & Copper
Cover.

In the Pastry: A Pair of Iron Dogs, Three old Chairs, A Table, An
Iron Peel, Two Iron Doors to the Ovens.

In the Larder: Two Flower Tubs & Covers, A Deal Table, A Parcell
of Earthen Ware, A Pewter Pastry Plate, Three round Brass Plates, An
old pair of Steeliards & Weights.

In the Wett Larder: Three Powdering Tubs, Two brass old Pans, Two
Wooden Trays.

In the Scullery: A Copper and two Plate Racks.

In the Bakehouse: A large Beam, Scales, Five half hundred Weights,
Five less Weights, Two Iron Peels, an Iron Lidd to the Oven, An Iron
Barr in the Chimney.

In the Meal House: A large Kneading Trough, A large Deal Bing, An
Iron Peel and a Coal Raker, One Wooden Peel.

In the Still House: A large Stone Mortar and wooden Pestle, Five
pewter stills with leaden Bottoms, the Ironwork fix'd of four of them,
the other in an Iron Frame, A Small Copper Stew Pot & Cover, Three
tin Boxes, a pair of Wafer Irons & A pair of Vauful Irons, Two old
Curtains & Rods, Three Copper Saucepans & Covers, A large Copper
Ladle, A Pint Pewter Pot, Two Pewter Ice Potts, A Hatchet, A Nutmeg
grater, A brass Drudge Box, An old large Knife for Plaister, An old
Brass Candlestick upon a Stand, A long Table, A Deal Table, Three old
Chairs, A large Parcell of Glass Bottles, Pickling Potts and Glasses,
About thirty Sieves of Several Sorts, About five Dozen of Sweet meat
Gally Pots, Some Earthen Ware, a Grate fix'd with an Iron back & a
pair of tongs, Two Irons fix'd to the Stoves.

In the Porter's Lodge: A Corded Bedstead with red Cloth furniture, A
feather Bed, Bolster, One Pillow, Four old Blankets, & a Rugg, Two old
Tables, An old pewter Bason, Seven old Chairs, The Bell upon the Top
of the Lodge.

Over the Great Hall: The House Clock

In the Closet to the Passage to Mrs. Perkins's Room:
China: Two large sugar Dishes & Covers, Two large Dishes Ditto,
Two Less Dishes Ditto, A Tea Pot and stand Ditto, Thirteen Octogon
Saucers, One Dozen Tea Cups Ditto, Eight handled Chocolate Ditto
with an odd Saucer All dark blue & white, Two Dozen of blue & white

water'd China Tea Cups with brown Rims & Saucers Ditto, Sixteen handled Coffee Cups Ditto, Twelve Saucers Ditto, Five Spoons Ditto, Three Slop Basons Ditto, Three Milk Porringers Ditto, Two Tea Potts Ditto, Three Stands Ditto, A Sugar Dish & Canister Ditto, Six Deep Plates Ditto, One white water'd Tea Pot Ditto, Six China Handled Coffee Cups Ditto, Twelve Saucers & fourteen Ditto, Twenty one Cups Ditto, Three Small handle Muggs, Two Sugar Dishes, A Stand and Strainers Ditto, All blue & white; Six Octogon Cups & Saucers colour'd, Two Delft Chocolate Cups & a pint Jugg and Cover, Thirteen large dark blue & white Tea Cups & Saucers Ditto, Ten handled Chocolate Cups Ditto, A Cawdle Cup & Cover, Three Sugar Dishes and Covers Ditto, A Tea Pot Ditto, Two Slop Basons Ditto, Two large Plates Ditto, Eight fine white China Cups, Nine Saucers Ditto, A Tea Pot and Stand Ditto, Two Sugar Dishes Ditto, a Slop Bason Ditto, A Spoon Boat, One large Saucer, One Milk Pot Ditto. In a Small Tray, Eleven large wrought white China Tea Cups with gold Rims, Nineteen Saucers Ditto, A Ribb'd Sugar Dish & Cover, A white wrought Tea Pot, A large Slop Bason Ditto, Fifteen blue & white China Cups & Saucers.

In the Brewhouse: A Wort Back over the Copper, A large Copper with a large brass Cock & Iron work, A large Mash Tun, A Pump in the Under Back, Four Troughs, Six Coolers, A Hop Basket, Three Leather Pipes with Brass Screws, Two Mash Rules, a false Bottom to the Mash Tun, A pair of Steps, A Leaden Pipe, with a large brass Cock to the Copper, A large Parcell of Turf to brew with, A Coal Raker, A Small Copper & Ironwork, A Small Mash Tun, Three small Coolers, Two Working Tubs, Eight Tap Tubs, A Small Under Back, A Small Tub, A Small Hop Sieve, A Funnel with an Iron Pipe, Five Pails, A large Hand Bowl, One Jett.

In the Cellar under the Brewhouse: Sixteen double Hogsheads with Iron Hoops Bull headed, Six Hogsheads, Twelve Drink Stalls.

In the Dairy: A large Milk Lead upon a Stand, Three Ditto without a Stand, Three Milk Pales, One Iron Hoop'd Pale, A large Cheese Tub, One Kimnel, One large Kettle, A large wooden Bowl, Nine large Earthen Milk Pans, A parcell of wooden Cheese Vats, Wooden Scales and a parcell of Earthen Ware, A Small Churn, A pair of Steps, A Cheese Rack, A broken cane Chair.

In the Bowling Green House: Sixteen Walnut Tree Chairs with Scarlet Morocco Leather Seats, Two Marble Slabs upon carved frames painted, A Walnut Tree Card Table inlaid, A Mahogony Tea Table, A Mahogony round Table with a Claw Foot, Three nine Inch brass Locks upon the Doors, A painted Blind for the Chimney.

In the Closet to the Bowling Green House: Two Corner Cupboards with Indian Pictures, A Mahogony Stand for a Tea Kettle, A Brass Lamp, Six Green Garden Chairs under the Piazza, A brass Tinder Box. In one of the Corner Cupboards – A colour'd China Tea Pot and Stand,

A brown Tea Pot & colour'd Stand, Twelve Colour'd Saucers, Nine Tea Cups Ditto, Eight Coffee Cups Ditto, Two Slop Basons Ditto, A Sugar Dish and Cover Ditto, A Milk Porringer Ditto, A Spoon Boat Ditto, One half pint Mugg Ditto, One blue & White Ditto, Six gilt Silver Tea Spoons in a Shagreen Case. In the other Indian Corner Cupboard – Two China Tea Pots & Stands, Two Sugar Dishes with Covers, A Milk Porringer & Slop Bason, A large handled Cup, Nine handled Coffee Cups, One odd Cup, Eight Cups, Eight Saucers, Three Spoon Boats, Two large Saucers being all blue and white, Two Indian Waiters, Two Stone Tea Pots.

In the Laundry Maid's Room: A Sacking bottom Bedstead with yellow Serge Furniture, A Feather Bed, Bolster & two Pillows, Four old Blanketts and a Red Rugg, One old Table, Two old Chairs & Matress, Two old Chairs & a large brass skillet.

In the Drying Room: All the Flair Lines, An Iron Dutch Stove for drying of Cloaths, A Parcell of Baskets & Flaskets.

In the Landry: A Napkin Press with fourteen Leaves, A large Deal Horse for drying of Cloaths, A Coal Grate, Shovel, Tongs, Poker and Cinder grate, A large long Iron for the Irons, Six Irons, Two Racks, A Deal Table, A Pail.

In the Wash House: A Copper and Ironwork, Ten Washing Tubbs, Three Wrincing Tubbs.

In the Small Beer Cellar: Four Upright New Hogsheads painted, with Bull heads, Nineteen Hogsheads, Seven drink Stalls, One brass Cock.

In the Ale Cellar: Thirteen Hogsheads, Four Drink Stalls, Four brass Cocks in Severall Cellars.

China
Twelve China handled Knives, Twelve China handled Forks with Silver Tines, In a Shagreen Case. Twelve more China handled Knives, Twelve China handled Forks with Silver Tines In a Shagreen Case. Nine large China Dishes of blue & white, Five Ditto 2nd size, Five Ditto 3rd Size, Five Dozen four Plates Ditto, Two Candlesticks Ditto, A large Monteith, Nine handled Coffee Cups, Nine Ditto of another sort, Six handled Chocolate Cups, Two Small Basons Ditto with Rims, Eight very Fine Cawdle Cups Ditto, Nine Slop Basons Ditto, One brown Ditto, Three Sugar Dishes with Covers the Rims Gilt Ditto, Thirteen Custard Cups Ditto, Eleven brown Edg'd Basons Ditto, Six brown Custard Cups, Two Small odd Basons Ditto, Six very fine Basons Ditto, A Tea Pot and Sugar Dish Ditto, Fifteen large Tea Cups Ditto, Eleven Tea Cups Ditto, Four Tea Cups and Saucers of a less size Ditto, Two Dozen of large Saucers Ditto, Three less Saucers, A Sugar Dish and Cover, One Porringer Ditto, One Tea Pot Ditto, Two Small drinking Muggs, Five odd Plates, Four large Saucers all blue & white China, Seven dark blue Cups Ditto, Six larger Cups Ditto, One Dozen of

colour'd China Cups & twelve Saucers Ditto, three Slop Basons Ditto, A Stand for a Tea Pot Ditto, Two Spoon Boats and Two Chocolate Cups Ditto, A Cream Porringer Ditto, Two blue & white odd Cups, Six blue & white Saucers gilt at the Edge, Six Cups Ditto, A Colour'd Boat for Spoons, Five Cups & Bason blue & white, An eight Inch brass lock upon the Door.

Mrs. James's Linnen Room: The Tapestry Hangings to the Room, One Matted Chair, A large pair of Brass Scales, Two pair of Small Ditto, Some small brass weights in a Box, A broken Looking Glass, A brass Tea Kettle, One small Table, One large Table, a Grate fixt to the Chimney with an Iron back, Shovel, Tongs, Poker Fender & Bellows, One Iron Trevit, Fourteen pieces of Tapestry Hangings; Two Flaggons, A Cup & Plate Silver Gilt belonging to the Communion Table in Leather Cases; Two Small Glass Mortars and Pestles, Six Dozen of Jelly Glasses, Nine Glass Basons, Twelve Glass Salvers, Fourteen blue Mohair Cushions, Eight Crimson Mohair Ditto, Eight Window seats Crimson Ditto, Two pair of Drab Colour Mohair Window Curtains & Valens, Part of a blue & yellow Silk Damask Furniture, the remainder up in the Wardrobe, Three Strip'd yellow & white camblet Window Curtains, A Yellow Silk Damask seat for the Boat, Seven Curtains Yellow Ditto for the Boat, and one Seat of Camblet Ditto, An Indian Susee of Yellow & White for a Settee Bed now in the Wardrobe, Four old blue Mohair Window Curtains, Four Curtains of Buff Colour'd Velvet & Valens, A Strip'd Callimancoe lined with blue Persian, the remaining part over against Bonafos's Room, Two green worsted Damask Curtains belonging to the Library, Eight blue serge Covers for Chairs, A Yellow Silk Counterpane adorn'd with a Small Silk Fringe, Two Pieces of black Velvet Embroider'd with gold and Silver & pannel'd with white Sattin Embroider'd with Silk, Nine breadths being of black Velvet Embroider'd with Gold, and Six pieces of white Flower'd Sattin, A Small Persian Foot Carpet, A Silk Carpet Ditto of the Lucas's Coat of Arms, A Worsted wrought Carpet Silk Fringe, A large old Carpet, A Turkey work'd foot Carpet, a piece of an old Carpet, Eleven Pieces of rich Tapestry Hangings, A Feather Bolster, A Parcell of Pieces of Severall Valens, A Feather Bolster, Some Tickin belonging to an Umbrello, A large Deal Press, A New Wainscot Close Stool and Pan, A Painted Blind for the Hall Chimney, An old Six leaved Screen, Two white Holland Quilts, A Pair of Down Pillows.

In the Duke's Closet: A Two foot Reflecting Telescope, A Spirit Level with a Telescope sight Two foot long by Wright, a Pair of brass Compasses one foot long and Case, a Cilinder Sun-Dial by Wright, Nine Fishing Rods, Seventeen yards of worsted Crimson Damask, Three white wax Candles, Two Umbrellas, About Twelve Small Prints roll'd up, Five Wooden Cases with bottles with glass Stoppers.

In the Duke's Closet: In the Bureau – A Telescope of Seven Joints about a foot each, A three foot Rule Box, A foot Sliding Rule Ditto, A pair of brass Compasses with Steel Joints, A two foot Rule of Box, A Travelling Screw Hasp for a Door, Fish and Counters for Cards, A Shagreen Pocket Book border'd with Silver Plate, Two pair of Steel Snuffers, One pair of Silver Scales & Weights, A China Funnel, Silver to an old Wooden Handle Weight 1 oz.18^{dwts}.; A Candle Screen with Silver in a brown Shagreen Case, A Lord Chamberlain's Gold Key, An Ivory foot Rule, An Engine to make Pens, Two pair of Spectacles, Two Reading Glasses, A hand Magnifying Glass, Some small Silver Wastecoat Buttons, Eight Mother of Pearl Tea Spoons, A set of Chessmen & Box.

Linnen:

Fifteen Second Sheets, Seventeen Servants Sheets, Six pair of new Second Sheets, Twelve pair of new Servants Sheets, Three Dozen of coarse Damask Napkins, Four Dozen of Birds eye Ditto, Two odd Ditto, One Dozen & a half of odd Servants Towels, One Dozen of Coarse Rubbers, Six Ditto, Ten Round Towells, Fifteen Holland Pillow biers, Two long Servants Table Cloths, A white Holland Quilt with Fringe, Ten old Table Cloths, Another white Holland Quilt, Ten old Curtains large and small, some Pieces of work'd Linnen belonging to the Furniture of a bed, A pair of white Curtains and Valens trim'd with Knotted Fringe, Some old pieces of Checkt Cotton, Eighteen pieces of old Sheets to mend others; One Trunk, One Chest, A Table & two old Chairs, Four Pewter Rims, A Basket for China Plates, Five gilt Pully Rods, A Moon Lanthorn, A new Umbrella.

More Linnen:

Two Dozen of Fine Damask Napkins,Two Dozen of Fine Diaper Ditto, Three Dozen of Fine Diaper Ditto, Two Dozen of good Diaper Ditto, One Dozen of fine Diaper Ditto, Two Dozen of Fine Diaper Ditto, One Dozen of fine Diaper Ditto, Eight very fine Damask Napkins, Ten Dozen of Birds Eye Ditto, Four Dozen of coarse Damask Napkins, Six Dozen of Birds Eye Ditto, Eight Dozen of coarse Damask Ditto, One Dozen of old Damask Ditto, One Dozen of Damask Ditto, Three Dozen of Birds Eye Ditto coarse, Two Dozen of Birds Eye Ditto, Four Dozen of Birds Eye coarse Ditto, Two Dozen of coarse Diaper Napkins, One dozen & two old Napkins, seven Dozen & ten of fine Tea Napkins, Eleven odd Small Towells, One Dozen of odd Fine Towells, Seven Dozen & ten Towells for the Head Servants, six Dozen Tea Napkins for the Steward's Parlour, One Dozen of Coarse Diaper Napkins, Three Dozen of very old Towells, Nine Very old Damask Napkins, Sixteen Diaper very old, Four Dozen & two great & Small Holland Pillowbiers, A Small white Window Curtain, Seven Muslin Twilights Strip'd and Flower'd, Twelve Fine Birds Eye Table Cloths, Nine Fine Diaper Table Cloths, Two fine Damask Ditto, Eleven Damask Table Cloths, Four Diaper Ditto, Four old Birds Eye Ditto, Three old Huccaback Ditto,

Five Damask Table Cloths Ditto, Two Diaper Ditto, Nine large Cloths for the Steward's Parlour, One Cloth Ditto, Nine pair of Fine Holland Sheets, Ten pair of Sheets Ditto.

In the Trunk: Eight Single Dimity Sheets and A piece of one, Three fine Damask Cloths for the Communion Table, Eight yards of Fine Diaper for Towells, Four pair and one 2nd Sheets, Four pair Ditto on the Beds, Nine pair and one Flaxen Sheets, Six Servants Long Table Cloths, Ten pair of Sheets in use.

In the Coachman's Room at the Stables: A Sacking bottom Bedstead, A Feather Bed, Bolster, Four Blanketts, Two very old Ruggs, Another Bedstead with a corded bottom green Linsey Furniture, A Feather Bed, Bolster, Three old Blankets, A pair of Sheets & a Coverlid, A Porridge Pot, A Saucepan, A Pair of Bellows, Fire Shovell, Tongs, A Grate fix'd, A Window Curtain & Rod, A long Towell.

In the Hill House

In the Great Room: Six long Garden Benches, Eight Cane Hall Chairs.

In the Closet to the East: A large Wainscot Oval Table, A corner Wainscot Table, Four Matted Chairs, A large Glass in a Walnut Tree Frame three feet one Inch by two feet four Inches, Two small Indian Corner Cupboards, A large Map being the Prospect of the City of London, A large Map of Paris, A Map of a Prospect of Versailles & Gardens, Thirteen prints of Heads, Six small Prints.

In the Closet to the West: Four matted Chairs, two arm'd Ditto, Seven large Prints being Prospects of Several parts of the Gardens of Versailles in black Frames & gold Beads, Three small Ditto, Six Small Prints in black Frames, A Picture of a half Length of Anthony Earl of Kent.

In the Stair Case to the South: A Print of the Prospect of Constantinople;Two Cane Elbow Dressing Chairs.

At the Top of the Stairs: A Head of Mr. Archer, A pair of glass Sconces.

In the Stair Case to the North: A Close Stool and Pewter Pan.

In the Great Room up one pair of Stairs: Eight Cane Elbow Chairs, A Large Glass over the Chimney with the Duke's Arms and Coronet, Three pair of gilt carved Arms, an Iron back in the Chimney, The Duke of Kent's Picture half Length.

In the Closet to the East; Five Chairs backs & seats alike, cover'd with yellow Caffoy & yellow Serge Covers, An old Broken Tea Table, Two corner Wainscot Tables fix'd, Two corner Cupboards with glass Doors three feet by twenty one Inches, A Picture over the Door, Lady Harold, Half Length, Lord Glenorchy's Picture & his Lady Ditto, Sixteen Prints with glass before them, Twelve other Prints.

In the Closet to the West: A large Stuft Couch cover'd with French Carpeting, Four Chairs Ditto back & Seats alike, A Picture of half length of Lord Harold in his University Habit, A large Print of the inside of St. Peter's at Rome, a black Frame and gold Bead, Six prints of other parts in Rome Ditto, Six Prints containing the Views of Several Citys in France, A large Print containing a View of Anguien, Five small Prints, A Wainscot Table.

In the North Stair Case: A Table Bedstead, A Close Stool cover'd with Velvet, Three Brass Locks, Seven Inches and a half upon the Doors.

In the Great Room of the Pavillion House: Twelve Chairs cover'd with Scarlet Morocco Leather, A handsome Stove Grate Iron Door.

In the Closet to the East: A crimson Mohair Couch with three Pillows Ditto, Two Matted Chairs, Gilt Leather Hangings, & Glass over the Chimney three feet five Inches by two feet two Inches, Two Walnut Tree Corner Cupboards with glass Doors three feet by twenty one Inches each, A handsome Steel Stove Grate with an Iron Door.

In the Closet to the West: A Couch cover'd with Scarlet Morocco Leather, two Pillows Ditto, Two Stools Ditto, A Red Japan'd Tea Table; A Teapot Stand and Slop bason, Eight large Tea Dishes & Saucers Ditto All blue & white China, Gilt Leather Hangings in the Room, A large Glass in a Walnut Tree Frame three feet four Inches by two feet one Inch.

In the Alcove to the West: Gilt Leather Hangings, Two Matted Chairs and a Small Wainscot Table.

In the Alcove to the East: Gilt Leather Hangings, two Matted Chairs, A Small Wainscot Table, Three ten Inch brass Locks upon the Doors.

More in the Closet over against Mrs Perkins's Room: A Measuring Wheel, A long Square Telescope, A large Pair of Backgammon Tables, Men & Dice, A Draught Board & Men, A Circular Astronomical Table with a Leather Cover, 6 Old Prints.

In the Closet: A large China Jarr & Cover, Two small Delf Potts.

An Account of the Silver Plate called Rest Plate lock'd up in a Chest in Mr. Hobbs's Room:

Eight Silver Salvers Scollop'd, 43 Ounces 0 Pennyweights, 41.12, 41.13, 41.15, 41.18, 39.18, 41.5, 40.1.

Three large Water Basons Scollop'd Ditto, 69 Ounces 12 Pennyweights, 70.9, 70.17.

Eight Salvers Ditto, 26 Ounces 10 Pennyweights, 28.0, 12.5, 15.8, 15.11, 19.5, 19.5, 12.2. Fourteen Candlesticks Ditto 16 ounces 9 pennyweights, 16.11, 17.11, 17.12, 18.4, 17.6, 16.16, 16.7, 14.5, 14.3, 12.9, 12.17, 13.7, 12.16.

A Snuffpan 10.7, Snuffers 3.0,

Sixteen Dishes Large and Small 73.3, 71.19, 72.14, 72.4, 58.0, 57.8, 53.0, 55.0, 44.19, 44.16, 44.9, 32.17, 32.13, 32.15, 32.13.

Five Dozen of Plates: One dozen 19.2, 19.4, 18.7, 19.13, 19.7, 19.5, 19.10, 19.6, 19.11, 19.5, 19.6, 19.6.

One Dozen More, 19.5, 19.11, 19.12, 20.6, 19.3, 19.3, 19.10, 19.1, 19.7, 19.5, 19.4, 19.9. One Dozen more, 19.4, 19.4, 19.13, 19.15, 20.0, 20.0,

20.2, 19.0, 20.0, 20.3, 20.0, 19.2. One Dozen more, 19.4, 19.6, 19.3, 19.13, 19.9, 19.1, 19.3, 20.10, 20.2, 20.0, 19.17, 18.17. One Dozen More, 18.18, 19.5, 19.16, 20.3, 18.17, 19.4, 20.5, 18.12, 19.2, 19.0, 19.5, 19.6 Eight broad rim'd Plates 17.9, 18.5, 18.5, 18.5, 18.0, 17.2, 18.0, 18.17. Two Basons Ditto 17.15, 23.16.
Four Sauce Boats 12.4, 12.19, 11.17, 12.18
Ten Salts weighing 39.2, A Preserving Pan 35.2, Six Saucers for Pickles weighing 19.14, A large Pastry Pan 196.0, A Coffee Pot 24.0, A Lamp 14.11, A Tea Kettle 48.7, A Lamp 44.12.
Four Castors 18.10, 18.8, 10.8, 8.14, A Warming Pan Ditto 54.5, A Coffee Pot with Silver Feet Ditto 25.10, An Apple Roaster Ditto 46.10, A Pudding pan Ditto 24.15, A Ring for the middle of a Table Ditto 29.15, Four Nossels Ditto 2.18, 2.18, 2.18, 2.15, One Pepper Castor Ditto 2.3, One Ditto & Small Spoon 2.9, A Toasting Fork, the Silver Mark'd 2.14, A Fire Shovel & Tongs with 5 large Silver Knobs, A large Silver Head for the Porter's Staff with the Grey Arms & Earl's Coronet fixt on a Cane Staff ,
Four Dozen of Silver handled Knives 61.10, Two Dozen & five 3 Tin'd Silver Forks, weigh'd [blank], Five Dozen and five Silver Spoons 158.3, Six Silver handled Forks with Steel Tines [blank], A Shaving Bason Ditto 19.15, An Ewer 15.5, A Silver Standish for the Library 27.17, A little Lamp for the Library to seal Letters 9.15, Another for the Duke's Room Ditto 10.18, A Reading Glass Set in Silver [blank], Five Chamber Pots 25.5, 21.10, 26.13, 28.4, 22.4, Three Tankards with Covers 17.10, 16.13, 13.1, Five Tumblers Ditto 6.13, 6.16, 7.2, 7.12, 6.14.
Three Skillets Ditto 22 Ounces 5 Pennyweight, 23.5, 8.4.
Two Soup Dishes alike 35.7, Basons Ditto 39.8, Three Soop Ladles 8.18, 8.3, 9.4. Two Egg Spoons 2.14, 4.4, One Egg Slice 2.17, Two large Wrought Salvers for Deserts 65.4, 65.9.

The above Inventory consisting of forty three Folios is a true Account of the Furniture, Goods, Plate, and Linnen belonging to the said Rest House As Witness Our hands this twenty fourth day of June One thousand seven hundred and forty.
per James Lucas, Daniel Milward, Robert Skinner[35]

BCRO: L 31/184/1

NOTES

1. James Collett-White's article *The Old House at Wrest* BM XXII pp.322–327 and XXIII pp.4–12. VCH II pp.325–328.
2. Chancery IPM 1 Edward II No.54 see VCH II 327 note 18.
3. Bedford Assize J.I. 1/24m23d, 26m20d.
4. VCH II p.331. Placito de Quo Warranto (Record Commission) 45.
5. A. Underwood p.11, R. Ian Jack *The Grey of Ruthin Valor 1467–1468* (BHRS Vol.XLVI) 1965.
6. G.W. Bernard *The Fortunes of the Greys, Earls of Kent in the Early Sixteenth Century* The Historical Journal 25.3 (1982) pp.671–685; L 24/455, 475–478.

7. L 24/16.
8. L 33/232/8.
9. L 26/232, L Jeayes 254 and L 26/1407. Transcript by John Thompson (Classification 130).
10. L 31/169.
11. Carew's poem is most conveniently available in S.R. Houfe's *Through Visitors Eyes: A Bedfordshire Anthology* pp.213–216.
12. L 31/170–178.
13. L 31/228.
14. L 31/194, L 31/230–241.
15. Illustrated in J. Kip's Engravings of c.1705–1708 (LL 1839) and J. Rocque's *Plan & View of Buildings and Gardens at Rest* 1735 (X 95/230) and 1737 [BL (Maps) K 70 p.11].
16. L 31/195 p.223.
17. Land Use Consultants *Historical Survey of Wrest Park*, 1983, and *Wrest Park Masterplan for Restoration & Management* comments on latter by James Collett-White and Mike Turner (Z 821/1–5).
18. L 33/57–63.
19. See Horace Walpole *Visits to Country Seats*, Walpole Society Vol.16 pp.69–71, most easily available in Simon Houfe's *Through Visitors Eyes* p.63.
20. Archer's portrait was in Hill House; see 1740 Inventory above. Leoni plans (L 33/46–48), Estimate (L 31/245)
21. Letters from John Gerard to Duke of Kent 1715–1717 (L 30/8/28/1–55) and Terry Friedman's *Lord Harrold in Italy 1715–16*, Burlington Magazine November 1988 pp.836–842.
22. L 33/148–149.
23. Horace Walpole p.62.
24. Sir Oliver Millar: *Van Dyck in England* (1982).
25. Brown's work at Wrest took from 1758 to 1760.
26. L 31/266–272.
27. BM. Add Mss 35693.135.
28. Richardson Collection.
29. L 31/277.
30. Earl de Grey's *History of Wrest Park*, edited by Alan Cirket, BHRS Vol 59 pp.66–67. S.R. Houfe's articles *Wrest Park Bedfordshire* (CL for 25 June 1970 pp.1250–1253 and for 2 July 1970 pp 18–21) concentrate on the present house.
31. L 33/146–147 and BHRS Vol 59 p.67.
32. Earl de Grey's *Memoirs April 1846,* edited by Alan Cirket in BHRS Vol 59 pp.66–67.
33. BHRS Vol 59 p.68.
34. BHRS Vol 59 p.70.
35. The rest of this volume is concerned with the changing of plate in 1743 and 1746

GLOSSARY

ALEMBIC/ALEMBICK: Apparatus used in distilling, consisting of gourd shaped vessel surmounted by the head whose beak conveyed the vapours to the receiver in which they were condensed.

AMBIRELLA: Umbrella.

ANDIRON: see Dog Irons.

BANYAN: Informal indoor gentleman's gown, knee length to full length, made of Indian cottons.

BATH STOVE: A hot grate with an iron plate just above the fire with a greatly reduced opening. Illustrated in Lawrence Wright HFB. p.87.

BATTLEDORE AND BLOCK: Flat wooden instrument for smoothing linen after washing, resembling a cricket back. M. Reed.

BEATING HORSE: Clothes horse for beating clothes on.

BEAUFETTA: Tea chest and hand board.

BELL GLASS: Glass in shape of a bell, used for forcing plants.

BELLMETTLE: Alloy of copper and tin used for making bells.

BIRDSEYE NAPKINS: It is not clear whether these are decorated with small flowers or merely spotted.

BIDET/BIDDET: A vessel on a low, narrow stand which can be bestriden for bathing purposes. O.E.D.

BLUE AND WHITE: Chinese porcelain with blue enamelled painting decoration. In the context of these inventories it was probably Kuang'si period (1662–1722) made for export.

BLUNDERBUS: Short gun with large bore firing many balls or slugs; used for small range fire only.

BOB WIG: Wig having bottom locks turned up into "bobs" or short curls.

BOLSTER: Long stuffed pillow or cushion used to support sleeper's head. O.E.D.

BOOT JACK: Shaped contrivance to help pull off boots. O.E.D.

BREAKFAST BOARD: Possibly a side table.

BRUSSELS CARPET: Type of carpet made at Brussels and elsewhere with a worsted warp brought to the surface in loops to make the pile. They were made on draw looms till 1825. PDDA.

BURNT CHINA: China that, after initial firing has extra decoration painted on, and is refired.

BUROE: Bureau—writing table or desk.

BUSTOS: Statues.

CABRIOLE: Leg (of furniture) curved outwards at the knee and tapering inwards below, terminated by a club, hoof, bun, paw, claw and ball or scroll foot: especially popular in first half of eighteenth century. PDDA.

CAFFA/CAFFOY: Probably the makers of these inventories used the meaning "painted cloth made in Dutch East Indies" OED.

CALICO: Cotton cloth, especially plain white unprinted. O.E.D. Calico was legislated against from 1722 to 1774. It could be manufactured after 1774 but not imported from India.

CALLIMANCO: Woollen stuff from Flanders, glossy on the surface, and woven with silk twill, chequered in the warp, so that the checks are only seen on one side. Millard.

CAMBRICK: Fine white linen, originating from Chambray in Flanders. OED.

CAMLET/CAMBLET: Costly Eastern fabric made from Angora goat hair or European substitutes (usually wool, silk and hair, especially at Brussels)—much used for eighteenth century bed hangings.

CAMP CHAIR: Folding chair.

CANOPY FURNITURE: see Tent Bedstead.

CANTERBURY: Stand with light partitions to hold music portfolios.

CAPITAL MESSUAGE: Chief house on a manor or estate.

CAT & CANDLE SHADE: Cat = rest for plates etc. to be kept warm near fireside, made of three rods joined crossways in the centre.

CAUDLE CUPS: Vessel from which warm spiced gruel called caudle or posset might be drunk. PDDA p.157.

CAVE: Ground floor in piano nobile room with domed ceiling.

CELARET/CELLERETT/COLLURETT: Case or sideboard to hold wine bottles.

CHAFING DISH: Dish for keeping food warm placed on a chafer; a small enclosed brazier containing charcoal or hot ash. M.Reed.

CHEANY/CHENEY/CHINA: Warp printed fabric, here used for curtains, the designs were initially of Chinese origin.

CHERRY WITH SEVEN DRAWERS: Furniture made out of Cherry wood.

CHIMNEY GLASS: Looking glass over a chimney piece.

CHINTZ: Cotton cloth fast printed with parti-coloured pattern, usually glazed. O.E.D.

CLAW: See pillar and claw.

CLOSE STOOL: Movable latrine, in eighteenth century superseded by pot cupboard or night table. PDDA.

COACH: Top.

COLANDER/COLLINDER POT: Metal vessel, closely perforated with small holes at the bottom to act as a strainer. O.E.D.

COMMERCE TABLE: Table for *Commerce,* a game in which exchange and barter play a prominent part. O.E.D.

COMMODE: Chest of drawers, especially of French pattern. Only in the mid-nineteenth century was it used as a name for a close stool.

COOKHOLD: Unclear—possibly a type of skewer.

CORDIAL GLASSES: Liqueur glasses.

CORNICHES: Cornices.

COVERLID: Coverlet.

CRANE NECK: Iron bar bent like a crane's neck uniting the back and front timbers in a carriage. Also used for the springs to which the thick straps supporting the coach body were attached.

CRANKEY: Checked linen.

CROWN GLASS: Technique in which after the bubble of glass was blown a rod was attached to the opposite side.

CULGEE: Figured Indian silk. OED.

CUPOLA/CUPALO: Diminutive dome rising above a roof. OED.

DAMASK: Fabric with woven pattern of contrasting textures from the interchange of warp and weft. Reversible and usually self coloured and can be in silk, linen or worsted.

DELF/DELFT WARE: Tin glazed earthenware initially produced in Holland in the late seventeenth century, centring on Delft. Imitation of Chinese Blue and White porcelain was the key feature of Delft ware produced in Holland and England at Southwark, Bristol and Lambeth.

DEVILS AND TAILORS: Probably table-top skittles game also known as "Devil among the Tailors".

DIAPER: Linen fabric with small diamond pattern in damask weave.

DIMITY: Stout cotton cloth woven with raised stripes or figures, used undyed for beds and hangings. Millard.

DOBING PANS: Probably dubbing pans for fat.

DOG IRONS: Fire Dogs/Andirons. Primarily used for stopping large logs rolling off the hearth. They could be used in kitchens for cooking. see Lawrence Wright HFB.

DORTER: Dormitory in a monastery.

DOILET/DOYLIES: Ornamental napkins used at desert.

DREDGER: Vessel with perforated lid, sometimes called as Castor.

DREDGE/DRUDGE BOX: Box for containing dredges (a comfit containing a seed or grain of spice); term probably used generally for spice boxes.

DROGGETT/DRUGGETT: Coarse woollen stuff used for floor or table coverings OED.

DUMB WAITER: Stand often of three tiers of revolving circular trays, placed near a dining table for self service; invented in England c.1740.

DUTCH TABLE: Important for development of Cabriole leg in the Age of Walnut. EF.

EARS: Part of a bell.

EARTHENWARE: Pottery fired up to a maximum of 1200° centigrade, needing glazing to make it non-porous.

ELBOW CHAIR: Chair with two arm rests.

ENAMEL'D CHINA: Porcelain with painted decoration over an initial glaze, followed by second glaze fired at much lower temperature.

EPERGNE: Table centre usually of silver. One dated 1764 illustrated in PDDA p.279.

ESCRITOIRE: Writing desk.

EWE: Yew.

EWER: Water jug with a wide mouth OED.

FERRETTING: Stout tape made out of silk or cotton.

FESTOON: Curtains arranged in a curved form between two points. OED.

FIELD BEDSTEAD: Portable or folding bed.

FINEER'D: Veneered.

FIRKIN: Small cask for liquids, butter or fish; half a kilderkin.

FISH KETTLE: Low oval dish with lid for boiling or baking fish. D. deHaan.

FLAIR BLANKET: Meaning obscure, possibly fleur blanket, i.e. blanket with flowers depicted.

FLASKETT: Either a shallow washing tub or a clothes basket. M. Reed.

FLOCK: Wool refuse used for stuffing mattresses, pillows etc.

FLY LEG TABLE: Table with a flap supported by a leg.

FLY TABLE: A table with a flap or leaf supported by a swinging bracket called a Fly Rail. E.F. page 212.

FOREST WORK: Embroidery of cross stitch on canvas, using trees as part of the basic design. See CL 14 March 1991.

FOWLING PIECE: Light gun.

FOX DUSTER: Probably made from a fox's tail or "brush".

FRATER: Refectory in a monastery.

GARRET: Attic.

GILL: A measure for liquids holding one quarter of a standard pint.

GIRANDOLES: Elaborate sconces, often Rococo. PDDA.

GOOLOON: Probably Galloon; braid or ribbon, much used as gimp in the finishing of upholstery.

GOUTY CHAIR: Chair with a leg rest for use of person with gout.

HAIRLINE: Bottle Grate.

HAIR LINE: Iron.

HALBERD: Spear and battle axe.

HANGING PRESS: Cupboard for hanging clothes.

HARRATEEN: Technically 'a kind of woollen moire made in Norwich' but in these inventories, it is used loosely to describe a linen fabric for curtains and bed furniture, as defined in the OED.

HEMP: Vegetable fibre used for coarse cloth.

HOGSHEAD: Large cask measuring 52½ Imperial gallons. O.E.D.

HOLLAND: Good quality linen, often imported from Holland. N. Evans.

HORSE PISTOLS: Large pistol carried at the pommel of the saddle when on horseback.

HOUSEWIFE: Sewing/mending kit.

HUCKABACK/HUCKABAG: Stout linen fabric with rough surface, for towels etc. OED.

INDIA: All oriental exports mid-sixteenth century—mid-eighteenth century were called Indian regardless of what particular country they came from.

IRON MAIDEN: Precise meaning not clear in this context. The word "maiden" is used by the Scots as an alternative to "guillotine".

ITALIAN IRON: Cylindrical with rounded end for crimping lace. OED.

JACK: see Smoke Jack.

JACONET: A variety of muslin originally imported from India.

JAPAN/JAPANNED: Imitation oriental Lacquer, usually decorated with Chinoiserie designs. PDDA.

KEEPERS: Probably Creepers, simple fire dogs to put behind or between more elaborate Andirons.

KILDERKIN: Cask for liquids, containing 16–18 gallons

KIMNEL: Household Tub. M. Reed.

LANDSKIP: Landscape painting.

LATH (CURTAINS): Rail for hanging curtains, usually flat or oval section.

LAZY BACK: A rod with serrated edge used for tipping a kettle over a fire without taking it off the pot hook, illustrated in Lawrence Wright HFB p.43.

LIGNUM VITAE: Very hard, heavy wood, greenish brown or black in colour; much used in seventeenth century by Dutch makers.

LIMBECK/LIMBICK: see Alembick.

LINDSEY/LINSEY: Coarse inferior cloth made from mixture of wool and linen. N. Evans.

LOO TABLE: Oval table designed for the game of Loo. EF p.286.

LUMBER: Superfluous furniture.

LUSTRE: Glass chandelier.

LUTESTRING: Glossy silk fabric; plain or figured weave for which the warp is heated and stretched to produce lustre and crispness.

MACARONE TABLE: Possibly a gaming table. OED.

MANCHESTER BED FURNISHINGS AND QUILT: Probably made out of cotton.

MANGLE: Apparatus used for smoothing linen, not for pressing the water out. de Haan.

MARSEILLES QUILT: Cotton fabric woven with a pattern to resemble quilting.

MAZARINE/MAZARENE: Flat pierced plate fitting into a larger dish, so that the liquid could be strained from boiled fish placed on it.

MESSUAGE: See CAPITAL MESSUAGE

MOHAIR: Fine Camlet from the hair of the angora goat. Millard.

MONA DRAM: Chest and stand.

MONTEITH: Wine glass cooler in form of a bowl, normally silver or glass with notched rim to hold the feet of wine glasses while their bowls were suspended in water; called after Monteith, a Scotsman. PDAA.

MOREEN: Cheap imitation in wool (or wool and cotton) of moiré.

MOROCCO: Goat leather used in fine upholstery.

MARTELLO/MORTELO: Small circular fort. OED. Its meaning is unclear in this context.

NANKEEN: Term used for export porcelain from Chinese port of Nanking, especially referring to cruder blue and white and richly enamelled wares being exported in quantity. PDDA p.544.

NIGHT STOOL: see Close Stool.

NIGHT TABLE: Bed side table.

OGEE: A moulding consisting of a continuous double curve, convex above, concave below.

OIL CLOTH: Waterproofed table cloth.

ORMOULU: From French *or moulu*, gilded brass or copper mounts. EF p.329.

OSNABURGH LINEN: Coarse linen originating in Osnabruck.

OTTOMAN: Cushioned seat, without back or arms for reclining on. OED.

PALLIASS: Straw-stuffed mattress.

PANTHEON STOVE: Probably stove with a dome in the shape of the Pantheon in Rome.

PAPSPOON: Spoon for semi-liquid or mashed food; used for children. OED.

PATTY PAN: Small tin pan for baking pasties. OED.

PEELING: Thin skin or fabric formerly used as dress material.

PEMBROKE TABLE: Stands on four legs and has two rectangular leaves supported by brackets hinged to the frieze. PDDA.

PERSIAN CARPET: Probably seen by the makers of the inventories as a flower design carpet.

PERSIAN LINING: Thin light silk in plain weave.

PESTLE AND MORTAR: Club shaped instrument and bowl used for pounding substances.

PEWTER: Grey alloy of tin and lead or other metal.

PHAETON: see Crane Neck.

PIANO NOBILE: Principal rooms on the first floor.

PIER GLASS: Tall narrow mirror made to hang between two windows.

PIGGONS: Pig irons.

PILASTER/PILLASTER: Shallow pier or rectangular column, confirming to classical orders.

PILLER AND CLAW TABLE: Table resting on a single pillar with feet depicting birds' claws. These were unfashionable after 1765. EF p.134.

PILLION: Saddle allowing second person, normally a woman, to ride on a horse. OED.

PILLOW-BIERS: Pillow case or slip. M. Reed.

PIPE: Large cask for beer, normally two hogsheads. M. Reed.

PLATE WARMER: Plates with hollow bottoms for hot water to keep the plates warm.

PORRINGER: Small bowl with one or two handles, generally silver or pewter. PDDA p.623.

PORTRAIT GLASS: Probably half length hanging mirror.

POTTAGE POT: Pot for making soup.

POTT HANGERS: Device for hanging pot or kettle over the fire.

POWDERING TUB: Used for salting or pickling meat. N. Evans.

PRESS BED: Bed constructed to fold up and put in a press. OED.

PURLIN: Horizontal beams which run along length of roof, resting on the principal rafters, which they cross at right angles, lending support to common rafters or boards of the roof. OED.

QUEENS WARE: Title originally given by Wedgwood (and subsequently used by other Staffordshire potters) for pale cream-coloured earthenware. Name prompted by Queen Charlotte's patronage.

RASP: Coarse file having separate teeth raised on its surface by means of a pointed punch. OED.

RED EARTHENWARE: Probably unglazed red stoneware called Redware, produced from c.1690 by Elers Brothers, illustrated in *English Ceramics* Nos. 107–110.

REGESTER/REGISTER STOVE: Stove fitted with register plate near funnel, designed to keep in warm air.

RERE DORTER: Area behind the sleeping quarters of the monks, often used for latrines.

RUMFORD STOVE: Brick built fireplaces with opening above the fire, for heat efficiency. Designed by Benjamin Thompson, Count Rumford (1753–1814). See Lawrence Wright. HFB p.113–118.

RUMMERS: Glasses called after German Römer. By end of eighteenth century used to describe a glass with a very capacious bowl, short stem and with a circular or heavy square foot. See illustration G. Savage p.65.

RUNLET: Cask or Vessel. Large runlets contained 12–18½ gallons and small runlets a pint–4 gallons.

RUSSIA LEATHER: Durable leather made of skins impregnated with oil distilled from birch bark. OED.

RUSSIA LINEN (Russia Crash): Coarse linen made from Russian hemp.

SALAMANDER/SALLAMANDER: Hot iron plate for browning omelettes.

SALOON: Principal reception room, often on piano nobile floor.

SARCENET: Light weight and easily draped silk often used for linings. It was very supple because it had fewer warp and weft threads. Courtaulds.

SARCOPHAGUS: Wine cooler, grate etc.; anything in shape of Egyptian sarcophagus.

SCALLOP/SCOLLOPT: Shape of a shell.

SCONCE: Wall light consisting of bracket candlestick with polished back plate or mirror to reflect light. PDDA.

SCOTCH TABLE LINEN: Cambric—fine white linen made in imitation of the French.

SCREWTORE: see Escritoire.

SCIMITAR/SCYMITER: Oriental curved sword usually broadening to a point.

SCUTCHEON: Ornamental brass.

SERGE: Durable twilled cloth of worsted.

SHAGREEN: Sharkskin used to cover boxes and ornamental items in the eighteenth century.

SHALLOON: Closely woven woollen material chiefly used for linings OED.

SHAMBRAY MUSLIN: Cambric muslin, loose weave fabric.

SHUFFLE/SHOVEL BOARD: A game in which a coin is driven by a blow of the hand along a highly polished surface, marked with transverse lines. OED.

SKILLET: Cooking pot with long handle and three feet to stand over fire.

SLIP SCONCE: Sconce of narrow or elongated shape.

SMOKE JACK: Horizontal multi bladed fan, hung in a narrow neck in the flue, is turned by the rising current and transmits power by gears to the spit. Illustrated Lawrence Wright HFB p.51.

SNAITH/SNEAD: Scythe shaft. see Joseph Wright *The English Dialect Dictionary* p.574.

SOY BOTTLE: Sauce bottle.

SPIDER LEG TABLE: Long thin legs like those of a spider. OED.

SPITTOON: Receptacle for spit, usually round flat vessel of earthenware or metal, sometimes having a cover in the form of a funnel. OED.

SPRIGG/SPRING: Design of a small spray of flowers or leaves, embroidered, woven or stamped on a textile fabric or applied to ceramic ware. OED.

SPATTERDASH/SPLATTERDASH: Long gaiter or legging of leather or cloth, etc. to keep trousers or stockings from being spattered. OED.

SQUABS/SWABS: Club like feet to furniture.

STANDISH: Stand for ink, pens etc; illustrated PDAA p.756.

STILL: Apparatus for distillation, consisting of a close vessel in which the substance to be distilled is subjected to heat, and of arrangements for the condensation of the vapour produced. OED. See ALEMBRIC.

STEELYARDS/STILYARDS: Short and long arms used in weighing.

STOCK: Close fitting neckcloth. OED.

STUFF: Fabric made of woollen thread, possibly used for lining material, but was also a general term used for any fabric.

STUMP BEDSTEAD: Bedstead without posts. OED.

SURTOUT: Man's great coat. OED.

SWING GLASS: Looking glass suspended on pivots. OED.

TAFFETA/TAFFERTY: A light thin silk or union stuff of decided brightness and lustre. OED.

TAMBOURN/TAMBORN: Chain stitch embroidery worked with a hook and called after the drum-like frame on which the work was stretched.

TAMMY: Cheap worsted cloth in twill weave, possibly originating from Tamworth, Staffordshire.

TEA WAITER: Probably tea table, which also could be called tea kettle stand. EF.

TENT BED: Small four poster resembling a tent with low canopy. EF.

TESTER: Canopy of four post or draped bed, either of wood or fabric. EF.

TICK/TICKEN: Hard linen used for cases of pillows and mattresses. N. Evans.

TIE WIG: Wig having the hair gathered together behind and tied with a knot of ribbon. OED.

TRIVET: Three-legged metal table or stand used near fireplace for warming dishes. EF p.443.

TRUNDLE BED: Low bed on wheels which could be pushed under higher bed when not in use.

TUNBRIDGE WARE: Small wooden objects lavishly decorated with parquetry patterns by a special method developed at Tunbridge Wells in late 17C.

TUNNING DISH/TUNDISH: Wooden dish or shallow vessel with tube at bottom fitting into bung hole of cask. OED.

TURKEY CARPET: Probably seen by the makers of the inventories as carpets with a geometric design.

TURNUP BEDSTEAD: Bedstead with a turn-up end.

VALENCE: Originally drapery of canopy of bed; later used to describe top of any drapery arrangement.

VAPOUR BATH: Form of Turkish Bath used throughout eighteenth century in England. OED.

VESTIBULE: Ante-chamber or hall.

WAINSCOT: Oak. Formerly a superior quality of foreign oak imported from Russia, Holland or Germany, especially used for fine panel work. OED.

WARMING PAN: Long-handled covered pan of metal (usually brass) to contain live coals, used for warming beds. OED.

WATER PLATES: Plates with hollow bottoms for water to keep food warm.

WINDSOR CHAIR: Chair made using bentwood back frame and wood seat with the legs pegged directly into the seat. They originated from near Windsor Castle between 1700 and 1725. EF p.461.

WORSTED: Fabrics made from carded and combed long wools, arranged parallel to one another.

WORT: Stage in the brewing process.

WROUGHT: With pattern embroidered or woven.

NAMES INDEX

Illustrations are shown in bold.

Adolphus, King of Sweden, portrait of, 163
Ailesbury,1st Earl, 106; 2nd Earl, 12, 106; 3rd
    Earl, 106; Dowager Countess, 12, 106
Allen, Elisha, 132
Alken, Seiffert,109
Altham, Lady, portrait of, 162
Ampthill, 3rd Lord, 197
Ampthill Park House 3, 6, 9, 13-22, **Cover**
Antonie, John, 35; Marc, 5, 7-8, 32-4; Richard,
    8, 35, 208; William Lee, 10, 40
Archer, Thomas, 13, 246, 270
Arkwright, Esmé, 208
Ashburnham, Jemima, Countess of, portrait of,
    257
Ashburnham, 1st Lord, 12; 2nd Lord, 247
Aspin, Anne, 205
Aspley Guise 1
Astry, Family, 89

Badeslade, Thomas, 212
Bartolozzi, Francesco, prints 214
Bayliss, Nathaniel, 107
Bedford, 4th Duke of, 4, 107, 109, 125, 193-
    204; 5th Duke, 110, 215
Bedford, Swan Inn, 110
Benn, Amabel, portrait of, 257
Benn, Sir Anthony, 3, 244, 260
Benn, Mary, portrait of, 256
Berrill, Thomas, 194
Bevan, Benjamin, 154
Bletsoe Castle 165
Bowes, Mrs, portrait of, 163
Brandreth, Family, 3, 123-131
Bridgman, Mr., Steward of Houghton House,
    107
Brittain, Baron, 73
Bromsall, Family, 5, 8, 184-6, 191-2
Brotherton, Thomas, 192
Bromham Hospital 80
Brown, Lancelot, (Capability), 76, 249, 273
Brown, William, valuer, 42, 52, 70, 72
Bruce, Lord Robert, 12, 106
Buck, Samuel & Nathaniel, engravers, 24
Buckingham House (Palace), London, 13, 89
Buckler, John, **250**
Buckler, John Chessel, **ii**
Bullock, John, **7**, 93, 205-8
Burge, William,194
Butcher, Thomas, 15
Butler, Arthur Stanley George, 136
Bing, Sarah, see Osborn
Bing, Family, see Torrington, Lord

Cainho, Clophill, 3
Carew, Thomas, 244
Cavendish, Lady Ann, portrait of, 257
Chambers, Sir William, 14, 107-9
Charles 1, portrait of, 151, 162-3
Cheney, Sir Thomas, 234
Chernocke, Sir Robert, 3
Chicksands Priory 4, 5, 23-31, 72, 212, **23, 25,
    26**
Clement XI, Pope, portrait of, 152, 162
Cleveland, Lord & Lady, 234; see Wentworth
Cloak, George, 41
Cobb, Family, 205
Cockayne Hatley 1
Cole, Martin, 77
Colworth House, Sharnbrook, 3-6, 8, 32-72, **39,
    43-5**
Conolly, Lady Anne, 237
Cooke, Ambrose, valuer, 126
Cooper, Family of Toddington, 237
Crew, Family portraits, 260; Sir Randolph,
    portrait of, 256; Thomas, Lord, portrait
    of, 257

De Grey, Thomas, Earl, 246, 250-1
Delabrière, Louis André, painter, 219
Derby, Countess of, portrait of,179, 256
de la Rue, Thomas, 78
Devis, Arthur, painter, 7, 94, 102
Dickinson, John, 154
Duel, John, portrait of, 256
Du Thé, Madame, 43

Edrop, John, 78
Egerton, Lord Chancellor, portrait of, 163
Elizabeth I, portrait of, 179; visit, 234
Ellis, T, 184
Ernle, Lord, 197
Eston, Negus, 52
Evelyn, Jane, portrait of, 260; John, portrait of,
    256

Ficcorony, Signor, portrait of,153, 162
Fisher, Thomas, 134, 166, 205, **25**
Fitzwilliam, 2nd Earl, 5, 13
Flitcroft, Henry, 193, 249
Fleury, Cardinal, print of, 262
Fossey, Thomas, 126
Fox, Charles James, 43
Franklyn, John, Steward of Leighs, 152; John
    of Northill, 186
Freart, author, 245

Garrard, George, 217
Gibbard, Family, 206, 208; see also Stileman-Gibbard
George I, portrait of, 163
Gibbs, James, 4, 147, 150
Glenorchy, Amabel portrait of, 257, 262
Gordon, William, cartographer, 3 see Maps
Gough, John, valuer, 231
Gowran, Lady, 13-4
Grey, Family of Wrest, 243; see also Kent
Grey, Jemima, Marchioness, 3, 148, 213, 219, 243, 273
Grierson, gunmaker, 183
Grumbold, Robert, 12
Guercino 79

Hardwicke, 2nd Earl of, 249
Harper, Lady, portrait of, 257
Harris, William & Joseph, mercers, 194
Harrold, Earl & Countess, portraits of, 257, 262
Hart, Sir Eustace, portrait of, 256
Harvey, Family of Ickwell Bury, 3, 11, 132-145, 186
Hartop, Elizabeth, portrait of, 257
Hasells Hall, Sandy, 3, 5, 8, 73-88, 208, **74, 79**
Hawksmoor, Nicholas, 13
Hayes, Thomas, carpenter, 36
Henri IV of France, portrait of, 259
Herbert, see Pembroke
Higham Gobion 3
Hinwick House, Podington, 3, 6, 10, 33, 89-102, 208, **90, 92, 94**
Hoddesdon, Christopher, 146, 151, 163
Holland, Henry, 4, 6, 40, 196, 214-6, 218-9; Henry 3rd Lord, 15, 112
Holt, Lady Leigh, portrait of, 162
Hooper, Thomas, 245
Hoppner, John, 169, 172
Houghton House, Ampthill, 103-122, **105-111**
Houghton Regis Manor House 3-5, 10, 12 123-131, 165, **123**
Howard, Admiral, 2 prints of, 262
Hulcote 3
Hunt, John, carver, 90
Huntley, Robert & Matthew, 194
Hyatt, Bartholomew, valuer, 52

Ickwell Bury, Northill, 2, 3, 6, 132-145, **132, 134, 136**

Jackson, Thomas Jobson, 112
Jacob, Hildebrand, 24
James, I, 103, 105, 165, 234, 256
Jeffreys, Thomas, cartographer, 184
Johnes, Reverend, 218, 220
Jones, Inigo, 3, 20, 104-6
Juvarra, Filippo, 246

Kent, Amabel, Countess of, 243, 273
Kent, Earls of, 243; Duke of, 3, 7, 8, 243-273; see also Grey
King, clockmaker, 183

Kingsley, Elizabeth, 73; Heylock, 5, 73, 75-6, 208
Knight, Richard, 33, 89, 91

Langley, Batty, 246
Langlois, Pierre, 109
Lawrence, Richard, sculptor, 39, 71; Sir Thomas, 169, 172
Lee, Dr John, 70; Sir William, 38, 71
Leicester, Countess of, portrait of,163; Earl of, 103
Leigh, Family of Leighton Buzzard, 5, 9, 146-164
Leighton Buzzard, Prebendal House, 4, 5, 146-164, **146**
Leoni, Giacomo, 246
Linnell, William, carver, 193-4
Livesay, Family, 3
Longueville, Lady Susan, portrait of, 260
Lovett, Mrs, portrait of, 162
Lowndes, Matthew, carpenter, 235, 237, 242
Lucas, Mary, Baroness, 244-5; Family, portraits of, 260; James, valuer, 272
Luke, 2nd Lord, 15
Lumley, John, 13

Magniac, Family, 45
Mary, II, portrait of, 93, 99; Queen of Scots, portrait of, 256
May, Hugh, architect, 245
Maynard, Lady Elizabeth, portait of, 256; Family, portraits of 260
Melchbourne House 4-6, 8, 165-183, **166, 171**
Melchett, 2nd Lord, 45
Milward, Daniel, valuer, 272; William, wood-cutter, portrait of, 256
Mintrin, builder, 78
Monmouth, Duke of, 235
Montagu, Family, 32, 71
Moore, Thomas, architect, 193

Nevill, Ann, portrait of, 260
Northill Manor 5, 10, 184-192
Nottingham, 2nd Earl of, 13

Oakley House 4, 6, 193-204, **195**
Orlebar, Family, 3; Frederica, 170; John, **94**
Orme, artist ,147-8, **146**
Osborn, Family, 24-27, 31
Ossory, 1st Earl of,14, 110; 2nd Earl of, 15; see also Gowran

Paine, William, of Podington, 3
Palladio, Andrea, 20
Palmer, Robert,197
Pearson, Thomas Hooke, 79
Pembroke, Mary, Countess of, 103, 106
Penrose, Francis Cranmer, 91, 96, 102
Phillips, John, carpenter, 193
Podington, see Hinwick House
Polwarth, Lord & Lady, 153, 213-4, 231; see Grey
Portland, 3rd Duke of, 231

Portland, Lady (widow of 1st Earl), 246
Price, Rebecca, authoress, 9, 125, 131
Pym, Family, 74-88

Read, artist of Bedford, 38; John, at Houghton
    House, 110
Redhouse, Samuel, 80
Reni, Guido, 79
Repton, Humphrey, 77
Reynold, Samuel William, 40-42
Richardson, Sir Albert, 112, 216
Richmond, Nathaniel, 76
Robinson, John, of Denston Hall, Suffolk, 186
Rockingham, Lady, portrait of,162
Rose, Joseph, 15
Russell, Constance & Romola, 15, 203-4

Scrivener, John, builder, 35
Sharnbrook House 6, 205-11, **206**; see
    Colworth House
Silsoe, see Wrest Park
Shaw, John, architect, 250
Shrewsbury, Countess of, portrait of, 256;
    Elizabeth, daughter of Gilbert, Earl of
    Shrewsbury, portrait of, 260
Skinner, Robert, valuer, 272
Smith, Elizabeth, portrait of, 256; John, valuer,
    126; John, architect, 249
Smythson , John, architect, 104
Southill Park 1, 4, 6, 9, 40, 212-233, **213, 215,
    217**
St John, Family, 165-183
Stallwood, Joseph, bricklayer, 235-7, 242
Stephens, Thomas, carver, 194
Stevens, Edward, 76, 249
Stileman-Gibbard, Family, 208
Strafford, 1st Earl, 235; 2nd Earl, 237; Lord,
    portrait of,163
Sumpter, John, the elder, 33; John, the
    younger, 35

Tatham, Charles Heathcote, 216, 218-9; Henry,
    167; Thomas, 41-2
Tavistock, Francis, Marquess of, 6, 8, 10, 40,
    105, 107-9, 113
Thorpe, John, architect, 104

Tompion, Thomas, 10, 14, 17, 132
Toddington Manor House 4, 234-242, **236, 238**
Torrington, 1st Viscount, 110; 4th Viscount,10,
    213, 215, 218; 5th Viscount, 77, 110, 112,
    212
Townley, Maximilian, 172
Trevor, Robert, 4th Lord, 194, 196-7
Turner, Thomas, valuer, 183

Vandyck, Sir Anthony, 151, 163-4, 248-9
Verney, Hon Miss, portrait of,162; Hon Mrs,
    portrait of, 163

Wagstaff, John, 32, 71
Walker, Paul, valuer, 231
Walpole, Horace, 246, 248, 273; Sir Robert,
    249
Ware, Isaac, 25, 212
Warren, Thomas, ironsmith, 89
Watkins, Samuel & Sills, valuers, 101
Waters, John, brickmaker, 78
Wayman, Daniel, carpenter, 91
Watson, William Clarence, 45
Wedgwood, Josiah, 39, 167
Wells, Col. H G, 136
Wensleydale, Lord, 15
Wentworth, Family, 234-5, 237, 242; see
    Cleveland
Weston, Sir William, 165
Weyland, Richard, tenant of Ickwell Bury, 133,
    137
Whitbread, Emma, 167; Family, 214-9; 232;
    Samuel II, 4, 6, 40;
William III, portrait of, 93, 99
Willaume, David, 8
Winde, William, 13
Wittenbrook, Moses Van, painter, 72
Woburn Abbey 4, 107, 193, 196, 249
Woolfe, John, 6, 38, 249
Worlidge, Thomas, engraver of gems, 214
Wouverman, Pieter, 7, 72
Wrest Park 3-5, 8, 11-2, 76, 154, 219, 243-273,
    11, 245, 247, 250
Wyatt, Sir Henry, 243; James, 25, 27, 133, 154

Young, Clyde, architect, 208

SUBJECT INDEX

Armour 133, 135, 139, 189; Cap 27; Helmet 139
Arras, see Tapestry Hangings
Astronomical Instruments 10, 268, 271

Bells & Bell Systems 20-1, 29, 47, 50, 53, 57,
    59, 66, 68, 70, 84, 100, 120, 126-7, 144,
    158, 188, 190, 208, 254, 257, 259, 261-2,
    264-5
Bird Cage 17, 49, 60, 97

Birds, Cases of, 135, 142-3, 159
Blinds, Silk, 54, 116; Venetian 53, 62-3, 67
Books 16, 51, 91, 101, 124, 127, 183, 219, 245,
    259
Building Trade, Bricklayer, 33, 35, 193, 235;
    Brickmaker 78; Carpenter 33, 78, 193, 235;
    Carver 90, 107, 193; Ironmonger 89, 193;
    Mason 33, 89, 112, 132; Tiler 33

Carpets, Brussels, 43, 53, 56, 61-4, 66-7, 135, 139, 177-9; Kidderminster 64, 135, 138, 142, 145; Persian 158, 262, 268; Scotch 221, 230; Turkey 43, 49, 53, 62, 98-9, 135, 138-9, 157-8, 177, 229, 244, 261, 268; Wilton 117, 135, 141, 143, 175; Window 48
Caudle Cup 20, 117, 266-7
Ceramics, Alabaster, 56, 207; Blue & White Porcelain 8, 14, 49, 51, 56-7, 59, 75, 85-6, 95, 97-100, 110, 117, 124, 128, 135, 144, 150, 155, 159, 178, 181-2, 249, 252-3, 255, 258, 265-8, 271; China, Enamelled 51, 55, 59, 75, 84-6, 100, 150, 159, 182, 210, 266; General 20-1, 34, 37, 42, 44, 67, 96, 188-9, 208; Jars 19-20, 56-7, 59, 98, 170, 179, 188, 258, 271; Vases 19, 39, 54-5, 67; Cream coloured ware 110, 117; Bow 8; Delft 5, 34, 37, 47, 95, 99, 189, 215, 220, 226, 249, 266, 271; Derby 172; Earthenware 8, 50, 57, 83, 100, 127,156, 160, 179, 190, 200, 255, 265-6; Ornamental Figures 14, 19-20, 37, 48-9, 59, 169, 179; Chelsea 8, 110; Queensware 215, 225-6; Redware 20, 129, 150, 159, 227, 229; Sèvres 110; Staffordshire 8, 110, 117, 150, 159; Indian China 8, 181; Japan China 98, 100, 110; Meissen 8; Nanking 8, 37, 52, 170, 181; New Hall 170; Stoneware 8, 83, 85, 100, 119-20, 127, 190, 230-1, 267; Wedgwood 110, 167, 179; Worcester 8, 169, 182
China, see Ceramics
Chocolate Service 49-51, 57, 84, 99, 117, 159, 181, 189, 200, 211, 228, 252, 255, 264-8
Cistern 21-2, 30, 53, 69, 78, 84, 119, 128, 158-9, 188, 191, 211, 224-5, 227, 229, 255
Clockmakers 10, 14, 17, 47, 49, 50, 132, 157, 160, 177, 183, 185
Clocks, Alarm, 10, 221; Stable 30, 100, 132; Chamber 17, 54-6, 62, 82, 128, 183, 187, 219, 262; Eight Day 29, 58, 66, 81-2, 98, 124, 128, 177, 185, 189; Pendulum 14, 117, 124
Coffee Mill 21, 29, 35, 58, 83, 100, 117, 143, 190, 225
Coffee Service 8, 14, 20, 34, 47, 49, 51-2, 59, 67, 84-5, 100-1, 118, 143-4, 159, 180-1, 227, 255, 266-7, 272
Costume, Men's Clothes, 95, 101, 121, 125, 130, 185-6, 191-2; Wigs 100, 118, 125, 130, 185, 191
Country Houses, Building Campaigns, 2-3, 32, 37-8, 40, 77, 102, 107, 132, 147, 166, 171, 184, 193, 196, 205, 207-8, 212, 215, 244, 246, 249
Country Houses, Demolitions,110-1, 126, 154, 186, 237, 251
Country Houses, Design Styles, Baroque, 3, 5, 89, 102, 148, 246; Chinoiserie 26, 36; Classical 90, 105, 167, 245; Elizabethan 32, 73, 89, 93, 205, 234; French 3, 6, 13, 32, 104, 106, 196, 216, 250; Gothic 26; Grecian/Greek Revival 78, 104, 147;

Italianate 3, 104-6; Palladian 3, 104; Rococo 6, 102, 194-6
Country Houses, Exterior, Cupola, 12, 236-7; Loggia 103-4; Tower 112, 237, 239, 245; Wing 147, 216, 245, 247, 249
Country Houses, Materials Used, Brick, 32, 78, 147, 166, 205, 244; Plaster 15, 32; Stone 35, 107, 166, 195, 205, 217, 238; Tiling 238-9, 241
Curtains, Festooned, 25, 54, 56, 61, 109, 113-6, 157-8, 173-5, 196, 198-9

Dress, see Costume
Drink, Beer, 121, 138, 182, 191, 214, 267; Brewhouse 108, 129, 136-7, 161, 182, 191, 266; Cider 21, 57, 121; Wine 121, 170, 182, 214; Wine Cooler 53, 57, 68, 72, 133, 138, 170, 172, 179

Embroidery, Irish Stitch, 24, 27-8; Turkish Work 24, 27; Wrought Work 56, 93, 140, 157
Estate Offical, Steward, 107, 172, 245, 251

Frames, Lacquered, 43, 47-8, 55, 61-2, 64-6, 81, 185, 188, 196; Japan 27, 53, 92, 98, 172, 176, 185, 188; Tabernacle 17-8, 20, 157
Furniture, Japanned, 18-20, 24, 57-9, 75, 88, 98, 100, 114, 117, 125-6, 135, 139-141, 144, 150, 158-9, 175-7, 179, 188, 196, 220-1, 225-6, 231, 253, 257-60, 271
Furniture, Materials Used, Bamboo, 114-8, 169, 176; Beech 113, 117, 135, 140, 142, 230; Cane 17-8, 24, 27, 29, 43, 47, 53, 55-6, 63, 75, 81-2, 97, 142, 150, 155-7, 161, 177-8, 187, 190, 211, 223, 230, 248, 251-2, 254, 256, 259, 261, 263, 270; Cedar 4, 8, 112; Cherry 125; Ebony 135, 189, 248; Lime 116; Mahogany 6-7, 14, 37, 42, 48-50, 52-3, 57-62, 64, 66, 68, 75-6, 79, 88-9, 93, 99, 109, 113-5, 118, 133, 135, 138-141, 143-5, 149-150, 158-9, 167-9, 172, 174-9, 181, 196, 198-9, 202, 206-7, 209, 214, 218, 220, 222-6, 230, 248, 253, 255-6, 258, 261, 266; Marble 5, 14, 18-9, 47-8, 56, 58, 68, 132, 171, 202, 210 218, 224; Oak, Norway 5, 34, 47; Oak, Wainscot 5-7, 14, 50, 62, 75, 100, 108, 114-5, 118-9, 133, 139-140, 143-4, 150, 155-6, 159, 168, 172, 176-7, 179, 181, 196-8, 200, 202, 220, 223-6, 229-230; Pear 109, 114, 117; Rosewood 43, 56, 62, 69, 79, 255; Satinwood 16, 42-3, 56, 62, 141, 168, 176-9; Wainscot, see Oak; Walnut 5-7, 14, 16-20, 24, 34, 37, 48-50, 62, 64-6, 75, 81-2, 93, 97-9, 139-40, 142-3, 150, 156-8, 168, 172-4, 185, 187, 189, 196, 198-9, 206-7, 209, 221, 248, 252, 257, 259-63, 266; Yew 42, 55, 179, 209
Furniture, Painted, 7, 19, 60, 62, 81, 117, 138-9, 141, 143, 174, 197, 200, 219, 223, 244, 263
Furniture, Seating Covers, Horsehair, 56, 59, 63; Leather 21, 27, 29, 42, 47-8, 57, 68, 81,

113, 128, 150, 178-9, 187, 196, 199, 209, 211, 223-4, 230, 252; Matted 18, 29, 96, 113, 117-8, 155, 159, 173, 176-8, 187, 197, 200, 252-3, 255, 258, 263, 268, 270; Morocco 53-4, 114, 138, 266, 271; Spanish Leather 54, 56

Furniture, Styles, Indian, 98, 124, 128, 156-7, 189, 253, 257-8, 263, 267

Furniture, Types, Beds, Corded, 15-16, 85, 161, 188, 254, 259, 262-5, 270; Field Bed 18, 51, 57, 60, 113, 173-4, 261; Four Poster 7, 18, 42-60-5, 68, 82, 96-8, 113-9, 140, 143, 169, 175, 197, 200-1, 209, 221-224, 226-7, 229; Half Canopy 97, 140, 197, 209; Half Tester 60, 88, 89; Settee/Sofa 66, 68, 126, 175, 220-1, 225, 226, 268; Trundle 205; Wardrobe 59-60, 62, 143, 268

Furniture, Types, Bookcase, 53-4, 62, 69, 93, 97, 109, 117-8, 138-9, 143, 168, 176-8, 189, 196, 218-9, 225, 230, 263

Furniture, Types, Bureau, 50, 62, 64, 66, 68, 75, 82, 114, 128, 139-140, 142-3, 157, 179, 189, 200, 202, 221, 223, 226, 252-3

Furniture, Types, Cabinet with Tortoiseshell Inlay, 50, 248, 261

Furniture, Types, Chairs, Fan Back, 117, 196, 199; Pembroke 115, 219; Smoking 48; Wicker 109; Windsor 16, 20, 116, 173, 179-180, 211, 256

Furniture, Types, Children's, 109, 113, 128, 140, 193, 169, 174, 176, 211, 221, 256, 263

Furnitue, Types, Cupboard, China, 54; Corner 49-50, 100, 126, 128, 143, 156, 189, 203, 255, 261-2, 266-7, 270-1

Furniture, Types, Dumbwaiter, 14, 18, 48, 57, 60-1, 68, 116, 133, 138, 158, 225

Furniture Types, Looking Glass, Chimney, 19, 42, 48-9, 51, 53, 55-6, 62-4, 66, 81, 98, 141, 154, 157-8, 189, 209, 219, 260, 263, 271; Pier 19, 47, 50, 55-6, 59-62, 64, 66, 82, 84, 139, 156-7, 168, 196, 199, 218, 222, 223-4, 257, 260; Rising 43, 62, 176; Swing 60-62, 64, 127, 140, 156, 169, 174-5, 209

Furniture Types, Reading Stand, 93, 97, 138-9, 142, 179, 199, 223, 253

Furniture Types, Settee/Sofa, 20, 29, 53-5, 63, 66, 80-81, 83, 93, 97-9, 109, 117, 139, 150, 158, 161, 176, 208, 223, 253, 255-6, 259, 262, 264, 270-1

Furniture, Types, Spittoon, 59

Furniture, Types, Tables, Commerce, 115; Commode 63, 109, 114, 199, 222, 253; Counting 93, 101; Fly 222; Lady's Work 43; Lady's Writing 20, 53, 56, 84-5, 109, 178, 187, 219, 248; Leaf 65; Kingswood 219; Night 62-3, 109, 113-5, 168, 175-6, 199, 222-3, 225, 258, 262; Pembroke 48, 53, 64, 66, 139, 174-9, 219, 222, 224, 230; Spider Leg 116, 198-9, 225

Furniture, Types, Stands, Pillar & Claw, 54, 56, 60, 75, 80, 114-5, 117, 142, 156-9, 168, 178, 181, 196, 199-200, 221, 224-5, 266

Games, Backgammon, 19, 54, 95, 99, 115, 127, 182, 219, 254, 271; Billiards 224, 246, 253; Bowls 226, Cards 269; Chess 219, 269; Devil &Taylors 224; Dice 115, 127, 219, 271; Draughts 54, 95, 99, 185, 189, 219, 224, 271; Loo 224; Pope Joan 219

Garden Equipment 121, 162, 231

Glass, Beakers, 20, 29, 60, 100; Flint 159, 259; Monteith 267; Plate 49, 53, 55, 60, 63-4, 268; Rimmers 160; Water 47, 50-51, 57, 60, 120, 125, 135, 159, 179, 181, 189, 192, 196, 200, 211, 226, 255, 265

Globes 83, 117, 169, 178, 189, 224, 263

Guns/Pistols, Blunderbus, 98; Cannons, 139; Fowling Pieces, 98, 118, 189; General, 50, 76, 84, 100, 130, 138, 157-8, 189; Horse Pistols, 226; Lock Gun, 226; Muskets, 189; Rifle 97

Heating, Pans, Warming, 47, 50, 84, 127, 144, 188, 190, 211, 228

Heating, Stoves, Bath, 10, 19, 44, 49, 69-70, 107, 141-3, 177, 215, 221, 223, 225-6, 231; Pantheon, 141, 174-7; Register, 44, 69, 139, 142, 169, 173-9, 181; Rumford, 60, 69-70

Higmergig 158-9

Horse Drawn Vehicles 121, 162

Horses 120-121

House Officials, Butler, 69, 85, 155, 172, 263; Chef 246; Cook 119, 155, 229; Footmen 161; Housekeeper 21, 59, 65, 69, 117, 138, 155, 159, 162, 181, 225, 264; Maids 29, 51, 60, 65, 69, 83, 97, 118-9, 225, 229, 267

Kitchen Equipment, Ovens, 41, 58, 265; Ranges 20-1, 69, 83, 99, 129, 160, 180, 201, 203, 228, 265; Smoke Jacks 9, 34, 69, 83, 99, 119, 129, 160, 180, 189, 201, 228, 264; Spits 9, 20, 34, 58, 69, 99, 119, 129, 144, 180, 189, 201, 211, 228, 264

Lighting, Chandelier, 6, 54-6, 68, 139, 158, 224; Girandole 6, 179; Jermes 223; Lamps, Globe 55, 61, 87, 115, 223, 226; Lamps, Patent 59, 68; Sconces 18, 48, 55, 81, 85, 127-8, 158, 189, 254-260, 263, 270; Slip Sconces 82, 98-9, 156-7

Lodges 41, 78, 80, 88, 103, 194, 243, 246, 251, 265

Maps, Bedfordshire, County, 13, 15, 49, 73-4, 89, 132, 134, 154, 183-4, 192, 212, 262; France 270; Houghton Regis 131; Huntingdonshire 259; Leighton Buzzard 170

Meteorological Equipment, Barometer, 99, 189, 208, 219; Thermometer 61, 252, 255; Weather Glass 19, 29, 48, 128, 139, 158, 252, 255

Money in the House 76, 87, 130

Music, Chamber Organ, 37, 48, 142; Hand Organ 54, 221; Harpsicord 95, 139, 223, 231

Paintings, see under artist's name in Names
Index; Battles 7, 141; Chinese 215, 226;
Classical Subjects 37, 54, 152, 162-3, 207;
Dutch 54, 61, 151, 163, 169, 179, 207;
Flower 49, 53, 152, 207; General 28, 48-9,
65-6, 96-8, 127-8, 135, 138-9, 141-3, 182,
185, 187, 224-5, 244, 248, 252, 254-6, 261-
2, 270-1; Indian 51, 124, 126-8, 162, 209,
251, 262, 266; Landscapes 7, 29, 65, 146,
162-3, 169, 179, 199, 209; Miniatures 115;
Pastoral Idyll 43, 53, 65, 151; Portraits 7,
37, 48, 53, 93-4, 99, 124-5, 151, 162-3, 169,
171, 179, 208, 215, 222, 257, 260, 262;
Religious 7, 49, 65, 79, 152, 162-3, 169,
179, 207, 209; Still Life 48, 153, 162
Plate, Gold, 57, 59, 87, 124, 125, 130, 151, 191,
269; Pewter 20-21, 50, 58, 84, 95, 99-101,
120, 128, 140, 144, 155, 161, 169, 181, 189,
200-201, 208, 211, 215, 227, 263-5; Silver
8-9, 14, 51, 67, 76, 86-7, 95, 124-5, 130,
135, 151, 158-9, 169, 180, 184, 191, 267,
269, 271-2
Quilt, Marseilles, 17, 141

Religious Houses, former, 23, 32, 165
Rooms & Outbuildings, Contents of, Alcove
Room 260; Arcade 17; Attics, Garrets 13,
15-16, 35, 46, 50-1, 64, 83, 113, 139-140,
154, 172, 186, 188, 197, 200-201, 209, 220,
254, 259, 263-4; Bacon Room 129;
Bakehouse 20, 30, 120, 182, 229-230, 265;
Ballroom 224; Bathing Room 17, 65, 225;
Bedchambers 13, 17-9, 24, 28, 37, 46, 50,
60-2, 66, 81, 96, 98, 114, 116, 119, 126-7,
141-3, 174, 182, 187, 197, 200, 209, 221-2,
252, 256, 259, 261; Bedroom Canopy 175;
Bedrooms, Principal 17-8, 61-4, 98, 113,
127, 141, 156-7, 175, 177, 198-9, 201-2,
224-5, 252, 258; Bedrooms Tent 143;
Billiard Room 253; Blacksmith's Shop 68;
Boiling House 265; Bottle House 192;
Boudoir 54; Bow Room 177; Bowling
Green House 266; Breakfast Room 53, 69,
139; Brewhouse 21, 30, 52, 85, 100, 108,
127, 136-7, 161, 182, 191, 266; Butler's
Pantry 20, 60, 85, 144, 159, 179, 200, 202,
226, 255; Butler's Room 69, 85, 155, 173,
262; Carpenter's Shop 85; Caves 226;
Cellars 30, 47, 85, 121, 127, 138, 160,
182, 191-2, 203, 229, 266-7; Chapel 24,
26-7, 259; Chapel Room 260; Cheese
Chamber 84, 127; Closet 29, 57, 67; Coach
House 162, 191, 241; Coachman's & Boys'
Room 85, 161, 270; Confectionery 255;
Cook's Room 119, 155, 229; Dairy 14, 21,
29, 50, 68, 84, 120, 137, 160, 191, 266;
Dining Room 138, 177, 239, 257; Dining
Parlour 4, 8, 53-4, 69, 99, 199, 201, 224;
Drawing Room/Withdrawing Room 14, 24,
27, 55-6, 66, 81, 114, 128, 139, 158, 162,
179, 189, 224, 255, 257; Dressing Room
14, 18-9, 28, 62-3, 69, 82, 84, 97, 114, 143,

156-7, 172, 252; Drying Room 161, 191,
267; Lady Duchess's Room 261; Farmer's
Room 119; Footman's Pantry 69;
Footmen's Room 161; Gallery 14, 16, 20,
28, 60, 83, 97, 139, 172, 187, 238, 240;
Long 256; Marble 258; Game Keeper's
Room 161; Garden House 231; Gardener's
Room 119; Great Hall, 14, 19, 24, 27, 47-
8, 116, 223, 256; Great State Room 239;
Great Room 270; Green Room 252; Hall
30, 66, 81, 99, 128, 139, 144, 179, 189,
210; Housekeeper's Room 21, 59, 65, 69,
117, 138, 155, 159, 162, 181, 225, 264;
Kennels 69; Kitchen 9, 14, 20, 29, 47, 49,
57, 69, 83, 99, 119, 128, 143, 160, 180, 189,
200, 203, 210, 227, 241; Kitchen Maids'
Room 119; Lady Maid's Room 118, 225;
Larder 30, 68, 84, 144, 181, 203, 265;
Laundry 21, 85, 128, 137, 161, 182, 190,
229-230, 241, 267; Laundry Maid's Room
118, 267; Library 14, 20, 25, 44, 54, 56, 95,
108, 113, 138, 178, 223, 253; Linen Room
268; Maids' Room 29, 51, 60, 65, 69, 83,
97, 118, 140, 229; Meal House 265;
Menagerie 230; Nursery 83, 97, 113, 126,
176, 188; Pantry 28, 50, 57, 69, 99, 117,
188; Parlour 29, 37, 47-8, 80-1, 84, 99, 128,
158, 162, 188-9, 199, 202, 209, 239, 255;
Passage Room 18, 29, 143, 163; Pastry 30,
84, 129, 190, 230, 265; Pavilion House 271;
Porter's Lodge 265; Powder Room 21;
Round Tower 239; Saddle Room 68;
Saloon 5, 158, 162; Scullery 144, 181, 190,
229, 265; Servants' Bedroom 30, 51, 60,
140; Servants' Hall 21, 47, 50, 59, 69, 85,
100, 120, 138, 180, 188, 200, 203, 227, 240,
254; Shoe Room 227; Sitting Room,
Private 56; Slaughter House 21; Slop
Room 226; Smoking Room 189, 259;
Spangle Room 256; Stables 68, 100, 120,
211, 241, 270; Staircase 49, 156, 163;
Staircase, Great 81, 145, 239, 257;
Steward's Dining Room 117, 158;
Steward's Parlour 254; Steward's Room
21, 30, 155, 158, 162, 200, 203, 225, 238,
251; Still Room 181, 230, 265; Stone
Parlour 14, 20, 116, 210, 238; Store Room
29, 83, 97, 119, 188; Study 49, 53-4, 69, 84,
138, 199, 210; Tapestry Room 97; Valet
Room 60, 65; Vestibule 14, 19, 223; Wash
House 30, 69, 85, 100, 120, 127, 137, 190,
192, 211, 227, 230, 241, 267; Wardrobe
Garret 263; Wet Larder, 227, 265;
Woodhouse 161; Wool Room 161; Yard
30, 121

Saddlery 28, 121, 162, 209
Sanitation, Bathing Room, 9, 13, 43, 76, 214;
Bathing Tub 20, 65; Bed Pan 29, 211, 228,
264, 270; Bidet 9, 60-1, 64, 66, 68, 141-2,
168, 173, 175-7; Chamber Pot 9, 21, 60,
99, 127-8, 161, 208, 226, 265, 272; Close

Stool 18, 28-9, 62, 68, 82-3, 88, 97-8, 127, 140, 142, 155-7, 168, 172-3, 187, 198, 205, 209, 222, 230, 251-4, 256-7, 259-64, 268, 270-1; Pot Cupboard 61-2, 65-6, 174-7, 199; Shower Bath 144, 173; Vapour Bath 169, 177; Water Closet 214

Schools 154

Sport, Fishing, 125-6, 268; Hunting 10, 40, 53, 108, 169, 193-4, 208; Real Tennis 239; Shooting, see Guns, Fowling Pieces

Tapestry 6-7, 19-20, 24, 27-9, 46, 93, 97-8, 113, 125, 127, 199, 234, 244, 248, 251-6, 260-3, 268

Tea Service 8, 34, 47, 49, 57, 85-6, 97, 99, 100, 117, 144, 180, 188, 190, 252-3, 255, 257-8, 265-7

Textile, Design, Check, 17, 65, 99, 113-5, 118-9, 157, 173-4, 197-8, 209, 222, 269; Stripe, 13, 17, 60-1, 63-5, 141, 143, 158, 172, 179, 215, 220, 224, 230, 256, 263, 269

Textile Type, Caffoy, 19, 226, 252-3, 262, 270; Callico 17, 27-9, 56, 63-5, 155, 189, 251, 261; Callimanco 35, 46, 48, 253; Callimaris 253, 268; Camblet 16, 18, 82, 124, 127, 154-6, 186, 209, 259, 264; Chintz 4, 9, 56-7, 61, 65, 187, 214, 222, 261; Cheney 197-8; Cotton 29, 57, 139, 143, 172, 175, 198, 215; Cranky 141-3, 172-7, 226-7; Damask 17, 19, 27, 47-50, 58, 76, 81, 85, 101, 109, 120, 126-7, 130, 155, 158, 170, 179, 182, 187, 192, 196, 199, 207, 209, 215, 224, 231,

234, 253, 255, 260, 263, 268-70; Diaper 86, 120, 130, 155-6, 182, 192, 269; Dimity 29, 60, 62, 64, 141-3, 173-7, 197, 221, 229, 251-3, 256-7, 270; Drugget 261; Flax 47, 101, 130, 155, 270; Fustian 114; Gooloon 56; Harrateen 18, 47, 49, 259-62; Hemp 101, 120, 155; Holland 47, 51, 56-7, 67, 85, 101, 120, 130, 141, 155, 183, 252-3, 257-8, 260-2, 269-70; Huckaback 51, 58, 85, 101, 120, 156, 182-3, 192, 269; Jaconet 56; Lace 46, 48; Lindsey 97, 252, 254, 264; Linen 16, 18, 47, 183, 257; Lutestring 224-5; Moreen 54, 114; Muslin 49, 56, 140, 156; Osnaburgh 155; Plaid 57, 60, 68, 135, 139, 260; Sacken 60, 88; Sarcenet 57; Satin 17, 49, 268; Serge 51, 89, 209, 259-60, 263; Shalloon 19; Shambray 56; Silk 19, 54-5, 64, 69, 82, 93, 98, 116, 127, 153, 158, 176, 187, 199, 253-4, 256; Stuff 27-8, 197-8, 231, 256; Taffety 19; Tick/Ticken 63, 65-6, 113, 259, 268; Velvet 16, 128, 158, 187, 219-20, 226, 244, 248, 252-4, 257-8, 261-2, 268; Worsted 47, 57, 63, 153, 252

Traps, Mouse, 186, 190; Rat 128

Umbrella 16, 19, 42, 48, 200, 211, 268-9

Valuers 7, 42, 52, 70, 101, 126, 231, 272

Weapons, Bow, 139, 158; Halberd 9, 27; Pikes 189; Scabbard and Swords 50, 98, 130, 189; Spear 139